CORN, COTTON AND CHOCOLATE

HOW THE MAYA CHANGED THE WORLD

By

James A. O'Kon P.E.

CORN, COTTON AND CHOCOLATE: HOW THE MAYA CHANGED THE WORLD

Copyright © 2017 by James O'Kon PE

All rights reserved. This book or any portion thereof may not be reproduced or used in any manner whatsoever without the express written permission of the publisher except for the use of brief quotations in a book review, or scholarly journal.

First Printing: 2017

KDP Publishing corporation

ISBN: 9781520813097

--

26104 Plantation Drive

Atlanta, Georgia 30325

jamesokon@okon.com

CORN, COTTON AND CHOCOLATE: HOW THE MAYA CHANGED THE WORLD

ACKNOWLEDGEMENTS

I wish to acknowledge the people who assisted me with the ideas and concepts presented in *Corn, Cotton, and Chocolate: How the Maya Changed the World*.

I want to thank the kind reviewers of the manuscript including Dr. William Barnhart, Dr. Mark Van Stone and Dr. Nicholas Helmuth.

Many of the ideas in this book came from years of interchange with friends, colleagues and collaborators. I wish to acknowledge the contributions to the laborious process made by George Stuart, Keith Merlin, Mark Van Stone, Carolyn Tate, William Barnhart, Philippe Kleinfelter, and Nicholas Helmuth.

In addition, I want to thank colleagues who have offered suggestions and criticisms that have been invaluable. These people include Kira Francklin, John Williams, Carl Stimmel and Julie Barnwell Lalor.

CORN, COTTON AND CHOCOLATE: HOW THE MAYA CHANGED THE WORLD

To Carol, my wife and my muse.

CORN, COTTON AND CHOCOLATE: HOW THE MAYA CHANGED THE WORLD

CORN, COTTON AND CHOCOLATE: HOW THE MAYA CHANGED THE WORLD

TABLE OF CONTENTS

Chapter 1: Columbus Introduces the World to Maya Cultivars — page 11

Chapter 2: The Mysterious Maya: The Phantoms of History — page 19

Chapter 3: Maya Agronomists Invent the Magic Cultivars — page 29

Chapter 4: Maya Cultivars Travel the World — page 37

Chapter 5: How Maya Cultivars Transformed History — page 43

Chapter 6: **Avocado**   Botanical: *Persea americana*   Maya: *oom* — page 45

Chapter 7: **Cassava**   Botanical: *Manihot esculenta*   Maya: *man* — page 55

Chapter 8: **Chicle**   Botanical: *Manikara zapota*   Maya: *lits* — page 63

Chapter 9: **Chili Peppers**   Botanical: *Capsicum*   Maya: *yic* — page 73

Chapter 10: **Chocolate**   Botanical: *Theobroma cacao*   Maya: *ka'kau'* — page 89

Chapter 11: **Common Bean**   Botanical: *Phaseolus vulgaris*   Maya: *bot* — page 103

Chapter 12: **Cotton**   Botanical: *Gossypium hirsutum*   Maya: *piits* — page 115

Chapter 13: **Henequen**   Botanical: *Agave sisalana*   Maya: *kih* — page 131

Chapter 14: **Maize**   Botanical: *Zea mays*   Maya: *ixi im* — page 141

Chapter 15: **Papaya**   Botanical: *Carica papaya*   Maya: *puut* — page 161

Chapter 16: **Peanut**   Botanical: *Arachis hypogaea*   Maya: *mani* — page 167

Chapter 17: **Pineapple**   Botanical: *Ananas comosus*   Maya: *anana* — page 179

Chapter 18: **Squash**   Botanical: *Cucurbita*   Maya: *kuum* — page 191

Chapter 19: **Sunflowers**   Botanical: *Helianthus annuus*   Maya: *lol* — page 203

Chapter 20: **Sweet Potato**   Botanical: *Ipomoea batatas*   Maya: *lis* — page 213

Chapter 21: **Tobacco**   Botanical: *Nicotiana*   Maya: *k'uuts* — page 223

Chapter 22: **Tomato**   Botanical: *Solanum lycopersicum*   Maya: *p'aak* — page 241

Chapter 23: **Turkey**   Botanical: *Meleagris gallopavo*   Maya: *uu lum* — page 253

Chapter 24: **Vanilla**   Botanical: *Vanilla planifolia*   Maya: *sool* — page 267

Chapter 25: Maya Cultivars as a Team and as Solo Act Change the World — page 277

Epilogue: Remember the Future and Anticipate the Past — page 301

For each cultivar, the English name is in bold letters, the botanical name follows and the Maya name is last.

CORN, COTTON AND CHOCOLATE: HOW THE MAYA CHANGED THE WORLD

CORN, COTTON AND CHOCOLATE: HOW THE MAYA CHANGED THE WORLD

PREFACE

The Maya were the longest-lived civilization in history. Their historic period lasted for 3500 years and traced parallel time lines with other civilizations in world history. The Maya began their civilization in 2500 BC on a parallel with the ancient Sumerians and terminated in around 900 AD during the reign of Emperor Charlemagne. The time-lines were parallel, but their histories did not converge because the Maya and other world civilizations did not know that each other existed. The Maya were the phantoms of history.

The Maya homeland was deep in the remote tropical rainforest of the Yucatán, far distant from other classic cradles of civilization. Their remote location deprived them of scientific contributions from other civilizations. The Maya conceived their sophisticated sciences, advanced technologies and unique agronomy without outside influence and independently developed their body of knowledge in total isolation.

The ancient Maya were avid sky watchers and after millennia of observation of the heavens they gained an uncanny knowledge of the harmonious composition of the cosmos. Their study of the vast expanse of the universe and the mysterious movements of astral bodies evolved into their quadripartite philosophy of the cosmos: A belief system that inspired the scientific culture guiding the Maya civilization.

Their advanced sciences included astronomy, mathematics and one of the five original written languages in the world. They constructed grand high-rise cities in the rainforest replete with otherworldly art and architecture, and developed technologies that were 2000 years in advance of comparable European achievements.

They were the greatest agronomists in world history. The bountiful cultivars produced by Maya agronomy are real inventions generated by their scientific methodologies. These unique inventions were not machines but are living organisms propagated by Maya agriculturists. These cultivars nourished the Maya culture and enabled their rapid growth into a society of profound thinkers. The Maya are actual proof of the scientific theorem that developing societies with an early start on bountiful food production accelerate their ascendency into an advanced civilization.

The Classic Maya developed advances in science, technology and agricultural that predated similar achievements in other civilizations. In the 21st century, ancient Maya scientific advances have been surpassed by centuries of scientific and technical achievements in the western world. However, the intellectual magic achieved by Maya agronomy sciences has not been surpassed.

Mathematicians proclaim that one of the singular accomplishments of the human era, and the greatest intellectual feat of the Maya, was the invention of the number zero. Their cultivation of unique cultivars was a comparable intellectual accomplishment. The creation of Maya cultivars was the result of conscious biological manipulation of native plants altered into productive specimens for food and fiber.

The Maya converted a native grass into a sophisticated high yielding grain called maize. Botanists consider this feat to be mankind's first and greatest achievement in the history of agronomy. Their feats of agronomy are timeless.

After European contact, the ingenious products of Maya agronomy were disseminated around the world. The integration of Maya cultivars into world cultures has altered the way that the world

CORN, COTTON AND CHOCOLATE: HOW THE MAYA CHANGED THE WORLD

is nourished and has changed the course of history. It is astounding that an isolated civilization in a remote tropical setting has had a significant influence on the contemporary world. Even more unique is that this inventive civilization collapsed over 1100 years ago.

Maya agronomy is a living invention created by the world's greatest ancient intellectual civilization. The Maya legacy lives on and has served as a catalyst for world change. Scholars have overlooked the importance of Maya cultivars inducing their historic changes and their role in shaping the modern world. This book will provide a narrative detailing numerous historical changes caused by Maya cultivars and relate them to lifestyles in the 21st century world.

European contact with the Americas altered the history of the world forever; it not only changed the Americas but changed the old world land masses of Europe, Asia and Africa. Since the 15th century Maya cultivars have affected world food security, politics, laws, intellectual thought, industrial development, modern technology, financial empires and have triggered economic and cultural booms.

Maya cultivars constitute most of the important food and fiber crops in the 21st century. Their increased value has forever changed the balance of financial worth between the Maya cultivar and the troves of precious metals taken from the Americas.

They now feed 60% of the world's population, clothe 90% of the world's population, have increased global population and are the world's favorite flavors, fiber, fruit, spice, grain and drug. Maya cultivars have started armed revolutions, overthrown monarchies, founded college systems, promoted deadly habits, sparked sporting empires, changed the speech, music and lifestyles of world cultures and have killed more people than all the wars in history.

One would think that all this multifaceted change is beyond the scope of Maya cultivars. After all, they are only members of the plant kingdom and not an inspired renaissance movement. We will trace the source of the New World cultivars and follow the trail of these Maya inventions as they play their part in changing the history of the world.

Maya cosmic philosophy was based on concepts of time and space. They believed in cyclic time as in "history repeating itself". This sophisticated philosophy enabled the Maya to: *Remember the future and to anticipate the past.* This volume will borrow a page out of Maya philosophy in our assessment of the historical changes promulgated by Maya cultivars. We will undertake the role of a futurist and will assume that we have the gift of remembering the future as we assess the impact of Maya cultivars on history and project their implications on the future.

The author describes how Maya cultivars have been involved in the lives of people around the world and have altered the human condition that in turn has affected the course of history. The book will fascinate historians, archaeologists, plant lovers, gardeners, foodies, bloggers, cooking schools, trivia buffs and the intelligent readers who enjoy a good read and are fond of the obscure facets that have changed our world

CORN, COTTON AND CHOCOLATE: HOW THE MAYA CHANGED THE WORLD

CHAPTER 1: COLUMBUS INTRODUCES THE WORLD TO MAYA CULTIVARS

"Tierra a la vista" came the excited cry from the crow's nest lookout posted high atop the main mast. Crewmen swarmed upward, climbing the shrouds, eager to see the new land. This call was the first declaration that a completely New World had been discovered.

It was October 20, 1492, and Christopher Columbus was elated. The "Great Navigator" had guided his fleet of three ships westward across the Atlantic. He was searching for a new trade route to the Orient, sailing to the west in hopes of reaching the rich treasures of the East. Christopher Columbus, however, did not reach India on this voyage nor would the "Admiral of the Ocean Sea" ever reach the orient on any of his other three voyages of discovery.

India was the ultimate destination for European merchants seeking the vast riches of the East. Trade with the orient offered gold, silk, and spices for successful merchants, but the trading routes were fraught with danger. Reaching the promised lands of the East was a difficult journey. The route required sailing eastward across the length of the Mediterranean Sea and forming caravans to cross the Afro-Eurasian landmass. The caravans trekked overland, traversing exotic lands with challenging environments and hostile inhabitants.

For protection, the caravan trains were accompanied by small armies. Byzantine and Muslim rulers poised along the trade routes demanded tribute for the privilege of traversing their lands. Marauding raiders and bandits coveting the merchants' treasures lurked along the route. The profitability of the traditional overland trade route was diminished by looting as well as the tax burden. In the late middle ages, European merchants began searching for a safer trade route to the East Indies, preferably a sea route.

It was 1492 and the last Moorish ruler, Emir Muhammad XII, had surrendered the Emirate of Alhambra to the Spanish monarchy. This treaty ended the 800-year reign of the Moors on the Iberian Peninsula. The Emir was forced to abandon his beloved snowcapped Serra Nevada Mountains and retreat across the Mediterranean to the desert kingdom of Morocco. The King and Queen of Spain, Ferdinand and Isabella, took up residence in the Alhambra, the exotic royal palace of the Moors.

Christopher Columbus, an Italian navigator, convinced the Spanish monarchy that he possessed a revolutionary strategy for navigating a new route to the Eastern hemisphere. Meeting with the royal couple, in the Hall of the Ambassadors at the Alhambra, Columbus secured the sponsorship of Queen Isabella of Castile and King Ferdinand of Aragon to undertake the mission. Spain was the new power in Europe and needed to seek riches to finance their status and power. Spain had a pressing need for a new route to the wealth of the Indies.

On May 5, 1492, sailing under the Spanish flag, his three-ship fleet departed from Protos de la Fonterra on the Spanish coast, sailing westward to find an alternate sea route to the East Indies; a route that would bypass the Byzantine and Muslim middlemen. The small fleet dropped anchor in the Canary Islands, putting in for provisions and repairs. On September 6, 1492, outfitted and re-provisioned, the ships set sail westward seeking the riches of the Orient.

Unlike most of his crew, who believed that the earth was flat, Columbus knew that the earth was a sphere. The concept of the earth as a globe, as well as the size of its circumference, was an accepted fact by learned men of the middle ages. He was confident that his concept of

CORN, COTTON AND CHOCOLATE: HOW THE MAYA CHANGED THE WORLD

combining logical navigation methodology with global geometry would lead to the new route. Sailing on a course to the west would ultimately lead to the same destinations achieved by sailing eastward. Medieval mapmakers were sure that a vast un-crossable ocean extended between Europe and Asia. They had no concept that a large landmass was positioned in the Ocean Sea, as the Atlantic Ocean was then known.

On October 20, 1492, after a voyage of five weeks, the Great Navigator's ships landed on an Island in the Bahamas. He was so sure that he had reached the shores of the Indian subcontinent, that he termed the dark skinned native Arawak culture as "Indians".

Christopher Columbus had made the most celebrated error in history. He had not just discovered a single continent, he had discovered two new continents. He had encountered a destination that was much more significant than India. He had discovered a whole New World, a land with more potential, resources and treasures than the whole of the Orient. More than just riches, the discovery of the New World and the exploitation of its resources would produce changes in Europe that would result in levels of new prosperity for all social levels.

Spanish discoveries were initially confined to the Caribbean Islands. However, Columbus and other Iberian explorers were disappointed with their discoveries in the Caribbean Sea. The discoveries were important relative to new knowledge of the world, but they did not encounter the anticipated riches. They became aware that the islands possessed little of value to trade with the Spanish. The long-anticipated treasure trove of gold and silver were not realized until the vast landmass of the Americas had been explored. At that time, more wealth than the conquistadors had ever envisioned became a reality.

During his four voyages of discovery, Columbus encountered only small amounts of gold. However, during his explorations, he discovered valuable treasures. Columbus recognized the value of Maya cultivars. The Great Navigator shipped Maya cultivars back to the Spanish court. He introduced corn, cotton, chocolate, pineapple, tomatoes, chilies and the turkey to Europe. Maya cultivars began changing the world as soon as they were introduced to Europe.

Columbus' discoveries brought the New World into the forefront of European attention. Major sea powers in Europe launched expeditions of discovery for the exploitation of its riches, building trade networks, colonizing the lands and converting the pagans. The span of centuries extending from the 15th to the 17th century became known as the Age of Discovery. This interval in historical time served as a cultural bridge between the middle ages and the modern era. During this era, Europeans explored the world by long-range maritime travel. They explored new lands including the Americas, Asia, and Africa. The expeditions searched for trade goods, trading locations and ports, but they all wanted a piece of the Americas. Exploration discovered dozens of new food cultivars unknown to Europeans. When these plants were adopted, they provided the basis of an unprecedented expansion of the world's food supply and changed history.

In the Americas, Spanish explorers encountered several indigenous civilizations residing in grand cities larger and more populous then those of Europe. These civilizations included the Aztec Empire, the Inca Empire and the Maya civilization. European expeditions, searching for riches, colonization and conversion, collided with native civilizations and the results were catastrophic. Warfare and European crowd disease enabled the Spanish to devastate the native cultures and the world has never been the same.

CORN, COTTON AND CHOCOLATE: HOW THE MAYA CHANGED THE WORLD

The chronology of their conquests, the treasures they looted and the disasters they wrought are a matter of history. The conquistadors first conquered the Aztec Empire and then the Inca Empire. The Maya were the last to be conquered. At the beginning of the conquest, the conquistadors did not find the treasure they sought, but colonization and familiarity with the resources of the native cultures revealed the true treasures that were to be found in the new lands.

THE CONQUEST OF THE AZTEC EMPIRE

The Aztec was the first of the indigenous empires to be conquered by the Spanish. They were a wandering tribe from the north of Mesoamerica until the 13th century when they found their way into the Valley of Teotihuacán.

They migrated to a small swampy island in Lake Texcoco. In 1325, they founded the city of Tenochtitlan, which would soon be the capital of a massive empire. The capital city grew to have a population estimated as high as 300,000. Of all the cities in Europe, only Constantinople was larger. The Aztec Empire contained a population of over 25,000,000 people; it was a mighty force. The capital city boasted monumental architecture, large pyramids and refined temples, the façades were festooned with fine sculpture and colored stucco.

The Aztec were an intelligent culture but did not develop mathematics or writing. They did develop a system of narrative books. These books are pictorial and were meant to symbolize spoken or written narratives. There was no explicit Aztec math; it is believed that they applied a Maya-derived math using different symbols for numbers. Rather than a bar and a dot, the symbols included a feather, a flag and a bag representing different numerical values.

The Aztecs were great agriculturists and had creative methods of farming. Maize was the principal crop cultivated by the Aztec. Maize and the other major Aztec agricultural crops were directly inherited from ancient Maya agronomists. Maya cultivars provided many Aztec foods including avocados, beans, squashes, sweet potatoes, tomatoes, chia, amaranth and chilies.

Hernando Cortez, a Castilian adventurer based on the island of Cuba, heard tales of gold that could be found in a great kingdom on the mainland. The ambitious Cortez launched an unauthorized expedition to search out the fabled riches. In February 1519, Cortez sailed from Cuba with 11 ships, 500 men, 13 horses and number of cannon. He landed on the shores of Mexico at the Yucatán Peninsula and proceeded north to Tabasco.

As he marched towards the Aztec capital he realized that his army of 500 men was not a large enough force to challenge the Empire and he searched out allies along his line of march. Cortez developed alliances with native armies as he traveled. He strengthened his force with 3,000 Tlaxcaltec troops and they became a force to be reckoned with. The Aztec emperor Montezuma welcomed Cortez and his troops into the heart of the Aztec Empire. Montezuma presented Cortez with lavish gifts of gold. The Spanish entered the city and were amazed by the size and magnitude of the city of Tenochtitlan. They considered it to be grander than any city in Spain.

In April 15, 1520, Cortez traveled to the Gulf Coast leaving the city in the hands of subordinates. During his absence, his lieutenants carried out a ruthless massacre of the Aztec elite in the main temple. Brutally hacking off heads and body parts, hundreds of leading Aztec citizens were massacred. The marauding Spanish looted the fallen nobility of large quantities gold. After the attack, the population of the city rose en mass against the Spanish. Fierce fighting broke out and Aztec troops attacked the Spanish who barricaded themselves in the palace.

CORN, COTTON AND CHOCOLATE: HOW THE MAYA CHANGED THE WORLD

Cortez raced back to the capital to pacify the Aztec populace. Attempting to calm the angry crowds, Cortez ordered Montezuma to address the angry crowd from a palace balcony. The emperor was jeered by the throng and stones began to fly. Montezuma was severely injured by a stone and died from his injuries.

On July 1, 1520, under attack from furious Aztec warriors, Spaniards and their allied troops retreated from the city using the causeways that connected the island city to the shore. They were attacked by Aztec forces on the landside and from war canoes in the lake. The retreat turned into a rout. Soldiers weighed down by body armor and looted gold were drowned or killed by the attacking Aztec troops. The Spanish escaped with the Aztec in hot pursuit. The retreating Spanish lost 600 soldiers and 1000 native allies.

The pursuing Aztec army overtook the Spanish and attempted to destroy them at the Battle of Otumba. A fierce battle ensued, but superior tactics by the Spanish cavalry and their cannonades made the difference in the outcome of the battle. The Aztecs broke off the fight and left the field of battle.

In April 1521, the Spanish marched back to Tenochtitlan with their native allies plus new Spanish reinforcements from Cuba. The allied forces lay siege to the capital. The new Aztec emperor, Cuauhtémoc, led the defense of the capital city.

The siege lasted for eight months. The Aztec isolated the city by cutting off the causeways crossing the lake to the island. The lake became a moat for the fortress city. Cortez' plan of attack included the launching of boats for a marine assault. When the assault began, his cannonades decimated the city. The Spanish and their warrior allies manned the boats, landed on the shore, stormed the city and overwhelmed the defenders.

No one was spared. They plundered the treasures, and razed the capital. They tore down the magnificent art and architecture of the city, stone by stone. The stone rubble and the fragmented artworks were cast into the lake. Cuauhtémoc was captured as he attempted escape in a canoe. The grand city finally fell, ending the Aztec empire. Cortez claimed the city for Spain and re-named it Mexico City.

Cortez' dreams of golden treasure became a disappointment. Gold did not have intrinsic value to the Aztec. Many of the gold objects were actually gold foil covering wood carvings. A quantity of the treasure was actually *tumbaga*, an alloy of gold and copper. Large quantities of the gold plundered from the massacre in the temple had been lost in the furious retreat from Tenochtitlan. However, the word got out and Cortez' conquest of Mexico and his overstated claims of gold treasure radiated outward on waves of exciting news. European sea powers rushed forward to launch expeditions capitalizing on the wealth of the New World. However, the real treasure trove was found in South America. The bloody conquests of the Inca Empire lead to the gold and riches coveted by the Spanish Crown.

THE CONQUEST OF THE INCA EMPIRE

The Inca were also newcomers to the heights of power in pre-Hispanic empire-building. During the 12th century AD, the Inca were a pastoral people residing in the western South America. In the early 13th century, the Inca emerged from the highlands of Peru. With Cusco as their capital they consolidated their power and formed an Empire. From 1438 until 1533 the Inca incorporated a large area of western South America into their power base, controlling the largest political area in pre-Hispanic America. Their empire ranged from present day Columbia south to

CORN, COTTON AND CHOCOLATE: HOW THE MAYA CHANGED THE WORLD

Argentina. The Inca did not develop a written language and did not possess mathematics or any basic sciences. The Inca used assemblages of knotted strings, known as Quipu, to record mathematical information, the exact interpretation of the meaning of the knots is no longer known. They had an advanced understanding of civil engineering technology, and constructed an excellent road network that extended over 24,000 miles. Their system of roads enabled the transport of goods throughout the empire. The Inca road system traversed tall mountain ranges, Inca engineers constructed long rope suspension bridges to cross over canyons, gorges and rivers.

Inca architecture consisted of buildings constructed of finely worked stone walls assembled without mortar and topped with a thatched timber roofs. Their architecture had little decoration, but was built with a backdrop of dramatic landscapes. Their agriculture was well suited to the high altitude, steep conditions and the aridity of their mountain environment. They developed efficient agricultural techniques that included terracing and irrigation systems. Their agriculture included nutritious cultivars suited to their high-altitude, including potatoes, peppers, quinoa, sweet potatoes, peanuts and maize that was inherited from the ancient Maya.

In 1529, Francisco Pizarro obtained permission from the Spanish monarchy to conquer the land they called Peru. In 1532, Pizarro arrived in Peru and traveled to the capital of Cusco. He had 168 men under his command, 106 in the infantry and 62 cavalry mounted on horses.

Pizarro invited the emperor to meet with him to discuss peace relations between the Spanish and the Inca. The emperor responded that he would attend the meeting, but he did have questions about the actual intent of the Spanish.

Prior to the meeting, Pizarro positioned his men and their weapons strategically around the plaza. When the grand emperor, Atahualpa Inca, entered the plaza with his twelve personal attendants and 7000 unarmed soldiers, he was met by Pizarro, his lieutenants, and priests. The Inca asked Pizarro from where the Spanish derived their authority and he was presented with a bible and was told that it contained the word of god. The Inca held the book, shaking it near his ear, said "why does it not speak to me?" He had never seen a book and he then threw the unfamiliar object to the side.

This anti-Catholic action of casting away the bible, gave the Spanish a reason to attack. The Spaniards unleashed a thundering cannonade directly into the vulnerable mass of unarmed Incas. The armor-clad Spanish surged forward in a concerted charge, wading into the mass of humanity. The effect of their weaponry was devastating, the shocked mass of Incas could offer no resistance and the battle became a massacre.

The attack included a cavalry charge against the massed Inca. the Inca had never seen horses nor heard the sound of gunfire. The combination of horses and gunfire resulted in horrific panic of the Inca. The Spanish onslaught was expedited by their steel swords, helmets and armor. The Inca suffered 2000 dead compared to five of Pizarro's men. Pizarro then executed the emperor's 12-man honor guard and took Atahualpa Inca as a captive.

The battle had a strategic importance in the conquest of Peru. The Inca Empire embraced a centralized chain of command extending directly to the emperor as the commander in chief. This system of organization for Inca armed forces meant that once the Spaniards captured the emperor, they effectively paralyzed all the Inca armed forces. As a ransom for the Emperor, Pizarro demanded one room filled with gold and two rooms filled with silver.

CORN, COTTON AND CHOCOLATE: HOW THE MAYA CHANGED THE WORLD

Pizarro allowed the gold and silver to flow in and to pile up in the rooms, but he had no intention of releasing the emperor. He needed the emperor's influence over his generals and the Inca people to maintain the peace and gain control of Peru.

By May 3, 1533, the Spanish received all the treasure requested. It was melted down and made into gold bars. The emperor was jailed until August 1533, when he was then tried by the Spanish, convicted and sentenced to death for anti-Catholic practices. He agreed to accept baptism to avoid being burned the stake. At his baptism, he received the Christian name of Francisco. On August 29, 1533, the emperor was garroted and died a Christian.

Having deprived the Inca Empire of leadership, Pizarro then led his men in an orgy of looting, pillaging and torture while searching for precious treasure. The situation of the Inca Empire went downhill quickly. The last Inca, Tupac Amaru, was executed in 1572 and by this time the Spanish had destroyed most of the Inca culture and proceeded to colonize and exploit the former empire.

The conquest of Peru took about 40 years for completion. The Spanish conquest was achieved through relentless force, legendary courage, remarkable cunning and untold cruelty, aided by factors like European crowd disease and a vast division in communications and culture.

Unlike Mexico, the Spanish lust for gold came to fruition in Peru; untold fortunes were collected, which was then shipped back to Spain. The vast treasure was squandered by the Spanish royalty on wars and religious campaigns. Spain spent enormous amounts of this wealth by hiring mercenaries to fight the Protestant Reformation and to halt the Turkish invasions of Europe. The real treasure to be yielded by the Americas had not been revealed. Maya cultivars were yet to step up and take their place in history.

THE CONQUEST OF THE MAYA

The Maya culture, located in the Yucatán Peninsula, was the last indigenous domain to fall before the conquistadors. The Maya were an ancient civilization with a 3000-year history before its collapse in the 10th century. By comparison the Aztec and Incas were newcomers to history; both empires were founded in the 13th century. The Aztec and the Inca empires experienced parallel development; each had less than 400 years of total history when they were conquered by the Spanish. They did not achieve the levels of science, technology, or a written language comparable with the Maya.

The 3000-year-old Maya civilization collapsed in the 10th century, over 600 years before the Spanish conquest. After the collapse of the civilization, their grand cities were abandoned to the rainforest and overgrown by the relentless tendrils of the jungle. The Maya and their literate culture survived for six centuries. The culture continued onward, complete with their libraries of books, sciences, and advanced agriculture methods. At the time of the Spanish Conquest, the Maya domain, located on the Yucatán Peninsula of Mexico, had a population of 2,000,000 people residing in 16 fiercely independent states.

The conquest of the Maya states followed a completely different scenario than the conquests of the Aztec and Inca Empires. The Maya domain, composed of independent polities did not have a central political control. This organization was the opposite of an Empire, where the central power is focused on the emperor. Overthrowing the imperial seat of power would terminate the collective resistance of the population. The conquest of the Maya culture required the total defeat of each of the states on a singular basis. The states fiercely resisted the onslaught of the

CORN, COTTON AND CHOCOLATE: HOW THE MAYA CHANGED THE WORLD

Spanish. The Maya did not go quietly. It would take 170 years after the fall of the northern Yucatán before the last Maya citadel was defeated.

The rich lands of the New World attracted the attention of conquistadors. Francisco de Montejo, a veteran of Cortez' campaigns against the Aztec, successfully petitioned the king of Spain for the privilege to conquer the Yucatán. In 1527, he arrived in the eastern Yucatán and was peaceably greeted by the Maya; however, as the Spanish moved into the interior they found deserted villages. The Maya were clever and resistant fighters. The Spanish were first harassed, then ambushed, then openly attacked by Maya warriors. Montejo did not have success in subduing the Maya this year. In 1528, defeated, he traveled to the north of Mexico to gather a larger army.

Francisco de Montejo was in his late sixties, and turned over his royal rights to conquer the Yucatán to his son, Francisco de Montejo, the younger. The younger Montejo invaded Yucatán in 1540. In 1542, Montejo set up his capital in the Maya city of Ti'ho, which he renamed Mérida.

Montejo gained an important ally when the lord of the Tutal Xiu Maya converted to Christianity. The Tutal Xiu Maya controlled the western Yucatán; their army had a large number of warriors that became a valuable asset to the Spanish. The allied forces of Spanish soldiers and Tutal Xiu Maya warriors conquered the combined armed forces of the Maya states of the northern Yucatán. In 1546, the conquest of the northern Yucatán was officially complete, but the remainder of the Yucatán was still in the control of the individual Maya states. It would be a long time before the complete Yucatán Peninsula became a part of New Spain.

Francisco De Montejo became Governor and Captain General of the Yucatán. The conquistadors had little interest in the ruins of the abandoned Maya cities because they did not contain booty for enriching the Spanish court. The Franciscan priests, escorting the conquistadors, were educated men of god who should have had some curiosity in the artistic treasures of the lost civilization. However, they consorted in the demolition of the ancient Maya cities, using the stone from buildings for building new churches. They burned thousands of Maya books containing the scientific and intellectual legacy of the sophisticated society.

The books were written by Maya intelligentsia and contained records of the history and the sciences of the Maya civilization. The books that survived the centuries before the conquest had been protected, copied, and updated by generations of Maya scribes; these educated men were still writing and reading Maya books after the conquest. The Franciscans were devoted to destroying the religion of the Maya and converting them to Christianity. Resistance was punished by hanging, burning alive and drowning. It was forbidden to practice the Maya religion under penalty of death.

The Maya culture did not go easy. The Itza Maya in the southern part of the Yucatán resisted the Spanish for over 150 years after the conquest of the northern Yucatán. Between 1618 and 1624, the Spanish attempted to overcome the Itza Maya and their capital, Tayasal. In 1696, a force of 60 Spanish soldiers marched from Mérida in an attempt to capture Tayasal, but they were also beaten back by fierce Itza Maya attacks.

The Spanish command in Mérida decided that a major force was needed to overcome Tayasal. In 1697, the command sent out a force of 235 Spanish soldiers accompanied by thousands of Tutal Xiu Maya warriors. The army was equipped with artillery, a large mule train of supplies and men to cut a path through the rain forest.

CORN, COTTON AND CHOCOLATE: HOW THE MAYA CHANGED THE WORLD

The fortress city of Tayasal was located on an island in Lake Petén Itza. The Spanish invaders established a fort on the shore of the lake. They had prefabricated a warship in Mérida; the vessel had been carried overland in sections. The invaders assembled the boat on the shores of the lake. On March 30, 1697, the allied Spanish and Maya forces carried out an amphibious assault on the last independent citadel of the Maya and conquered the Itza Capital of Tayasal.

The Itza capital capitulated 150 years after the fall of the northern lowlands. When Tayasal fell to the Spanish, the literate scribes were still maintaining the classic period books. When the city fell, all the Maya books were burned and the scribes were put to death. There is no way to estimate the number of Maya books burned in the name of Christianity during the conquest. Only four Maya books survived the wrath of the zealous priests. These books are now known as "codices".

In 1697, at the time of the fall of Tayasal, the United States was a British colony and Harvard University was 63 years old. Somehow, we are connected.

At the beginning of the conquest in Mexico, the prime motivation of the conquistadors was the acquisition of precious metal. Initially the conquistadors had little interest in the Yucatán, its geology lacked metallic ore including gold and silver. However, in the Yucatán when the dreams of gold eventually faded, the reality of royal land grants became attractive. Land grants were a sure bet to promote colonization and bring wealth to the conquistadors.

It was not long before the Spanish adventurers became focused on royal land grants in the Yucatán. The goal of the Spanish crown and the purpose of the royal land grants were to develop a viable colonial presence in the Yucatán. The first efforts to establish a Spanish colony in the Yucatán began in the early sixteenth century. The program of land grants was awarded principally to conquistadors. This system of royal grants began what is now termed the Hacienda System.

Under the program of colonization, the Spanish begin to live within the indigenous community. The colonists grew familiar with the lifestyle of the local culture and the cultivars that were an integral part of the Maya patrimony. Large plots of farmland were planted with indigenous cultivars. The colonists became aware of the trading value of the rich cultivars available in the Maya habitat. These Maya cultivars included tobacco, cotton, henequen, maize, tomatoes, beans, squash, chocolate, vanilla, chilies, avocados, pineapples and other agricultural products. It became apparent that these unique products of Maya agronomy were valuable assets that could be transported as trade goods to the rest of the globe. These cultivars would make them rich.

Ships returning to Europe were not filled with gold but were filled with agriculture products harvested in Mesoamerica. These cultivars were Maya inventions that would change the world. They would make a more lasting impact on civilization, culture, and geopolitical aspects of the human condition than gold and silver would ever make and prove, in the long run, to be of more value than all the precious metals taken from the New World. The agronomy of the ancient Maya civilization would become a catalyst that would change the world forever.

CORN, COTTON AND CHOCOLATE: HOW THE MAYA CHANGED THE WORLD

CHAPTER 2: THE MYSTERIOUS MAYA, THE PHANTOMS OF HISTORY

The Maya civilization had small beginnings, first settling in small farming villages and flourishing into a scientific civilization that resided in grand high-rise cities. Maya intellectuals developed remarkable sciences in astronomy, mathematics, calendrics and writing. Maya engineers created technologies that were millennia in advance of European discoveries. However, from the beginning, the strength of the Maya civilization was all about their agriculture. The most enduring inventions of Maya intellectual efforts were in agronomy. Their great bounty of nutritious agricultural products produced a well-nourished population. Creative agronomy was the principal reason that the Maya flourished into a sophisticated scientific culture, enhancing their wealth and acquiring the capability to support an oversized population.

When placed in historical perspective, the long-term duration of the Maya era is incomparable. They had the longest-lived civilization in history. The Maya civilization stayed the course for 3500 years; its term extended from ancient biblical times to the European Middle Ages. Their time depth predated Hammurabi's code, Nebuchadnezzar and his hanging gardens, the rise and fall of the Egyptian kingdoms. They outlasted the classic Greek culture, marshaled on during the rise and fall of Rome, and terminated during the reign of Charlemagne. However, none of these historic people had any knowledge of the existence of the Maya civilization. Their time lines paralleled, but their histories do not converge because the Maya and other world civilizations did not know of the existence of each other. The Maya were the phantoms of history.

The Maya dominion was located in Southeastern Mesoamerica, a geographical area located in the Central American isthmus. This culturally defined area is an amoeba shaped region that extends from the northern Mexican highlands southward to the rainforests of Honduras. The most complex and advanced pre-Columbian cultures of the Americas flourished within the bounds of Mesoamerica. It is the most remote cradle of civilization on the planet.

The Maya scientific civilization developed in the isolation of the Yucatán. Their civilization was influenced by other Mesoamerican cultures predating or paralleling their ascendancy to the primary indigenous culture of the area. Mesoamerica was the incubator of precocious civilizations other than the Maya. These cultures included the Olmec, Zapotec, Teotihuacán, Toltec, and Aztec cultures. None of these cultures achieved the elevated levels of science, technology or agriculture that were realized by the Maya. It is impossible to create a mosaic reflecting the complete history of the numerous cultures that have emerged and declined in Mesoamerica since time immemorial. The names, achievements, and contributions of these ancient unknown cultures are lost in the mists of time.

THE EVOLUTION OF THE MAYA COSMIC PHILOSOPHY

The ancient Maya were avid sky watchers; they peered into the transparent night sky with fascination and awe. To them the vast array of lights in the heavens appeared to be in close contact with earthly affairs. After millennia of observations and study of the heavens they gained an uncanny knowledge of the harmonious composition of the cosmos.

For centuries before the Classic period, they observed the panoply of brilliant lights arrayed across the firmament; they studied the roaming motion of the planets, the orbs of fixed stars, the most remote of celestial spheres and the slow motion of our galaxy. Their thoughts roamed beyond our solar bubble and out into interstellar space. Their understanding of the roaming of astral bodies combined with millennia of profound thinking generated an innate knowledge of time and space.

Their knowledge of time and the universe grew into the veneration of the cosmos and the development of their quadripartite cosmic philosophy. This belief system inspired the scientific culture that guided their civilization.

Maya astronomers calculated the periods of astral bodies in terms of days and years, and then enumerated the cycles of various heavenly bodies into countless repetitions of the cycles that extended into periods of hundreds, thousands and millions of years. Their profound thought process stimulated the development of astronomy, mathematics, and innovative methods of written record keeping.

The skills of Maya scientists in astronomy, calendrics, mathematics and a comprehensive written script enabled the preservation of records including calculations of astronomical observations, historical narratives and scientific practices. Their written language enabled the Maya to enhance their scientific skills and preserve their knowledge for future generations.

MAYA SCIENCES

The Maya were the last of the great ancient civilizations on our planet to be discovered. They were "overlooked" and they only became known in the mid-nineteenth century. In the Yucatán, the Maya were never succeeded by another indigenous culture. The physical remains of the cities and the logic of the Maya culture have remained intact and fixed in time.

Since the re-discovery of the Maya in the nineteenth Century there has been great public interest in the civilization. The Maya have been studied and their advanced levels of scientific disciplines have amazed the Western world.

Their scientific and technological achievements were more advanced than any other contemporary culture on the planet. They have been compared to the Egyptians for the use of hieroglyphic-like characters in their writing, to the Greeks for their development of advanced sciences, to the Romans for construction of well-drained paved highways and to the Phoenicians for long-range trading in sea going vessels. In astronomy, they computed the time of earth's revolution around the sun to an accuracy that was more precise than that calculated by modern scientific instruments. The Maya created written almanacs of solar and lunar cycles containing accurate predictions of eclipse cycles. Their almanacs charted cycles of Venus, Mars, Mercury, Jupiter, and Saturn with great precision.

The mathematical system of the Maya was unique and well suited for the calculation of large array numbers The Maya mathematical system used a base of twenty rather than a base of ten used in European mathematics. Their mathematical system enabled the calculation of massive numbers using only three symbols. The mathematic system of the Maya used mathematics for everyday basic mathematical functions and their positional mathematics permitted the calculation of numbers in magnitudes of the hundreds of trillions.

Calculation using their mathematical system is flexible and exquisite for large magnitude astronomical calculations as well as minute calculations for practical applications in bookkeeping, census taking, record keeping and engineering calculations. The Maya mathematical system was vastly superior to that of the Roman, Greek, and Egyptian mathematical systems. These other mathematical systems were limited in their scope of

CORN, COTTON AND CHOCOLATE: HOW THE MAYA CHANGED THE WORLD

functions and were confined to numbers in the positive numerical range. The Maya understood the concept of the number zero and the computation of large array numbers in the negative number range, 900 years prior to European mathematicians.

The Maya writing system, a unique development of this brilliant civilization, is one of the world's five original written languages. The intricate and artistic flow of the characters creates a brilliantly derived art form for their language that enabled them to write anything they could speak. The Maya script was the thread that bound together the interdisciplinary sciences of astronomy, mathematics and calendrics.

Maya masters of the written word not only chronicled the history of the Maya and executed daily correspondence that managed the city-state, but they wrote thousands of books dealing with numerous and diverse subjects including astronomy, mathematics, calendrics, technology, medicine, law, ritual, music, and natural history.

During the Classic period, from 250 AD to 900 AD, the sophistication of Maya arts and sciences soared while Europe stumbled through the Dark Ages. When the Maya were enjoying the good life in their grand cities with populations of 100,000, London was a swampy river trading town with 9000 inhabitants.

MAYA TECHNOLOGY

The scientific accomplishments of the Maya were revealed through translations of their surviving books, painted ceramics and carved and painted inscriptions. Their achievements continue to astonish the academic world. However, scholarly research devoted to the Maya has completely overlooked the technological achievements of Maya engineers.

Technological achievements enabled the survival, health, and advantageous lifestyles of the inhabitants who populated the world's densest urban centers. Technology enabled the survival and growth of the Maya society despite their precocious tropical environment. Their culture suffered from an inconstant supply of rainwater, a lack of surface water, poor soil conditions and porous rock. They also had no beasts of burden or utilitarian metal ore.

The Maya, America's first engineers, met these challenges and overcame the obstacles. They fabricated tools of materials harder than steel, created cast-in-place concrete structures, built high-rise buildings, designed an efficient water management infrastructure system, devised land and water transportation systems, and developed productive agricultural systems that overcame the problematic environment and enhanced the power of their city-states.

Maya civilization and its technological developments were greatly influenced by the diversity and demands of their natural environment. The interaction of the lithosphere, biosphere and hydrosphere of the Yucatán presented unique and complex challenges to Maya engineers. The prospering of the Maya civilization, the survival of their densely-populated cities and their agricultural bounty was dependent on technological solutions for resolving adverse environmental conditions.

Technological solutions were solutions to the challenges of the Maya environment and it is apparent that the effects of the adverse environment were the impetus that inspired and motivated Maya technology. This technology created innovative solutions that enabled the high numbers of their populations of cities to lead a sophisticated urban lifestyle.

CORN, COTTON AND CHOCOLATE: HOW THE MAYA CHANGED THE WORLD

Maya technology overcame the absence of native metallic ore. They developed specialized tools that were harder than iron and were used for the fine shaping of stone and wood. Maya tools were fabricated from jadeite, a material harder that steel. These tools enabled Maya builders and artisans to construct structures in a grand architectural style replete with finely carved stone friezes. They fabricated fine cutting blades made from obsidian, a volcanic glass. Obsidian produces the world's sharpest blades.

Maya technicians invented the methodology for producing hydraulic cement from native limestone. This cement was used to produce cast-in-place concrete. Cement was the technological "glue" used to hold the Maya cities together and enabled their structures to persevere over 1,200 years of history while resisting a harsh environment. The Maya fabrication techniques for cement were invented 2,000 years in advance of European methods for manufacturing cement.

The classic Maya cities were the world's most populous cities of their historical time. High-rise buildings reaching into the tropical sky presented a spectacular profile against the backdrop of the rainforest canopy. These monumental landmarks would not have been possible to construct without the structural mechanisms developed by Maya engineers. Innovative Maya technicians invented the vaulted arch, high-rise structural systems and other mechanisms that enabled the construction of long span, high-rise buildings which characterized the skyline of Maya cities.

The Maya developed a series of unique technical solutions to satisfy the threat of dehydration for the population of large cities as well as water for agricultural systems. Maya engineering solutions included shaped cityscapes designed to divert storm water into storage facilities, underground reservoirs for urban water supplies, water filtration systems and efficient irrigation systems for agriculture.

To solve transportation issues relating to commerce, military movements, and agriculture, Maya engineers developed a system of elevated paved highways that connected Maya power centers. These all-weather roads, known as *sacbeob* or white roads, provided the Maya society with a reliable road system that could be used as transportation all year-round.

The Americas did not possess native animals that could be domesticated for use as beasts of burden. The horse, oxen and other beasts of burden were European imports to the Americas. However, the Maya had large amounts of well-fed manpower to do anything they needed done. The Maya understood the principal of the wheel, using them on toys, but the wheel was not practicable for use on carts that used the kinetic energy of manpower. Maya creativity developed man-powered transport systems that were more efficient and economical than animal powered transport. The adventurous and resourceful Maya were long-range sea traders. Their technology developed large sea-going cargo vessels that traversed long-range trade routes over the sea lanes of the Caribbean Sea, Gulf of Mexico and even the Pacific Ocean.

How did the Maya achieve these amazing accomplishments in the isolation of the Yucatán without the influence of outside cultures? What motivated their thirst for knowledge? What were the influences that aided their formula for success? The answer is "home cooking", a culturally motivated striving for achievement motivated by the need to overcome their complex tropical environment while keeping their gaze turned to the heavens.

CORN, COTTON AND CHOCOLATE: HOW THE MAYA CHANGED THE WORLD

MAYA AGRICULTURAL SCIENCES

The Maya lifestyle and success was all about agriculture. The Maya practiced efficient methods of agronomy for millennia. The variety of their cultivars increased as the Maya agronomists entered their Classic period. Technological innovations enabled the population to expand at a rate that outstripped capabilities for feeding the populace using traditional agriculture methods. Maya technicians met the challenge by developing new cultivars and improved methods of agriculture systems to satisfy the needs of the growing population. Agronomy sciences made significant contributions to agricultural systems for producing larger quantities of food by developing sustainable long-term growth strategies.

By 8,000 BC, the cultivation of domestic agriculture products and creative agronomy began in Mesoamerica. A great variety of agriculture products and efficient agriculture methods were developed by the Maya. These agriculture innovations evolved into the successful farming methods which produced the rich harvests of the Classic period. The technology of the ancient Maya resulted in diverse and sophisticated methods of agriculture production. Maya agriculture methodologies overcame the adverse environment and enabled enhanced food production.

Their first great contribution to agriculture was the domestication of maize. Maya agronomists were able to alter *tenocinte*, a wild native grass, into the high yielding grain. This was a pivotal step forward in the agronomy of the Maya.

The lifestyle of the Maya led to the skillful domestication of plants and animals, increasing agriculture yields. The only solution for agricultural success was to depart from traditional methods and develop new methods to increase the agriculture yield. This secure food supply allowed the Maya make the transition from hunters and gatherers, to settle down, adopt a sedentary lifestyle, advance their culture, and grow their population. The sedentary lifestyle and the abundance of agriculture led to the establishment of villages and towns. These settlements became the focus of their newly formed society.

Maya engineers combined agricultural technology and cultivars developed by their agronomy sciences to increase the food supply. Maya engineers created fertile new agricultural land areas that included the use of reclaimed wetlands, terraces, raised fields and new irrigation methodologies.

As the Maya population grew, the demand for increased agriculture yields became a constant challenge to be satisfied. Higher crop yields meant a demand for more water. Maya water management technology met the challenge of that demand with a multidiscipline effort to generate abundant agriculture yields for the needs of the Maya population.

MAYA HISTORY AND THE DEVELOPMENT OF THEIR PATRIMONY

The chronology of the colonization of the Americas is surrounded by controversy and speculation. It is generally theorized that, 20,000 years ago, at the end of the Pleistocene Era, hunters and gatherers of Siberia crossed over the frozen Bering Sea to a new continent. These migratory nomads colonized the Americas. This was not a purposeful southward migration, but a natural expansion into new territory that attracted the newcomers.

During this period, giant mega fauna still roamed the Americas, including giant ground sloths, mammoths, gomphotheres, saber tooth tigers, camels and wild horses. Bands of nomadic

CORN, COTTON AND CHOCOLATE: HOW THE MAYA CHANGED THE WORLD

hunters-gathers migrated toward southern Mesoamerica; they liked what they saw, made camp, and began their evolution into the Maya civilization.

During their Archaic period, 8000 BC to 2500 BC, the proto-Maya culture in southern Mesoamerica began to practice sophisticated agricultural practices, including agronomy and agriculture sciences. The ecosystem of the Maya world was an excellent environment for the growth of maize as well as a wealth of other agriculture products.

The establishment of towns with an increased population base enabled the emergence of industrial and trading skills which enhanced the development of their technical arts. The technical arts flourished and created a new class of artisans who developed new techniques including loom weaving, basketry, stylized pottery, and specialized tool making. These new industrial products and the surplus of agriculture products created a merchant class and the opportunity to initiate long-range trade routes to other parts of Mesoamerica.

The Maya of the pre-Classic period, 2,000 BC to 250 AD, optimized the wealth they derived from the hybridization of valuable cultivars. The advancement of the technological arts was applied to develop their society and economy. The social culture of the towns became more stratified as the new merchant and artesian classes merged synergistically with the ruling elite.

During the classic period, 250 AD to 910 AD, the Maya organized their domain into individual city-states. Over fifty city-states were founded in the 125,000-square mile Maya region. The Maya world did not follow the political philosophy of the empire builders; they espoused a more finite method of political subdivision. Their political organization was based on small independent polities. The basic political unit of the Maya was a sovereign city-state.

The Maya placed emphasis on individuality and the independent city-state suited this political philosophy. The urban centers of their city-states were home to tens of thousands of inhabitants including the elite ruling classes, scientists, merchants, engineers, artisans, and specialists.

The sprawling Maya city-states were more than technically dazzling examples of art and architecture that were conceived to overwhelm the observer with a sense of wonderment. These cities were centers of power, incubators of science and technology, seats of learning, and the hub of big business operations that generated the wealth of the kingdom.

Some cities were larger and more powerful than others and became were more influential. The larger classic cities had greater influence on the development of the cultural, scientific, and technical advances of the Maya culture. The scale and influence of the leading cities reflected their great wealth which led to enhanced commercial power and universities offering a wide diversity of learning skills and the generation of scientific knowledge. Dissemination of scientific knowledge was dispersed by the more powerful city-states through their larger trade networks, political influences, and dominance.

The population of the inhabitants of large classic cities is uncertain. Scholars have developed estimates of the population based on the remnants of dwellings in the urban area. For instance, it has been estimated that the city of Tikal had a population of 100,000 people.

The Maya enjoyed the height of their golden age during the ninth century. Their Classic cities featured dramatic architecture with high-rise pyramids smoothly coated in stucco and painted in brilliant colors laid out around grand plazas. Stepped pyramidal structures, topped by temples, towered over art-adorned palaces, universities, ball courts, and public buildings.

CORN, COTTON AND CHOCOLATE: HOW THE MAYA CHANGED THE WORLD

These large cities were planned urban spaces with nodes of artistically styled buildings connected by elevated paved roadways. These paved roads crossed the cityscape and extended out of the city into the hinterlands. This all-weather road system traversed the root-tangled and marshy jungle floor, smoothing the way for travelers as well as the intercity transportation system required for trade and communication with other city-states.

The Classic period saw the flourishing of the scientific, technical and artistic capabilities of the Maya civilization. The powerful city-states, fueled by wealth from bountiful agriculture, multi-faceted industries and a long-range trading network produced a cultured environment. The sophistication of the Maya intellectual elite was motivated by their cosmic philosophy and long-term cognitive thought. This combination of salient factors enabled scientists to advance their disciplines and to enhance their sphere of knowledge. The scientific and technical levels achieved by the Maya during the classic period pre-dated similar achievements of European scientists by a thousand years.

The ninth century saw the golden age of the Classic Maya burning brightly and then enigmatically the brilliant society was extinguished. The Maya had enjoyed over three thousand years of civilization during their Pre-classic period and six centuries of unparalleled enlightenment and prosperity during the Classic period. As the tenth century approached, the classic civilization of the Maya collapsed when the worst drought in 3,000 years resulted in catastrophe. Their magnificent cities were abandoned, surrendered to the encroaching rain forest and crumbled into decay. The civilization that achieved intellectual heights for millennia was no more.

Analysis of paleo-climatic and meteorological historical data concurrent with this period indicates that the root cause of the failure of the Maya society was an environmental disaster combined with the inability of Maya technology to overcome the natural crisis. The root cause of the demise of the classic cities and the death of the Maya civilization was not due to "The barbarians at the gates" syndrome, the revolt of slaves, or invasion from outside forces that had been surmised by some scholars, but the end of days was caused by an apocalyptic environmental disaster.

Maya advances in agriculture technology replete with great water reservoirs failed to overcome the devastation of the Great Drought. The failure of engineered systems and the inability of Maya technology to cope with the vagaries of Mother Nature resulted in the death of 98% of the Maya population and the collapse of the Maya civilization.

During the Post-classic period the Maya slowly came back and the culture survived. The rebirth and dominance of cities in the northern lowlands, including Uxmal, Mayapan and Chichen Itza was the result of the outside cultural influence of the Toltec from Central Mexico. These cities owed their survival to the accessibility of a reliable water supply from the aquifer. The products of their agronomy survived the collapse and were foisted on the Post classic period.

The Toltec and Maya cultures interacted to construct new cities with a composite art and architectural style reflecting both Maya and Toltec stylistic modes. The brief blossoming of these cities extended until about 1,200 AD. At that time, Chichen Itza was sacked by the city of Mayapan. Mayapan was the last remnant of the Maya Civilization when it fell to a revolt in 1460.

The Maya scientific heritage did not survive into the Post-classic period. However, thousands of Classic period books survived. These volumes containing the collective knowledge of the Maya were inscribed by the intellectual elite. They were preserved over the centuries and copied by

CORN, COTTON AND CHOCOLATE: HOW THE MAYA CHANGED THE WORLD

literate Maya scribes. The work of preservation extended beyond the Post classic period and into the time of the Spanish conquest.

The Spanish conquest extinguished the indigenous cultures of Mesoamerican. The great Maya Classic period had collapsed more than six centuries before conquistador Hernando Cortez landed on the Mexican coast. The ancient cities of the Maya were degraded by the passage of time and jealously hidden by the encompassing veil of the rainforest tendrils. The conquistadors had no interest in the ruins and their resplendent artwork. They were seeking gold and treasure.

While the Spanish colonial government attempted to suppress the traditional culture of the Maya, the knowledge of the Maya sciences lived on through the books carefully protected by the Maya elite. These priceless treasures of scientific knowledge, which had survived hundreds of years, were destroyed by the Spanish colonial government during the period from 1563 to 1697.

As the centuries passed the Spanish colonial government suppressed all outside references to the lost cities of the Maya. The Maya continued to be the phantoms of history. The exploration of the ancient cities was forbidden by the Spanish until the 1820 Mexican Revolution. Since the discovery of the Maya civilization in the 1840s, the achievements of Maya science and technology have been revealed and the world has been amazed at their accomplishments.

REDISCOVERY AND DECIPHERMENT

The grand cities of the Maya civilization lay buried beneath the luxuriant vegetation of the tropical jungle for six centuries before the conquistadors landed on the coast of Mexico. A millennium would pass after the Maya collapse before the outside world knew of their existence. The discovery jump started the effort to uncover the wonders of the constructions of the Maya cities. However, the riddle of Maya writing would stay a mystery for an additional century after the discovery of the ruined civilization. When the Maya writing code was broken, it revealed the amazing truths of their philosophy, history, and scientific accomplishments.

Prior to the discovery of Maya cities, images of pre-Colombian art included in European publications were derived from the minimal descriptions of pre-Columbian cities derived from the letters and accounts of conquistadors. Scholars pursued the misconception that pre-Colombian civilizations had European roots. They could not conceive that that an isolated indigenous civilization could create the levels of art and construction discovered among the ruined cities.

Spain's New World colonies won their independence during the early part of the 19th century. Gone was the xenophobic policy of New Spain. The Maya homeland in Mexico and Central America was opened to explorers and scholars of antiquity. In 1841, world history was changed when two explorers published accounts of their adventures in the rainforest of the Yucatán. The books contained incredible descriptions and images of the art and architecture of the lost cities of the Maya civilization.

On October 3, 1839, John Lloyd Stevens and Frederick Catherwood boarded a ship in New York harbor and set sail for the Bay of Honduras. Little did this talented pair know how much this adventure would change their lives and result in the re-writing of world history.

The pair traveled to ancient Maya sites and recorded their observations of the amazing art and architecture. Stephens's narrative of the art and architecture of in the classic cities, and the daily incidents of their travels were chatty, well organized, and clearly written accounts of the adventure. Catherwood's splendid drawings of the art and architecture in the ruins were talented and faithful depictions of their beauty.

Stephens was familiar with the recent decipherment of Egyptian hieroglyphics by the French scholar Jean François Champollion, who had deciphered the Rosetta stone. Stephens was convinced that the carved inscriptions on the monuments were a hieroglyphic script that described the historical records of the civilization that had constructed the cities. This leap of consciousness was a direct link derived from their knowledge of the writing systems of ancient civilizations.

Previous European volumes describing Maya art and architecture had cost thousands of dollars. In 1841 Stephens two-volume sets of his books sold for five dollars and were affordable to the general American reading public. *Incidents of Travel in Central America, Chiapas and Yucatán* sold 20,000 copies in the first three months of publication. Stevens' clever narrative and the precise engravings by Catherwood produced works that fueled popular imagination and became best sellers throughout the world.

In 1843, the pair published a second two volume set relating to the Maya, *Incidents of Travel in Yucatán*". The second set, equally popular as the first, related to their exploration of Maya sites in the Yucatán in more depth. These popular books resulted in the re-writing of the history of the Americas and opened the Classic Maya civilization to exploration and fields of study. Today, these books are as popular with aficionados of archaeology as they were in the 19th century

The most brilliant breakthrough of Maya writing decipherment, arguably the greatest linguistic achievement since the translation of the Rosetta stone, did not come from the ivory towers of an Ivy League university. The breakthrough started in the war-torn streets of Berlin during WWII.

In May 1945, the Soviet Army had overrun Berlin and was sacking the capital of the Third Reich. On that night, Yuri Valentinovich Knorosov, a young Russian artillery spotter, found himself in front of the Prussian National Library. The library was being pillaged by the victorious Red Army. That fiery night, Yuri encountered his comrades throwing thousands of rare books into the burning pyre. It was fate that guided his hand to a random book lying at the edge of the conflagration. He snagged the book from the inferno and then slipped away into the darkness. The random book that Yuri collected was a rare 1933 publication containing facsimiles of Maya books. Fate had guided him to a volume containing copies of the only Maya writings existing: the Paris, Dresden, and Madrid Codices.

Knorosov, a scholar in ancient written scripts, was well prepared to decipher the Maya code. His background in ancient languages and writing systems prepared him well for the task of breaking the Maya code much better than Western scholars. His brilliant work became the most significant effort in deciphering the Maya script. In 1952, he published the paper "Ancient Writing of Central America." Then, the real work in decipherment, based on Knorosov's work, began in earnest.

Further progress in the decipherment accelerated exponentially during the 1960's and 1970's. Breakthroughs in reading the Maya script were advanced by a series of conferences that assembled talented epigraphers and Mayanists. These conferences; including the Palenque Round Table and the Texas Maya Meetings combined with a new breed of "young Turks" and "born again" veterans created unique and advanced breakthroughs in unveiling the secrets of the Maya. Archaeologists are now able to decipher 85% of the Mayan hieroglyphics.

CORN, COTTON AND CHOCOLATE: HOW THE MAYA CHANGED THE WORLD

The cities of the lost Maya civilization lay hidden in the dense rain forest; their structures had suffered the toll wrought by time and the environment. As explorers and archaeologists located the remnants of this intellectual culture and reported the glory of the art and architecture of the cities and their scientific accomplishments, readers across the globe became intrigued by the Maya. During the past century, universities, museums, foundations and governments have cleared the sites of the ancient ruins and consolidated the monumental structures to permit a view of the ancient Maya cities.

Tourists and aficionados of Maya culture have flocked to the ancient cities to gaze in awe at the skyscraping pyramids and ornate sculptures constructed by artisans who have long passed into history. The numbers of international visitors have increased until they now count in the tens of millions each year who pay homage to their beloved Maya.

MAYA CULTIVARS THAT HAVE CHANGED THE WORLD

Maya inventiveness and their cognitive thought process created prodigious works in science, technology, art and agricultural sciences. Their creativity in agronomy and agricultural sciences resulting in the development of valuable cultivars that continues to affect the fortunes of the world and its populations. The conquistadors quickly recognized the value of Maya cultivars and transported the Maya agricultural products to Europe and Asia.

These Maya cultivars were diffused around the globe for three centuries prior to the discovery of the lost Maya civilization by explorers in the rainforest. They have been a part of the world's bounty of foods for such a long time that many countries have forgotten that are from the New World and have assumed that they originated in their own countries.

Maya foodstuffs have changed the tastes of many countries and, today, the world benefits from Maya agriculture in many ways. One can imagine the change in Thai, Indian or Hungarian cooking without chili peppers. Roaming the aisles of a modern supermarket, the agricultural legacy of our brilliant Maya antecedents becomes apparent. Observe the commercial offerings contributed by the Maya: maize, tomatoes, chocolate, vanilla, squash, chilies, beans, peanuts, avocados, chicle, sweet potato, papaya, pineapple, jicama, sunflower seeds, and a wide variety of other agricultural products like cotton, tobacco, and sisal. The influence of Maya cultivars goes well beyond the food consumed by the world.

The influence of Maya cultivars has changed the world and they are still evolving global cultures and politics. Maya cultivars have started wars, incited revolutions, changed geopolitical borders, modified language, enriched and caused the financial collapse of nations, ensconced themselves in popular arts, and have been the cause of the death of millions of people.

This book describes the methods Maya agronomists used in producing their cultivars, traces the paths of the world traveling Maya cultivars and details the effects that Maya cultivars have had altering the history of the world.

CORN, COTTON AND CHOCOLATE: HOW THE MAYA CHANGED THE WORLD

CHAPTER 3: MAYA AGRONOMISTS INVENT THE MAGIC CULTIVAR

The Maya were the ancient world's greatest agronomists. Their history of agricultural achievements extends in time more than 8000 years. Their agronomists created cultivars of unequaled quality by combining science with innovative environmental management and selective plant breeding. The cultivars produced by Maya agronomy are real inventions generated by their scientific civilization. These unique inventions were not machines but living organisms. The goal of their agronomy was to develop cultivars that enhanced the lifestyle of their populace.

A cultivar is native plant that has been intentionally altered by humans for specific characteristics and converted into a valuable food or fiber product. The achievements of their agronomy were the greatest and most enduring creations of the Maya civilization. This creative endowment has been passed down over millennia and now provides the majority of the world's agricultural food supply. These Maya inventions have influenced the world's social-political history and have altered the tastes, beliefs, and mores of the modern lifestyle. Maya cultivars have changed the world.

Their 3500-year history gave the Maya ample time to perfect their agronomy. Nowhere in the world was so much energy invested in domesticating plants and the effort has proven its worth. These cultivars provide the majority of foods that constitute the modern diet. Their mastery of agriculture made the Maya the greatest of the world's ancient agronomists and arguably the best in world history. The Maya produced exquisite cultivars that have outlasted their civilization by 1100 years.

Compared with Maya advances in science and technology, their greatest inventions were in agronomy and agriculture sciences. Their bounty of agricultural cultivars was the primary reason that Maya technology soared and accelerated their evolution into a sophisticated urban civilization.

Long before their Classic period, Maya agronomists developed cultivars that provided food and clothing for their population. The final characteristics and appearance of these cultivars bore no resemblance to the original native plant. Maya agronomists converted a native grass into a sophisticated high-yielding grain called maize. Botanists consider this feat to be the greatest achievement in the history of agronomy.

The magnitude of scientific knowledge generated in the modern world has surpassed Maya in advances science and technology. However, innovations by Maya agronomists have not been surpassed. Modern agronomists have genetically altered Maya cultivars, but the level of quality and variety of cultivars originally developed by the ancient Maya has not been surpassed.

The influence of Maya cultivars on the course of history has been overlooked by scholars. These cultivars have induced a synergistic influence on the world's society comparable to similar influences which enabled the Maya to develop their advanced civilization. This symbiotic influence adheres to a classic anthropological concept: a sufficient food supply is required for a culture to accelerate their advance into a great civilization. Simply put, food security enables the

CORN, COTTON AND CHOCOLATE: HOW THE MAYA CHANGED THE WORLD

refinement of culture, urban development, domination over the natural environment and the growth of advanced ideas. Maya cultivars initiated a green revolution that has altered the world.

THE MIRACLE OF MAYA AGRONOMY

Maya farmers practiced agronomy for millennia. They applied a combination of plant genetics, meteorology, and soil sciences to alter plant characteristics. Their mission was to produce a superior cultivar capable of producing nutritional foods and quality fibers. The science of agronomy was developed and mastered by the Maya through a process of intense agricultural activities.

The Maya were fortunate to inhabit an environment that ranged from rainforest to alpine climate. This diverse environment was the locale of a broad range of plants that possessed important innate nutritional characteristics. These wild specimens became prime candidates for manipulation into a valuable cultivar.

They used a variation of the scientific method for the development of a cultivar. Their methodology involved systematic observation, experimentation by testing, and the evolution of a native plant into a useful specimen of nutritious food bearing plants. Maya cultivars were the results of conscious biological manipulation of native plants. Their expertise in developing cultivars started when a Maya farmer noticed that the seeds of certain specimens were different from other typical plants in his field. Selected seeds of the aberrant specimen were saved and propagated. This process of selection, maintenance, and cultivation of a particular plant would be reiterated until the optimized cultivar was produced. The cultivar was introduced and adopted as a mainstay of the basic Maya diet.

The science of agronomy played an active role in Maya culture throughout their history. This practical science began well before their pre-Classic period. By the dawn of their pre-Classic period, the Maya had achieved significant breakthroughs in the cultivation of plants. They developed agronomy into a broad based and finite science.

Motivated by their cosmic belief system, Maya agronomists adopted a dedication for developing cultivars that enabled feeding large populations. They acquired the unique ability to identify wild plant specimens and convert them into valuable cultivars. This capability of breeding plants evolved into a cornucopia of astounding Maya cultivars. These unique Maya inventions assumed a life of their own and they have survived and prospered over the millennia.

THE FIRST CULTIVAR

The transformation of a native grass into high yielding maize, which we call corn, is the best-known Maya cultivar. The modern manifestation of this ancient plant bears little resemblance to its ancestor. The ancestor of maize was a wild grass called *teosinte* from southern Mesoamerica. The transformation from an inconspicuous grass into a diverse, highly evolved, and productive food plant is a story of co-evolution and interdependence between humans and maize that has spanned thousands of years.

Teosinte is a tall, drought-tolerant grass that produces an enclosed husk with fruiting spikes that are filled with two rows of small, dark triangular-shaped seeds. After discovering that teosinte seeds were edible, Maya farmers began selecting teosinte seeds from spikes with promising

CORN, COTTON AND CHOCOLATE: HOW THE MAYA CHANGED THE WORLD

traits and planting them in cultivated plots. The plants from selected seeds were grown in isolation away from wild teosinte growing in the surrounding fields. Isolation was required in order to avoid cross-pollination. Thus, the process of intentional evolution of maize had begun.

The oldest known evidence of maize "corncobs" that are distinctly different from teosinte, are estimated to be 5400 years in age. The cobs have rows of kernels firmly attached to the cob, which are only one-inch in length. At this point, the program of evolving teosinte into maize had progressed for 2000 years of human manipulation. The long-term program of evolution changed the characteristics of teosinte and altered their grain spikes into the cobs of the transformed maize plant. The process of genetic evolution continued over millennia until maize assumed characteristics similar to the familiar modern grain of corn.

The attachment of kernels to a central cob and the lack of a hard, inedible coat around the seed are the key factors that have inextricably bound maize propagation to human involvement. Human hands are required to reproduce maize. Because of the firm attachment of the kernels to the cob, the kernels must be manually removed from the cob and stored until the following planting cycle.

THE THREE SISTERS

Maya agronomists developed cultivar support systems that further enhanced their ability to produce quality crops. Maize was joined by two other Maya cultivars to form the most important food group in Maya culture. The second most important crop in Maya agriculture is the squash. Chronologically, the squash plant was domesticated over 10,000 years ago; it was a cultivar before maize.

The common bean was a major food source for the Maya and became the third plant in the basic food support group. Beans were an early product of domestication. Bean cultivars were adapted as early as squash and maize. It is apparent that these three crops were the first domesticated cultivars, they became more than just a self-supporting team, they became the stuff of legend known as the "three sisters".

These three cultivars formed the nucleus of Maya agriculture. Maize, beans, and squash provided the Maya with a troika of complementing nutrients. Each of the cultivars contributed some part of the essential mix of amino acids and vitamins that human beings require for survival.

Additional beneficial characteristic of the three sisters includes planting them together to create synergistic benefits. Together they form a support system vital to their growth process. These self-helping cultivars are known as "companion plants". They form a mutual benefit system that enhances the supply and retention of soil nutrients while protecting the triad from pests and disease while the maize stalks provide vertical supports for the bean runners.

Maya agronomists realized that the same plant breeding procedures that were used to modify maize, squash and beans could be used to alter other native plants. They accelerated their efforts to introduce additional nutritious cultivars into the food supply. Their success with the science of agronomy was a smash hit. Productivity soared and population growth blossomed.

CORN, COTTON AND CHOCOLATE: HOW THE MAYA CHANGED THE WORLD

THE SEASONAL DESERT AND THE GEOLOGY OF THE ENVIRONMENT

Nothing came easy to the Maya, they learned early in their history to overcome environmental adversity. The success achieved by the brilliant and patient Maya agronomists is more impressive when one considers slthe negative environmental and geological factors that had to be overcome to achieve success in agricultural sciences. The negatives are not easily perceived to the eye of the casual observer.

Maya agronomists faced a triple whammy of adverse environmental obstacles that impeded their achievements. Negative issues included inadequate soil conditions, the nature of the subsurface geology, and the capricious rainfall in the Yucatán.

Geographically, the Maya domain lies in some of the most diverse topography of the tropics. The Yucatán Peninsula is the principal geographic landform of the domain. Bordered by the Pacific Ocean on the west, it extends northward, jutting outward from the mid-America isthmus and forming a landmass that separates the Gulf of Mexico and the Caribbean Sea. Geologically, the Yucatán peninsula is a broad flat shelf of karstic limestone that extends on a north-south axis from a range of massive volcanic mountains as they curve southward along the Pacific Coast.

The climate of the Maya world is one of the most diverse on the planet. It is a complex combination of ecosystems, environmental areas, and topographical zones. The hot tropical climate of the lowland rainforests is in stark contrast to the temperate climate located in the high volcanic mountains of the southern highlands

The Maya world experiences some of the heaviest rainfall in the tropics and this heavy rainfall has both positive and negative factors. Approximately 75% of the yearly rainfall occurs during the six-month rainy season. The dry season has a significant lack of rain. The reduced amount of precipitation during the dry season creates drought-like conditions for the Yucatán. This phenomenon of alternating periods of heavy rain and drought-like conditions turns the Yucatán peninsula into a "seasonal desert".

The cyclic wet-dry contrast of the seasons is the result of a meteorological phenomenon stemming from the seasonal migration of precipitation associated with the inter-tropical convergence zone. This inter-tropical convergence zone migrates to the South during the winters leaving the Yucatán in drought-like conditions for six months. This atmospheric condition, known as the meteorological equator, results in a northern shift of the zone during the summer and with this shift, heavy rains come to the Yucatán.

The Maya were faced with alternating conditions of deluge or drought each year. For survival, Maya society and its agriculture required a dependable year-round source of water. The development of water management methodologies presented a challenge for Maya agriculture technology.

In addition to the precocious rainfall, the Maya had to overcome additional environmental adversities. These included a thin layer of infertile soil overlaying a limestone subsurface. The subsurface of the Yucatán is composed of karstic limestone, a porous material that directly absorbs rainwater permitting it to flow downward into the aquifer. The flow of rainwater travels down through the thin soil layer, passes through the porous limestone stratum and into the deep aquifer. This disposition of the rainfall directly into the aquifer, results in the lack of surface water in the Yucatán. The absence of natural bodies of surface water in the form of rivers or lakes deprived the Maya population with a natural supply of surface water to exploit during the dry season.

It is a wonder that the lush rainforests thrive in the drought-like dry season. During the rainy season, the dense tropical vegetation of the rainforest drinks in large amounts of precipitation. During the dry season, the rainforest trees draw moisture from deep taproots. The roots extend deep down through the limestone into the aquifer. The lack of surface water leaves the area without a source of water during the dry season. A seasoned explorer knows that one can easily die of thirst during the dry season while wandering in the lush, humid rainforest.

SOLVING THE ENVIRONMENTAL ISSUES

Maya lifestyle was all about agriculture. The quantity and variety of their cultivars accelerated as the Maya entered their Classic period. It was the right idea at the right time. Population growth ballooned due to the urbanization of the city-states. This population growth induced the need for increased food production. The solution for increasing crop production required departing from traditional farming methods and developing new techniques based on a combination of water management technology, soil management and enhanced cultivars.

The traditional Maya farming methods used the classic "slash and burn" technique of clearing land for agriculture. This ancient method was inefficient and produced a low crop yield. Slash and burn agriculture requires cutting down a section of forest and burning the accumulated cut vegetation. The ashes from the burned vegetation were scattered over the plot providing nutrients for the soil

After 2 to 5 years of farming activity the thin infertile soil of the Yucatán became depleted. When the traditional farming cycle is complete, the land is then planted as an orchard garden and allowed to return to its natural growth. The natural recovery of fertility for a depleted plot may take a period of 5 to 15 years. In the meantime, a new plot of land is cleared, the vegetation burned and another cycle of cultivation begins.

The Maya combined agricultural technology with proven cultivars to create new agriculture methodologies. New agriculture technology required that Maya engineers introduce innovative management systems that enhanced the production of crops.

The Maya developed water management methodologies that overcome the foibles of precipitation in the Yucatán. Maya engineers solved the issue of inconstant rainfall by capturing the massive volume of storm water that fell during the rainy season. They developed engineered systems to collect and store water during the rainy season to provide an ample supply of potable water during the dry season.

Maya civil engineers faced up to Mother Nature's challenge and applied their ingenuity to develop viable solutions for locations with disparate water sourcing issues. Varied solutions involved optimization of aquifer-fed water supply systems, collection of storm water using

CORN, COTTON AND CHOCOLATE: HOW THE MAYA CHANGED THE WORLD

underground storage reservoir structures, storage in surface water reservoirs, and agricultural-integrated water supply systems.

The heuristic technology of the Maya civilization triumphed over the fickleness of Mother Nature. Maya engineers optimized their technology and overcame the lack of water created by the seasonal desert.

AGRICULTURAL TECHNOLOGY OVERCOMES ENVIRONMENTAL BARRIERS

As the Maya population grew, the demand for increased agriculture yields became a challenge. Higher crop yields required a dependable and sufficient supply of water, improved soil conditions, and enhanced agriculture systems. Maya agricultural sciences rose to the challenge. The demand for a dependable water source was met with a multidiscipline effort. They applied the principals of hydrology and agricultural sciences combined with agronomy to increase agricultural output.

As the Maya entered their Classic period, urbanization and technological innovations caused the population to expand at a rate that outstripped traditional capabilities for feeding the populace. Maya technicians faced the challenge of developing new agriculture methods to satisfy the needs of the growing population.

Agriculture technology was needed to produce greater quantities of food. The Maya developed sustainable long-term growth strategies for agriculture systems including the development of high yielding cultivars, replenishment of soil, irrigation and fertilization, cultivation of hillside terraces, raised fields in wetland agriculture and irrigation dams.

RAISED FIELD AND WETLAND AGRICULTURE

A large proportion of the Maya domain consisted of wetlands. The Maya discovered the fertility of swamp bottom sediments and developed a system of fertile agricultural platforms in the wetlands. To develop arable fields for planting they elevated the surface of the swamp into soil platforms that rose above the water level. To achieve the desired geometry, they collected the soil from the swamp bottoms and placed this sediment fill upon adjacent areas. They developed platforms bordered by a series of irrigation ditches constructed in a Cartesian grid pattern. The ditches formed a system of canals between the raised soil platforms.

The bottoms of the canals were often sealed with clay to prevent the loss of water into the porous limestone substrate. The water filled canals transcribed the limits of the rectangular raised fields. Irrigation water that collected in the canals sustained the crops and made them independent of the rainy season.

Cultivated plots on the platforms were planted and cultivars were harvested. As the cycle of crop growing progressed, soil was eroded from the raised fields and flowed into the canals. This eroded soil became mixed with organic matter in the bottom of the canals. The organic matter was formed from the spoilage of animal, plant, and aquatic life living in the canals. Maya farmers maintained the canals by mucking out the ditches and used this material as fertilizer by placing the enriched soil on the surface of the raised field. This enriched sediment increased the nitrogen and other nutrients in the soil.

CORN, COTTON AND CHOCOLATE: HOW THE MAYA CHANGED THE WORLD

With the raised field system, Maya farmers produced yields of crops that was greater than four times the yield using traditional farming methodologies. The increased yield included crops planted on the surface of the raised fields during the rainy season and additional crops that were grown in the muddy and nutrient rich bottom of the canal during the dry season. The canals were used as aquaculture systems, supporting a habitat for turtles, fish, amphibians, and editable water plants that supplemented the diet of the Maya.

The agro-ecosystem of canals and raised fields proved to be a long-term strategy for feeding the population and enabled the added advantage of producing up to four crops per year.

AGRICULTURE TERRACES

Initially only the level portions or bottomland of the area was cultivated. Later, the innovative use of sustainable agricultural terraces was introduced to areas with hilly terrain. Terraces were hydrological structures constructed on a sloped hillside. As the demand for foodstuffs increased and additional arable land was required, agriculture terraces were constructed on the hillsides rising above the bottomland. The terraces were designed to optimize the development of horizontal arable land as the structures stepped down the slope.

Stepped terraces were developed by constructing cut stone masonry retaining walls founded on the limestone bedrock. The retaining walls were then backfilled with fertile soil that was placed level with the top of the downhill wall and filled up to the base of the upper retaining wall. This geometry developed a large mass of soil behind the wall.

In addition to creating additional land for cultivation, the terraces reduced erosion on the downhill slopes. With the terrace system, storm water was slowed as it flowed down the face of the retaining walls and across the level section of the terraces. Storm water flow was therefore absorbed and captured by the soil mass. This water was retained by the deep mass of soil and helped to maintain moisture in the soil for the crops during the dry season.

The terrace system had the advantage of creating new agricultural space, capturing water for use during the dry season and enabling Maya farmers to harvest multiple crops throughout the year. Multiple crop cycles greatly accelerated the process of genetic alteration.

FOREST GARDENS

The catalog of Maya cultivars included not only grains, vegetables and fibers but also included tree-borne fruit. The Maya devised an agricultural management system for genetically altering trees within the surrounds of the rainforest. The perimeter of trees and the rainforest canopy offered protection for the sensitive cultivars, providing shade, wind shielding and pollen isolation. The forest gardens sustained biodiverse habitat that enabled agronomists to alter specimens meeting a wide array of human needs.

The botanical forest gardens were a variegated garden of genetically altered cultivars of tree species including avocado, cacao, chicle, mango, papaya, and vanilla. The forest garden was highly dependent on human interaction for the sustainable management of its natural resources.

MAYA CULTIVARS THAT CHANGED WORLD HISTORY

CORN, COTTON AND CHOCOLATE: HOW THE MAYA CHANGED THE WORLD

Although there are few agricultural artifacts surviving from this historical period, the agronomy of the Maya involved the manipulation of plant characteristics and the selective breeding of native plants to develop cultivars that could be grown under diverse environmental conditions producing fruit, vegetables, and fiber.

The greatest intellectual feat performed by the Maya is considered to be the invention of the number zero. A feat that mathematicians claim was one of the singular accomplishments of the human era. Modern agronomists consider the development of maize to be mankind's first and greatest feat of genetic engineering. Using this logic, the cultivation of maize by the Maya could be considered an intellectual accomplishment comparable to the invention of the number zero.

One of the overt changes in world habits promulgated by Maya agricultural genius is the alteration of global nutrition and food habits. The conquistadors were the first traders to transport Maya agricultural products across the globe. Maya foodstuffs have changed the tastes of many countries. Can one imagine the taste of Thai, Indian or Mexican food without chili peppers? Roaming the aisles of a modern supermarket, the agricultural legacy of our Maya becomes apparent. The commercial offerings contributed by Maya cultivars would include: avocado, tomatoes, corn, squash, chilies, beans, sweet potato, papaya, chocolate, peanuts, vanilla, pineapple, jicama, guava, sunflower seeds, and a variety of other lesser known foodstuffs.

Maya cultivars can claim a key role in the shaping of modern culture. The changes are extensive and will surprise and enlighten the reader. They have altered civilization and made a difference in the historical process. Maya cultivars have proven to be a source of power and, great wealth, but have also produced poverty, misery, and exploitation. They have started wars and initiated rebellions; overthrown monarchies and altered political boundaries; inspired industrial, technical and scientific revolutions. They have started college systems, promoted deadly habits, sparked sporting empires and changed cultural speech, music and lifestyles.

One may think that all this change is beyond the influence generated from plants. How did Maya cultivars alter human behavior and affect the course of history? In this book, we will see how the cultivars influenced wars, political boundaries, social behavior, and addictions. We will follow the trail of these historic Maya inventions as they play their part in changing the history of the world.

The chronicle of how Maya cultivars changed the world unfolds in the following chapters. The narrative of how they infused their character into world historical scenarios shifts like a kaleidoscopic image. The recounting of their influence begins with a discussion of the diffusion of Maya cultivars across the globe. It will then detail each individual cultivar with historical descriptions and the cultural influence that the cultivar had on the world. Finally, the book will provide a composite analysis of the synergistic changes to world history initiated by Maya cultivars.

CORN, COTTON AND CHOCOLATE: HOW THE MAYA CHANGED THE WORLD

CHAPTER 4: MAYA CULTIVARS TRAVEL THE WORLD

Maya cultivars changed the course of history when they became world travelers. The agricultural prowess of the Maya civilization was indeed amazing. Mother Nature had generously endowed the ecosystem of the Yucatán with indigenous plants that had the potential to become valuable cultivars. Maya agronomists exploited these wild inedible plants and changed them into high yielding cultivars. They were an agriculture-based society that turned the cultivation of crops into a science.

The environmental largess of native plants combined with the Maya's scientific approach to cultivation enabled them to become the finest agronomists on the planet. Their hard work and agricultural production was recognized during their time. Before European contact, Maya cultivars swept across the lands of the New World and were adopted by other cultures of the Americas. This was a harbinger of their acceptance by the world at large.

What were the mechanisms enabling these plants from an ancient culture to become world travelers? How did they become an integral part of world history and play such a critical role in feeding the majority of the modern world? Maya cultivars were recognized as unique and became a valuable commodity during the era preceding European contact. They were dispersed by Maya traders and became a hit with America's pre-Columbian cultures.

The popularity of the cultivars blossomed after European contact; foreign traders roamed the seas and disseminated them across the globe. They spread across the oceans into every realm. The foods and fibers produced by Maya cultivars assumed an important role in the habits and mores of the world. Maya cultivars played a key part in the shaping of modern culture and became an influential factor in the historical process.

Unraveling the influence of the Maya cultivars on world history is a tale of cultural interchange and European exploitation. The tale involves the weaving of the strands of their ecological, political and agricultural effects on history into a fabric reflecting worldwide change. The Maya cultivars introduced amazing effects for their new owners.

DIFFUSION OF MAYA CULTIVARS TO THE AMERICAS

Trading was a major component in the Maya economic system. Maya economics functioned on simple supply and demand and the economy of the Maya civilization depended on profitable trading operations within the realm of the Maya and with distant cultures. The Maya participated in trading with multiple Mesoamerican cultures, including Teotihuacan, the Zapotec and the Olmec.

The Maya trading network disseminated their cultivars throughout North America, Mesoamerica, the Caribbean, the Mid America Isthmus, and cultures living on the fringes of South America. This wide-ranging trade network allowed Maya merchants to trade a variety of sustenance and prestige goods. Sustenance trade goods are items used daily such as cultivars, textiles and salt. Prestige items included jadeite, feathers and semi-precious stones. Maya trading activities disseminated their cultivars to the remainder of the Americas. They carried out trading operations while traversing land and sea trade routes.

Maya merchants trekked overland transporting their trade goods in manpowered pack trains. They carried trade goods using the tumpline, which are backpacks supported by a strap stretched across the forehead of the porter. The tumpline can transport a load that is more than

CORN, COTTON AND CHOCOLATE: HOW THE MAYA CHANGED THE WORLD

the weight of the porter. The line of porters followed rugged trails leading to distant trading destinations across the land mass of America.

Trade goods were also shipped through seagoing voyages. Maya sea traders traversed the Caribbean, the Gulf of Mexico, and the Pacific Ocean connecting with trading partners accessible by sea routes. Large Maya seagoing cargo vessels plied the open seas and ventured eastward across the turquoise waters of the Caribbean. Their vessels traveled north to the far reaches of Mesoamerica, east to Florida, south to Panama and to other ports positioned along the Mid-America Isthmus. Maya sea traders traveled far and encountered trading partners with valuable resources that could be exchanged for the products of Maya agronomy and industry.

Beginning about 2500 BC, maize began to be propagated throughout the Americas. The people of the New World were being nourished by Maya cultivars including the miracle grain of the Maya. Maize was adopted by numerous cultures and was the prime source of grain for America's native peoples. The Maya handed off the baton of their magic cultivars to other cultures and the three sisters were reunited by Maya traders.

DIFFUSION OF MAYA CULTIVARS ACROSS AMERICA BY CULTURAL TRADERS

Maya cultivars and a wide variety of other goods were disseminated to foreign cultures living on the coastal areas of South America and North America. The cultivars were then dispersed into the interior of the hemispheres by domestic trading networks.

Chronologically, Maya cultivars were introduced to South America before they were dispersed into North America. The ancient South American cultures trading with the Maya then introduced maize and other cultivars to the cultures living in their interior. The ancient cultures that first adopted maize have passed into the mists of time and their identity is unknown to archaeology.

However, maize has been the prime cultivar that left a trail of evidence. This evidence has been assessed by archaeologists to determine the earliest cultivation of maize in South America. The Maya cultivar has provided a definitive time line for its cultivation and consumption in South America.

The earliest culture introducing maize to South America predated the Inca by 3700 years. These cultures also predated the Wari, a culture that rose around 600 AD and collapsed around 1100 AD. The Wari were predated by the Moche Culture and the Moche predated by the Chavin who ruled from 900 BC to 200 AD. At the rise of the Chavin culture, maize had been a longtime staple of earlier and nameless cultures for 1500 years.

Archaeologists have learned that during the Late Archaic period, maize was a primary component in the diet of ancient cultures living in the Norte Chico region of Peru. The region is believed to be the place where the cultural evolution in the Andes emerged from simple hunting and gathering cultures and became a complex agriculture society.

Traders were tardy in their introduction of Maya cultivars to North American cultures. It was not until the first millennium AD, that cultivars spread by Maya traders bartered with their Native American counterparts. These Native American traders subsequently introduced Maya cultivars to areas of the present Southwest United States. In the following millennium, North American traders introduced Maya cultivars to the northeast United Stated and southeastern Canada. The Maya cultivars included maize, squash, beans and tobacco. The new cultivars transformed the cultures from hunter-gathers into sedentary agriculture-based culture.

CORN, COTTON AND CHOCOLATE: HOW THE MAYA CHANGED THE WORLD

Trading relationships had covered the North America for 1000 years prior to European settlement. When the Pilgrims arrived in the New England, the fields of the Eastern American tribes were filled with stalks of maize, squash and beans. The three sisters had traveled from the Maya realm to their new home in North America.

When the Pilgrims reached the shores of Massachusetts in 1620, they were ill provisioned for survival. They did not possess the capability for producing enough food to feed the Plymouth colony. Maize had been growing in Europe for over 100 years. However, the Pilgrims did not transport maize to the New World, maize was provided to the colony by Indians. The Maya cultivar had come full circle and provided the basis for survival of some of America's first settlers.

EUROPEAN DIFFUSION, THE AGE OF DISCOVERY AND THE COLUMBIAN EXCHANGE

At the time of European contact, the Maya trading network had disseminated their cultivars to populations throughout the Americas. Their popularity extended from North America, south to the Aztec Empire in Mesoamerica and below the equator to the Inca in South America. Numerous cultures of the New World were being nourished by Maya cultivars. Greater success for Maya cultivars was yet to come when the remainder of the world became converts to these tasty Maya inventions. Maya cultivars became world changers and the agricultural conqueror of the world.

Long-distance maritime travel by European ships had a deep history before the fifteenth century voyages of discovery. With the discovery of America, voyages of exploration increased dramatically and produced new knowledge of the earth's geography. This era became known as the "Age of Discovery", a period which started in the early 15th century and extended to the 17th century. The Age of Discovery was a time of great historic change. It is considered to be the end of the medieval period and a time bridge that extended into the modern era.

During this period, European explorers proved that there was open water around southern Africa and that Europe could be linked to Asia by sailing eastward around Africa. They demonstrated that the western Atlantic was not land-locked, and there was open water to the south of the Americas leading to Asiatic destinations. With this new knowledge of navigation, European ships could reach Asia by sailing east or west from Europe.

The values of nautical destinations were revolutionized as new and exotic lands were encountered. European explorers, learning about foreign lands, brought back the knowledge of a larger world to the courts of Europe. The long unrealized dream of reaching all parts of the world from Europe became a reality. Access to global trade changed the world.

Christopher Columbus' first voyage to the Americas in 1492 launched the era of large-scale contact between the Old and the New Worlds that resulted in a social, political and ecological revolution that changed history. Columbus was the first explorer to introduce Maya cultivars to Europe and he was received as a hero in Spain. Returning from his first voyage he transported Maya cultivars and animals to the Spanish Court including tobacco, pineapple, tomato, chili peppers and the turkey.

As the 16th century unfolded, explorers crisscrossed the Caribbean Islands, the Yucatán Peninsula and the balance of Mesoamerica. Their explorations enabled them to encounter scores of Maya cultivars being grown in these areas. They were impressed by the quality and flavor of these fruits and vegetables. They were fascinated with cotton fiber and the taste of

CORN, COTTON AND CHOCOLATE: HOW THE MAYA CHANGED THE WORLD

tobacco. They made a conscious decision that these Maya inventions had great potential as lucrative trade items and assets for their country. The dissemination of Maya cultivars to other countries was rapid and the adoption of the cultivars by peoples in Europe and Afro-Eurasia altered history.

The newly discovered sea routes became busy channels of contact between the New World and Afro-Eurasia. Trading activities increased during the early 16th century and circulated Maya cultivars. Explorers traveled to ports of call around the world transferring Maya cultivars which became very important crops in Afro-Eurasia. They began to change the world.

In the 16th century, the adoption of Maya cultivars by cultures across the globe came rapidly. Tomatoes were growing in Italy by 1530; maize was an African crop by 1590; papayas were grown in Asia by 1530 and tobacco in 1520. In 1550 Europeans introduced cassava and the peanut to tropical Southeast Asia and West Africa, where they flourished. The early history of dissemination, adoption and application of Maya cultivars exhibits just how smoothly they became part and parcel of world cultures

Greater success for the Maya cultivar maize was yet to come when the remainder of the world became converts of the Maya inventions. Maize became the agricultural conqueror of the world. It now has the greatest production tonnage of any grain in the world.

THE COLUMBIAN EXCHANGE

The most striking aspect of the Age of Discovery was the enormous extension of networks of communication and exchange that tightly linked individuals and societies. Every region of the world became intricately connected. After 1492, the world's ecosystems collided and mixed as European vessels carried numerous species of plants, animals and microbes to new homes across the oceans. This exchange of cultivars, animals and ideas become known as the Great Exchange or the Columbian Exchange after Christopher Columbus. Scholars believe that the ecological transformation set off by Columbus's voyages was one of the events that established the modern world. The traveling Maya cultivars played an important role in the Columbian exchange and their role in changing world history.

The Columbian exchange is part of the reason why Europe rose to world predominance, and that China, once the richest most advanced societies on earth, fell behind. Why was it that the United Kingdom launched the Industrial Revolution? These questions are connected in crucial ways to the Columbian Exchange and Maya cultivars.

WORLD TRADE AND BIOLOGICAL EXCHANGES BEFORE 1492

The discovery of the proof of a scientific truth, previously thought to be a legend, is the stuff usually reserved for the literature of fantasy or tall tales spun around the campfire. This was true of contrary theories related to continental drift, plate tectonics, the spherical shape of the earth and the heliocentric theories believing that the earth revolves around the sun.

Rarely is truth stranger than fiction, but detective work and research into the mystery behind the origins of Maya cultivars found growing in another hemisphere before the discovery of America follows a winding path between science and ancient history. The back-story of the truth behind the sources of the world traveling Maya cultivars involves proofs derived from botany sciences, archaeology, ancient linguistics and nautical technology.

CORN, COTTON AND CHOCOLATE: HOW THE MAYA CHANGED THE WORLD

How did Maya cultivars reported to be growing in another hemisphere during ancient times ever come about? Maya cultivar plants are indigenous to the Yucatán so how did they make the voyage to another continent? The only solution for this conundrum would be the transport of the plants via transoceanic travel. It would have to be trans-Atlantic travel that occurred thousands of years before Columbus reached the shores of America. But these voyages, according to some scholars, were impossible.

The truth behind the origin and history of plants found growing on more than one continent has now explained using multidiscipline scientific research. In the book, *World Trade and Biological Exchanges Before 1492*, authored by Dr. Carl L. Johannsen and Dr. John L. Sorenson, the authors develop scientific proof that certain species found growing on two different continents must have a single source of origin. Evidence of the existence of an organism living in a specific historical setting includes archaeological discovery of plant residue *in situ*, historical documents, ancient text, explorer's reports and lexicons. Artifacts can indicate positive knowledge of a species being cultivated in a hemisphere where it did not originate.

The authors trace the travels of plants that were involved in transoceanic travel prior to 1492. Of the plants Included in the studies the majority are Maya cultivars that began their world travels thousands of years before Columbus landed on the Americas. The body of proof comes from archaeological, historical, linguistic, ancient art and biological sciences. The worldwide distribution of cultivars could not have been due merely to natural transfer mechanisms such as birds' flight or seed flotation, but were by intentional means by human devices.

Their book offers conclusive evidence that nearly 100 species of plants, most them cultivars, were present in both the eastern and western hemisphere prior to European contact. Over half the plant transfers consist of flora of American origin that spread to Eurasia or Oceana at early historical dates.

The logical explanation for these findings is that a considerable number of round trip, trans-oceanic voyages were carried out over the 7000 years between the sixth millennium BCE and European contact with the Americas. The expanding knowledge of early maritime technology and its potential for oceanic travel increasingly provides confidence that the vessels and the navigators possessed nautical skills capable of traveling long distance ocean travel.

Biologists believe that any given species arises only once in the course of evolution. This is because any new species evolves in a unique set of environmental parameters that is only found in a single geographic location on the planet. The chances that any two-isolated species can evolve in exactly the same way with the same characteristics are incalculably low. The odds are low because no two localities on earth are exactly alike considering the physical geographical conditions governing the evolutionary process, all species arise in a single place at a given historical time.

When evidence confirms that a species existed in the New World as well as an ocean apart in other hemispheres, it presents a paradox. The unraveling of a paradox demands a rational explanation. It may be assumed that the seeds of a species traveled over the oceans via a natural means. The odds for successful natural transport of plants are so slim that a scholar assuming or claiming a passive natural mode of transport for such an improbable feat must demonstrate the methodology of transport rather than asserting a fact.

Historical records around the globe are replete with accounts of sailing voyages that were carried out thousands of years in time depth. Records indicate the existence of watercraft

CORN, COTTON AND CHOCOLATE: HOW THE MAYA CHANGED THE WORLD

capable of trans-oceanic voyaging as early as the fifth millennium B.C. Nautical history and modern experimental voyages have demonstrated that oceanic voyaging in early times was not as daunting as many modern researchers might have supposed. Sea voyages apparently did not intimidate certain adventurous mariners.

In recent time periods, oceans have been successfully crossed hundreds of times in a variety of unlikely watercraft ranging from small sailboats, sailboards, rowboats, rafts, and canoes. Transatlantic travel and survival on the high seas apparently does not present a sense of fear in the hearts of amateurs or technologically limited voyagers as landlocked scholars might anticipate.

Despite well documented historical evidence well as technological proof of ancient capabilities for nautical travel, a negative attitude has persisted among scholars that have been labeled "American thalassophobia" (illogical aversion to considering the sea as a possible route), and "intellectual mal de mar". Those that possess this phobia cannot abide the concept of ancient sea travel as a consideration for a mode of communication. This attitude has prevented virtually all New World archaeologists from inquiring whether ship travel could enable the spread of ancient cultures over long distances.

This flies in the face of historical accounts of sea battles and long voyages that were carried out by ancient ships. Re-creations of ancient vessels including large sea-going ships that were the work horses of the naval fleets of the Greeks, Romans, Egyptians, Phoenicians, Arabs, and Chinese have been built and sailed. The re-created ships averaged over 170 feet in length, yet scholars are comfortable with the fact that the ships of Christopher Columbus averaged about 65 feet in length, or nearly a third the length of the ancient ships of classical navies. When Columbus went aboard a Maya sea-going cargo vessel in 1504, he noted in one of his accounts that the Maya craft was 80 feet in length and was longer than his ship. Possibly the doubting scholars should watch the History Channel.

Scholars have now begun to realize that voyagers using simple marine technology could have reached the New World millennia ago. Our present state of knowledge about ancient nautical capabilities allows for oceanic voyages that could account for the presence of maize, the pineapple and the peanut growing in both America and Asia during pre-contact periods.

Biological studies of Maya cultivars found on other continents have provided significant evidence that these viable plants were transferred using trans-oceanic methods. Evidence has come from the archaeological discovery of plant remains including pollen and DNA. Another source of conclusive evidence comes from historical documents including descriptions of plants in ancient texts, or lexicons of appropriate date that show a knowledge of the species in the hemisphere where it did not originate. In addition, depictions of plants in ancient art can also be a determinative factor.

The list of cultivars with hard evidence that the organism was present in both the eastern and western hemispheres before Columbus first made contact is replete with Maya cultivars. The list of Maya cultivars with decisive evidence of being transferred include: maize, squash, chili peppers, beans, cotton, sweet potato, agave, pineapple, papaya, sunflower, cassava, and jicama among others.

CORN, COTTON AND CHOCOLATE: HOW THE MAYA CHANGED THE WORLD

CHAPTER 5: HOW MAYA CULTIVARS TRANSFORMED HISTORY

In the 500 years since Maya cultivars were introduced worldwide, they have unleashed a synergistic phenomenon that has proved to be a source of power and wealth, but has also caused poverty, misery, and exploitation. The effects of Maya cultivars on the world's societies has become a stimulant that has altered history. The phenomenon was initiated by the discovery of America and has released catalysts with worldwide implications. The Columbian landfall on America was the pivotal point that changed the history of the world.

The discovery of the Americas stimulated world-changing principles including the Columbian Exchange, the Age of Discovery, and globalization. Each of these factors was influenced by Maya cultivars; Maya cultivars became instruments of change that altered history and generated the advanced technology of the 21st century.

THE COLUMBIAN EXCHANGE

The Columbian Exchange was the widespread exchange of ecology, agriculture, and culture occurring after European contact. It involved the transport and transfer of a wide variety of ideas, plants, animals, foods, human populations and communicable diseases between the Eastern and Western hemispheres. The Columbian Exchange between the Americas and the Afro-Eurasian hemispheres followed the discovery of the Americas and was a pivotal point in history accelerating the Age of Discovery and then to globalization. In addition to the exchange of ideas, the Columbian Exchange resulted in a great influx of Europeans into the Americas, widespread colonization, slavery and the destruction of great American civilizations including the Maya, Aztec, and Inca. The Columbian Exchange was the major factor in the dissemination of Maya cultivars across the world.

THE AGE OF DISCOVERY

The "Age of Discovery" signaled the end of the middle ages, triggered the early modern period and initiated the rise of European nation states. During this time, European overseas expansion led to enhanced contact between the Old and New Worlds. The contact implemented the Columbian Exchange, one of the most significant global events in history. The Age of Discovery enabled European powers to explore the Americas, Africa, Asia and Oceana and resulted in the ascendency of European states. European exploration allowed the global mapping of the world, resulting in a New World-view with the acknowledgement of distant civilizations. Voyages of discovery and trading spread the Maya cultivars to diverse cultures.

GLOBALIZATION

Globalization began when Columbus landed on an island in the Caribbean. Globalization refers to processes that enhanced worldwide exchanges of national and cultural resources. Early in the 15th century Europeans made discoveries that promoted globalization. They explored the oceans and stimulated transatlantic travel to the New World inducing the global movement of people and ideas. Since the start of globalization, the transmission of communication, goods, ideas and technology have expanded over the centuries.

The new forms of transportation and telecommunications have compressed time and space with increasingly rapid rates of global interchange. Intermodal transport and air travel has made transportation easier and faster. The advent of digital communications including mobile phones,

CORN, COTTON AND CHOCOLATE: HOW THE MAYA CHANGED THE WORLD

the internet and social media have connected billions of people around the globe into a "small world" community. We are now all connected by only six degrees of separation.

Globalization is not just an economic and cultural mechanism but is also a biological phenomenon. Some biologists state that globalization has initiated a new biological era. This era is called the Homogenocene, which constitutes a new geological epoch for the lithosphere. We have transitioned from the Pleistocene through the Holocene and are now in the Homogenocene epoch. This epoch is the product of globalization. It is the mixing of substances of the New World with Old World substances to create a uniform blend. Organisms from separate hemispheres can now travel, and prosper in locations halfway around the world.

THE MAYA CULTIVARS AND THEIR EFFECT ON HISTORY

The greatest lasting impact of the Columbian Exchange lies in the introduction of Maya cultivars to the rest of the world. Salient cultivars include tobacco, cotton, turkeys, maize, sweet potatoes, tomatoes, peanuts, cassava, cacao, chicle, henequen, sunflower seeds, papaya, vanilla, chili peppers, beans, and squash. Maya cultivars have made important changes to the food security of the entire world. Maize has energized South America, Europe, Africa, and China. The introductions of new crops from the New World have had a dramatic impact on demographics. Maya cultivars now feed 60% of the world's population daily and have resulted in large population increases.

Maya cultivars affected food supplies, politics, laws, customs, technology and financial Empires. They have started armed revolutions, initiated rebellions, altered political boundaries, inspired industrial, technical and scientific revolutions, started college systems, promoted deadly habits, sparked sporting empires and changed cultural speech, music and lifestyles. One would think that all this change is beyond the capabilities of agriculture products. This book follows the trail of these historic Maya inventions as they play their part in changing the history of the world.

Maya agronomists cultivated scores of valuable cultivars for food and fabric. However, this document will evaluate eighteen specimens of Maya cultivars which have been identified as important players as history changing cultivars.

The following chapters include a detailed background on each of these selected cultivars. Each dissertation will impart information relative to its character and its influence on the world. Each narrative starts with the impressions from my youth on how Maya cultivars influenced my life and affected contemporary culture. Then we provide an overview of the methodology used by Maya agronomists to domesticate that specimen and describe how the specimen was used by the Maya. The account then describes the dispersion of that specimen across the earth and usage of the cultivar as a food, fiber, spice or narcotic by the world. The narrative then recounts how that cultivar influenced international cultures and made its impact on world history.

Finally, we will describe how the Maya cultivars as a group changed history. Including their impact on world food security, population growth and the mass of the human body. The last chapter will detail how Maya cultivars contributed a greater number of specimens to the world food supply than any other continent, changed the legend of wealth generated from the New World from gold to green, why Maya cultivars are the world's favorite drug, flavor, fiber, fruit and spice and how Maya cultivars turned the USA into a world superpower.

CORN, COTTON AND CHOCOLATE: HOW THE MAYA CHANGED THE WORLD

CHAPTER 6: THE AVOCADO

Botanical name: *Persea americana* **Maya name:** *oom*

Memories of a youth

You will always remember your first real job. My first real job was working in a grocery store in a lowly position described as a "sack boy". I was 13 years old and working for Harris Brothers Super Market. I was paid the princely sum of 35¢ per hour. I had worked for several years at various jobs, helping out on the back of vegetable trucks, working in gardens, and even pushed an ice cream cart. However, this was my first opportunity to acquire a Social Security card and receive a real paycheck.

I was fascinated by the varieties of foods offered in the store; there were canned, packaged, fresh and frozen foods. The produce department, with its great variety of fresh fruits and vegetables, was an amazing experience. I was familiar with local fruits and vegetables from Georgia, but I was bewildered by the exotic imported produce. I was at a complete loss when trying to identify the curious looking imported fruits and vegetables.

My primary job was being stationed at the checkout counter where I placed groceries into paper bags and helped customers carry out their bags of groceries. I was also assigned to restock the shelves. I cheerfully carried out these assignments, but I was fascinated by the fresh fruits and vegetables available in the produce department.

One day, as I was looking over the array of exotic fruits and vegetables in the produce department, I picked up a beautiful red fruit with a spiked surface. Apparently, I appeared to be puzzled. A mellow voice behind me spoke, "that's called the dragon fruit and it's delicious."

"Thank you," I said. I turned to face the white-haired man who had spoken to me; I could see that he was a fellow employee. I then picked up another unfamiliar fruit and, looked up at him in puzzlement.

"That's a kiwi fruit,". he answered.

I looked at him and said, "How do you know all about these exotic fruits?"

He said, "I haven't always worked in a produce department. When I was younger, I operated a motorized dragline while building railroads for the United Fruit Company down in Honduras. When I lived there, I came to appreciate tropical fruits." He reached out his hand and introduced himself. "My name is Bob, and yours is Jimmy." I don't know how we knew my name, but he did. I shook his hand. I felt very grown up.

Bob walked over to a produce stand and picked up a green fruit that was oval shaped like a football. Holding up the unusual spherical fruit, he said, "In Honduras, they call this an *aguacate*. Some people call it an alligator pear. But in the United States it's generally called an avocado. This is the most flavorful and versatile fruit grown in the tropics."

"It's beautiful," I said. "How does it taste?"

Gesturing with the smooth green fruit he said, "Young man, it's time you learned about dining down in the tropics. Let's take a couple of these avocados and use them to make our lunch."

CORN, COTTON AND CHOCOLATE: HOW THE MAYA CHANGED THE WORLD

"Really? Well, it's almost lunch time," I said.

"Great," he said. "We will need a few more ingredients for preparing our lunch". He walked about the produce department gathering additional items. He selected two juicy red tomatoes, one onion, a lime and another avocado.

We went into the stockroom and Bob worked his magic. He opened the avocado, removing its large seed. Then removed the flesh and sectioned the avocado, cut up the tomato and the onion. He combined the ingredients into a bowl. He squeezed a quantity of lime juice into the mixture and mashed the contents of the bowl together into a multicolored heap. He opened a bag of chips, offered me the open bag and said, "dig in."

I scooped up the avocado mixture with the chip and inserted it into my mouth. Ka-boom! An explosion of flavor burst into my mouth, it had a savor taste combining the flavors of the tomatoes, onion, and lime awash in the luscious buttery flavor of the avocado. It was a total surprise to my senses. I thought it was the most delicious food I'd ever put in my mouth.

It's been a long time since I retired from my career as a sack boy, but I will never forget the experience of tasting my first guacamole. Bob did not call our lunch guacamole. He didn't have to place a name on that wonderful concoction, it was delicious by any name.

That was the beginning of my lifelong love affair with the avocado. I have enjoyed sliced avocado, avocado salads, avocado soup, avocado smoothies, avocado ice cream and every style of guacamole. I've enjoyed this delicious fruit in the USA, Europe and in the Yucatán where the avocado started life as a Maya cultivar. Sliced, diced, mashed or in a salad the avocado has a uniquely sophisticated character and they cannot be compared to any other fruit.

I will always be grateful to the Maya agronomists who cultivated the wonderful avocado tree in the forest gardens of the Yucatán. How would they know that enjoying a football game would be much less of a pleasure without guacamole and tortilla chips?

THE MAYA AND THE AVOCADO

The avocado is a cultivar that came out of a very different time, a time when long extinct creatures roamed Mesoamerica. Avocado trees are an ancient species and the fruit was at its evolutionary prime during the beginning of the Cenozoic Era. During this Age of Mammals, the avocado co-evolved with the giant mammals. This was a time when mega fauna, including mammoths, giant ground sloths and gomphotheres roamed the Yucatán. The gomphothere was a giant creature similar to an elephant but smaller than their cousins the mammoths. Gomphotheres were once widespread in North America and roamed Mesoamerica.

SURVIVAL OF THE AVOCADO AS AN ECOLOGICAL ANACHRONISM

The co-evolution of the avocado and the gomphothere meant that the giant mammal became a part of the process of propagating the avocado. These immense herbivores had the capability to eat and swallow whole avocados without noticing the large seed passing through their interior. Avocado pulp evolved to contain natural laxatives which quickened the passage of the seed through their digestive tract. The animals would then wander away from the tree that provided the fruit and in the course of time, they would deposit the seed in a totally different location along with a pile of fertilizer.

CORN, COTTON AND CHOCOLATE: HOW THE MAYA CHANGED THE WORLD

The avocado is haunted by the ghosts of mega fauna who evolved along with the avocado tree. These great mammals disappeared forever from the face of the earth about 10,000 years ago. No extant native North American animal is large enough to effectively disperse avocado seeds in this evolutionary fashion. After a cataclysmic shift in the population of giant land mammals, the wild avocado required a method of seed dispersal, which makes its survival somewhat of an ecological anachronism. How did it survive?

Recent evidence has determined that the mammoth and the gomphotheres became extinct in a time period parallel with the arrival of the proto-Maya population. Without larger mammals like the gomphothere to disperse their seed, avocado fruit would rot where they fell below their tree. If these seeds sprouted in place, beneath their parent tree, they would be in competition for light and growth. The seedling would wither and die which would limit the survival of the species. For the avocado to survive the Maya had to take an active part in their cultivation.

The avocado enjoys a symbiotic relationship with the Maya. Once *Homo sapiens* got involved with the ancient fruit to the point where man could cultivate the species, the fruit had the chance to thrive again. Maya began serving as surrogates for the gomphothere and became the disperser of the avocado seed resulting the survival of the fruit.

Back when the giant mammals roamed the earth, the avocado possessed a larger seed with a small fleshy area. Through the magic of cultivation, Maya agronomists changed the avocado into a fruit with a greater amount of the edible flesh. Human interaction bulked up avocados so there is more of the delicious flesh to eat.

THE AVOCADO AS MAYA FOOD

The first archaeological evidence of human cultivation of the avocado dates to 8,000 to 10,000 BC. At this stage, human populations were collecting wild avocados and consuming them after minimal processing. Eventually the avocado became a staple and one of the favorite foods of the ancient Maya.

The avocado was an important part of the Maya diet. To enjoy its buttery taste, it was eaten raw or with tortillas. They were mixed with corn flour and shaped into tamales or mashed, or mixed with onions and cilantro. The avocado was combined with maize, tomatoes and other ingredients and made into main dishes. The seeds, leaves and bark of the avocado tree were used for medicine. Avocado oil was used for cooking in the Maya kitchen.

The transformation of avocados into a cultivar became a vital part of Maya agriculture. The early Maya were quite successful at cultivating and harvesting fruit from the avocado trees. Avocado trees were grown in forest gardens. The Maya believed that avocados were a fertility fruit. Maya families would not allow their virgin daughters outside of the house during the avocado harvesting season. The Maya also reserved avocados for royal tables of luxury. *Yum Caax* was the Maya God of Agriculture. He was the protector of wild plants and dined on avocados.

AVOCADOS AS PART OF MAYA LIFE

The avocado became an important part of Maya life and its culture. The 14th month in the Maya calendar, *K'ank'in*, is represented by the glyph for the avocado. The city emblem for the Classic

CORN, COTTON AND CHOCOLATE: HOW THE MAYA CHANGED THE WORLD

Maya city of Pusilha includes the glyph of the avocado and the city was known as the Kingdom of the Avocado.

The Maya believe that their ancestors are reborn in avocado trees and the trees were planted over the graves of their ancestors. The Maya surrounded their houses with avocado trees. The avocado is a very tall tree with a large diameter trunk. The trunk of the tree was used by Maya boat builders to carve out their long seagoing cargo vessels. It's large diameter and length was advantageous to the construction of the large vessels.

The avocado was widely distributed by Maya traders prior to European contact. The fruit had been introduced to Mesoamerica, the Caribbean, Central America and South America.

THE AVOCADO MEETS THE WORLD

Worldwide distribution of the avocado followed the Spanish conquest. The world quickly accepted the delicious fruit. European traders distributed the plant to Europe in the 16th century and it was introduced to Indonesia in 1750 and Brazil in 1809. By the 19th century the avocado was an important product grown in every country in the tropics.

The Spanish conquistadors enjoyed the delicious fruits, but discovered a unique use for the avocado seed. The seed yields a milky liquid that becomes red when exposed to air. The Spaniards found they could use this reddish brown indelible liquid as ink to be used on documents. Some of these documents are still in existence today.

The avocado was also quite popular with seamen. European sailors in the 1700s called it "midshipman's butter" because they liked to spread it on hardtack biscuits. The popularity of the avocado was indicated in published accounts of the conquest. The first published record of the avocado was early in the conquest. The fruit was defined in the book, *Suma De Geografia Que Trata De Todas Las Partidas Del Mundo*. The book was written in 1516 by Martin Fernandez de Enciso, a Spanish conquistador and cosmographer.

In 1526, Fernandez de Oviedo, historian to the conquistadors, wrote about the avocado trees he saw along the north coast of Colombia: *"In the center of the fruit is a seed like a peeled chestnut, and between this and the rind is the part which is eaten, which is abundant and is a paste similar to butter and of very good taste."*

The taste and preparation of the avocado was described by William Damplier, an English travel writer and an adventurer who realized that not all wealth coming from the New World came in the shape of gold; he discovered that his books could bring wealth. He commented on the avocado:

"This fruit (the avocado) hath no taste of itself, and therefore it is usually mixt with sugar and lime juice, and beaten together in a plate, and this is an excellent dish. The ordinary way is to eat it with a little salt and a roasted plantain; and thus, a man that's hungry, may make a good meal of it. It is very wholesome eaten any way. It is reported that this fruit provokes to lust, and there is said to be much esteemed by the Spaniards."

CORN, COTTON AND CHOCOLATE: HOW THE MAYA CHANGED THE WORLD

ALL THE WORLD LOVES THE AVOCADO

In the 21st century the avocado is loved around the world. They are grown on every continent on earth except Antarctica. The conditions for cultivation of the avocado lie in a balanced environment for growth of the cultivar. Where these conditions are satisfied, the avocado has prospered. These soil and climate conditions are available throughout the tropics from South Africa to South America, southern India, Sri Lanka, Australia, the Philippines, Malaysia, Central America, the Caribbean, Mexico and parts of the United States.

The annual world production of the avocado exceeds 4,000,000 metric tons. Mexico leads the world in the production of the delicious fruit but the commercial farming of the succulent fruit is a success in numerous countries located in the tropics. The following is the summary of the production from the leading countries that produce avocados in metric tons.

TOP 20 AVOCADO PRODUCING COUNTRIES IN METRIC TONS

RANK	COUNTRY	PRODUCTION
1	Mexico	1,467 837
2	Dominican Republic	387 546
3	Colombia	303 340
4	Peru	288 387
5	Indonesia	276 311
6	Kenya	191 505
7	USA	175 226
8	Chile	164 750
9	Brazil	157 482
10	Rwanda	148 823
11	Venezuela	113 842
12	China	112 000
13	Guatemala	95 977
14	Israel	91 904
15	South Africa	89 999
16	Cameroon	75 989
17	Spain	69 400
18	Congo	65 500
19	Haiti	53 000
20	Australia	52 982

THE AVOCADO IS A WONDERFUL FRUIT, ERR BERRY

The avocado (*Persea americana*) is a fruit and not a vegetable! It is actually a member of the berry family. The avocado is a tall tree that grows to heights of 66 feet (20 m). It is native to Mesoamerica and is classified in the flowering plant family *lauraceae*.

CORN, COTTON AND CHOCOLATE: HOW THE MAYA CHANGED THE WORLD

The term avocado also refers to the fruit. The flowers are small, inconspicuous, greenish-yellow. The fruit is large, pear-shaped and green-skinned with a fleshy body and a large central seed, the avocado is a climacteric fruit (similar to the banana), which means it matures on the tree, but ripens off the tree.

Avocados are commercially valuable and are cultivated in tropical and Mediterranean climates throughout the world. The subtropical species needs a climate without frost and with little wind. High winds reduce the humidity, dehydrate the flowers, and affect pollination. The trees also need well-aerated soils, ideally more than one meter deep. These soil and climate conditions are widely available in the tropics.

The native, undomesticated variety is known as a *criollo*, and is small, with dark or black skin, and contains a larger seed. While dozens of different cultivars of avocado are grown, the Hass avocado is the most common. It produces fruit year-round and accounts for 80% of cultivated avocados in the world.

THE AVOCADO TRADE AGREEMENT: A REAL MEXICAN STANDOFF

Things do not always go as smooth as the buttery flesh of the avocado. A curious battle emerged between the USA and Mexico over the importation of the succulent fruit from Mexico into the USA. After the North American Free Trade Agreement (NAFTA) went into effect in 1994, Mexico tried exporting avocados into the USA. A backlash ensued when the USA put restrictions on the importation of the fruit from Mexico. The avocado introduced a big change in the trade relations between the countries.

The U.S. government used the excuse that importing the avocado would introduce the Tephritidae fruit fly to the USA, and this fruit fly would destroy California's avocado crops. The Mexican government responded by graciously inviting USDA inspectors to Mexico to observe the situation, but the U.S. government declined the invitation, claiming that a fruit fly inspection was not feasible. This was a flimsy excuse.

The Mexican government then proposed they would only sell avocados to the northeastern U.S. and only in the winter. The fruit flies cannot withstand extreme cold weather and the cold would kill the fruit flies. This gracious and logical solution was also refused by the U.S. government.

Then the Mexican government countered by suggesting that there could possibly be issues with corn grown in the USA that was imported into Mexico. Mexico started erecting barriers to the importation of American grown corn into Mexico. The issue then became a classic Mexican standoff. Uncle Sam was caught off-guard. The USA did not expect that that Mexico would dare place an embargo on the huge tonnage of corn they imported from the USA. The logic worked, the USA blinked first and gave the green light for importation of the Mexican avocado.

Time has shown that the U.S. position has proved to be spurious. Presently, avocados imported from Mexico are allowed in all 50 states. That is because USDA inspectors visited the Mexican State of Michoacán, inspected fruit and found no evidence of the dreaded fruit fly. Viva Mexico.

CORN, COTTON AND CHOCOLATE: HOW THE MAYA CHANGED THE WORLD

YOU SAY AVOCADO, THEY SAY AQUACATE

People across the globe call the avocado by various names. The names are as divergent as the language of those countries. The Maya word for avocado is *oom*. Since the Spanish did not make contact with the Maya until after the Aztec were conquered, the Spanish learned about the avocado from the Aztec. At the time of the conquest of the Aztec, the avocado was sold in the open markets held in Tenochtitlan, the Aztec capital. Several Spanish colonial documents report that the Aztecs accepted avocados as tributes from subject regions where this plant was abundant.

The Spanish couldn't pronounce the Aztec word for the fruit, known as *ahuacatl*, meaning "testicle" because of its shape. This is most likely because the avocado, growing in pairs, resembled the body part. After the arrival of Spanish conquistadors, Spanish speakers substituted the word "aguacate" for the Aztec (Nahuatl) word because they could not pronounce *ahuacatl*.

The Spanish name, *aguacate*, was first used by Pedro de Cieza de Leon, a Spanish historian. Writing in a journal of his travels in 1550, he noted that the avocado grew in Panama, Ecuador, Colombia, and Peru. In Spain, it is known as *abogado* and in France it is *avocat*. In some countries of South America, such as Argentina, Bolivia, Chile, Peru, and Uruguay, the avocado is known by its Inca Quechua name, *palta*. In other Spanish-speaking countries it is known by the Mexican name, *aguacate* and in Portuguese it is *abacate*.

The word avocado is an English derivation from the Spanish word "aguacate". The English living in Jamaica called the avocado an alligator pear. Some speculate that they were comparing the skin to that of an alligator. Trinidad and Tobago, it is called "zaboca".

DELICIOUS TREATS MADE FROM THE AVOCADO

The avocado is consumed in a wide variety of ways and has changed the tastes of the world. The fruit is not sweet, but rich, and distinctly yet subtly flavored. The flesh has a smooth, almost creamy texture. It is used in both savory and sweet dishes. The avocado is very popular in vegetarian cuisine, as a substitute for meats in sandwiches and salads because of its high fat content.

A ripe avocado yield to gentle pressure when held in the palm of the hand and squeezed. The flesh is prone to enzymatic browning which means it turns brown quickly after exposure to air. To prevent this, lime or lemon juice can be added to avocados after they are peeled.

One of the most popular avocado dishes is guacamole. It has become part of American cuisine as a dip, condiment and salad ingredient. In Mexico, it is traditionally made by mashing ripe avocados with a *molcajete* (mortar and pestle) with sea salt. Some recipes call for tomato, onion, garlic, lime juice, chili, yogurt or additional seasonings.

In Mexico and Central America, avocados are served mixed with white rice, in soups, salads, or on the side of chicken and meat. Avocado slices are frequently added to hamburgers, *tortas* (Mexican sandwiches), hot dogs, and *carne asada*.

CORN, COTTON AND CHOCOLATE: HOW THE MAYA CHANGED THE WORLD

In Peru, they are consumed with cheesy breadsticks or *tequeños,* as a dip, served as a side dish with grilled meats, used in salads and sandwiches, or as a whole dish when filled with tuna, shrimp, or chicken. The Chilean version of Caesar salad contains large slices of mature avocado.

In some countries, the use of avocados varies widely but the usage always takes advantage of the rich flavor and nutritional value of the fruit. In Australia and New Zealand, avocado is commonly served in sandwiches, with sushi, on toast, or with chicken. In the Philippines, Brazil, Indonesia, Vietnam, and southern India avocados are frequently used in milkshakes and added to ice cream and other desserts. In Indonesia avocado milkshakes with chocolate syrup are popular.

AVOCADO FESTIVALS

The avocado was introduced to California from Mexico in the 19th century, and has become a successful cash crop. About 59,000 acres, some 95% of United States avocado production, is located in Southern California. Fallbrook, California, claims the title of "Avocado Capital of the World", and hosts an annual avocado festival.

Since the 1960s, tens of thousands of avocado lovers converge in Fallbrook, located in San Diego's North County, to sample avocados, check out the crazy cooking contest entries, buy funky avocado-themed gifts and enjoy bands, live entertainment and friendly beer gardens. Come to the festival prepared with your best guacamole recipe. There is a race where the cars are made from avocados. If you have never seen a giant, inflatable avocado, just come on over to the Fallbrook Avocado Festival in California and see it in living color-green, that is!

THE MOST INTIMIDATING TEAM MASCOT EVER: THE GREEN MONSTER FROM THE GUATEMALA SOCCER TEAM

Imagine being responsible for coming up with a mascot to be adopted for your soccer team, a mascot you would consider tough and fierce. You might select types of animals that would strike fear into the hearts of opponents. *Au contraire.* A soccer team from Antigua, Guatemala selected a frightening, vicious green colored mascot: The Fighting Avocado! Yes, that is an avocado, the most intimidating mascot in the world. Well, almost.

The avocado is not a frightening mascot, but in the city of Antigua, avocados enjoy a special place in the hearts of the population. Antiguans are known as "green bellies" because they grow and eat so many avocados. Hence, the origin of the mascot. Evildoers, beware the Fighting Avocado.

THE AVOCADO AND HUMAN ALLERGIES

Some people have allergic reactions to avocado. There are two main forms of allergy. Those with a tree-pollen allergy who develop local symptoms in the mouth and throat shortly after eating avocado; the second, known as latex-fruit syndrome is related to latex allergy and symptoms include generalized hives, abdominal pain and vomiting and can sometimes be life-threatening.

AVOCADOS AND THEIR TOXICITY TO ANIMALS

CORN, COTTON AND CHOCOLATE: HOW THE MAYA CHANGED THE WORLD

The other bad news is that the avocado leaves, bark, skin, or pit are documented to be harmful to animals. Cats, dogs, cattle, rabbits, rats, guinea pigs, birds, fish, and horses can be severely harmed or even killed when they consume parts of the tree. The avocado fruit is poisonous to some birds, and the American Society for the Prevention of Cruelty to Animals (ASPCA) lists it as toxic to many animals.

THE MIRACLE OF AVOCADO OIL

Avocado oil is an edible oil pressed from the fruit of the avocado. As food oil, it is used as cooking oil and as an ingredient in other dishes. Avocado oil functions well as a carrier oil for other flavors. It is high in monounsaturated fats and vitamin E.

Avocado oil is used in cosmetics, where it is valued for its supposed regenerative and moisturizing properties. Avocado oil was originally, and is still extracted for cosmetic use because of its very high skin penetration and rapid absorption.

HOW THE AVOCADO CHANGED THE WORLD.

The avocado has become loved by people around the world, it is popular as food or dip. Guacamole is America's favorite food when watching football on TV. Each year, 4,000,000 metric tons are produced and it is grown on every continent except for Antarctica.

CORN, COTTON AND CHOCOLATE: HOW THE MAYA CHANGED THE WORLD

CHAPTER 7: CASSAVA

Botanical name: *Manihot esculenta*   **Maya name:** *man*

Memories of a youth

I loved dessert. While I did not have a real sweet tooth, any sweet dish that topped off a meal seemed to me to be the best part of dinner. In the early 1940s, during World War II, the available desserts were limited by rationing. You could serve cakes, pies and various kinds of puddings. Cakes and pies took a lot of time to prepare and were reserved for Sunday dinners and birthdays.

For everyday meals, my mother would prepare some type of pudding like rice pudding, banana pudding or a Jello-based dessert. Instant puddings had not been introduced during World War II. Jello was always a treat when combined with a fruit filling, but my favorite dessert was tapioca pudding. Tapioca pudding is one of those comfort foods that conjure up childhood memories.

However, tapioca was a casualty of the World War. The delicious product is derived from the cassava root and was principally grown in the islands of Java. Tapioca was missing from our grocery shelves due to the Japanese occupation of the islands. The supply of tapioca from Java was terminated after the Japanese invaded the islands. The Japanese held the islands until their surrender in September 1945. The only supply of tapioca during World War II came from Brazil, and it was in short supply. However, my mother was able to purchase several boxes of tapioca which she stretched out over the war years until the supply was depleted.

It was a special occasion when my mother served this delicious comfort food. Forget the cakes and pies, tapioca pudding was the real treat. Mother prepared her version of tapioca pudding with coconut. Coconut gave the pearly lustered dish a very special taste, a taste that elevated the dessert to a higher level.

Tapioca is a starchy substance extracted from the root of the cassava plant and turned into pellets which are used to prepare the pudding. The finished dessert is studded with gelatinous spheres like tiny pearls. These tiny pearl-like components made the desert more attractive in to my childhood memories. The pudding was not only utterly delicious but gave the impression that you were devouring precious pearls.

To place a spoonful of this ambrosia into my mouth was soothing and delicious. Just the thought of that delicious pudding brings back the nostalgic memories spent with my mother and my family.

Over the years, I have sampled various desserts, but they cannot compare was my mother's tapioca pudding made with shining pearls of the cassava. Little did Maya agronomists know what a delicious comfort food would produce when they domesticated cassava.

THE MAYA AND CASSAVA

Cassava has recently joined the ranks of the most important Maya cultivars. Its value to the Maya civilization was unrecognized for a long time. The scholarly study of Maya food staples had long held that maize was the principal Maya food crop. However, mounting evidence indicated that something was missing from the equation of Maya food staples.

CORN, COTTON AND CHOCOLATE: HOW THE MAYA CHANGED THE WORLD

The ancient Maya elevated maize to the highest level of food sources. Maize was the royalty of Maya food crops, and was the undisputed staple of the Maya. It was the reliable source of calories, providing the complex carbohydrates that enabled the Maya to develop their civilization.

During the Classic period when Maya population expanded, maize alone could not supply sufficient calories to support the population. The concept that the Maya powered their society on the triad of maize, beans and squash became suspect to archaeologists. To survive, the Maya required an additional staple for feeding the masses, a cultivar that could provide the large source of calories required to feed the burgeoning cities in the domain.

Enter cassava into the big game. This root vegetable had the capacity to deliver the additional nutrients that allowed the densely-populated cities to flourish.

The concept of cassava as a food staple was based on the inability of maize to feed the population serving as a standalone cultivar. However, as a team, cassava and maize combined to meet those needs. Evidence for this teamwork was lacking because traces of cassava rarely survive in the archaeological record.

After recent discoveries, archaeologists now consider cassava to be the missing staple crop of the Maya, cassava has been identified as the forgotten cultivar in the Maya food panoply. Over historical time cassava has proved that it had the right stuff. In the 21st century it provides daily food for over 500 million people.

Cassava is a hardy plant that produces a plain tasting root that is versatile and can be made into anything from tortillas to moonshine. The root can be cooked like a potato, and the leaves of the plant are high in protein. It can grow anywhere and produces six times more calories than maize.

The species *Manihot esculenta* likely originated further south in Brazil. However, in the late Archaic period, the Maya assumed the responsibility of cassava domestication and the modern Maya continue to cultivate the nutritious tuber.

Today, the growing of cassava is a common sight in fields across the Maya domain. Until recently there was little direct evidence of its cultivation before European contact. Recent discoveries, suggest that the Maya cultivated the crop and cassava has now proven to be a staple in the ancient Maya world.

By 6,600 BC, evidence of cassava pollen appears in the Maya lowlands. Cassava pollen has been found at Maya archaeological sites in Belize and Mexico, but it was not known whether it was cultivated as a major crop or the pollen was the just remnants of a few garden plants. This concept has been altered and valid proof has been found of extensive cultivation of cassava by Maya farmers.

The oldest direct evidence of cassava cultivation comes from a 1,400-year-old Maya site at Joya de Cerén, in El Salvador. The site was buried beneath 17 feet of ash by a volcano eruption around AD 600. This Maya settlement in El Salvador, now known as America's Pompeii, appears to have answered the riddle of how the Maya civilization fed its multitudes. Archaeologists found a 1,400-year-old field of cassava buried beneath the deep volcanic ash.

CORN, COTTON AND CHOCOLATE: HOW THE MAYA CHANGED THE WORLD

THE MAYA PROVIDE THE TECHNOLOGY FOR DEFUSING CYANIDE IN CASSAVA.

The Maya discovered that the consumption of cassava has a dangerous pitfall. The tuber contains cyanide located in cyanogenic glycosides which can be deadly to the unknowing consumer. Maya technicians developed a simplistic method of extracting the cyanide as part of cassava's food preparation process.

The safe processing method used by Maya cooks was to mix cassava flour and water into a thick paste and then spread the mix in a thin layer over a basket. The basket and cassava mix was allowed to stand in the shade for five hours. The process removes the cyanide and makes the flour safe for consumption. The cassava can then be made into tamales for the evening dinner.

THE MAYA WAY TO PREPARE CASSAVA FOR COOKING

Maya villagers living in the Yucatán today prepare their cassava in a fashion similar to the ancient Maya. Cooks have a long tradition of preparing their cassava by cutting the roots into small chunks, drying the chunks for eight days, then grinding them into a fine, flour-like powder known as *almidón*. The flour is then treated for cyanide.

The cassava flour can be stored almost indefinitely, and was used by ancient Maya cooks for making tamales, tortillas and as a thickening agent for stews. Cassava was also used to brew alcoholic beverages. The Maya enjoyed the good life.

CASSAVA TRAVELS AND CHANGES HOW THE WORLD IS FED

Early in the 16th century, cassava was first encountered by European contact. It was introduced to Africa in the 16th century and to the Philippines in the 17th century. It traveled from the Philippines to Malaysia in the 18th century. The traveling cassava also changed the way the world was fed.

Cassava is extensively cultivated for its starchy tuberous root in tropical and subtropical regions of the world. Cassava root is a major source of carbohydrates; however, it is a poor source of protein. After maize and rice, cassava is the third largest source of food and food carbohydrates in the tropics and is the basic daily food source for 500,000,000 people in the world. Since being introduced in the 16th century, maize and cassava have replaced traditional African crops as the continent's most important staple food crop. Cassava is sometimes described as the "bread of the tropics".

The cassava plant gives the highest yield of carbohydrates per cultivated area among all crop plants, except for sugarcane and sugar beets. Cassava plays a particularly important role in agriculture in developing countries, especially in sub-Saharan Africa. Cassava is one of the most drought-tolerant crops, and can be successfully grown in poor soils, soil conditions that are common in certain parts of Africa and South America.

Introduction of cassava to the world has changed the metrics of populations. After introduction to China, the population, which had been held in check by a shortage of irrigable rice fields, got a boost from cassava. Cassava proved that it could be grown on marginal land, the rest is history.

CORN, COTTON AND CHOCOLATE: HOW THE MAYA CHANGED THE WORLD

THE WORLD LOVES CASSAVA

Cassava is widely cultivated in tropical and sub-tropical regions of the world, and mainly in Africa, Asia and Latin America. Cassava producing countries grow over 300 million metric tons of cassava every year. African countries are producing more than half of the total world production of Cassava, second is Asia and then Latin America, Nigeria is leading the world in production of cassava with its annual production of 54 million tons. Here is a list of the top cassava producing countries in the world during 2015.

THE TOP 20 COUNTRIES PRODUCING CASSAVA IN METRIC TONS

RANK	COUNTRY	PRODUCTION
1	Nigeria	54 000 000
2	Indonesia	24 177 372
3	Thailand	29 848 000
4	Democratic Republic of the Congo	16 000 000
5	Ghana	14 547 279
6	Brazil	23 044 557
7	Angola	10 636 400
8	Mozambique	10 051 364
9	Viet Nam	9 745 545
10	India	8 746 500
11	Cambodia	7 613 697
12	United Republic of Tanzania	5 462 454
13	Uganda	4 924 560
14	Malawi	4 692 202
15	China	4 560 000
16	Cameroon	4 287 177
17	Sierra Leone	3 520 000
18	Madagascar	3 621 309
19	Benin	3 295 785
20	Rwanda	2 716 421

CASSAVA THE PLANT

Cassava is also known as yucca, manioc, or mogo. It is a woody shrub of the *Euphorbiaceae* (spurge family). The cassava root is long and tapered, with a firm, homogeneous flesh encased in a detachable rind, about 1mm thick, rough and brown on the outside, just like a potato. Commercial varieties can be 2 to 4 inches (5 to 10 cm) in diameter at the top, and around 6 to 12 inches (15 cm to 30 cm) long. A woody cordon runs along the root's axis and the flesh can be chalk-white or yellowish. Cassava leaves are a good source of protein (rich in lysine), but deficient in the amino acid methionine and tryptophan.

CORN, COTTON AND CHOCOLATE: HOW THE MAYA CHANGED THE WORLD

CASSAVA AS A POPULAR FOOD

As a food, cassava, has changed the tastes of the world. As the daily food for half a billion people a wide variety of methods for preparation have been developed. This popular cultivar contains anti-nutrition factors and toxins. The root must be properly prepared before consumption. Improper preparation of cassava can leave enough residual cyanide to cause acute cyanide intoxication and goiters, and may even cause ataxia or partial paralysis.

Cassava-based dishes are widely consumed wherever the plant is cultivated and some have regional, national, or ethnic importance. Cassava can be cooked in various ways. The soft-boiled root has a delicate flavor and can replace potatoes as an accompaniment for meat dishes, or made into purées, dumplings, soups and stews. Cassava is commonly used in Western cuisine as an alternative to wheat. There is great potential in the use of cassava flour as it may be considered as a replacement for wheat flour. Since cassava is gluten free, it is perfect for use as gluten-free, grain-free baking and cooking.

AFRICA:

In Africa, *fufu*, or cassava bread, is made by first pounding cassava in a mortar to make flour, which is then sifted before being put in hot water to become *fufu*. *Fufu* is eaten by making a small ball in one's fingers and then dipping into an accompanying soup or sauce.

Gari is a delicacy in Nigeria, Cameroon, Congo, Ghana and other parts of Africa. *Gari* is a creamy-white, granular flour with a slightly sour, fermented flavor made from fermented, gelatinized fresh cassava tubers. One can simply soak *gari* in cold water, add a bit of sugar and roasted peanuts to taste, and add whatever quantity of evaporated milk one desires.

In the Democratic Republic of the Congo, cassava leaves are washed with hot water, pounded in a mortar, and boiled. During the boiling process, the pot is not covered, enabling the release of hydrogen cyanide. The pot is then covered when ingredients such as, onion, fish, and other ingredients are added, and only opened as needed for stirring. The sauce produced by the process is eaten with rice, and is called, *sombe* in Swahili. Cassava root flour is also used to make a cassava bread by boiling flour until it is a thick, rubbery ball called *bukari* in Swahili.

THE PACIFIC:

In the Philippines cassava cake is one of the most popular homemade delicacies. Made from grated cassava it is mixed with coconut milk, eggs, and butter and topped with a creamy milk mixture.

In Indonesia, *Singkong or Ketela* (cassava) is an important food. It can be cooked by frying or boiling, or processed by fermentation to make *tapai* and *getuk* cake, while the starch is made into *krupuk* crackers.

SOUTH AMERICA:

In Brazil, a crunchy meal called *farinha de mandioca* is produced for use as a condiment, a base for *farofa*, or a stand-alone side dish. Cassava roots are ground to a pulp called a *massa* and squeezed with a device called a *tipiti* to dry it out. The dried *massa* is then toasted over a large copper stove to produce the dried meal. Fried cassava is a typical dish in Brazil where it can be found as a substitute for French fries. It is commonly served in bars as appetizer and side dish for beer.

CORN, COTTON AND CHOCOLATE: HOW THE MAYA CHANGED THE WORLD

ITS MILLER TIME

Cassava is one of the richest fermentable substances known to produce alcohol. The crude alcohol of cassava is described as average in quality and has a disagreeable odor, but it can be improved if the first and last fractions in the distillation process are discarded.

However, modern cultures have created numerous efficient methods for making cassava into an alcoholic beverage. The type and methodology used varies with the country and the continent.

Most concoctions are from Latin countries, but *kasiri* is popular in Sub-Saharan Africa and *Impala* hails from Mozambique. Latin American alcoholic beverages made from cassava include *Cauim* and *tiquira* from Brazil, *parakari* or *kari* from Guyana, Nijimanche from Ecuador and Peru and *chicha de yuca*, from Panama.

TAPIOCA, THE SWEET SIDE OF CASSAVA

Tapioca is a product of the cassava root and is used for desserts. To prepare tapioca, cassava flour is treated to form flakes, seeds, and pearls of tapioca. Pearl tapioca, rather than the quicker cooking flake kind, is preferred for tapioca pudding. Tapioca granules, flakes or pellets are used to make tapioca pudding and to thicken pie fillings.

Tapioca has traditionally been considered a healthy food because this form of starch is easy to digest. In 19th century America, tapioca pudding was often prescribed for the young, old and the sick.

THE MANY USES OF CASSAVA

Cassava has changed the way that the world looks at a root vegetable. In addition to feeding the world, cassava has multiple uses as a biofuel, an animal food, a medicine and a starch.

BIOFUEL

Generally accepted sources of raw material for biofuel production are cereal grains such as corn, wheat, rye, barley, sorghum grains, rice, potatoes, apple wine, and others. Cassava has now become a leader in ethanol production because of its high crop yields (30-80 ton/hectare) and high starch content. Because of high yields and high starch levels, compared to wheat, corn or sugar cane, cassava produces high amounts of ethanol per ton. Cassava yields amounts up to about 200 liters per ton and is 96% pure ethanol.

In many countries, significant research has begun to evaluate the use of cassava as an ethanol biofuel feedstock. In the People's Republic of China, the target is to increase the application of ethanol fuel by non-grain feedstock to 2 million tons, and that of biodiesel to 200 thousand tons. This will be equivalent to a substitute of 10 million tons of petroleum.

ANIMAL FEED

Cassava is used worldwide for animal feed. Cassava hay is produced at a growth stage of three to four months, harvested when about 30 inches (30–45 cm) above ground, and sun-dried for one to two days until it has final dry matter of less than 85%. It is used as a good roughage source for dairy or beef cattle, buffalo, goats, and sheep by either direct feeding or as a protein source in the concentrate mixtures.

ETHNO MEDICINE

CORN, COTTON AND CHOCOLATE: HOW THE MAYA CHANGED THE WORLD

Cassava has multiple applications in medicine and in health. Its bitter leaves are used to treat hypertension, headache, and pain. In Cuba cassava is commonly used to treat irritable bowel syndrome; the paste is eaten in excess during treatment. In folk medicine, the cassava plant is promoted for treating snakebites, boils, diarrhea, flu, hernia, inflammation, conjunctivitis, sores, and several other problems including cancer.

CASSAVA STARCH AS AN ADHESIVE:

The application of cassava for use in adhesives is one of the most important uses of the cultivar. Cassava starch is used in the manufacture of glue with the help of chemicals. The following are some of the major uses of cassava adhesives in industry

Corrugated cardboard manufacture: Used in the manufacture of cartons. boxes and other packing material.

Re-moistening glues: Used for adhesives that are coated and dried on surfaces, such as postage stamps and envelope flaps

Wallpaper: Starch-based products are used as adhesives for wallpaper and other domestic uses

Paper industry: In the paper and board industries, starch is used in large quantities at the end of the wet treatment, at the size press and in the coating operations.

Textile industry. In the textile industry, starches occupy an important place in such operations as warp sizing, cloth finishing and printing

HOW CASSAVA CHANGED THE WORLD

Cassava has changed how the world eats. The cultivar now feeds 500,000,000 people in the tropics every day. Cassava is now grown in tropical and subtropical countries across the world. Over 300,000,000 metric tons are produced each year. s changed the agriculture in countries that produce the vegetable because it is a very drought-tolerant crop and can be successfully grown on marginal soils, conditions that are common in parts of Africa and South America. It has multiple uses in addition to food including bio-fuel medicine and industrial applications.

CORN, COTTON AND CHOCOLATE: HOW THE MAYA CHANGED THE WORLD

CHAPTER 8: CHICLE

Botanical name: *Manikara zapota* **Maya Name**: *lits*

Memories of a youth

In our little town in Georgia, a baseball card collection was a must for all boys. The cards had value as a collectable item and intrinsic value as a treasure coveted by other boy collectors. They brought great entertainment and pleasure to a boy as he fondled and examined his collection. Trading baseball cards produced an adrenaline rush when interacting with other boys. The very act of trading released the sneaky gambler that dwelt in their little hearts as they used their best skills at bartering the valued cardboard rectangles.

A collection of baseball trading cards began with the purchase of a pack of bubble gum because a complimentary card was included within the package. Baseball cards were made of a cardboard rectangle featuring a photo and vital statistics of a big-league baseball player. Each card came with a delicious stick of bubble gum. The gum was produced by either the Bowman or Tops chewing gum companies

The front of the card displayed an image of the big-league player with identifying information, including the player's name and team affiliation. The back of the card displayed baseball statistics and biographical information.

Rather than go for collecting a complete set of cards, our neighborhood gang collected cards featuring individual star players. When you bought a packet of gum, you strived to add the biggest stars to your collection. When opening a pack of bubble gum, there was always great mystery and suspense because you could not tell the identity of the player whose card was in the packet. The suspense would end when the packet was opened and you could see the name on the card. Your excitement was unparalleled when you got lucky and obtained one of your favorite players.

From 1948 to 1952, the Bowman company was the major producer of baseball cards. Topps began to produce large sets of cards in 1951. Chewing gum companies were not the first to produce the cards. Baseball cards were first introduced in the early 20th century by the tobacco industry. Cards were included with a package of cigarettes. Baseball cards were missing during World War II, when the war effort demanded the raw materials. Production of baseball cards was re-started in 1948.

Major league baseball players of my boyhood era were an amazing group of overachieving athletes. Now, seven decades later, they are still the finest men that ever played the game. We knew that these men were the best players of our time; but little did we know that they would be the best players of all time. This was the start of baseball's golden years, both leagues contributed great players to our dream teams. The players included Joe DiMaggio, Jacky Robinson, Bob Feller, Stan Musial, Ted Williams, Hank Greenberg, Willie Mays, Eddie Mathews, Duke Snyder, Mickey Mantle and Warren Spahn among other giants in the game.

We collected individual cards of players that were playing with star quality and rookie players for whom we tried to predict a bright future of becoming stars. I usually had difficulty in predicting a successful future for a rookie, but I scored big with a Yogi Berra rookie card in 1948.

CORN, COTTON AND CHOCOLATE: HOW THE MAYA CHANGED THE WORLD

During baseball's Golden Era, baseball cards were collected by boys for fun. As a result, they were fondled, stuffed in pockets, traded for other boyhood desirables and playfully installed in bicycle spokes to make faux motors. Because of their "mistreatment", cards from these years became increasingly difficult to find in collectible condition.

The value of trading cards has skyrocketed during the 21st century. The baseball trading card of a 1917 Pittsburg Pirates shortstop, Honus Wagner sold recently for $2.1 million, a record for any baseball card. Mickey Mantle's true rookie card was a 1951 Bowman issue and is the ultimate card to own of the post-war era.

However, chewing the bubble gum contained in the pack was immediate gratification, and was suited for bubble blowing competitions. The gum was made with real chicle from the Yucatán. It was the same gum that was chewed by the Maya 1500 years ago. This was before 1960 when synthetic chicle was substituted for the real thing in many brands of gum.

Chewing the hard chunk of bubble gum to form a bubble took a little patience. As you chewed the gum it becomes soft and pliable, then came the moment of truth. When the wad of gum was properly masticated, you were ready to form a bubble. Arranging the soft mass of gum around your tongue, forming an indentation in the gum, you pursed your lips and blew into the mass. Eureka, you produced a perfect bubble.

What could be better? A beautiful baseball card and a perfect bubble formed from chicle harvested from trees in the rainforest. Maya agronomists would have been proud of my perfect bubble.

THE MAYA AND CHICLE

The Maya were not the first people in history to habitually chew a gum-like substance, but they were the first to use chicle as a chewing gum. Forms of chewing gums were used in Ancient Greece. The Greeks chewed gum made from the resin of the mastic tree. Chicle is derived from the sap of the sapodilla tree, a tropical evergreen native to the Yucatán. Maya chicle was the gum that changed the world's habits and the etiquette of gum chewers.

The largest concentration of indigenous sapodilla trees is found in the state of Quintana Roo on the Yucatán Peninsula. When the bark of the sapodilla tree is cut, the tree produces a milky fluid that forms a protective film over the damaged area. This milky fluid is a natural polymer known as chicle latex. This material has been used as a chewing gum for millennia by pre-Columbian peoples.

The Maya refer to the sapodilla tree as *tzicte' ya'*, meaning "wounded noble tree" this descriptive name reflects the methodology used by the Maya to collect chicle. The Maya harvested the chicle by cutting slashes in a zigzag pattern down the tree trunk.

This cutting pattern allows the chicle to run down the tree following the zigzag path into collection vessels. After the chicle is collected it is dried and treated. This method of preparing the chicle has been used for thousands of years. The ancient Maya recognized that chicle is a rubbery resin that when chewed could be enjoyed for its high sugar content and sweet flavor but it also served to freshen breath, quench thirst, stave off hunger and keep teeth clean. Chicle was also used by the Maya as a filling for tooth cavities.

The Maya used chicle latex for many practical applications including use as an adhesive or sealant. The wood of the sapodilla tree was also highly prized for its high strength and density.

CORN, COTTON AND CHOCOLATE: HOW THE MAYA CHANGED THE WORLD

The wood resists degradation for centuries. The wood was used for shaping the timber beams and carved lintels in the construction of monumental buildings in their grand cities. Archaeology has greatly benefited from the durable quality of the sapodilla wood. Over time, organic objects in humid tropical climates become degraded but sapodilla wood is an exception. Artifacts made from sapodilla wood remain intact.

CHICLE CHANGES THE HABITS OF THE WORLD

Unlike other Maya cultivars, chicle was not spread worldwide through commercial trading. The Spanish observed the use of chicle by the Maya and the Aztec, they found its usage to be curious, but did not grasp its appeal to the individual users of the gum. Therefore, the use of chicle as a chewing gum was confined to the Yucatán and was not introduced to the outside world for 370 years after first contact. Then in the late 19th century, a strange twist of history changed the market for chicle and the art of chewing gum changed the habits of the world.

Antonio Lopez de Santa Anna was Mexico's leader during the 1840 Mexican-American war. As the eleven-time president of Mexico, he was the leader of the Mexican forces in 1836 against the Texas Republic at the Alamo. He had a famous name but he was unsuccessful in the wars against Texas and the USA. He had mixed results as president of Mexico and he was exiled from Mexico. In 1869, he moved to the United States and was living in Staten Island, New York. The hand of fate placed Santa Anna in Staten Island and where he became acquainted with Thomas Adams.

In the 1860s, Thomas Adams had been a photographer and an inventor. He was unsuccessful at the profession of photography. However, his fortunes turned around when Adams encountered Santa Anna. Santa Anna was in New York trying to raise money to finance an army to return to his country and take over Mexico City.

During his time in New York City, Santa Anna introduced the first shipments of chicle to the U.S. It was Santa Anna who suggested that the unsuccessful but inventive photographer experiment with Mexican chicle. Santa Anna arranged to have two tons of the chicle latex sent to Adams for experimentation.

Santa Anna felt chicle would be in high demand among Americans because he believed it could be used as an additive to natural rubber, making rubber a less expensive material. This hybrid mixture could be used to manufacture all kinds of items using rubber, primarily carriage tires. Santa Anna planned to make a fortune selling chicle to Americans.

Adams spent more than a year experimenting and trying to make practical items from chicle including rain boots, toys, masks and bicycle tires, but found chicle unsuitable as a rubber substitute. Adams tried unsuccessfully to vulcanize the chicle, but he could not produce a usable product. After a year's work of blending chicle with rubber, the experiments were regarded as a failure. Santa Anna lost interest in the experiments and returned to Mexico City, where he died in 1876. He died senile, impoverished, and totally unaware that the chicle latex he left behind would change world history.

The disappointed Thomas Adams intended to throw the remaining chicle into the New York Harbor. However, fate again stepped in before he disposed of the chicle. By chance, Adams visited a neighborhood drugstore. While he was there, a little girl came into the shop and asked for chewing gum that cost one penny. After the child left the store, Adams asked the druggist what type of chewing gum the little girl had purchased. He was told that it was made of paraffin

CORN, COTTON AND CHOCOLATE: HOW THE MAYA CHANGED THE WORLD

wax and was called White Mountain. Then Adams remembered that General Santa Anna chewed chicle as a gum, just as the Mayan people did for thousands of years. He asked the druggist if he would be willing to try selling an entirely different kind of gum, the druggist agreed.

When Thomas Adams arrived home that night, he spoke to his son, about his idea. Thomas junior was very much impressed, and suggested that they make up a few boxes of chicle chewing gum and give it a name and a label. They decided that the name of the gum would be "Adams New York No. 1". The gum was made of pure chicle without any added flavor. It was made into penny sticks and wrapped in colored tissue papers. On the cover of the box was a color picture of New York City Hall. Adams produced a batch of chicle-based gum and delivered the gum to the druggist. The gum sold out the first day. Soon thereafter Adams opened the world's first chewing gum factory on a $55 investment

By February 1871, Adams New York Gum could be found on sale in drug stores around New York for a penny. In 1888, a Thomas Adams' chewing gum called "Tutti-Frutti" became the first gum to be sold in a vending machine. The machines were located in a New York City subway station. Thomas Adams sold the gum with the slogan "Adams' New York Gum, No. 1, Snapping and stretching." By the end of the 19th century the firm became the nation's most prosperous chewing gum company. It built a monopoly in 1899 by merging with the six largest chewing gum manufacturers in the United States and Canada, and achieved even greater success when he introduced "Chiclets".

The best-known chewing gum manufacturers worldwide is Wrigley. Wrigley was founded by William Wrigley in 1892 in Chicago. It became known as Wrigley's Spearmint Gum and within four years was the bestselling gum in the U.S. The average American chewed 300 sticks per year. Chewing gum had truly become part of the American way of life.

Historically, during World War II, the image of an American soldier chewing a piece of Wrigley's gum became an icon in American media. Wrigley began donating their gum to the troops because it was regarded as a stress reliever and a healthier alternative to smoking. By the end of the war, sales of Wrigley's gum had doubled and it had become popular among the youth of America.

It was William Wrigley Jr. who established an international market for the chewing gum industry, he stretched his empire to 37 countries. His factories produced 280 million sticks of gum a week. His name became synonymous with chewing gum throughout the twentieth century. He introduced several brands and flavors to the industry and became one of the ten wealthiest men in the United States.

CHICLEROS, THE MEN WHO HARVESTED CHICLE

During the first half of the 20th century, as the popularity of chewing gum spread worldwide, the demand for chicle increased. This demand resulted in chicle becoming one of Mexico's largest exports. The hard work of collecting chicle from the rainforest fell to a cadre of Maya men who were a breed like a page out of the American wild west.

The Sapodilla tree did not lend itself to being planted in plantations. To collect chicle, the trees had to be searched out deep in the jungle. The men who searched the jungle collecting chicle were called *chicleros*. The *chiclero* was a wild and woolly individual, they had notorious reputation as violent, promiscuous criminals.

CORN, COTTON AND CHOCOLATE: HOW THE MAYA CHANGED THE WORLD

Their lifestyle permitted unsupervised work in the jungle as a lone wolf. This was the perfect position for individuals running from the law or those shunned by their villages. Wages were low, the workdays were long, conditions were dangerous, and chicleros lived in constant debt to the company store. The company store provided their equipment and food at inflated prices.

These rough and tumble men have been accused of many sins. They were known as hardworking drunks, murders and rapists. Despite their sins, they were men of the forest, naturalists, and especially advisors and guides for archaeologists. They had an excellent working knowledge of forest plants and habits of wildlife. During their daily explorations for untapped sapodilla trees, chicleros came across unknown archaeological sites hiding in the jungle.

Chicleros played a significant role in archaeological discovery. They have been responsible for discovering some of the most important archaeological sites in the Maya area. For over a century, if It was not for their explorations in the jungle, many important sites would still be unknown.

This misunderstood group of Maya men played a significant role in a truly American industry. They wandered the forest collecting the key ingredient for a product that was enjoyed by millions around the world. They collected chicle that changed the world, and because of their explorations they opened the ancient world of the Maya for all the world to see.

SAPODILLA, THE TREE THAT PRODUCES CHICLE

The sapodilla tree can grow to more than to a height of 100 feet with an average trunk diameter of 5 feet. It is wind-resistant and the bark is rich with the white, gummy latex called chicle. The ornamental leaves are medium green and glossy. The white flowers are inconspicuous and bell-like, with a six-lobed corolla.

The fruit is a large ellipsoid berry, averaging 3 inches in diameter, containing two to five seeds. Inside, its flesh ranges from a pale yellow to an earthy brown color with a grainy texture akin to that of a well-ripened pear. The fruit has an exceptionally sweet, malty flavor. The seeds are black and resemble beans, with a hook at one end that can catch in the throat if swallowed. The trees can only survive in warm, typically tropical environments, dying easily if the temperature drops below freezing. From germination, the sapodilla tree will usually take anywhere from five to eight years to bear fruit.

WORLD PRODUCTION OF GUM, THE BAD HABIT TAKES OVER THE WORLD

America was the gum chewing capital of the world until the 1940s when the world changed into passionate gum chewers. The worldwide habit of chewing gum was spread by American troops during WWII. Over 500 million sticks of gum, every year, were chewed by American soldiers. The gum was provided as part of their rations.

The troops found that they could win over European civilians during WWII by handing children a stick of gum. Gum chewing caught on and worldwide market in chewing gum spread rapidly after WWII. Chewing gum became a wildly successful product because its producers sold something that was popular and in demand. They created the desire for a product that has no real value and the chicle industry in the Yucatán was becoming rich.

CORN, COTTON AND CHOCOLATE: HOW THE MAYA CHANGED THE WORLD

American philosopher, Elbert Hubbard, is credited with stating, "We will never be a great country until we expend more money for books than we do for gum," and the craze for gum truly did take over the country. Children throughout the country could not stop buying the product, and sales increased even more when illustrated cards were included in the packs. The cards depicted American celebrities, including baseball players. These cards encouraged kids to chew as much gum as possible and build a large card collection to trade with and brag about to their friends.

The habit of chewing gum has enveloped billions of people worldwide. Globally, a total of 3.74 trillion sticks of gum are chewed each year, producing a worldwide chewing gum industry worth $19 billion. There are 115 chewing gum companies scattered across the world with 30 companies in the USA. Turkey has the highest number of companies with a total of 60. These companies produce 100,000 tons of gum annually.

The chewing of gum has been called "The cause of the downfall of the western world." This comment was made by people who are disgusted by gum smacking individuals and by "gum chewing do-nothings".

BUBBLE GUM OR I'M FOREVER BLOWING BUBBLES

The ubiquitous bubble-blowing youngster did not come onto being until 50 years after the onset of chicle based chewing gum. There were early attempts at making bubble gum at the turn of the 20th century; however, these bubble gums failed because they were too wet and usually broke before a nice bubble was formed.

It was in 1928 that Walter Diemer happened upon just the right gum recipe to make the very first successful bubble gum. This was a special type of chewing gum that allows the chewer to blow bubbles. At the time, 23-year-old Diemer was an accountant for Fleer Chewing Gum Company.

As a hobby Diemer experimented on new gum recipes in his spare time. Diemer accidently hit upon a formula that was less sticky and more flexible than other chewing gums; these were the actual characteristics required that allowed the gum chewer to form bubbles.

Diemer used a pink dye for his new gum because pink was the only color available at the Fleer Chewing Gum Company. Today, the pink color remains the industry standard for bubble gum. Fleer Chewing Gum Company marketed Diemer's new gum as "Dubble Bubble." To help sell the new bubble gum, Diemer himself taught salespeople how to blow bubbles so that they in turn could teach potential customers.

During World War II, Dubble Bubble was distributed to the military. Sugar and latex became scarce due to the war effort and bubble gum manufacturing was halted in 1942. After the war, Fleer resumed manufacturing Dubble Bubble and the popularity of its gum grew steadily. Over time, Fleer extended its reach and expanded distribution of its products overseas. Dubble Bubble remained the only bubble gum on the market until Bazooka bubble gum appeared on the market after World War II.

CHICLE INVENTS BASEBALL CARDS

Trading baseball cards was a popular boyhood past time for the American youth of the 1950's, 1960's and 1970's. These boys are now adults but they are still collecting the cardboard rectangles. Except now, the cards are not just for collecting they are in the big-time bucks. A

CORN, COTTON AND CHOCOLATE: HOW THE MAYA CHANGED THE WORLD

Honus Wagner card recently sold for $2,100,000, and that's a lot of moola to pay for a card included as a freebee in a pack of gum. Actually, the Honus Wagner card was the prize in a package of cigarettes.

That was in 1909, before chewing gum got into the baseball trading card business. The gum companies did not distribute baseball cards until the 1930's when Babe Ruth and Lou Gehrig cards were included in packs of chewing gum. In contrast to the plain, black and white designs common in earlier decades, the card sets of the 1930s featured bright, hand-colored photos of players on the front of the card. The backs provided brief biographies, statistics and personal information such as height, weight, and birthplace.

The distribution of baseball cards was interrupted by WWII and production did not return until 1948. This was the beginning of the golden age of baseball that extended from the 1940s until the 1970s. Baseball card production resumed with trading card issues by the Bowman Gum and the Leaf Candy Company. Baseball card collecting became very popular again.

Bowman was the major producer of baseball cards from 1948 to 1952. In 1952, Topps began to produce large sets of cards as well. The 1952 Topps set is the most sought-after post-World War set among collectors because of the scarcity of the Mickey Mantle card. This was the first Mickey Mantle card issued by Topps. Although it is not his true rookie card, that honor belongs to his 1951 Bowman card, it is still considered the ultimate baseball card to own of the post-war era.

Over the years, baseball cards in the United States have gone through numerous changes in everything from production and marketing to distribution and usage. Traditionally, boys would collect the cards by buying individual packs of gum rather than whole sets of cards. Hoping to get lucky and pick their favorite player or players from their hometown teams. Once they had a collection, they would trade cards of favorite star players with their friends. What would happen to the cards of no-name rookies? They were put to utilitarian use as an "improvised motor" for bicycles, by affixing the card to the frame of the bike and letting the spokes hit them, simulating the sound of a Harley Davidson motorcycle.

Collecting cards was for fun and part of the excitement in collecting was that every new spring brought exciting new cards. Boys waited to collect cards in anticipation for the upcoming baseball season. Now that the boys have grown into men, collecting is now judged by the card's worth in monetary terms.

Vintage baseball cards have been a prime focus of countless collectors and historians of America's favorite pastime. Some baseball card collectors pay large sums of money to gain possession of these cards and they expend a lot of time devoted to collecting. Since rare baseball card are difficult to find, collectors seek ways to become aware of the rare cards that enter the trading or selling market. Baseball card collectors normally obtain them from other card collectors or from specialized dealers.

A wag once said that the United States pays billions of dollars per year for chewing gum, a substance which has no practical use. That may be true of the disposable chewing gum contained in the package, but the some of the precious baseball cards that were part of the package now sell for a fortune. They cost millions of dollars exceeding the price of a fine painting by Picasso.

CORN, COTTON AND CHOCOLATE: HOW THE MAYA CHANGED THE WORLD

CHICLE CHANGES WORLD LAWS: BAD CHEWING HABITS MEET RESISTANCE

Maya chicle has changed laws of the world. There is a strictly enforced ban on importing chewing gum into Singapore. Since 2004, only chewing gum of therapeutic value that is prescribed a doctor is allowed.

In Singapore, chewing gum was causing serious maintenance problems throughout the city. Vandals were disposing of spent gum in mailboxes, inside keyholes and even on elevator buttons. Chewing gum left on floors, the seats of public buses, stairways and pavements in public areas increased the cost of cleaning and damaged cleaning equipment. It was then reported that vandals had begun sticking chewing gum on the door sensors of Mass Rapid Transit trains, preventing the door from functioning properly and causing disruption of train services. Culprits were difficult to apprehend. In January 1992, the Prime Minister, signed a ban on importing gum into Singapore.

WALKING AND CHEWING GUM AT THE SAME TIME

The history of chicle is full of quotes about the futility of chewing gum. However, the most infamous quote relating to the practice of chewing gum comes from a comment made by former President Lyndon Johnson about former U.S. President Gerald Ford. Johnson said: *"Gerald is so dumb he can't walk and chew gum at the same time.... He's a nice fellow, but he spent too much time playing football without a helmet."*

GUM CHEWING ETIQUETTE

The proper art and etiquette of chewing gum has been hotly debated for many years. Researching the opinions of etiquette experts for advice has varied results. People chew 3.74 trillion sticks of gum per year. That's a lot of people and a lot of gum. What standards exist to guide gum chewers in the proper etiquette of chewing?

The ultimate expert on etiquette, Emily Post, at first refused to even discuss chewing gum. By the 1950s, she would only say that it was a bad habit and that a lady should not engage in it. In the 1960s, she ranted about chewing gum and stated that it made a person look like a cow chewing its cud. That was her last word: Ladies should not chew gum, particularly if they appear to be chewing their cud, popping the gum and smacking with an open mouth.

Some doctors and dentists state that chewing gum has its benefits. One is as an aid to digestion, another is assisting people in clearing their ear drums when ascending or descending in an airplane. In fact, doctors have found that gum strengthens weak jaws, reduces muscular tension and helps the chewer relax. Many people use gum to help refresh their breath after a meal.

These practical applications can be done very privately and can be accomplished in a minute or two quietly. One does not need to be walking down the street smacking gum and blowing bubbles. That's unacceptable behavior at any age.

Here are a few suggestions from the experts on when not to chew gum.

CORN, COTTON AND CHOCOLATE: HOW THE MAYA CHANGED THE WORLD

When you are at your work place. Avoid chewing gum during any professional meetings, at job interviews and in any presentation where your participation is required. Eliminate gum chewing in any working environment where you're in constant contact with customers or clients.

Avoid chewing gum during church and weddings, this is especially for true bridesmaids and groomsmen. Do not chew when on stage at graduations or during school presentations.

You should spit out your gum when in a situation in which you'll be talking with many people Chewing gum is like chewing food, do not do it with your mouth open. This will help you avoid looking like a grazing cow.

When eating, or drinking, discard your gum and get a new piece afterwards. Do not affix your gum to your plate or cup to "save for later".

While in public, do not blow bubbles with your gum. Do not chew gum during phone conversations. It's the same as chewing right into someone's ear.

The best time to chew gum is when you are alone or with friends or family in an informal setting. Chew gum when you are in your car, at home, while reading or anytime you're not carrying on a conversation with others on the phone or in person. Beware, though, sometimes your friends can be irritated if you "crack" your gum so fast and loudly that it sounds like a drive-by shooting.

DISPOSING OF GUM PROPERLY

When it comes to disposing of "ABC" (already been chewed) gum, it is not advised to drop the "ABC" gum on the street, in the grass, in a water fountain, in a urinal, or stick it to the underside of something. The best solution to do is to keep the gum wrapper and use that wrapper as a sanitary method to transfer the gum from your mouth to the trash. Sometimes gum doesn't come in a wrapper so try to find something similar like a tissue or piece of paper to use in this situation.

Should you be without paper to wrap the gum, use your fingers. If you are near a trash can, but have nothing to wrap your gum with, it is more polite to use your fingers to throw the gum into the trash than to spit it straight from your mouth. Spitting your gum out directly into the garbage is acceptable but only when done with the utmost discretion. This is not something to be done in front of others.

REALLY? CHEWING GUM IS GOOD FOR THE BRAIN?

A study carried out in England has found that the act of chewing gum improves short and long-term memory by as much as 35 percent. The type of gum being chewed doesn't matter. The key to better brain power is the repetitive chewing motion, according to the study, which was presented at the British Psychological Society's Annual Conference.

"The results were extremely clear; specifically, we found that chewing gum targeted memory," says Andrew Scholey, a scientist with the university's human cognitive-neuroscience unit who carried out the study. "People recalled more words and performed better in tests on working memory."

CORN, COTTON AND CHOCOLATE: HOW THE MAYA CHANGED THE WORLD

Why does chewing gum stimulate one's memory? Scientists don't know for sure, but they are working on two theories. One is that the gentle exercise of chewing raises a person's heart rate, which increases the flow of oxygen to the brain. Another is that chewing triggers the release of insulin, a natural chemical that stimulates a sector of the brain involved in memory.

The results of the study were welcomed by chewing gum manufacturers worldwide, who said they always had known there were positive benefits to chewing gum. Proving that people can chew gum and walk at the same time.

FUNCTIONAL CHEWING GUM, CHICLE AS A MEDICINE

Finally, a positive use for gum chewing. Functional chewing gum is the name given to types of chewing gum which impart some useful function other than the usual chewing pleasures. Examples include nicotine gum which is used to aid smoking cessation and caffeine gum to resist fatigue.

Nicotine gum is a type of chewing gum that delivers nicotine directly to the body. It is used as an aid in nicotine replacement therapy (NRT), a process for the cession of smoking and smokeless tobacco. The nicotine is delivered to the bloodstream during the chewing process via absorption by the tissues of the mouth. Sleep researcher Gary Kamimori invented caffeine gum. During WWII, the U.S. Army readily supplied this gum to its troops to help resist fatigue through the rigors of military operations. Each piece contained caffeine that was roughly the equivalent of a six-ounce cup of coffee.

OH NO! I CAN'T SEEM TO GET THAT SONG OUT OF MY HEAD.

We are all familiar with the earworm. What! You didn't know that having a song stuck in your head had a name. We've all been victims of the earworm: this is a catchy piece of music that gets stuck in your head and you can't seem to dislodge it.

Earworms are incredibly common; 90% of us suffer from earworms at least once a week. And while they're not actually harmful, they can be distracting. But fear not! Researchers have come to the rescue with a scientifically backed earworm prevention weapon: chewing gum.

Yes, scientists at the University of Reading, say the best way to treat earworms is to chew gum. "The key is to find something that will give the right level of challenge," Dr. Ira Hyman, a music psychologist at Western Washington University, told the Telegraph newspaper. "If you are cognitively engaged, it limits the ability of intrusive songs to enter your head."

HOW CHICLE CHANGED THE WORLD

Chicle changed the world when it introduced a nasty habit, one that altered etiquette. The habit of chewing gum has enveloped billions of people worldwide. Globally, a total of 3.74 trillion sticks of gum are chewed each year, producing a worldwide chewing gum industry worth $19 billion. Chicle introduced baseball trading cards and bubble gun to American boys. Maya chicle has changed laws of the world and proved that some people can't walk and chew gum at the same time.

CORN, COTTON AND CHOCOLATE: HOW THE MAYA CHANGED THE WORLD

CHAPTER 9: CHILI PEPPERS

Botanical name: *Capsicum* **Maya Name:** *yic*

Memories of a youth

Chili peppers are currently the world's favorite spice. However, during the 1940s chili peppers were almost unheard of in my home state of Georgia. Mexican or Thai restaurants did not exist until many years later. So, my experience with the heat of that savory spice did not begin until I traveled to Mexico during the 1960s.

By the early 1970s, I was well familiar with chilies. I ate them and cooked with them and considered them to be the food of the gods. My most memorable experience with the capsicum critters took place not in Mexico, but in the hallowed halls of Harvard University.

I was part of an architectural team that was selected by Harvard University to design a new student athletic facility. In the spring of 1975, our team was meeting with the university. The evening before the conference, we were having dinner in a hallowed dining hall of Harvard. Our team consisted of men from different design disciplines. One of the outstanding talents on our design team was an architect whose roots were in Texas. Jimmie Hagan had an infectious personality, but true to his Texas roots, he tended to make his talking points by speaking loudly.

We were seated directly across from each other reviewing the menu. I was perusing the bill of fare and noticed that *chili con carne* was suggested as a favorite dish.

Speaking out loud but mostly to myself, I said, "I wonder what kind of beans they use in their chili con carne"

Imagine this scenario set in the hushed halls of a sacrosanct Harvard University dining hall. Students and faculty members were quietly dining and conversing in hushed tones. Then like a clap of thunder came a crystal-clear shout in a distinct Texas accent.

"Ain't no stinking beans in no f***ing chili." Everyone in the hall went silent. Startled, they all looked up at Jimmie Hagan, who had just commented on the quality of the university recipe for chili con carne. I was a little stunned, but after all, I had incited the mini chili riot.

"Jimmie", I said with a stage whisper, "keep it down. Let's try the chili, maybe they prepared it properly."

Things calmed down, we ordered the chili con carne, but as we anticipated, the otherwise delicious bowl of red contained beans. Hell, what did we expect, we were in Boston?

Jimmie then proclaimed. "I can make better chili then this."

My life experience included experience as a chili chef. I responded, "I can also make better chili then this."

"Well put your money where your mouth is. I bet I can make better chili then you can," retorted Jimmie.

That was it! He had thrown down his gauntlet. He challenged me to a chili cook off. I accepted and we set the date for the competition. Afterwards, when the enormity of the challenge sunk in,

CORN, COTTON AND CHOCOLATE: HOW THE MAYA CHANGED THE WORLD

I realized that I had accepted the challenge for a chili cook-off from a real Texan. I knew if I had a chance in hell to win, I had to get my chili con carne recipe absolutely perfect.

I carried out extensive research; I was not going to use a commercial chili powder. I knew a jalapeño from a habanera and I was going to make my chili con carne from scratch using genuine Mexican spices and real chili peppers. In preparation for the event I prepared a recipe for chili that included the real ingredients. I used top sirloin steak, tomatillos, chopped tomatoes, onions, garlic, olive oil, sea salt, lime juice and black pepper. The piece de resistance was my own chili seasoning made from chipotle, jalapeño peppers, cayenne peppers, ancho peppers and oregano.

A week prior to the Saturday night of the cook off, we send out invitations to our friends. They were not just going to be guests for dinner but they would be judges to decide the best chili. Several days before to the event I began my preparation and the recipe was assembled two days before the event. I allowed my marvelous pot of chili to simmer on the stove for 48 hours. By the evening of the event, my chili was just right. I was ready!

Jimmie arrived early with this large pot of Texas chili. He placed the pot side by side with my chili simmering on the stove. Our guests arrived, we joined the party.

After two hours, it was time to serve dinner. Everyone lined up by the dining table, which contained the pots of competition grade chili con carne. All the guests were eager to sample the two pots of chili. Our guests each ate two bowls, one from each pot. I was amazed at their interest in partaking of the competing chilies. After sampling the two chilies, our guests cast their ballots for the best pot of chili. The winner was going to be either Jimmie or Jimmy. In any event a Jim was going to win.

When the ballots were cast and the votes were counted by an impartial panel, the big winner was announced. The announcement was stunning. I had actually won! Hooray! I could not believe it. I had beaten a genuine born and bred Texas chili cook.

Jimmie Hagan gave me a big hug and said, "Hell, Jimmy I even liked your chili better than mine."

What a great evening, I won the competition and had a real Texan tell me he liked my chili con carne. The Maya cultivar that changed the tastes of the world had led me to victory in the Harvard chili con carne contest.

THE MAYA AND THE CHILI PEPPER

The chili pepper is now the world's most popular spice, and has been determined to be the oldest spice utilized in the Americas, and one of the oldest seasonings in the world. The chili pepper, a plant native to Mesoamerica, was domesticated by Maya agronomists over 7,000 years ago.

When cultivating the chili pepper, Maya agronomists were aided by migrating aerial collaborators. Scientists believe that, prior to domestication, birds were responsible for the spread of wild chili peppers. Over the centuries birds developed a symbiotic relationship with chili peppers. Birds do not have receptors in their mouths that feel the heat from the chilies and passage of the seed through a bird's digestive system does not harm the germination qualities of the pepper seed. So, birds became the first cultivators of chili peppers. They would consume the small colorful fruits and disperse the seeds as they flew across the Yucatán. The seeds

CORN, COTTON AND CHOCOLATE: HOW THE MAYA CHANGED THE WORLD

would then sprout into new chili plants. The wild chili peppers were collected and domesticated by Maya agronomists.

CHILIES USED BY MAYA IN THEIR FOODS

In archaeological sites where chili pepper residue has been found, researchers also detected remnants of maize. That suggests that the domestication of the two foods went hand in hand. This includes their use as partners in the preparation of food. Chiles were used by the Maya as a source of food and flavoring. Chili dishes were prepared in many forms, including fresh, dried, crushed, cooked, roasted and as a spice for other dishes. It was sprinkled over sauces, ground into maize dough, and boiled with beans, providing tastes as well as great quantities of vitamins A and C. Chiles were used as a flavoring when combined with maize, beans, and squash. The chili pepper was featured as the spice in numerous types stews including vegetable, turkey, and dog meat and in chili-spiced tomato salsa.

The use of the chili pepper is fundamental to Mesoamerican cuisines and perhaps is positioned second only to maize. The peppers from capsicum plants can be used in a fresh or dried state. A dried chili pepper is stronger and more effective than a fresh chili.

Chilis were also as a flavoring to chocolate, when prepared as a beverage. Archaeologists found capsicum in a vessel in the shape of a spouted jar, used for pouring a liquid. Archaeologists suggest that the jar may have been used to prepare spicy beverages or for condiments much like the bottles today that have a very narrow opening to sprinkle out the spice.

Chilies were an important ingredient in the Mayan diet. The Maya used chilies as a part of almost every meal, from breakfast, which was a hot cereal of ground maize spiced with chili peppers called *atole or pozol,* to the evening meal of various stews spiced with chilies. Chilies also played an important role in nutrition and the health of the Maya. Capsaicin, the principal enzyme in chilies, reduces the bacterial growth in un-refrigerated foods.

THE MAYA DOMESTICATED ALL TYPES OF CHILIES.

The Maya domesticated the entire spectrum of types of capsicum. The cultivated chilies varied in shapes and color from yellow, green, orange, red and to yellow and in heat intensity of from very mild to volcanic. There are four major species of cultivated capsicum developed by Maya agronomists: *Capsicum annuum, Capsicum Baccatu, Capsicum Chinense,* and *Capsicum Pubescena.* All chili peppers have their origins in the Yucatán.

THE CHILI AS MAYA MEDICINE

Medicine among the ancient Maya was a complex blend of, religion, ritual and science affecting both mind and body. While important to all, medicine was practiced only by a select few, who inherited their positions and received extensive medical education from the elders. Maya shamans used chili peppers containing capsaicin for various medical purposes. Capsaicin was used as a salve to relieve muscle and joint pain, used to relieve headaches and taken internally as an intestinal stimulant. Chili peppers were also used to treat wounds by inhibiting bacteria.

CORN, COTTON AND CHOCOLATE: HOW THE MAYA CHANGED THE WORLD

CHILIES AS MAYA WEAPONS

The Maya used the chili pepper as a chemical weapon during warfare. They used the toxic qualities of the capsaicin in chili to create a pre-Columbian version of the hand grenade. The toxic weapon was fabricated from a hollowed-out gourd, pumpkin or calabash. The hollowed-out calabash was then filled with hot ashes and ground up chili peppers.

The missile was tossed into the midst of the enemy. When the grenade hit the ground, it smashed and burst open, creating clouds of toxic smoke. The toxic smoke disrupted the enemy causing choking and irritation of the eyes and throat. Maya warriors used this type of grenade against the Spanish in battles during the conquest.

CHILI PEPPERS ARE INTRODUCED TO THE WORLD

Chilies have become the world's most popular spice. The cultivar was widely disseminated by Maya traders prior to European contact. By the time of the conquest, the Maya trade network had spread the chili pepper to all of Mesoamerica, the Caribbean and Central America.

When Columbus first encountered the chili, he named it "pepper" as it was the closest spice to black pepper that Columbus encountered in the New World, although it is not at all similar. It served as an all-purpose spice to flavor all types of dishes; it fulfilled the role of black pepper quite well, because like the familiar black pepper, it had a spicy hot taste.

Upon their introduction into Europe, chilies were grown as botanical curiosities in the gardens of Spanish and Portuguese monasteries. Christian monks experimented with the culinary potential of chili peppers and discovered that their pungency offered a substitute for black peppercorns, which at the time were so costly that in some countries, they were used as legal currency.

Dr. Diego Álvarez Chanca, a physician on Columbus' second voyage to the West Indies in 1493, brought the first chili peppers to Spain and first wrote about their medicinal effects in 1494. After Columbus' discovery, chilies were disseminated and cultivated around the globe.

The spread of chili peppers to Asia was carried out by Portuguese traders because Lisbon was a port of call for Spanish ships. The Portuguese became aware of the trade value of chilies and introduced them as part of their dominance of the Asian spice trade routes.

There is direct correlation between the dissemination of chili peppers to India and the presence of Portuguese traders in the subcontinent. In 1498, the Portuguese explorer Vasco da Gama reached the shores of India and his ships were transporting the pungent spice. Goa, located on the west coast of India, became a Portuguese colony. The chili pepper became popular in Goan cuisine. Chilies were introduced into India, where they became celebrated. Chili peppers then journeyed from India, through Central Asia and Turkey, to Hungary.

Exactly how the plant spread from South Asia to China and Southeast Asia is not recorded in detail, but it is assumed that Arab and European traders carried the chili via traditional trading routes.

Like the tomato, the chili pepper took a round trip across the Atlantic before arriving in America. It was almost 200 years before the chili was introduced back into America. Despite being grown by the Maya in the Yucatán for millennia, it was not until the slave trade was active that the chili was introduced to North America.

CORN, COTTON AND CHOCOLATE: HOW THE MAYA CHANGED THE WORLD

By the 17th century, chili peppers had become such a crucial part of the African diet that slave traders were required to transport large quantities of chilies. Furthermore, to maintain the eating habits of slaves, plantations began to grow chili peppers. It was not until the 17th century that the chili peppers found a place in the kitchens of America. Since then the chili has grown in popularity and has become an integral part of American cuisine and culture.

THAT'S A WHOLE LOT OF CHILI PEPPERS

As the world's favorite spice, chilies are big producers in countries where they are a favorite spice. World production of chilies exceeds 26,000,000 metric tons. China is the world's largest producer, followed by Mexico. However, India appears to be the largest consumer of chili peppers.

TOP 5 CHILI PRODUCING COUNTRIES IN METRIC TONS

RANK	COUNTRY	PRODUCTION
1	China	14,026,272
2	Mexico	1,890,428
3	Turkey	1,759,224
4	Indonesia	1,128,790
5	Spain	1,059,500

DO YOU SAY CHILI, CHILE, CHILLI OR JUST SIMPLY PEPPER?

Confusion constantly reigns over what to call the fruit of the capsicum plant. Do you call it chili, chili pepper or what? Confusion is appropriate because the dictionary spells the fruit three ways. The three primary spellings of the popular spice are *chili*, *chile* and *chilli*, all of which are recognized by dictionaries and all of them are acceptable.

The generic name *capsicum* is derived from the Greek word kapto, meaning "to bite" or "to swallow." The original Mexican name, chili came from the Nahuatl word chilli or *xilli*, referring to the larger capsicum variety.

The term "chili" is widely used in the United States and Canada. However, this spelling is discouraged by some since it is also commonly used as a short name for "chili con carne".

"Chile" is the most common Spanish spelling in Mexico and several other Latin American countries, as well as some parts of the United States and Canada, which refers specifically to this plant and its fruit.

"Chilli" was the original Romanization of the Náhuatl language word for the fruit and is the preferred British spelling per the Oxford English Dictionary, although it also lists chile and chili as variants.

WOW! THERE ARE MANY TYPES OF CHILIES BUT THEY ARE ALL MAYA

Chili pepper comes in many forms, shapes, colors and levels of heat. The chili pepper is a berry and is the fruit from the genus *Capsicum*. After the Columbian Exchange, multiple cultivars of

CORN, COTTON AND CHOCOLATE: HOW THE MAYA CHANGED THE WORLD

chili peppers were spread across the world and are now used in food, medicine, weapons and other purposes. It has induced changes in world cultures.

There are four major species of cultivated capsicum. They are all Maya cultivars. The species and varieties are manifested in different shapes, colors, flavors and heat levels. Following is a listing of the major species and examples of the various types of chilies:

Capsicum annuum: includes bell peppers, wax, cayenne, jalapeños, and chiltepin

Capsicum frutescens: Includes malagueta, tabasco and piri piri.

Capsicum chinense: includes scotch bonnet. naga, habañero, Datil and Scotch bonnet

Capsicum Pubescena: includes rococo peppers

THERE IS BIG HEAT IN CHILES OR JUST HOW HOT IS HOT?

Nearly everyone has had the sensation of the fiery burn produced in your mouth when biting down on a chili pepper or being singed by hot chili sauce. The chili pepper is a member of the *capsicum* family, but the culprit in causing the pain is *capsaicin*. Yes, they do sound alike. This alkaloid is contained in the chili pepper and supplies the intensity of flavor, aroma and heat.

When consumed, capsaicinoids bind with pain receptors in the mouth and throat that are responsible for sensing heat. Once activated by the capsaicinoids, these receptors send a message to the brain that the person has consumed something hot and spicy. The brain responds to the burning sensation by raising the heart rate, increasing perspiration and release of endorphins.

The Scoville scale is the measurement of the pungency or spicy heat of chili peppers. The heat levels are reported in Scoville Heat Units (SHU) and they are a function of capsaicin concentration. The scale is named after its creator, American pharmacist Wilbur Scoville. His method, devised in 1912, is known as the Scoville Organoleptic Test.

In Scoville's method, a measured amount of alcohol extract of the capsaicin oil of the dried pepper is produced, then a solution of sugar and water is added in increments until the "heat" is just barely detectable by a panel of tasters, usually five. The degree of dilution gives its measure on the Scoville scale. Thus, a sweet pepper or a bell pepper, containing no capsaicin at all, has a Scoville rating of zero, meaning no heat detectable. The hottest chilies, such as habañeros and nagas, have a rating of Scoville rating of 300,000 or more, indicating their extract must be diluted over 300,000 times before the capsaicin presence is undetectable. Pungency is now determined more reliably by high-performance liquid chromatography, whose results are reported in Scoville units.

Like computers, superhot chilies are evolving their capsicum levels upward at a rate that outstrips the phenomena of just a few years ago. Botanists in several countries have developed new very hot cultivars of chili peppers. India has developed the Bhut Joloka measured at 1,600,000 SHU and Trinidad developed the Moruga Scorpion measured at 2,000,000 SHU. Pure Capsaicin is measured at 16,000,000 SHU.

The standard for hottest pepper was raised several times in the 21st century. In 2012, the Carolina Reaper was rated as the world's hottest chili pepper by Guinness World Records, averaging 1,569,300 SHU on the Scoville scale with peak levels of over 2,200,000 SHU. The previous record-holder was the Trinidad Moruga Scorpion. The Carolina Reaper has been stated to be able to "strip the chrome off a trailer hitch."

The optimum chilies are called Superhot and come in the brightest colors and are formed in bizarre shapes. Their given names, invoking doom and pain are: Carolina Reaper, Naga Viper, Armageddon, Borg 9, Naga Morich, and Brain Strain. They sound as though the names were made up by the demons that cause the pain in the mouth. Trinidad 7-Pots chilies are so called because it's said that one of the chilies is enough to season seven pots of stew.

If you happen to bite into a particularly hot specimen, don't gulp a glass of water to douse its fire, it will only make matters worse. The capsaicin oil in the chilies and water do not mix. Yogurt or milk will give you the needed relief.

CHILI HEADS OF THE WORLD UNITE

It may sound bizarre, but some people are addicted to the effects of capsaicin, the more potent the chili the better they rate. In fact, their ultimate goal is an attempt to consume the chili pepper or hot sauce that has the highest SHU ratings. People with this strange addiction are known as "Chili Heads". These devotees to the power of the chili pepper are mostly American, British, and Australian. Their actions and tastes conform to the motto, "From the inane to the insane."

Chili heads show up in droves at fiery-food events ranging from chili cook offs to hot sauce exhibitions; they seek the hottest chilies available. Chili peppers, in general, are things of beauty; they are colorful and are aesthetically shaped. There is a good reason that no one makes Christmas lights in the shape of rutabagas. Chili peppers represent a perfect symbology as the trademark of Chili Heads. The image appears as decorative patterns on shirts, on coffee mugs and a myriad of other objects used by Chili Heads.

The subculture even has its own language: Chile Heads speak in Scoville Heat Units (SHU), or Scovilles, as in: "At 3 million Scovilles, this sauce is nuclear!" Chili Heads are gaining in such numbers that hot sauce production is one of the fastest growing industries in the United States.

PSYCHOLOGY OF THE CHILI HEAD

Psychologist Paul Rozin suggests that eating superhot chilies by a Chili Head is an example of a "constrained risk" like riding a roller coaster, in which extreme sensations like pain and fear can be enjoyed because individuals know that these sensations are not actually harmful. This method lets people experience extreme feelings without any risk of bodily harm. Research finds that Chili Heads tend to have a penchant or psychological drive for thrill seeking. Think in terms of extreme sports, skydiving, fast cars and action flicks.

A HUNGARIAN TEAM WITH A MAYA PEPPER AND WINS THE NOBEL PRIZE

The discovery of vitamin C was a spectacular medical breakthrough and a great boon for mankind. The world-shaking breakthrough involved the chili pepper, a Maya cultivar. The serious medical condition known as scurvy was a widespread issue across the globe. Sailors, typically, developed scurvy during long sailing voyages. This was a disease characterized by weakness, pains in the joints, loose teeth and blood spots appearing all over the body, and finally sudden death "in the middle of a sentence" from the bursting of a main artery. However,

CORN, COTTON AND CHOCOLATE: HOW THE MAYA CHANGED THE WORLD

even desperately ill men would recover in 10 days or so after reaching land, where they could be given fresh fruit or salad greens. Fresh fruit and vegetables seemed to hold the solution to preventing and curing scurvy.

Scientists found that vitamin C was the solution for preventing and curing the condition. However, the isolation of pure vitamin C from the sugars in citrus fruit presented a difficulty. Then the chili pepper came to the rescue. Paprika is a popular Hungarian spice made from the ground, dried fruits of *capsicum annuum*, usually bell pepper or another type of chili pepper.

In 1933, Hungarian scientist Dr. Albert Szent- Györgyi began locating natural sources for the study and isolation of vitamin C. Szent-Györgyi solved the problem by making imaginative use of the local Hungarian specialty, paprika. Hungary is the paprika capital of the world, where matching salt and paprika shakers are found on every restaurant table.

One night, Szent-Györgyi recalled, his wife served him fresh red paprika for supper. He wrote in his autobiography, "I did not feel like eating it so I thought of a way out. Suddenly, it occurred to me that this is the one plant I had never tested. I took it to the laboratory, and about midnight I knew that the chili pepper was a treasure chest full of vitamin C."

Within several weeks Szent-Györgyi had produced three pounds of pure crystalline ascorbic acid. He proved that the acid was equivalent to vitamin C when fed to vitamin C-deficient guinea pigs.

Just four years after his discovery of vitamin C, Szent-Gyorgyi received the Nobel Prize for his seminal work. That year, in 1937, the deliberations in the Nobel Committee centered on whether the Prize should go to Szent-Györgyi alone or be shared with several other scientists who had conducted similar work. In the end, the Prize was given to Szent-Gyorgyi.

So, the vital vitamin C, its discovery and its isolation as a lifesaving medical and preventive medicine was a joint venture between two mysterious cultures: the Hungarian and the Maya. Both have mysterious beginnings and languages.

HOT SAUCE ANYONE?

Hot sauce is adored by Chili Heads, preferred by aficionados, and abhorred by others. The words "hot sauce" alone can make some people salivate, while they make others cringe.

Humans have used chili peppers and other hot spices for thousands of years. One of the first commercially available bottled hot sauces appeared in Massachusetts during 1807. However, of the early brands from the 1800's, few survive to this day. Tabasco sauce is the earliest recognizable brand in the hot sauce industry, appearing in 1868 and it has become synonymous with the term "hot sauce". As of 2010, it was the thirteenth best-selling condiment in the United States. Today hot sauce is an emerging global business. The industry is among the 10 fastest growing in the US, now rakes in over $1 billion a year in global sales.

So why do hot sauces keep getting hotter and hotter? The extreme chile-heads are clamoring for more and more heat. Throughout the 2000's there was a "hot sauce race" when everybody was trying to make the hottest product. The advent of super-hot chile peppers has allowed the sauce makers to make their sauces hotter and hotter.

CORN, COTTON AND CHOCOLATE: HOW THE MAYA CHANGED THE WORLD

There are many recipes for hot sauces but the only common ingredient is the chili pepper. Many hot sauces are made by using chili peppers as the base and adding salt and vinegar while other sauces use some type of fruits or vegetables as the base and add the chili peppers to make them hot.

The production of hot sauce differs in the United States and Mexico. Hot sauce made in the United States is typically made from chili peppers, vinegar and salt. The varieties of peppers that are used could be cayenne, chipotle, habañero and jalapeño. Some hot sauces, notably Tabasco sauce, are aged in wooden casks like the preparation of wine and fermented vinegar.

The Mexican hot sauce typically concentrates more on flavor than on intense heat. In Mexican sauces, vinegar is used sparingly or not at all. Chipotles are a very popular ingredient of Mexican hot sauce where the individual flavors of the peppers are more pronounced, although the sauces tend to be hot.

WHAT'S HOT IN A HOT SAUCE?

For the chili lovers, out there, there's no such thing as being too spicy, and hot sauce producers keep finding more and more ways to pack more capsaicin into their products. A concept of the SHU level of spicy hot sauces that are available compared to the SHU level of hot chilies is indicated in the following table.

Scoville Heat Units (SHU)	BRAND/CHILI PEPPER/HOT SAUCE
16,000,000	Pure Capsaicin and Dihydrocapsaicin
16,000,000	Blair's 16 Million Reserve
7,100,000	The Source
5,300,000	Police grade Pepper spray
4,000,000	Mad Dog 44 Magnum Pepper Extract
1,001,304	Naga-Bih Jolokia pepper
1,000,000	Cool Million Pepper Extract
1,000,000	1 Million Scoville Pepper Extract
5,000 - 10,000	Chipotle, a Jalapeño pepper that has been smoked
3,600	Cholula Hot Sauce
3,400	El Yucateco Chipotle Hot Sauce
2,500 - 5,000	Jalapeño
2,500 - 5,000	Original TABASCO® brand Pepper Sauce
2,085	FRANK'S® REDHOT® XTRA Hot
1,500 - 2,500	TABASCO® brand Chipotle Pepper Sauce

CHILIES HAVE CHANGED THE TASTES OF THE WORLD

Maya chilies have made a great difference in the tastes of food around the world. What would Indian or Thai food be without chilies? The food of numerous countries changed when chili peppers were introduced into their cuisine. The change of tastes had a worldwide impact. Chilies became a part of national dishes ranging from China, India, Thailand, Italy, Hungary, Poland and countries across the continent of Africa. Signature dishes in various countries are familiar to natives, tourists and guests in ethnic restaurants. To provide an overview of the culinary impact that chilies have had in influencing the cuisine of countries across the globe, we offer the following examples.

Mexico: The legacy of chilies joined with Mexican food is thousands of years old. Mexican food owes its flavors to the chili pepper. Mexican restaurants offer popular chili flavored dishes in their numerous locations throughout the world. It is unfortunate that the popular food served in Mexican restaurants in the U.S. is more Tex-Mex than authentic Mexican cuisine.

Spain: In Spain, the cuisine benefited from the discovery of the New World chilies. it would be very difficult to untangle Spanish cooking from chilies, garlic and olive oil. Ground chilies or paprika are a key ingredient in chorizo, rice dishes, and added to gazpacho as a garnish.

Hungary: Paprikash, also known as paprika, uses significant amounts of mild, ground, dried chilies in a braised chicken dish.

Poland: Paprykarz szczeciński is a fish paste with rice, onion, tomato concentrate, vegetable oil, chili pepper powder and other spices.

Italy: Puttanesca sauce is a tomato-based sauce for pasta including dried hot chilies.

India: Curry dishes are popular, usually containing fresh or dried chilies.

China: Kung Pao Chicken (also spelled Gong Bao) from the Sichuan region of China uses small hot dried chilies, briefly fried in oil, to add spice to the oil which is then used for frying.

Thailand: Som Tam, is a green papaya salad from Thai/Lao cuisine. Traditionally, it has a fistful of chopped fresh hot Thai chili powder, pounded in a mortar. Nam Pla Phrik is a traditional Thai sauce prepared with chopped fresh Thai bird's eye chili in fish sauce and lime juice.

CHILIES AS MEDICINE

The chili pepper has been used for medicinal purposes for thousands of years. The extract from the chili peppers, capsaicin, has many applications as a medicine ranging from muscle pain relief, to use as an anesthetic and for cancer prevention. The Maya had it right when using chilies for medical purposes. Modern medicine has proved the beneficial effects of capsaicin.

Capsaicin as a treatment for migraine headaches

Capsaicin is a safe and effective topical analgesic agent for the managing the pain of migraine headaches. The link between how skin reacts when rubbed with chili oil and what happens in the brain during a migraine has attracted the world's largest biotechnology company, seeking to create medicines for the more than 36 million Americans who suffer from migraines.

Capsaicin as a treatment for joint and muscle pain and diabetic neuropathy

Capsaicin has been successfully used as a topical application for joint pain, muscle pain and diabetic neuropathy. It is used in topical pain-relieving creams and patches (some of which contain the equivalent of 10 million SHU). Capsaicin helps alleviate pain in part by depleting a chemical component of nerve cells that is involved in transmitting pain signals to your brain. It also works by de-sensitizing sensory receptors in your skin.

Capsaicin as an agent to treat wounds

Modern research has found that capsaicin has varying degrees of inhibition against *Bacillus cereus, Bacillus subtilis, Clostridium sporogenes, Clostridium tetani,* and *Streptococcus pyogenes.*

Capsaicin as an anesthetic

An injection that combines capsaicin and a local anesthetic may provide localized numbness without the loss of muscle control caused by traditional anesthetics such as Novocain (procaine), according to a study conducted by researchers at Harvard Medical School.

Capsaicin as a cancer curative

A team of researchers from the Samuel Oschin Comprehensive Cancer Institute at Cedars-Sinai Medical Center found that capsaicin induced 80 percent of the human prostate cancer cells injected into mice to decrease and die. They also found that prostate cancer tumors in mice fed with capsaicin were about one-fifth the size of tumors in non-treated mice.

Capsaicin as a heart disease control

Under laboratory conditions five groups of hamsters were fed a high-cholesterol diet, however, four of the groups were fed varying amounts of powdered capsaicinoids while the fifth group consumed no capsaicinoids. After six weeks, the researchers measured the cholesterol in the five control groups.

Total cholesterol in all the hamsters was elevated, but hamsters in the control group that did not eat capsaicinoids had their total cholesterol rise three times as high as those in each of the other groups. Hamsters in the control group that did not eat capsaicinoids also had aortic arteries that were more rigid and less relaxed, compared with the capsaicinoid groups. The research tended to indicate that capsaicin can be a powerful tool in controlling cholesterol and heart disease.

CHILI PEPPERS AS A DETERRENT FOR MAN AND BEAST

The higher the SHU number in a chili pepper, the more potent the pepper is to human and animal receptors. These receptors are in the mouth, the nose and the eyes. With the rise of the capsaicin levels in superhot chilies, more purposes for use of the capsaicin as a deterrent or a defense have been identified.

Anti-elephant protection defense

More than 600 people have been killed by wild elephants in the Assam state of India in the past 16 years, and villagers have reacted with an anger that has shocked conservationists. Conservationists have turned to the power of the chili to deter elephants from invading their crops.

Conservationists working on the experimental project said they have put up jute fences made of strong vegetable fiber and smeared them with automobile grease and bhut jolokia chilies. These peppers, also known as ghost chilies, have been certified as one of the world's hottest by the Guinness Book of World Records.

Wildlife experts also were using smoke bombs made from chili powder to keep away elephants. They mix ground up chilies with straw to make torches, the burning straw and chilies deter elephants who cannot stand the toxic smoke.

Chilies in anti-terrorist grenades

The Indian government has developed anti-terrorist hand grenades to disperse terrorists. The hand grenades are made with the bhut jolokia chilli. Upon detonation, the grenades emit very toxic fumes that are a rapid deterrent.

Capsaicin as a spray is a deterrent for criminals

Extract of capsaicin in an aerosol can, usually known as capsicum or "pepper spray", has become widely used by police forces as a non-lethal means of incapacitating a person, and in a more widely dispersed form for riot control, or by individuals for personal defense.

THE WORLD FAMOUS "BOWL OF RED", OR CHILI CON CARNE

Chili con carne is much more than just a dish prepared with hot chili peppers. It is not just a food but it is a symbology, one that represents a way of life, a philosophy and has a pedigree that is defended to the death by chili con carne aficionados. The dish has inspired debates, duels, cook offs and multiple arguments both verbal and written extolling the merits of the famous "Bowl of Red."

Chili con carne, which are the Spanish words for chilies with meat, are more commonly known as simply "chili". Traditional versions of this stew are made using chili peppers, garlic, onions, and cumin, along with chopped or ground beef. Variations on the basic recipe involve different types of meat, but certain ingredients are forbidden in the authentic formula, especially beans. The variant recipes provoke disputes among aficionados, some of whom insist that the word "chili" only applies to the basic dish of chilies and meat.

The rules of the road for Chili Heads are established by Chili Societies. The Chili Appreciation Society International specified that, among other things, cooks are forbidden to include beans, marinate any meats, or discharge firearms in the preparation of chili for official competition.

THE LEGEND OF CHILI CON CARNE

Chili con carne is not a Mexican dish. It has a Tex-Mex or Texas-Mexican origin. Mexicans do not claim the spicy recipe but rather distain the dish. The only thing certain about the origins of chili is that it did not originate in Mexico.

Chili, as we know it in the U.S., cannot be found in Mexico today except in a few spots which cater to tourists. If chili had come from Mexico, it would still be there. Mexicans, especially those of Indian ancestry do not change their culinary customs from one generation, or even from one century to another.

If there is any doubt about what the Mexicans think about chili, *Diccionario de Mejicanismos,* published in 1959, defines chili con carne as "Detestable food passing itself off as Mexican, sold in the U.S. from Texas to New York."

CORN, COTTON AND CHOCOLATE: HOW THE MAYA CHANGED THE WORLD

Legend has it that the first documented recipe for "chili con carne" is dated September 2, 1519. The ingredients were to be boiled tomatoes, salt, chilies and meat. Bernal Diaz del Castillo, one of Hernan Cortez's captains and the source of the recipe, states in his book, *The Discovery and Conquest of Mexico,* that the Cholulan indians, allied with the Aztecs, were so confident of victory in a battle against the conquistadors, that they had "already prepared cauldrons of tomatoes, salt and chilies" in anticipation of a victory feast. The one missing ingredient, the meat, was to be furnished by the conquistadors themselves in the form of their flesh. The conquistadors won the battle. The Cholulans were disappointed that their chili did not receive the anticipated meat.

The chili recipe used by American frontier settlers consisted of dried beef, suet, dried chili peppers and salt, which were pounded together, formed into bricks and left to dry, which could then be boiled in pots on the trail.

During the 1880s, brightly dressed Mexican women known as "chili queens" began to operate around Military Plaza and other public gathering places in downtown San Antonio. They appeared at dusk, when they built charcoal or wood fires to reheat cauldrons of pre-cooked chili. They sold it by the bowl to passersby. The delicious aroma of the chili was a potent sales pitch and mariachi street musicians joined in to serenade the eaters. Some chili queens later built semi-permanent stalls in the Mercado. But all good things must come to an end. In 1937, the San Antonio health department required that the chili queens adhere to the same sanitary facility rules as regular restaurants. The colorful chili queens disappeared overnight.

The San Antonio Chili Stand, in operation at the 1893 Columbian Exposition in Chicago, introduced people from other parts of the country to the taste and appreciation of chili. San Antonio became a significant tourist destination and helped spread Texas-style chili con carne throughout the South and West.

Chili con carne is the official dish of the state of Texas as designated by the House Concurrent Resolution Number 18 of the 65th Texas Legislature during its regular session in 1977.

WHAT? YOU PUT BEANS IN THE CHILI?

The question of adding beans to chili has been controversial. Beans are a staple of Tex-Mex cuisine; however, they have been associated with chili as far back as the early 20th century. The question of whether beans "belong" in chili has been a matter of contention among chili cooks for a long time. It is likely that in many poorer areas of San Antonio and other places associated with the origins of chili, beans were used rather than meat, or in addition to meat. But purists including Chili Heads are adamant, "There ain't no beans in Chili".

THE MYSTERY OF THE ORIGIN OF CHILI POWDER

Chili historians are not exactly certain who first "invented" chili powder. It is agreed that the inventors of chili powder deserve a slot in history close to Alfred Nobel, the inventor of dynamite. A "Noble Prize" would be appropriate.

WHAT PROVIDES THE REAL HEAT IN CHILI CON CARNE?

Chili con carne is usually made with the chief's favorite blend of chili powder and some other chili heat including cayenne pepper. However, the real chili heads provide the heat in their chili con carne by making the rich flavor from scratch. They use a blend of whole dried peppers for

CORN, COTTON AND CHOCOLATE: HOW THE MAYA CHANGED THE WORLD

their recipe. They use Anaheim peppers for sweetness, arbol peppers for their heat, chipotles for their smoky flavor and ancho peppers for their addition of rich and fruity flavors. A great chili is reputed to open eighteen sinus cavities unknown to the medical profession.

TEXAS STYLE CHILI

Texas style chili may or may not contain beans and may even be made with no other vegetables whatsoever besides chili peppers. The choice of meat that is added to the recipe has many options. For example, at a chili cook-off the contestants added a varied choice of meat in addition to beef, there was pork, venison, possum, rattlesnake, shrimp, and armadillo. In some areas, versions with beans are referred to as "chili beans" while the term "chili" is reserved for the all-meat dish. Small red beans are commonly used for chili, as are black-eyed peas, kidney beans, great northern beans, or navy beans.

COMMERCIALLY PREPARED CHILI

Most commercially prepared canned chili includes beans. Commercial chili prepared without beans is usually called "chili no beans" in the United States. Some U.S. manufacturers, notably Bush Brothers and Company and Eden Organic, also sell canned precooked beans (with no meat) that are labeled "chili beans." These beans are intended for consumers to add to a chili recipe and are often sold with spices added.

CHILI ADDED TO A DISH

The attraction of the piquant taste of chili has drawn many cooks across the nation to include chili as an ingredient of other dishes. Chili has become a basic part of American cuisine and is added to everything from hot dogs to potatoes and spaghetti.

Chiliburger: A burger topped with chili (usually without beans). In California, this is sometimes referred to as a "chili size." Chili is also served on top of a ground beef patty alone.

Chili cheese fries: Chili is added to French fries and cheese to make chili cheese fries, or Coney Island fries.

Chili and rice: In southeast Texas, some people eat chili served over white rice. Chili over rice (frequently with beans) is also common in Hawaii (where it is known as chili rice) and is eaten this way in the United Kingdom and, to some extent, Australia.

Chili Spaghetti: This dish involves a Texas and Italian combination. Chili spaghetti started in Cincinnati and is a unique combination of flavors. The combo involves spaghetti topped with chili con carne and cheese. Additional flavors are added with onions and beans.

Chili mac: Is a dish made with canned chili, with the addition of macaroni or some other pasta. Chili mac is a standard dish in the U.S. military and is one of the varieties of Meal, Ready-to-Eat (MRE). A small bottle of Original TABASCO® brand Pepper Sauce, is packaged in each MRE and with NASA meals eaten in space.

Frito pie: This treat typically consists of a small, single-serving bag of Fritos corn chips with a cup of chili con carne poured over the top, usually finished off with grated cheese, onions and jalapeños and sour cream. Frito pies are popular in the southwestern United States.

CORN, COTTON AND CHOCOLATE: HOW THE MAYA CHANGED THE WORLD

Chili baked potato: A chili stuffed baked potato is a large baked potato stuffed with chili and possibly with other ingredients, such as butter, cheddar cheese, or chopped onions.

Chili Poutine: A poutine is a Canadian dish which usually consists of french fries covered with gravy and cheese, substituting chili con carne for the usual gravy.

THE BIGGEST GAME IN TOWN: THE CHILI COOK OFF

A chili cook-off is more than a social event, it is a lifestyle, it is a battle of wits, of guarded recipes and a competition between fierce competitors who are the ultimate Chili Heads. They possess special recipes with secret ingredients. They prepare their own particular recipe in special way for their unique pot of chili con carne. After the chili is prepared they submit their masterpiece to the judges for taste testing. A cook-off may be an informal gathering with the simple goal of enjoying food, or it may be a large-scale event with an official panel of judges and substantial prizes for the winners.

The Chili Appreciation Society International (CASI) and the International Chili Society (ICS) are the principal groups that organize chili cook-offs. These two groups sanction hundreds of annual cook offs that raise millions of dollars for charity. They sponsor the annual Terlingua International Chili Championship (CASI) and the World Championship Cook Off (ICS).

THE RULES OF THE CHILI COOK OFFS

The basic Rules and Regulations for a cook at the World's Championship, State, Regional and District cook offs vary slightly, but the major rules are similar.

1) Traditional Red Chili is defined as any kind of meat or combination of meats, cooked with red chili peppers, various spices and other ingredients, except for beans, which are strictly forbidden. Meat may not be precooked in any manner. All other ingredients must be chopped or prepared during the preparation period at the location of the cook-off.

2) The cooking period will be a minimum of 3 hours and a maximum of 4 hours. The exact starting and ending of the cooking period is to be announced by each local sponsoring organization. Cooking time during the cooking period is at the discretion of the contestant.

3) Each contestant must cook a minimum of two quarts of competition chili prepared in one pot which will be submitted for judging.

4) Judges are instructed that they should vote for chili, as defined by the International Chili Society, based on the following major considerations: good chili flavor, texture of the meat, consistency, blend of spices, aroma and color.

THE BIGGEST CHILI COOK OFF IS? WHERE ELSE, TEXAS

The most famous chili competition is the "World Championship" cook-off in Terlingua, Texas. During the first weekend in November, over 10,000 people, converge onto the tiny former mining town in the Texas desert. Each year the town, with a normal population of no more than a few dozens, plays host to two of the largest chili cook offs in the world. That's right, two.

CORN, COTTON AND CHOCOLATE: HOW THE MAYA CHANGED THE WORLD

This was a real mining town that went bust and the miners walked away, leaving their homes behind. Today you'll find a ghost town made up of decaying buildings, mineshafts, tall tales, ruins, crotchety old-timers, a three-legged dog, too much cactus, and semi-friendly rattlesnakes.

Instead of a competitive shootout, it seemed simple enough to determine who made the best chili. There would be a contest. It worked, too, for a while. But now, in addition to arguing about which chili is better, everybody's arguing about which cook off competition is better. So, you have to try 'em both.

It's not really about chili anyway. Both cook offs have turned into a gigantic party and now there are competing parties. And, don't forget to try the chili, because whatever your tastes, the best damn chili in the world is in Terlingua, Texas

MAYA CHILI PEPPERS AND THEIR PART IN CHANGING HISTORY

Maya Chili peppers are the world's most popular spice. They have largely altered the cuisines of the world and the tastes of cultures. The chili won the Noble Prize for the discovery of vitamin C in the chili pepper. Chilis are used as a toxic weapon throughout the world and are also used in medicines throughout the world. The chili pepper has become the stuff of legend with its chili con carne, chili heads and its cook-offs. Competition for the worlds "hottest" chili peppers has spurred the world's interest.

CORN, COTTON AND CHOCOLATE: HOW THE MAYA CHANGED THE WORLD

CHAPTER 10: CHOCOLATE /COCOA

Botanical name: *Theobroma cacao* **Maya Name:** *ka'kau'*

Memories of a youth

Easter Sunday was always a big affair in our family. We went to bed early on Saturday night. Awaking on Easter Sunday morning was eventful, we found treasures in our Easter baskets and we had a great Easter Sunday feast. However, my most memorable experience was finding my hidden Easter basket laden with a variety of really good offerings from the Easter Bunny. Yes, the Easter Bunny. I believed in him. He lived and breathed and came to our house when we were asleep. He would bring large elaborate baskets filled with a nest of cellophane grass for chocolate bunnies. It was the best of all the holidays. He was a champion of goodies for children on Easter Sunday.

The Easter Bunny had a logistics problem during Easter of 1944. All the chocolate and sugar supplies were being shipped overseas to supply our servicemen with vital foodstuffs. The home front was not provided with confectionery ingredients to make Easter goodies. It was a sad truth, but this rule also applied to the Easter Bunny who relied on chocolate from the Maya to make chocolate figures and sugar for his marshmallow chicks and duckies. The only available component of traditionally Easter offerings was hard-boiled eggs.

The country had devoted all its resources to winning the war. Using the logic that an army travels on its stomach, all essential food products were shipped overseas and were rationed on the home front. The basic C-ration of the soldier in the field consisted of a meat, bread and a nutritious sweet. This was usually a chocolate bar.

The Easter Bunny was stumped; he had a choice of eggs, eggs or eggs. How would he solve the dilemma of the missing chocolate? I was horrified. What would I find in my Easter basket on Sunday morning. Surely the Easter Bunny could perform some magic, but I knew that servicemen needed the chocolate and the Easter Bunny was shut out.

When I went to bed on Saturday night, I was deep in gloom, there was no way that the Easter Bunny could come through. I fell asleep expecting the worst, there would be nothing in my Easter basket in the morning.

Awakening the next morning, I slowly got up and begin to search for my hidden Easter basket. The search included myself and three siblings all searching and expecting to find nothing in our baskets. When we entered the living room, we were shocked. There were four baskets chock full of Easter goodies. I looked at my basket. It was topped by a large brown standing rabbit and was surrounded by baby chicks and decorated Easter eggs. He did it! The Easter Bunny pulled it off!

The Easter Bunny had been amazing and creative. The large standing rabbit was not made of chocolate, but was a large baked cookie. The exterior was decorated with multicolored frosting framing his outline and detailing his cute little outfit. I was elated! The bunny was not chocolate, but the symbology was present. It was a large brown cookie complete with elaborate trim.

The Easter Bunny had come through and I had received a large standing rabbit that looked like chocolate. The Maya agronomists who developed the cocoa tree would be proud of their helper

CORN, COTTON AND CHOCOLATE: HOW THE MAYA CHANGED THE WORLD

with the big ears. That old rabbit had delivered the goods when chocolate was missing from the home front. However, I think my creative mother had a hand in the magic solution.

THE MAYA AND CHOCOLATE

The love affair between the Maya and chocolate extends back in time four millennia. They were enjoying chocolate when Europe was in the Bronze Age. The Maya grew cacao trees in their forest gardens and collected the seeds from the trees to make a frothy, bitter drink from it.

Chocolate played a large role of the life of the ancient Maya. To the Mayas, cacao pods symbolized life and fertility. Chocolate had an extremely important place in the religious, spiritual and cultural life of the Maya. Maya hieroglyphs describe how chocolate was valued and used for ceremonial purposes. It was used as a gift to the deities and presented at royal burials to ensure comfort in the afterlife.

COCOA AS A BEVERAGE AND AS A FOOD

The Maya are given credit for creating the chocolate beverage over 3,000 years ago. Cocoa was used in chocolate-based drinks, the most common of which was a frothy beverage that was served to royals. There are several mixtures of cacao described in ancient texts for ceremonial and medicinal uses as well as culinary purposes. Some chocolate mixtures included maize, chili, vanilla, peanuts and honey from the native stingless bee. Chocolate was also mixed with a variety of flowers, and sometimes was thickened with *atol*, a maize gruel.

Archaeologists reported finding evidence of the oldest known cultivation of the cocoa tree and use of cacao at a Maya site in Puerto Escondido, Honduras, dating from about 1,100 to 1,400 BC. These are not the oldest traces of chocolate located by archaeologists, older samples were found in other sites dating 1,000 years earlier. The significance of this find is that it may provide insight as to the dietary customs in the era. The find lead experts to believe that there are ancient roots connected to Maya traditional dishes that are prepared today. Indicating that the pre-Hispanic Maya may have eaten foods made with cacao sauce, similar to the mole sauce made today.

COCOA IN MAYA HISTORY

The Maya passed down their knowledge of cacao in stonework, pottery and descriptions found in their intricate multicolored codices that extolled cacao and documented its use in everyday life and rituals. Sculpture from their monumental buildings reveals numerous carved images of cocoa pods, and the pods are depicted on vases, murals and other works of art.

Maya literature refers to cocoa as the god's food. The cacao tree, called "Madre Cacao," has the botanical name, *Theobroma cacao,* meaning "Food of the Gods". A name coined by the Swedish Scientist Carl Linnaeus in the volume *Systema Naturae*. He merged the Greek words "*Theo*" god and "*broma*" food with the Maya *cacao*. The word cacao originated from the Maya word *ka'kau'*, as well as the Maya words *chocol'ha* and the verb *chokola'j* meaning "to drink chocolate together".

CORN, COTTON AND CHOCOLATE: HOW THE MAYA CHANGED THE WORLD

THE YUCATAN, THE HOME OF THE COCOA TREE

Cacao was native to the Americas and was popular in both Mesoamerica and South America; however, cultivation, cultural elaboration and use of cacao were more extensive in Mesoamerica. Although some have argued for a South American center of domestication, other scholars have noted there is insufficient evidence to support this thesis because the wild ancestors of cacao found in the Maya region are genetically distinct from South American cacao plants. The South American subspecies *T. cacao spaerocarpum* has a smooth, melon-like fruit. In contrast, the Mesoamerican cacao subspecies has ridged elongated fruits. They are not the same and the agronomy prize goes to the Maya as the cultivators of the cocoa tree.

The Maya originally harvested cocoa beans from the rain forest trees. They later cleared areas of the forest to make way for cocoa plantations. The Maya agronomists cultivated the earliest known cocoa plantations in the Yucatán.

The Maya drank their chocolate hot and frothy. The foam was produced by pouring the drink back-and-forth from vessel to vessel from a height or with a beater. One of the earliest images of this froth-producing process is shown on a Maya Princeton Vase from the Late Classic. Chocolate was very useful in the Maya medicine, both as a primary remedy and as a vehicle to deliver other herbal medicines. Cocoa's soothing qualities were also discovered early on and it was used for the treatment of coughs, fever and even discomfort during pregnancy.

SCIENTIFIC ANALYSIS OF ANCIENT CHOCOLATE POTS

Cacao gets its punch from nearly 200 different chemicals, including a dash of caffeine, but the primary jolt comes from quantities of theobromine, a mild stimulant and vasodilator. Chemical analysis of residues from the interiors of four ceramic vases from an Early Classic period (AD 460-480) tomb at Rio Azul in northeastern Guatemala has revealed the presence of theobromine and caffeine. As cacao is the only known source from Mesoamerica containing both compounds, it seems likely that these vases were used as containers for cacao drinks. In addition, cacao is named in a hieroglyphic text on one of the vessels, a stirrup-handled pot with an intricately locking lid.

PARDON ME, DO YOU HAVE CHANGE FOR A COCOA BEAN?

The cocoa bean itself was highly valued as a commodity and served as currency. An early explorer visiting Guatemala found that in Maya culture, one cocoa bean could buy a large tomato or a ripe avocado, a turkey egg was 3 beans, 4 cocoa beans could buy a pumpkin, 100 beans could buy a rabbit or a good turkey hen, and 1000 beans would purchase a slave.

Maya merchants often traded cocoa beans for other commodities, such as cotton cloth, jade, obsidian and ceremonial feathers. Maya farmers transported their cocoa beans to market by canoe or in large baskets strapped to their backs in the form of a *mecapal* or tumpline. This is a band supported by the forehead and fastened to the basket which is carried against the back. Wealthy merchants traveled further, using large canoes and employing porters with tumplines to transport the cargo over land.

CORN, COTTON AND CHOCOLATE: HOW THE MAYA CHANGED THE WORLD

CHOCOLATE MEETS THE WORLD

The Spanish loved chocolate and kept the secret of the delicious drink to themselves for one hundred years after the conquest. Both Christopher Columbus and Hernando Cortez were familiar with the cacao bean and both brought samples of the cocoa bean back to Spain.

Despite being the first European to discover cocoa beans on his fourth voyage to America in 1502, Christopher Columbus dismissed the potential worth of cocoa. Columbus brought the cacao beans back to Europe as curiosities and their value was initially overlooked by the Spanish King and his court.

Twenty years later, in 1524, the first European records of cocoa importation came from the Spanish conquistador, Hernando Cortez, who brought three chests of cacao beans back to Spain. This time the beans were recognized as a real treasure and the exotic Maya drink was introduced to the royal court.

The cocoa beans brought to Spain by Cortes were hidden away in Spanish monasteries where they were processed into the chocolate drink. Its formula was kept a secret and became a fashionable drink which only the wealthy and Spanish nobility could afford to enjoy. The drink became very popular when chocolate was sweetened with sugar.

In 1585, the first shipment of cocoa beans that was intended for the general market landed in Spain. However, the King considered chocolate to be too good to share with other royal courts. The Spanish kept this delicious drink to themselves; there is no record of cacao being mentioned in any writings other than Spanish texts for almost hundred years. In 1609, the first book devoted entirely to chocolate was published, *Libro en el cual se trata del chocolate*, and the book came from Mexico.

In the early 17th century news of chocolate spread across Europe. With the decline of Spain as a world power, the secret of cocoa finally leaked out to other Europeans. It was an Italian traveler, Antonio Carletti, who, in 1606, discovered the Spanish secret of chocolate and took it to other parts of Europe.

Not everyone was eager to accept the mysterious new drink. In France, chocolate was met with skepticism and was considered a "barbarous product and noxious drug.". The French court was doubtful and accepted chocolate only after the Paris Faculty of Medicine gave its approval.

In 1643, the French court readily embraced chocolate. When the Spanish Princess Maria Theresa was betrothed to Louis XIV of France, she gave her fiancé an engagement gift of chocolate, packaged in an elegantly ornate chest. Eventually, the sugared chocolate drink found its way into other courts of Europe, becoming a huge hit among the elites.

Doctors of the times proclaimed its apparent aphrodisiac properties. This was the start of the tradition of gifting ladies with chocolates on Valentine's Day. Doctors claimed other medical miracles, and the merchant trade of cacao became a large part of the economy of Europe. In 1650, the chocolate craze, which now included candy, took hold in Paris and then conquered the rest of France. Chocolate's reputation as an aphrodisiac flourished in the French courts. French art and literature was thick with erotic imagery inspired by chocolate.

CORN, COTTON AND CHOCOLATE: HOW THE MAYA CHANGED THE WORLD

It was during this time that a group of nuns in France started making a solid chocolate, the precursor to the modern-day chocolate bar. They probably would have had a big seller on their hands, but for the intrusion of the Pope himself. Apparently, church delegates who had visited the cloistered convent claimed that the nuns weren't properly performing their daily chores and were behaving in a covetous and gluttonous manner in all matters concerning chocolate.

The Pope was so distressed at hearing of their performance that he banned chocolate by Papal decree, threatening excommunication to anyone involved in the manufacture of this devil's food. Needless to say, the black market that dealt chocolate to the nobles became a booming industry. Eventually the papal furor died down, and once again chocolate began to be mass-produced.

Within a few years, the knowledge of chocolate spread through France, Britain, Belgium, Germany, Switzerland, Austria and Italy. Several of these nations established their own cocoa plantations, effectively bringing an end to Spain's monopoly of the chocolate trade.

By the mid-1600s, the chocolate drink had gained widespread popularity in France and in 1657, an enterprising Frenchman opened the first chocolate house in London. This was even before coffee shops became popular. In 1689, a noted physician developed a milk chocolate drink which was initially used only by apothecaries.

London chocolate houses became the trendy meeting places where the elite London society savored their new chocolate-based luxury drink. The drink was foamed, not using the Maya method of pouring it from one cup into another, but by using a wooden whisk-like tool that is twirled between the palms of the hands. As the popularity of chocolate grew, England imposed an excessive duty of 10-15 shillings per pound. The duty was comparable to approximately three-fourths its weight in gold. It took almost 200 years before the duty was dropped.

Because of its high cost, chocolate was initially considered a beverage for the elite class. In England, by the 1700s, there was a chocolate house for every type of clientele: politicians, gamblers, literati and the beautiful people. Charles II tried unsuccessfully to suppress these establishments which he considered "hotbeds of sedition". However, in the mid-nineteenth century some chocolate houses were transformed into more respectable "clubs for gentlemen".

For hundreds of years, the chocolate making process remained basically unchanged. However, when the Industrial Revolution came about, many changes were introduced in the processes that brought the sweet chocolate to life. The transition from handmade chocolate products to industrialized applications was hastened by the advent of the steam engine. This process mechanized the cocoa grinding process and developed mills that squeezed out cocoa butter, which in turn helped to create hard, durable chocolate. By 1730, industrialization caused chocolate to drop in price from three dollars or more per pound to a price within the financial reach of all.

Chocolate companies began advertising the new inventions to sell many of the chocolate treats seen today. When the chocolate treats were mass produced, people began experiencing and consuming chocolate worldwide.

In 1755, chocolate made its appearance in America. The first American chocolate factory was constructed in 1765. The production of chocolate proceeded in America at a faster pace than

CORN, COTTON AND CHOCOLATE: HOW THE MAYA CHANGED THE WORLD

anywhere else in the world. Pre-Revolutionary New England set the pace of chocolate production for the world. During 1780, the first machine-made mixer for the chocolate drink is produced in Barcelona. By 1810, Venezuela cocoa plantations were producing one-half of the world's cocoa beans and one-third of the finished product was consumed by the Spanish.

The New World countries, Mexico, Costa Rica and Venezuela, were the world's main suppliers of Cacao until the start of the 20th century when the center of cultivation moved first to the Caribbean and then to Africa and Asia. By then, as cocoa plantations spread to the tropics in both hemispheres, the increased production lowered the price of cocoa beans and chocolate became a popular and affordable beverage to all classes everywhere.

In 1828, the cocoa press was invented. The press helped to improve the quality of the chocolate beverage by squeezing out part of the cocoa butter. Drinking chocolate now had a smooth consistency and a more pleasing taste.

In 1875, milk chocolate came of age and after eight years of experimentation, Daniel Peter, from Switzerland, placed the first milk chocolate on the market. In 1879, Rudolph Lindt of Berne, Switzerland, invented "conching", a means of heating and rolling chocolate to refine it. Chocolate then becomes "fondant" which means it melts in the mouth.

By 1900, Switzerland took the leadership role in producing chocolate. They are still the foremost producer of chocolate leading the world with sales of about 19 pounds per capita. However, this statistic may be inflated by tourist purchases of Swiss candies.

In 1900 Milton Hershey, a Mennonite from Pennsylvania, possessing an anti-alcohol attitude, saw chocolate as a good, profitable alternative to booze. Hershey began producing milk-chocolate bars and "kisses" with great success. In less than ten years he was able to buy two entire towns and name them after himself. Thus, the company headquarters is located in the city of Hershey, Pennsylvania.

During World War II, the U.S. government recognized chocolate's role for supporting the Allied Armed Forces. It allocated valuable shipping space for the importation of cocoa beans and the distribution of chocolate bars, which would provide strength for war weary soldiers. The U.S. Army D-rations include three 4-ounce chocolate bars. Chocolate has even been carried into space as part of the diet of U.S. astronauts.

CHOCOLATE HAS CHANGED THE SWEET TOOTH OF THE WORLD

The Maya cocoa bean has changed the "sweet tooth" of the world and changed the tastes and fortunes of numerous countries. This narrative has followed the Maya cultivar from the rainforest forest gardens to a scenario that took chocolate from the divine food of gods, through the European Royal's thirst for the drink and the quest for monopolies on mild drugs for high society, into respectability, common usage and finally to popular candy.

Chocolate has remained popular in Europe and the remainder of the world. After World War II many Belgian and French Chocolatiers specialized in making exceptionally fine, high grade chocolate. Now the chocoholic can enjoy their passion as solid dark chocolate candy, milk chocolate or white chocolate. Now all the Christian holy holidays are celebrated with chocolate, a product that was once the property of the heathen Maya.

CORN, COTTON AND CHOCOLATE: HOW THE MAYA CHANGED THE WORLD

CHOCOLATE BECOMES A COMMODITY GROWN IN THE TROPICS

Chocolate was introduced to Europe by the Spanish, and became a popular beverage by the mid-17th century. The Spanish introduced the cacao tree into the West Indies and the Philippines. It was introduced into the rest of Asia and into West Africa by other Europeans.

Cocoa plantations have spread across equatorial areas in Africa, Asia and South America. Now, more than 4,000,000 tons of cocoa are produced each year. Côte d'Ivoire and Indonesia produce more than half of the world's cocoa, producing 1.24 and 0.84 million metric tons respectively. Over 50,000,000 people worldwide rely on cocoa for their livelihood. The largest cocoa bean-producing countries in the world are shown in the following chart.

TOP 10 COCOA PRODUCING COUNTRIES IN METRIC TONS

RANK	COUNTRY	PRODUCTION
1	Ivory Coast	1.242
2	Indonesia	0.844
3	Ghana	0.632
4	Nigeria	0.360
5	Cameroon	0.264
6	Brazil	0.235
7	Ecuador	0.132
8	Togo	0.102
9	Dominican Republic	0.058
10	Peru	0.057

MAYA CHOCOLATE HAS BECOME A REALLY BIG BUSINESS

The cocoa bean considered by the Maya to be the food of the gods has now become the food for everyman. The chocolate confection industry is a 98-billion-dollar a year business. Yes, that is billion with a B. That makes the industry's value larger than the Gross Domestic Product (GDP) of more than 130 nations on earth. Hershey kisses, boxes of Godiva chocolate and cups of hot chocolate are worldwide favorites and add up to a huge industry.

Europeans account for nearly half of all the chocolate consumed in the world, according to the International Cocoa Organization. The Swiss lead with 24 pounds per capita. The Norwegian and British chocoholics follow with an average of 17½ pounds of chocolate per capita. Next in line, Belgians, Dutch, Germans and Austrians, are averaging more than 14 pounds per person each year. United States residents average 10 pounds per capita. Hey! We are not chocoholics.

Men's love of chocolate is on par with women's preference for the treat. A British research study revealed 91% of all women admit to eating chocolate, with the men at more than 87%. The production industry leaders include: Mars, Inc. with sales of $17.64 billion and Mondelez International, formerly Kraft Foods, with sales of $14.86 billion.

CHOCOLATE INVENTS THE MICROWAVE OVEN

CORN, COTTON AND CHOCOLATE: HOW THE MAYA CHANGED THE WORLD

The microwave oven started out as a machine that was more than five feet tall, weighed 750 pounds, and cost about $5,000. The first microwave oven, the Radarange, built by Raytheon Corporation in 1947, was based on an accidental discovery of a melted chocolate bar.

Several years prior to Raytheon's first attempt at the microwave oven, a scientist, Percy Spencer, was experimenting with a new magnetron, a vacuum tube that releases energy to power radar equipment.

Spencer happened to be a big fan of chocolate and while working with the device, he noticed that the chocolate bar in his pocket had started melting. He attributed it to the microwaves and, like any good scientist, he conducted more tests.

He quickly put two and two together and realized that the microwaves issued from magnetrons might be able to heat up food at incredibly fast rates. First, Spencer tried corn kernels. After they successfully popped, Spencer tried heating more foods. The results led engineers to contain the microwaves in a safe enclosure and violá, the microwave oven was born.

The countertop microwave oven in all American kitchens today was first introduced to the public in 1967 by the Amana Corporation. An invention that was invented with the assistance of Maya chocolate.

WHAT? YOU ARE OUT OF CHOCOLATE? CALL THE TOLL HOUSE INN FOR A NEW TYPE OF COOKIE

Chocolate chip cookies are the most popular cookie in America. Would you believe that America's favorite cookie was invented by accident? Then all praise Ruth Graves Wakefield for her mistakes in the kitchen.

Wakefield and her husband, Kenneth, owned Toll House Inn in Whitman, Massachusetts. Ruth prepared the recipes for the restaurant and cooked for the inn's guests. The favorite cookie that Ruth baked was her scrumptious Butter Drop Do cookie.

One day in 1930, Ruth had a problem that turned into a serendipitous invention. She found that she was out of baker's chocolate for her Butter Drop Do cookies and she was sure that her guests would be upset. She had a problem to solve and quickly came up with a solution. She had a bar of Nestle's semisweet chocolate that she had never used for her cookies. She broke the bar into tiny chunks and mixed them into the batter. She assumed that the chocolate would melt, as it baked and spread into the dough, and create a chocolate-flavored cookie just as the baker's chocolate had done.

That, of course, didn't happen. When Wakefield took the cookies out of the oven, she noticed that the chocolate chunks only melted slightly, holding their shape and forming a creamy texture. She served the cookies with the chocolate chips in them and the guests loved them.

Wakefield's chocolate chip cookies began attracting people from all over New England. After her recipe appeared in a Boston newspaper, Nestle gained a huge spike in sales. Everyone wanted Nestle's semisweet chocolate bars to make Wakefield's cookies.

And so, a marketing deal was struck, Andrew Nestle agreed to give Wakefield a lifetime supply of the chocolate in return for her recipe printed on every Nestle semisweet chocolate bar. Nestle kept their word even although Ruth died in 1977 and the Toll House Inn burned down in 1984. Ruth's recipe is still printed on every package of Nestle Chocolate.

CORN, COTTON AND CHOCOLATE: HOW THE MAYA CHANGED THE WORLD

I AM CONFUSED, WHAT ARE THE DIFFERENT TYPES OF CHOCOLATE?

When you shop for chocolate in the form of candy or are shopping for baking supplies, it is sometimes confusing when reviewing the type of chocolate you are buying. Why are there so many types and what are their purposes?

There are several different types of chocolate available. The main types of chocolate are milk chocolate, semisweet chocolate, bittersweet chocolate, white chocolate and unsweetened chocolate. The composition of the mixture, the source of cacao beans, the treatment, and roasting of beans, and the types and amounts of additives will significantly affect the flavor and the price of the final chocolate product.

MILK CHOCOLATE

Sweet chocolate which normally contains 10-20% cocoa solids (which includes cocoa and cocoa butter) and more than 12% milk solids. It is seldom used for baking, except for chunks in cookies.

DARK CHOCOLATE

Sweetened chocolate has a high content of cocoa solids without milk or with very little milk, and may contain up to 12% milk solids. Dark chocolate can either be sweet, semi-sweet, bittersweet or unsweetened.

SWEET DARK CHOCOLATE

Like semi-sweet chocolate, it is not always possible to distinguish between the flavor of sweet and semi-sweet chocolate. It contains 35-45% cocoa solids. If a recipe calls for sweet dark chocolate, you may also use semi-sweet chocolate.

SEMI-SWEET CHOCOLATE

This is the classic dark baking chocolate which can be purchased in most grocery stores. It is frequently used for cakes, cookies and brownies. It has a good, sweet flavor and contains 40-62% cocoa solids.

BITTERSWEET CHOCOLATE

A good quality bittersweet chocolate usually contains 60% to 85% cocoa solids depending on brand. If the content of cocoa solids is high then the content of sugar is low, giving a rich, intense and more or less bitter chocolate flavor. Bittersweet chocolate is often used for baking or cooking.

WHITE CHOCOLATE

White chocolate is made with cocoa butter, sugar, milk, emulsifier, vanilla and sometimes other flavorings. It does not contain the dark colored parts of the cacao bean which produce the dark color. It has a mild and pleasant flavor and can be used to make desserts or candies.

UNSWEETENED CHOCOLATE

CORN, COTTON AND CHOCOLATE: HOW THE MAYA CHANGED THE WORLD

A bitter chocolate which is only used for baking. The flavor is not good, so it is not suitable for eating alone. Use it only if a recipe specifies 'unsweetened chocolate'. It contains almost 100% cocoa solids and about half of it might be cocoa butter fat.

HOW WOULD YOU LIKE YOUR SCORPION, SIR? WITH OR WITHOUT CHOCOLATE COVERING?

The world of chocolate varieties available to the chocoholic is complete with every kind of candy bar, chocolate kisses, exotic boxed chocolates, chocolate syrup, chocolate toppings, shaped chocolates for holidays and even sugar free chocolate.

But the ultimate chocolate lover has turned up the game a notch or two. They have gone over the top by dipping the most curious items in chocolate, and devouring these strange and exotic chocolate combinations with much gusto.

The aficionados started by dipping some items in chocolate that sounded like a good combination of taste and composition: chocolate covered peanuts, chocolate covered pretzels, chocolate covered bananas and chocolate covered strawberries. These became popular because they were familiar foods to pair up with chocolate.

The next wave of developing exotic taste treats was more daring. Things were dipped with chocolate that were not usually associated with the sweet tasting treat but were edible. For example: chocolate dipped bacon, chocolate flavored chilies, chocolate covered pickles, chocolate covered onions, chocolate covered pumpkin seeds and chocolate covered jerky. These tasted pretty good, but the ultimate chocolate game was not over.

Chocolate lovers were searching for a taste thrill and thus came wasabi flavored chocolate, curry flavored chocolate and violet flavored chocolate. The thrill seekers then reached for a higher plateau. Entomophagy, the use of insects as food, caused them to dip insects in chocolate and devoured this new treat. Thus, the eating of chocolate covered crickets, chocolate covered ants, chocolate covered grasshoppers, and chocolate covered bees became the rage.

Well, I did leave out one obnoxious critter that is consumed: Chocolate covered scorpions. I omitted this scrofulous insect because it is just too ugly to eat, even covered in chocolate. However, chocoholics have further outdone themselves with the unspeakable chocolate covered morsel that is not only too ugly to eat, but its gummy squishy flesh is a contradiction to the flavor and crisp crunch of the delicious chocolate covering its body. The unspeakable creature is chocolate covered squid. Ugh!

COULD YOU HUM A BIT OF THAT POPULAR TUNE ABOUT CHOCOLATE?

It is not surprising that a popular treat like chocolate would have poetry, paeans, and songs written about its deliciousness. It is surprising how many published and recorded songs have been written about the product of the cocoa bean. Well over a hundred are listed on the internet, and these do not include that advertising jingle for a candy bar that rattles around in your head for hours at a time.

Many of the songs are downloadable from the internet and were written, sung or composed by a wide array of artists ranging from blues singers to recording stars and world famous classical composers.

CORN, COTTON AND CHOCOLATE: HOW THE MAYA CHANGED THE WORLD

Just selecting a few songs to list was quite a task. The list starts with a low-down whiskey voiced blues singer and runs the range of musical types and completes with a song from the Nutcracker Suite.

Tom Waits: *Chocolate Jesus,* A song written by Tom Waits and performed on his 1999 album, *Mule Variations.*

Sammy Davis, Jr.: *The Candy Man,* a song from the 1971 film: *Willy Wonka & the Chocolate Factory* and sung on his album, *Sammy Davis, Jr., Now.*

Madonna: *Candy Shop*, a song performed on her album, *Hard Candy.*

Pyotr Ilyich Tchaikovsky: *Chocolate, the Spanish Dance.* Act II of Tchaikovsky's Nutcracker Suite features a macho trumpet solo.

These are some of the compositions relating to the salutes to the charms of chocolate. They are symbolic of the way that chocolate from the Maya cocoa bean has conquered all class levels around the world.

HEATHEN CULTIVARS HAVE TAKEN OVER THE CHRISTIAN HOLY DAYS WITH CRAVEN IMAGES MADE FROM CHOCOLATE

Accounts of how chocolate has changed modern culture would be not be complete without a description of chocolate-centered celebrations including Saint Valentine's day, Easter Sunday or any of the holidays that involve celebration chocolate. Considering chocolate was first domesticated by the Maya, who by Christian dogma are heathens, chocolate has changed the major Christian Holidays.

CHOCOLATE FOR EASTER

Easter, the greatest feast day in the Christian calendar, celebrates the Resurrection of Christ. It is a religious high holiday and a day of gifting children with a tradition of baskets filled with specialty candy. The Easter Bunny is a legendary anthropomorphic character. However, the Easter Bunny, or Easter Hare, dates from ancient history.

Molded chocolate Easter eggs and standing bunnies have become popular in the past century. These chocolate representations of Easter are appropriate because of the springtime celebration of rabbits and eggs are linked with rituals of fertility. The first mass-produced chocolate eggs appeared in England in 1873 when Cadbury created their first Easter egg. It wasn't until the early 1900s that milk chocolate Easter eggs became widely available.

Americans spend roughly $1.9 billion on Easter candy, second only to Halloween in candy consumption. Ninety million chocolate Easter bunnies are produced each year.

CHOCOLATE FOR VALENTINE'S DAY

Saint Valentine was a martyr who died on February 14th, 269 AD. The tradition of gifting a box of chocolates on Valentine's day, marking his martyrdom, has become well established in the United States and Europe for many years and this Christian holiday is taking a strong hold in other parts of the world.

Saint Valentine's day now accelerates chocolate sales not only in the United States but also in Japan, where it had become a business obligation for women to present gifts of candy to their

CORN, COTTON AND CHOCOLATE: HOW THE MAYA CHANGED THE WORLD

male colleagues on Valentine's Day. The result is a merchandising bonanza of chocolate worth some $50,000,000 a year, with boxes of exquisite, elegant Japanese chocolates selling for as much as $300 a box.

MOTHER'S DAY CHOCOLATE

Mother's Day is not a religious holiday, but is the celebration of appreciation for everyone's Mother. If you're a mother, you're entitled to receive great chocolate on Mother's Day and if you're the child who brings the chocolate, you're entitled to share. Mothers are pleased to receive just a card, flowers or candy, but they better be part of a great brunch.

CHOCOLATE FOR HALLOWEEN

Halloween is the Eve of the All Saints Day. Halloween has its roots in ancient festivals with pagan roots, but has become part of the Catholic calendar. The night is associated with death, evil and monsters. It is celebrated with scary costumes, haunting of eerie places and the famous ritual of "trick or treat". Halloween is just not for kids. In addition to the chocolate treats given to children, chocolate makers have produced sophisticated products for adults that make this one of Americas best selling candy holidays.

CHOCOLATE FOR THE DAY OF THE DEAD

Since pre-Colombian times, Mexican people have celebrated El Dia de los Muertos (the day of the dead), a ritual in which the living remember their departed relatives. From October 31 through November 2, family graves in Mexico are tended and decorated with offerings and families expect a visit from loved ones who have passed. Offerings dedicated to the deceased are usually foods and beverages. Foods offered as tribute to the dead include chocolate beverages, chicken with chocolate mole sauce, and human skulls made from sugar and chocolate inscribed with the names of the deceased.

CHRISTMAS EVE IN FRANCE

Instead of gathering around the Christmas tree, French families gathered around a Yule log burning in the fireplace. Sometime after 1870, a Parisian patisserie was inspired by the festivity to create the first Bûche de Noël ("Christmas Log"), from a chocolate frosted cake. To imitate the log, a roll of Genoese sponge cake is covered in chocolate butter cream textured to resemble tree bark. The presentation of the Bûche de Noël is the desert highlight of the French holiday meal.

CHRISTMAS DAY

Christmas, the celebration of the birth of Christ, is a grand holiday for religious and commercial enthusiasts. Christmas is a time for giving boxes of luxury bonbons and collections of fine chocolate bars. Hot chocolate is a tradition not only for Santa but for all the family. Chocolate Santas, reindeer and bags of chocolate coins join the other chocolate treats for this holiday.

The Maya cultivar, that was the food of the gods, has found its place in modern celebrations honoring different gods.

MAYA CHOCOLATE'S PART IN CHANGING HISTORY

Maya chocolate is the second most popular flavor in the world and it has changed the world's "sweet tooth" and the fortunes of numerous countries. The cocoa bean, considered by the Maya

CORN, COTTON AND CHOCOLATE: HOW THE MAYA CHANGED THE WORLD

to be the food of the gods, has now become the food for everyman. The candy or chocolate confection industry is a 98-billion-dollar a year business. The pagan cultivar has high-jacked the Christian holidays by being the favorite gift offered on those celebrations.

CORN, COTTON AND CHOCOLATE: HOW THE MAYA CHANGED THE WORLD

CHAPTER 11: THE COMMON BEAN

Botanical name: *Phaseolus vulgaris* **Maya name**: *bot*

Memories of a youth

Some of the best memories of my youth were the lessons learned as a Boy Scout. The Scout movement had goals of responsible citizenship, character development and self-reliance

Well, those are the formal goals of scouting. In terms of my personal life experiences acquired through scouting, I owe my sense of teamwork, leadership and other important life skills that I gained while I navigated scouting adventures.

Merit badges are awarded in the scouts for learning specific skills. As you earned the iconic cloth patches, you grew nearer to your goal of success. A total of 21 merit badges must be earned before you qualify as an Eagle Scout.

During my time as a scout, I earned merit badges in first aid, swimming, rifle shooting, archery, canoeing, bugling, cooking, lifesaving, weather, astronomy, communications, and wood carving and others.

If one considers the core merit badges that I earned, some are especially important including first aid, lifesaving and cooking. These merit badges teach critical skills that you retain for the remainder of your life. The Boy Scout motto is to "be prepared" and the core skills learned enable a scout to be prepared to respond to all emergencies.

The skills I learned as a boy scout taught me about taking care of others. Cooking over a campfire was about taking care of others. It is a skill learned through the experience of feeding a group of boys on camping trips. To illustrate what a Boy Scout cook had to experience during a camping trip, consider the cooking responsibilities that were required to be performed while being a chef around a campfire.

Camporees were the name given to competitions between Boy Scout troops displaying their camping skills. Points were awarded for setting up camp including: properly pitching a tent, the alignment of the camp, latrine construction and preparing cooking facilities. The job of cooking included proper construction of the campfire, setting up your pots and pans and a display of the meals prepared for the scouts. We were graded on everything, we knew that our troop had superior skills in laying out a camp, pitching pup tents and latrine construction, but we knew that our cooking skills would sweep the field.

I had the responsibility of being the cook for the Panther Patrol of Boy Scout Troop 52. By coincidence, I was also the leader of the Panther Patrol. This was a task that I took seriously. The Camporees usually lasted three days and the cook had to prepare three meals a day. The Panther Patrol consisted of six scouts including myself. I had to prepare a menu that was inexpensive, wholesome, and easy to prepare over a campfire.

My cooking centered on easily prepared foods. The mainstay of my prepared dishes was canned beans. Of course, I would introduce a variety of other dishes into the menu. I did a lot with pancakes, cans of spam and canned fruits. The menu for a typical day would start out with pancakes and beans for breakfast; spam sandwiches and beans for lunch; and a dinner of a stew consisting of hot dogs, vegetables and beans. All slow cooked in a Dutch oven. Dessert consisted of pies made from canned fruit; this was simply two slices of bread their middle filled with fruit and baked in a cast iron pie iron.

This menu may sound monotonous, but considering the circumstances, it was great food enjoyed by hungry boys. I would be the first to rise in the morning, rekindling last night's coals into a cooking fire. One by one, my fellow scouts would crawl out of their warm sleeping bags and toast themselves by the fire. By this time, I would have a pot of beans simmering on the fire and have prepared my pancake batter.

Before you knew it, I would be serving pancakes and beans that were washed down with hot chocolate. I never had any complaints. Setting the table for a meal was easy, everyone had their own plate; consisting of a WWII army surplus mess kit. Everything we used was war surplus: our pup tents, canteens, mess kits and other camping tools were purchased from Old Sarge's Army-Navy surplus and were refugees from the recent war.

An important part of being a good cook was preparing a simple menu, one that featured multiple cans of beans. The brand of beans chosen was very important. Not just any type of beans would suffice. We were slaves to Van Camp's Pork and Beans. This brand with its trademark flavor and quantity of pork was a runaway favorite but there was also competition between Campbell's and Bush's pork and beans. We preferred the taste of Van Camp's Pork and Beans over the competition. Van Camps had enough spices built into their mix so that additional seasoning was not required to bring out the flavor.

Van camp's pork and beans went well with pancakes, as a side for sandwiches and as a basis for the stew for the evening meal. I liked to say that, "our food was brown and hot, and we had plenty of it." After dinner, we would sing our rendition of "Beans, Beans the Musical Fruit."

My memories of an enjoyable meal around the campfire came from dining upon a stew made from pork and beans followed by dessert of a fruit pie. All prepared upon my wood cooking fire. My band of brothers who shared the meal made the memories more enjoyable. Just to hear one of them say, "that was good stew, I think I'll have another helping," was my reward. I owed my cooking technique to the beans domesticated by Maya agronomists. Beans that feed the world and gave pleasure to my fellow scouts in the Panther Patrol.

MAYA AND BEANS

The Maya domesticated the common bean 7,000 years ago, and archaeological research clearly indicates a Mesoamerican origin of the common bean. Maya agronomists developed numerous varieties of beans, including some that are now extinct. Maya agronomists cultivated varieties of beans including: pinto, red beans, black beans, lima beans, runner bean, navy beans, and kidney beans. Many types of bean cultivars are unknown commercially or outside of Mexico, but are cultivated and eaten in Mexico.

In 2012, work by a group of geneticists made an argument for a Mesoamerican origin of all beans. The investigators examined the nucleotide diversity for five different genes found in all forms of beans, wild and domesticated, including examples from the Andes and Mesoamerica. Their study looked at the geographic distribution of the genes.

This study suggests that the wild form of bean originally spread from Mesoamerica, and then into the Andes. Along with squash and maize, beans were part of the "three sisters" that provided the foundation of Maya agriculture. The three complement one another in providing all

CORN, COTTON AND CHOCOLATE: HOW THE MAYA CHANGED THE WORLD

the necessary nutrients for a balanced diet. The Maya diet focused on four domesticated crops: maize, squash, beans and chili peppers.

THE BEAN AND MAYA COOKING

Beans were a major source of protein and a staple in the Maya diet. Maya methods for cooking beans are time honored and many of their methods are still used today. Maya cooks prepared dishes made from both mature beans and immature beans, or what we call "green beans".

When beans are mature, they appear as individual bean seeds in a pod and were prepared in an abundance of dishes. The old-school method for cooking mature beans uses an *olla*, an earthenware cooking pot. Beans were then served, along with their liquid, in small bowls. Beans were scooped up from the bowl with tortillas.

Beans would also be mashed up and wrapped inside tortillas to make something like a burrito. Beans, especially black beans, were made into soups and into bean patties which were cooked on a griddle-like flat surface, called a *comal*, heated over a fire. Chilies were used as condiments to spice up the flavor of the beans.

Green beans were also popular with the Maya. All green beans are immature beans, picked before they are ripe. They are still in their green pods and are eaten as string beans. They were fried on a *comal* with an egg coating, or added to soups and stews.

THE COMMON BEAN IS INTRODUCED TO THE WORLD

By the time of European contact, Maya traders had disseminated the bean throughout the Americas. Spanish traders were introduced to the common bean during the conquest of Mexico. Beans were first seen by a European when Christopher Columbus found them growing in cultivated fields.

Beans were introduced into Europe in the late 15th century by Spanish explorers returning from their voyages to the New World. Spanish and Portuguese traders carried beans to Africa and Asia.

The English dubbed Maya beans as "kidney beans" to distinguish them from their Old-World cousins. These hardy New World legumes soon became a popular crop in Europe because they were both highly nutritious and easy to grow. Because of their nutritional value and ease of storage when dried, they became a primary source of food for sailors, which is how the "Navy bean" got its name.

Beans are a very inexpensive form of good protein and they have become popular in cultures throughout the world. Beans were used as a meat substitute for the poor, and rarely graced the tables of the upper classes. During times of hardship, like the Great Depression in the United States, inexpensive beans were promoted as a source of protein when meat was scarce.

World War II increased the demand for beans when they became a staple in the C-rations supplied to United States servicemen. After the war, as the United States' food relief efforts around the world intensified, so did dry bean production.

CORN, COTTON AND CHOCOLATE: HOW THE MAYA CHANGED THE WORLD

In the United States, with its increasingly health-conscious society, beans were a welcome addition to the pantry of mainstream America. They are one of the most nutritionally complete foods available. In fact, they are the only food that fits into two food groups on the USDA Food Guide Pyramid: vegetable and protein. Studies confirm that a diet incorporating beans, with their low caloric count and high fiber content, helps to lower cholesterol. The combination of indisputable health benefits and incredible variety of flavors and textures ensures the bean's prominent place at the modern table.

In the 21st century, the bean is a popular food across the world and 42 million metric tons are grown each year. The bean is enjoyed in the cuisine of over 100 countries and it continues to be the brunt of humor for the flatulence produced by digesting the bean.

BEANS ARE ENJOYED BY PEOPLE AROUND THE WORLD

Whether refried, baked in a casserole or complementing a nice Chianti, the humble bean has long been a part of gourmet fare as well as everyday food in cultures around the globe. There are a few things we always keep in our pantry: a can of whole tomatoes, good olive oil, and pasta can usually be found. Next to those items, without fail, rests a can of beans. Beans are one of those versatile foods that find themselves at home in almost any dish, and make the dish more nutritious.

This Maya cultivar began its journey around the world at the beginning of the 16th when Europe had only fava beans, which are not common beans, and chick peas. Conquistadors transported the bean to Spain, where it spread across Europe and was disseminated by the Portuguese to Africa and Asia. It did not take long for cultures around the world to adopt the bean as part of their diet. Cultures prepared the bean according to their culinary traditions and new recipes were born by performing alchemy with beans and spices that blended with the tastes of that culture.

The recipes for beans have become legion. The bean is a favorite food across the world in countries ranging from China to France and Ghana. A discussion of the roles that the common bean has assumed in countries with a diversity of tastes would be lengthy and complex. It would include a range of dishes like bean salad in France, red beans with plum sauce in Russia, beans and bacon in Germany, Danish lima beans, South African beans and potatoes, Indian kidney bean curry and Szechuan wok fried green beans. The list of creative dishes is endless.

Think about the opportunities that the bean has been offered for inventing new recipes changing the tastes of world cultures. The most important beans from the New World include the common bean (*Phaseolus vulgaris*) which includes pinto beans, kidney beans, navy beans, and black beans. New World beans include lima beans (*Phaseolus limensis*), runner beans (*Phaseolus coccineus*), tepary beans (*Phaseolus acutifolius*), and butter beans (*Phaseolus lunatus*). Pinto beans are the most highly consumed dried bean in the United States.

THE BEAN, A MAYA CULTIVAR, EARNS AN ITALIAN PEDIGREE

In 1523, conquistadors Hernan Cortez sent a bag of beans back to the Spanish court. King Charles V was impressed with the New World cultivar and sent the bag of beans as a gift to Pope Clement VII. In turn, the Pope gifted the beans to Brother Pietro Valeriano, a monk from Belluno, a village in the region around Venice. The monk planted the beans in pots around the Abbey and had a bountiful crop of beans. Brother Pietro generously gave his surplus beans to

CORN, COTTON AND CHOCOLATE: HOW THE MAYA CHANGED THE WORLD

farmers living in the Lamon region near Venice. This bean has been given the name "lamon" and a Lamon Bean Festival is held every September in Belluno.

The Italians, the first Europeans to wholeheartedly embrace the tomato, adopted the Maya bean. In Italy, you can eat them in stews with polenta and in salads. This bean has become such a quality cultivar for the Venetian region that it was given a pedigree by the European Union. In 1993, a Consortium for its protection was created and in 1996 earned its "Protected Designation of Origin" status which is similar to the coveted "Denomination of Origin Controlled" (DOC) of French wines.

THE BLACK BEAN EPISODE: DON'T PICK A BLACK BEAN, OR YOU WILL BE SORRY

President Santa Anna of Mexico was a cruel man, but he may have had a little bit of a soft side. In a precursor to the Mexican-American War, 176 soldiers from the newly formed Republic of Texas escaped internment only to be recaptured by Mexican forces. Insisting that he was showing mercy, Mexico's President Antonio Lopez de Santa Ana decided not to execute the whole bunch of prisoners, opting instead to only shoot ten percent of the captives.

He devised a sinister scheme to determine who were the lucky captives who would be spared. Santa Ana held a "bean lottery," placing 17 black beans in a pot along with 159 white ones. Those Texans who drew the black beans were killed on the spot, while the others remained imprisoned.

WORLD PRODUCTION OF BEANS.

The commercial production of beans is well-distributed worldwide, countries in Asia, Africa, Europe, Oceania, South and North America are all among the top bean growers. Brazil and India are the largest producers of dry beans while China produces, by far, the largest quantity of green beans, almost as much as the rest of the top ten growers combined.

TOP 10 DRY BEAN PRODUCING COUNTRIES IN MILLION METRIC TONS

RANK	COUNTRY	PRODUCTION
1	India	4.87
2	Brazil	3.20
3	Myanmar	3.03
4	China	1.53
5	United States	1.44
6	Mexico	1.16
7	Tanzania	0.95
8	Uganda	0.46
9	Kenya	0.39
10	Argentina	0.34
	TOTAL	**23.23**

CORN, COTTON AND CHOCOLATE: HOW THE MAYA CHANGED THE WORLD

A whopping total of 42 million metric tons of dry and green beans are produced worldwide each year. That's 84,000,000,000 pounds of beans each year or 12 pounds for each inhabitant on the planet. There's a lot of Maya beans consumed each year.

TOP 10 GREEN BEAN PRODUCING COUNTRIES IN MILLION METRIC TONS

RANK	COUNTRY	PRODUCTION
1	China	13.03
2	Indonesia	0.88
3	Turkey	0.59
4	India	0.58
5	Thailand	0.30
6	Egypt	0.27
7	Morocco	0.20
8	Italy	0.18
9	Spain	0.17
10	Mexico	0.10
	TOTAL	**16.30**

PORK AND BEANS

Pork and beans is one the favorite ways to eat beans, served hot or cold, a dish of pork and beans is a convenient and favorite food. The flavor filled composition is a meal ready to go at any time. Many people have their first experience with the delightful concoction while camping or in the Boy scouts. The dish had its start as army rations during the American Civil war.

Gilbert Van Camp, Sr. is one of the originators, of canned food as it is known today. In 1861, Van Camp, who once was a tinsmith, was familiar with the technology of producing tin cans. Mr. Van Camp came up with the idea of putting vegetables and fruit into tin cans so they could be preserved for later use. At that time, Van Camp ran a grocery store in Indianapolis.

Van Camp saw the potential of a lucrative business in supplying canned beans for use to the United States Army. Beans were already a staple of army rations, in the form of dried beans but not in canned form.

Providing beans cooked with tomato sauce, ready prepared in cans provided the armed forces with a tasty food. A food which was available to eat at any time. Van Camp canned beans could be consumed either hot or cold. During the Civil War, Van Camp was able to get a lucrative contract with the U.S. Government for supplying canned beans to the army.

The lucrative army contract enabled Van Camp to establish a reputation for canned fruits and vegetables. Especially an enhanced reputation for canned beans with tomato sauce. During the next 70 years, Van Camp's canned food did quite well. In 1933, Van Camp Canning was still in business, and in that year, the company was sold to James and John Stokely. The name of the company became Stokely-Van Camp Inc.

CORN, COTTON AND CHOCOLATE: HOW THE MAYA CHANGED THE WORLD

The brand name of Van Camp's pork and beans is still around today, using the same name Van Camp used during the Civil War. Gilbert Van Camp's son Frank, who took over the business along the way, is credited with a new recipe which added pork and replaced the tomato sauce with ketchup. The legend of pork and beans lives on today as mainstays in the pantry and with campers on the trail.

THE BEAN AND FLATULENCE IN SONG AND JOKES

Flatulence is funny and fart humor has ancient beginnings. Not only in song and rhyme, but in jokes. The basis of song and fart humor in general is the sound produced from the high number of oligosaccharides present in beans. Bacteria in the large intestine digest these sugars; these bacteria produce carbon dioxide and hydrogen. The gases are expelled from the body as flatulence. They enable one to toot their stuff.

THE LONG HISTORY OF FLATULISTS AS ENTERTAINMENT

Enough entertainers performed with their flatus that the term flatulist was coined. There are several scattered references in historical texts about ancient and medieval flatulists, or professional farters. This was an entertainer, usually a comedian, that could produce various rhythms and pitches with their intestinal wind.

Saint Augustine mentions some performers who did have "*such command of their bowels, that they can break wind continuously at will, so as to produce the effect of singing.*" The professional farters of medieval Ireland were called *braigetoír*. As entertainers, these *braigetoir* ranked at the lower end of an entertainment scale headed by bards and harpers.

One medieval flatulist is mentioned in the 13th-century English Book of Fees. It lists one called Roland the Farter. Every Christmas, Roland was obliged to perform one jump, one whistle, and one fart annually at the court of King Henry II. But professional farting was not restricted to the aristocracy. The last known farting artist was Le Pétomane, a Frenchman, who was a professional flatulist around the start of the 20th century.

This is now a lost art. Today, they are only heard on hunting, fishing and camping expeditions. Usually performed by overweight men with a three-day beard. Let us not forget the whoopee cushion, a joking device invented in the early 20th century for simulating a fart. The act of farting be used as a humorous supplement to a joke especially among children, as the uncle saying to the child, "pull my finger".

SONGS RHYMES AND JOKES ABOUT FARTS

There are numerous songs and jokes that find humor about the gas produced after eating beans. There are a few examples that are popular enough and funny enough to include for the pleasure of the reader

SONGS ABOUT FARTS

"Beans, Beans, The Musical Fruit" is a schoolyard expression and a children's song about the capacity for beans to contribute to flatulence. The song is also variously known as "Beans,

CORN, COTTON AND CHOCOLATE: HOW THE MAYA CHANGED THE WORLD

Beans, the Magical Fruit", "Beans, Beans, the Miracle Fruit", and "Beans, Beans, the Wonderful Fruit".

Various versions of the" Beans, Beans" song exist, but our example is the standard.

Beans, beans, the musical fruit
The more you eat, the more you toot
The more you toot, the better you feel
So, we have beans at every meal!

This is a song about farts that occur on a highway and produces a supersonic event.

Going down the highway,
Going eighty-four,
Johnny cut a gasser
And it blew me out the door!
The engine, it exploded,
The chassis fell apart,
All because of Johnny's
Supersonic fart!

LIMERICKS ABOUT FARTS
One of the oldest forms of humor is the limerick. The word fart has a humorous connotation but it is an easy word to rhyme. We add a couple of funny examples.

There once was a man from Rangoon
Whose farts could be heard on the moon;
When you'd least expect 'em
They'd burst from his rectum
With the force of a raging typhoon!!

There was a young fellow from Sparta.
A really magnificent farter.
On the strength of one bean
He'd fart "God Save the Queen,"
And Beethoven's Moonlight Sonata.

FART JOKES

George Carlin said:
If two people are in an elevator and one person farts, everyone knows who did it.

Once, when Dorothy Parker was at a dinner, a man burped quite loudly. she is reported to have looked at him and said, "why didn't you use the other end and save your teeth?'"

Rodney Dangerfield said,
"Hey, did somebody step on a duck?"

CORN, COTTON AND CHOCOLATE: HOW THE MAYA CHANGED THE WORLD

A Scottish joke:
"Well, there's no point in having an arse if you can't let it rejoice in song!"

There are two flies sitting on a pile of poop. When one fly farts, the other fly looks at him and says, "Hey do ya mind? I'm eating here!"

Confucius say, "Crowded elevator always smell different to midget."

MAYA BEANS GAVE THE NAME TO BEAN TOWN AND MAINTAINED A RELIGION

Boston baked beans have a long history with the people of New England. Baked beans were prepared and enjoyed by Native Americans long before European contact. Today, Baked Beans are a popular dish, typically sweetened with molasses or maple syrup and flavored with salt pork or bacon.

Native Americans in North America made corn bread and baked beans. The Pilgrims of Plymouth Colony learned these recipes from the Native peoples in the early 1620s. The bean dish supplemented their diets. As time passed, the cooks of New England improved the dish. Molasses became a part of the baked bean recipe in the 1700s when the triangular Trade routes were established. The Triangular Trade of slaves helped to make Boston an exporter of rum, which is produced by the distillation of fermented molasses.

Molasses was added to the local baked bean recipes, creating Boston Baked Beans. In colonial New England, baked beans became an institution especially with the pilgrims. It was traditionally cooked on Saturdays and left in the brick ovens overnight. The Puritan Sabbath lasted from sundown on Saturday until sundown on Sunday, and this time was reserved for quiet piety and refrained from any exertion, including cooking. The beans were still hot on Sunday evening. Baked beans provided an easy-to-prepare dish for the Puritans, allowing people to indulge in a hot meal and still comply with Sabbath restrictions.

Brown bread and baked beans were a popular meal on Saturdays and Sundays in Massachusetts until at least the 1930s. Boston earned its nickname "Bean town" for the wide consumption of baked beans by its residents.

MEXICAN JUMPING BEANS

The jumping bean is not a bean, but is a spurge. They are from the shrub Sebastiania pavoniana. They are seed pods that have been inhabited by the larvae of a small moth (*Cydia deshaisiana*). The "bean" hops or jumps when heat is applied to the "bean". The movement occurs when the larva spasms in an attempt to roll the seed to a cooler environment to avoid dehydration and consequent death. The peculiar jumping bean is native to Mexico.

THERE AIN'T NO STINKING BEANS IN CHILI

The concept that chili con carne contains beans is spurious. A serious chili head will raise a protest if they find beans in their chili con carne. Even the suggestion of adding beans to chili con carne will cause a ruckus. Please refer to the chapter detailing the chili pepper to learn about the proper way to prepare chili con carne.

CORN, COTTON AND CHOCOLATE: HOW THE MAYA CHANGED THE WORLD

WHY BEANS ARE GOOD FOR YOU

Beans are nature's health food. They have an exceptionally high fiber content, and they're a fine source of protein, as well as calcium, iron, folic acid, and potassium.

Beans are rich in plant protein, fiber, B-vitamins, iron, folate, calcium, potassium, phosphorus, and zinc. Most beans are also low in fat. Beans are like meat in nutrients, but with lower iron levels and no animal fats. The high protein and other nutrients in beans make them a great option in the place of meat and dairy products. Vegetarians often substitute beans for meat.

Beans are a great source of fiber and help you have regular bowel movements. Just 1 cup of cooked black beans will give you 15 grams of fiber, which is about half of the recommended daily amount.

Beans are packed with nutrients. They are low in calories, but make you feel full. They are wonderful for people with diabetes since they do not increase your blood sugar very much. The body uses the carbohydrates in beans slowly, over time, providing steady energy for the body, brain, and nervous system. Eating more beans as part of a healthy diet can help lower blood sugar, blood pressure, heart rate, and other heart disease and diabetes risks. Beans and legumes contain antioxidants that help prevent cell damage and fight disease and aging. The fiber and other nutrients benefit the digestive system, and may even help to prevent digestive cancers. Green beans not only provide health benefits to our bodies, they keep our skin smooth, bolstering it with antioxidants proven to prevent premature skin aging.

The protein in beans can help build lean muscle, and it's a plant protein so you're getting the benefits of protein without having to eat meat, which often comes with added fat, calories, and cholesterol. Beans are also a rich source of antioxidants, which will help protect your cells from free radical damage and help you from experiencing many of the problems that can occur as you get older.

JACK AND THE BEAN STALK. IS THIS STORY APPROPRIATE FOR CHILDREN?

We all know the fairy tale about a boy named Jack and his encounter with a giant. Jack is a young boy sent to market to sell a cow. On the way, he is hustled by a man who gives him some "magic" beans for the cow. Jack comes home and his mother is shocked by the trade and throws the beans out into the yard.

Well, you know the rest of the story about the beans sprouting into a beanstalk, which jack climbs. At the top, he encounters a giant and winds up stealing the giants hoard of gold. The giant pursues Jack. Jack chops down the bean stalk and the pursuing giant falls to his death.

The earliest surviving written version of the tale is *The History of Jack and the Bean Stalk,* a book printed by Benjamin Tabart in 1807, but the story is certainly much older. A burlesque entitled The Story of Jack Spriggins and the Enchanted Bean was included in the 1734 second edition of *Round About Our Coal-Fire.*

Let us analyze the real truth behind this story. First, whoever, wrote the story plagiarized the works of William Shakespeare. The giant's battle cry: "Fee! Fie! Foe! Fum, I smell the blood of an Englishman". Was lifted directly from Act 3, Scene 4, of William Shakespeare's King Lear. The line in the play reads: "Fie, foh, and fum, I smell the blood of a British man." Second, Jack was a juvenile delinquent. The original story portrays Jack as a "hero" gaining the sympathy of

CORN, COTTON AND CHOCOLATE: HOW THE MAYA CHANGED THE WORLD

the giant's wife, hiding in his house, robbing and finally killing him. This just not the right way for a nice boy to behave.

The Maya bean has no responsibility in this matter. The beans were magic and naturally grew into a stalk. They were innocent of theft and murder. In fact, they had not even been properly introduced to Jack. However, with this yarn, Maya beans entered the storybooks of England and the world.

HOW THE MAYA BEAN HELPED TO CHANGE HISTORY

Maya common bean is a favorite food across the world and it changed the diet of billions of people. It is enjoyed in the cuisine of over 100 countries and 42 million metric tons of dried and green beans are grown each year. A Maya bean was given a pedigree by the European Union. The beam continues to be the subject of jokes due to the flatulence produced by ingesting the cultivar.

CORN, COTTON AND CHOCOLATE: HOW THE MAYA CHANGED THE WORLD

CHAPTER 12: COTTON

Botanical name: *Gossypium hirsutum*   **Maya name**: *piits*

Memories of a youth

Saturday was always a special day. Dad would give us our allowance. We would each be presented with one dime. It may seem odd in today's financial perspective that a thin dime caused so much excitement, but it was our magic passport to a Saturday full of adventure. The dime represented a tour of the town square and an afternoon of motion picture magic. My sisters, Janice, two years older, and Mary Rita, two years my junior and I would walk the few blocks to the town square. Saturday was always an exciting day for the denizens of our town. People would flock to the town for shopping and gathering for socializing and gossip. Plus, there would always be mule wagons circling the square.

As central features, the tree covered square boasted a beautiful Victorian gazebo and a bronze statue of Alexander Stevens Clay, a local hero. There were two movie theaters located on the square. However, our favorite movie palace was the Strand Theater on the corner of Cherokee Street. The movie theatres were always our ultimate destination on our Saturday outings.

We were fascinated with the activities going on in the town center. The hustle and bustle of people circulating around the square included the mob of shoppers, politicians lounging around the red brick courthouse and mule wagons loaded with bales of cotton.

There were always a lot of mule wagons transporting their loads to the cotton gin. Most of the cotton farmers drove their rigs quietly through the town. However, there were always the countrified exhibitionists that attracted attention. These show off farmers, mostly younger men, would stand at the front their wagons and crack their long whips over the heads of their mules. This noisy display of mule driving always disturbed the peace.

Older farmers and town folk would look disapprovingly at these showoffs. Younger viewers may have been impressed because these boisterous drivers cracking their bullwhips over their mules created quite a stir. They were a nuisance. The outrageous actions of the whip-cracking drivers evolved into a special nickname for them. It became the source of the slang term that eventually became a synonym for a white Southerner. They were called "crackers" because of the loud sound of the cracking whip. This name was not all bad, and it had nothing to do with race, and it actually became the name of our beloved Atlanta baseball team.

Our tour around the square involved a review of the movies offered by each of the theaters. While traversing the square, we read all the movie marquees and paused to look at the movie posters, but somehow, we always wound up at the Strand Theater. We had our thin dimes secured in our pockets ready to the hand to the lady in the box office for our admission to the theater. For those movie fans under 12 years old our ticket to paradise cost a mere 9¢. That's correct 9¢. For this meager amount, you had the opportunity to view a cowboy movie, a detective movie, coming attractions, cartoons and several serials.

This was a day's worth of entertainment for less than a dime. Oh yes, that penny we received in change was a valuable asset. For this thin copper coin, you could purchase a variety of delicious candies. You could choose between Kits, two packages of four caramels each, a Tootsie Roll, or Mary Janes. If properly managed these sweets could last you through the first movie. The actual time that the movie began or the subject of the first movie was irrelevant to us, because we

CORN, COTTON AND CHOCOLATE: HOW THE MAYA CHANGED THE WORLD

always sat through all the movies at least twice. The cowboy movie may have featured Roy Rogers, Gene Autry, Tex Ritter, Lash La Rue, or the Durango Kid. The detective movie mysteries were solved by Boston Blackie, Bulldog Drummond or Charley Chan.

As each year rolled into the fall, the days became shorter. The movies, if watched twice around, usually lasted four or five hours, but we had to be careful that we would not exit the theatre after the sun began to set. We had to be home before dark. On a particular Saturday in October, we overstayed our time at the movies.

When we exited the theater, the sun was setting, the shadows were growing long, the streetlights were on and our greatest fear was realized right before our eyes. Standing beneath the marquee of the theater, we watched the Ku Klux Klan parading around the square. we were frozen stiff. They were riding in convertible automobiles and pickup trucks. We had seen the Ku Klux Klan before, but never this close and never so many of them. They were sitting on the backs of the seats in their convertible cars and standing in the back of the pickups, holding flaming torches aloft. They were wearing their flowing white robes with tall hoods and masks. We were horrified!

The Klan was greatly feared by all black Southerners, and most white Southerners, especially Catholics and Jews. We were catholic. I was an altar boy, which placed a higher price of my head. We knew that we had to exit the square and head for home leaving the Klan behind us.

Light from the flickering torches cast eerie shadows on the wall of the theatre. Whispering our escape plan to each other, we slowly and casually walked toward the corner. Luckily the theater was on the corner of Cherokee Street. This street was our exit from the square and the safe route back home.

Out of the corners of our eyes, we kept the parade of Klansmen in sight. When we reached the corner, Janice, my older sister, said "let's run like hell!" and she took off like a bat out of hell. We had a clear field before us and the enemy behind. It was a simple matter of "feet do your stuff". I followed Janice like an Olympic sprinter; however, since she was two years older and taller, her long legs enabled her to quickly increase the distance between us.

I just hit my top speed when I realized that I had forgotten my little sister. "Wait, Jimmy, wait for me", came her little voice. Resisting all natural impulses to maintain my frantic escape, I stopped and turned. I saw her approaching with her little legs churning and making every attempt to catch up. She was only seven years old but she knew what the Klan was all about.

She was scared. During my pause, I looked up the street for the Ku Klux Klan. They were not in sight. I reached my hand out and Mary Rita caught hold. I could hear her breath coming in gasps, caused both by the run and terror of the Ku Klux Klan. With the enemy no longer pursuing us, we could walk more slowly. Janice had already disappeared around the corner of Forest Avenue. Mary Rita and I walked home, hand in hand, safe from the evil forces circling the town square.

That was over 60 years ago, I do not remember my little sister ever holding my hand again. However, the events of that night and the level of fear we experienced has never been replicated. As we turned down Forest Avenue for home and safety, little did I know that the crackers driving their mule wagons, loaded with bales of cotton, and the Ku Klux Klan were the results of Maya cotton and the way it changed the world.

CORN, COTTON AND CHOCOLATE: HOW THE MAYA CHANGED THE WORLD

MAYA COTTON

Early in their civilization Maya agronomists recognized the value of an indigenous wild cotton plant and began the cultivation of what would become history's most valuable and productive vegetable fiber.

Nowhere else in the world, but in the Yucatán Peninsula, was so much energy invested in domesticating plants. For thousands of years Maya agronomists altered the DNA of the cotton plant through selective breeding. They delivered a cultivar that is soft and fluffy, has strong fibers and is almost pure cellulose. Cotton fabrics discovered by archaeologists in Mesoamerica have been dated to 5800 B.C.

This species of cotton, *Gossypium hirsutum*, is indigenous to the Yucatán and its homegrown status made it a definitive selection as an important Maya cultivar. Maya agronomists developed the *Gossypium hirsutum* into the most versatile vegetable fiber on earth. It has high quality fibers, is easily cultivated and produces greater yields per acre than any other cotton. The Maya had invented a surefire winner.

The Maya had a long time to get the cultivar just right. Their 3,000-year history in cultivating the plant rewarded them with a product that has become the most valuable fiber on the planet. To satisfy the high demands for cotton products, the Maya increased the yield of their cotton crops through advanced genetics and agriculture technology. The ancient Maya practiced strategies of agriculture technology as diverse as terracing, raised fields, canals, and continuous cultivation involving crop rotation.

The Maya discovered that quality cotton textiles were an invaluable resource for trading. Therefore, Maya production of cotton and woven textiles had to be sufficient for domestic applications, plus the lucrative profit from trading operations across Mesoamerica and their wide seaborne trade network. This trade continued into the Spanish colonial period.

THE PRODUCTION OF MAYA TEXTILES

In Maya society, men traditionally grew and harvested the cotton plant while women processed the fiber and created textiles for clothing and other utilitarian products. Fabrics and their designs played a significant role in ancient Maya life, art, social symbolism and religious beliefs.

In the fabrication of textiles, the first step is preparing the fiber. The preparation of cotton for spinning was labor intensive. The fiber had to be washed and picked clean of seeds. The loose fibers are then spun into threads by hand, with spindles, a long stick-like device for holding the thread, and whorls, a weight held on the spindle that increased the speed of its rotation.

Maya women wove cotton fabric using classic back strap looms. This weaving device employs wood rods and straps worn around the waist to create tension in the lengthwise threads for the loom. Bone picks were used to weave the weft, or the crosswise threads, which created the design patterns.

They used different woven designs to signify family or regional relationships, in addition to religious and ceremonial affiliations. These designs were passed on from generation to generation. Weavers used natural dyes for creating clothing designs. Examples of colors available to the ancient Maya dyers include green, purple, black, blue and red. In addition to designs embedded into the fabric, other decorative elements included embroidery and brocade.

CORN, COTTON AND CHOCOLATE: HOW THE MAYA CHANGED THE WORLD

The woven pieces used to make clothing are woven to the required size and are never cut. Despite its simplicity, the blackstrap loom permits more types of techniques and designs to be woven into the cloth than other type of loom. Most of the fabrics have designs woven into them, especially cloth destined for ceremonial clothing. The decorative elements can signify history, cultural identity, religious affiliation, social status or something personal about the wearer. Since most indigenous people come from agricultural societies, clothing designs generally relate to the natural world.

THE SIGNIFICANCE OF MAYA COTTON CLOTHING.

Mayan clothing was needed less for protection from the tropical elements and more for personal adornment and identification. Clothing and its adornment indicated socioeconomic or political status, the regions in which they live, their own religious power, and other factors. Maya priests and the elite wore luxurious elaborate outfits and were adorned with jewelry.

Elite women were also responsible for the task of weaving textiles for their families; however, they had the additional responsibility of producing luxurious textiles and garments for tribute to other elites and rulers. To do this, their cloth was of the finest quality both in the production of the spun threads and in the elaborate dying and embellishments. They used bird feathers, pearls, jade or other precious stone beads combined with the most elaborate brocade and embroidery.

In the hot, humid environment of the ancient Maya, almost all their cotton clothing has deteriorated. Instead of actual cotton artifacts archaeologists interpret the fashion sense of the ancient Maya by utilizing Maya artifacts including paintings on ceramic ware, carvings, ceramic figurines, murals and the historical records of Spanish conquistadors.

A common theme painted on Maya vases is the scene of the royal audience. These vase paintings provide details of cotton clothing and decorative accessories made of cotton fabric. The *ahau* or lord is characteristically depicted, receiving visitors, while seated cross-legged. On various vase paintings, the names of the *ahau* and his visitors are provided by glyphs. Some of the most interesting information painted on the vases are the details of the clothing styles, decorative patterning, face painting, masks worn, gestures made and so forth. Many vases indicate the style of interior decor with its throne, cotton curtains and sumptuous pillows.

The ancient Maya had a concept about clothes that was different from contemporary clothing design. Their tropical climate was hot and humid, and they never made clothes that fit close to the body. Clothes fit loosely about the body, to increase ventilation and clothing tended to be held in place by being knotted by belts made of cloth or other materials. Cotton was the perfect fabric for the tropical climate.

Maya men's clothing included a kind of breechcloth that was, according to archaeologists, "five fingers wide" and between eight and ten feet long. This breechcloth was wrapped around the waist repeatedly before being passed between the legs. For the upper classes, they were commonly decorated with feather work on the ends of the cloth. Lower class men wore an undecorated breechcloth.

The most prevalent and influential item of women's clothing in ancient times is the *huipil*, like a loose blouse-like dress; it is still worn in Maya areas today. The *huipil* is a loose rectangular garment, made from combining two lengths of back strap loom fabric, with a hole in the middle

CORN, COTTON AND CHOCOLATE: HOW THE MAYA CHANGED THE WORLD

for the head. The *huipil* could be worn loose, extending to the ankles or tucked into a skirt that was made from a single length of fabric wrapped and tied around the waist.

The *huipil* is usually white with colorful designs woven or embroidered into the cloth around the neck. *Huipils* were important in displaying one's religion, family ties and community affiliation. Different communities tended to have different designs and colors. *Huipils* used for ceremonial purposes were more elaborate. Both traditions still exist today.

Maya farmers wore minimal clothing. Men wore plain breechcloths or a band of cloth wound around their waists. Women in farming communities wore a length of minimally ornamented material with holes made for the arms and head known as a *kub*.

COTTON AND ITS MULTIPLE USES BY THE MAYA.

The Maya used cotton as a woven fabric and a quilted fabric for various diverse applications. The uses ranged from decorative accessories such as pillows and curtains to utilitarian purposes such as body armor for warriors and as padding for ball players.

DECORATIVE ACCESSORIES

The scenes painted on vases and murals depict a wide assortment of activities of Maya elites and of everyday life. The vases depict the use of cotton fabric for pillows, cushions, drapery and coverings for doorways. Cotton was also used for the fabrication of hammocks. The decorative accessories are used in ways similar to contemporary applications.

PROTECTIVE WEAR FOR BALL PLAYERS

Numerous Maya sculptures and figurines depict ballplayers and their equipment. They played the game against competing teams on a long, narrow ball court between sloped stonewalls. The stone ring goals were located at mid-court. The 10 to 12-inch solid rubber ball weighed 6 pounds. The complete rulebook for the game is unknown, but it was illegal to handle the ball or to strike the ball except with the elbows, hips, knees or head. This was a dangerous game with vicious body contact, striking the heavy ball and slamming into the wall required protection for the player.

Quilted cotton padding was used for protective gear on the chest, knees, forearms, elbows, hips and head. Quilted cotton padding along with other materials was ergonomically designed and fabricated into protective gear for the players. Like the pioneering Maya, quilted cotton padding was used by American football players in the first half of the 20th century.

ARMOR FOR THE WARRIOR

Figurines and murals depict the Maya warrior with his quilted-cotton body armor and wooden shield as the very picture of the well-dressed Maya fighting man. This quilted armor was more effective than one would assume. The quilted armor was worn over the shoulders and covered the torso, the arms and the head was protected by a helmet fabricated from cotton.

The use of this cotton armor extended past the Classic period, the Post Classic period and was the front-line armor used by the Maya soldiers throughout the 170 years of conflict against the Spanish conquistadors.

The Spanish initiated their conquest of the Maya in 1527 and the last Maya citadel fell in 1697. During this period, the Spanish soldier grew to respect the fierce Maya warrior and his armor.

CORN, COTTON AND CHOCOLATE: HOW THE MAYA CHANGED THE WORLD

The effectiveness of the quilted cotton armor was verified by a conquistador who stated that the cotton armor could resist the slashing blow from his steel sword and survive. Because imitation is the highest form of flattery, when conquistadors as well as their war dogs adopted the quilted cotton armor, the Maya must have been flattered.

MAYA COTTON MEETS THE WORLD

Maya cotton made its debut and the opportunity to show it qualities to the world, when the Great Navigator encountered the Maya miracle fiber. During his fourth voyage to the New World in 1504, Christopher Columbus boarded a large Maya trading vessel near the coast of Honduras. It was serendipitous that Columbus was not only the Admiral of the Ocean Sea, but was from an Italian family that was in the weaving business. He really knew his fabrics.

Fernando, the son of Christopher Columbus, wrote about the incident in his journal:

"Fortune there arrived at that time a canoe long as a galley and eight feet wide, made of a single tree trunk like the other Indian canoes; it was freighted with merchandise from the western regions around New Spain. Amidships it had a palm-leaf awning like that on Venetian gondolas; this gave complete protection against the rain and waves. Underneath were women and children and all the baggage and merchandise. There were twenty-five paddlers aboard, but they offered no resistance when our boats drew up to them.

The large canoe was loaded with trade goods, the "costliest and handsomest" of which were "cotton mantles and sleeveless shirts embroidered and painted in different designs and colors, long wooden swords edged with "flint knives that cut like steel" copper hatchets and bells; and a crucible for melting copper. Notably, they also had:

"...many of the almonds [cacao beans] which the Indians of New Spain use as currency; and these the Indians in the canoe valued greatly, for I noticed that when they were brought aboard with the other goods, and some fell to the floor, all the Indians stooped to pick them up as if they had lost something of great value..."

Columbus boarded the vessel and took the valued cargo on board his ship. He was particularly interested in the cotton cloth. He declared that the fabric was more precious than gold. Columbus was an amazing prognosticator; cotton did turn out to be more valuable than gold.

MAYA COTTON CHANGES WORLD HISTORY

Maya agronomists developed a native cultivar that has become the world's most widely used vegetable fiber. Cotton is truly a miracle fiber and has been spun, woven, and dyed for 7000 years. Maya cotton, the species, *Gossypium hirsutum* is a newcomer. The species is indigenous to the Yucatán and its homegrown status made it a perfect selection for a Maya cultivar. It has high quality fibers, is easily cultivated and produces greater yields per acre than any other cotton species. Maya cotton now provides textiles that clothe 95% of the world.

Maya cotton is also known as upland cotton. Gossypium hirsutum is the raw material for a vast variety of textile products and this species is considered the most important of the cotton-yielding plants. Of the four-cotton species, commercially available today *Gossypium hirsutum* provides 90% of current world production. *Gossypium barbadense*, also New World cotton that provides 3-4% of world production. Both *Gossypium arboreum* and *Gossypium herbaceum* are Old World cottons and together they provide only 2% of world production.

CORN, COTTON AND CHOCOLATE: HOW THE MAYA CHANGED THE WORLD

The use of cotton for fabric dates to prehistoric times and artifacts of cotton fabric dated from before 5000 BC have been excavated by archaeologists in Mesoamerica and in the ancient Indus Valley Civilization located in Pakistan. Arab merchants first brought cotton cloth to Europe about 800 A.D. The English name for "cotton" reflects its long term and winding travels. The English name derives from the Arabic *(al) qutun*, which began to be used around 1400 AD. The Spanish word, *"algodón"*, is likewise derived from the Arabic term.

During the late medieval period, cotton from India became popular as an imported fiber in northern Europe, without any actual knowledge of how cotton was produced, other than that it came from a plant. Europeans came to believe an improbable myth about its sourcing. Noting its similarities to wool, the medieval population (who also believed in witches and werewolves), came to believe that cotton was produced by plant-borne sheep, which grew on a wonderful tree which sprouted tiny lambs on the ends of its branches. These branches were pliable so that they bent down to allow the lambs to feed on grass when they were hungry. This legend was finally put rest by explorers to the New World. This myth is retained in the name given to cotton in many European languages, such as German *Baumwolle*, which translates as "tree wool"

When Columbus encountered cotton plants and woven cotton fabric, he disseminated the plant to the world market. By the end of the 16th century, cotton was cultivated throughout the warmer regions in Asia and the Americas. Cottonseeds are believed to have been planted in Florida in 1556 and in Virginia in 1607. By 1616, colonists were growing cotton along the James River in Virginia. The Maya cultivar was spreading across the world and introducing a new versatile textile to its populations.

The cultivation of cotton became popular in the Southern region of the United States where the climate and soil conditions were well suited for the growth of cotton. In addition, the use of slave labor reduced the cost of production. Several other factors contributed to the growth of the cotton industry of the United States. These included the increased demand for cotton raw material by the British Industrial Revolution, inexpensive fertile land, and the cotton gin. The growth of cotton expanded and by the early 1830s the United States produced most the cotton in the world. Cotton exceeded the combined value of all other United States exports. Maya cotton was on the way to become "King Cotton".

In 1860, The wealth from cotton growing led the South into the bloody Civil War. "King Cotton", was a phrase used by Southern politicians before the Civil War. The term arrogantly verbalized their belief that an independent Confederacy would be economically successful, assuring the South's victory in a war. They were dead wrong.

in 1865, after the end of the Civil war, cotton remained a key crop in the Southern economy. Sharecropping evolved across the Southern states. This was a farming system in which landless black and white farmers farmed land owned by others in return for a share of the profits. Until the 1950s when mechanical cotton pickers were developed, cotton farmers needed additional labor to hand-pick cotton. Picking cotton was a source of income for families across the South. Rural and small-town school systems had split their vacations so children could work in the fields during "cotton-picking time."

In 1912, the British cotton industry was at its peak, annually producing eight billion yards of cloth. During World War I, cotton could not be exported to foreign markets. To meet their

CORN, COTTON AND CHOCOLATE: HOW THE MAYA CHANGED THE WORLD

demands, some countries built their own factories, particularly Japan. By 1933 Japan introduced 24-hour cotton production and became the world's largest cotton manufacturer.

It was not until the 1950s that reliable harvesting machinery was introduced. Prior to this, cotton-harvesting machinery had been too clumsy to pick cotton without shredding the fibers. During the first half of the 20th century, employment in the cotton industry fell, as machines began to replace laborers and the South's rural labor force had dwindled during the World Wars. Cotton remains a major export of the Southern United States.

In the 21st century, textile mills have moved from America and western Europe to lower-wage countries. Industrial cotton textile production is currently located in countries like India, Bangladesh, China, and Latin America. In these regions labor is much less expensive than in the first world, and attracts poor workers.

21ST CENTURY COTTON AND WORLD PRODUCTION

The demand for cotton has doubled since the 1980s. The cotton growing nations produce 26,000,000 metric tons per year. The leading producer of cotton is China with 6,841,593 tons, followed by India with 5,323,467 and the United States with 3,598,853 tons. Following is a chart showing the top cotton producing countries.

TOP 10 COTTON PRODUCING COUNTRIES IN METRIC TONS

RANK	COUNTRY	PRODUCTION (MT)
1	China	6,841,593
2	India	5,323,467
3	United States of America	3,598,853
4	Pakistan	2,216,932
5	Brazil	1,639,537
6	Uzbekistan	1,053,742
7	Australia	976,475
8	Turkey	853,831
9	Argentina	214,371
10	Turkmenistan	199,358

MAYA COTTON TEAMS WITH THE COTTON GIN TO BECOME A WORLD POWER

The Industrial Revolution began in Britain in 1733 and changed the technological character of the world. The Industrial Revolution mechanized the textile industry, when cotton spinning machinery was powered by steam engines, and the power loom increased the output of a textile worker. The Industrial Revolution and technology continually expanded with the invention of new machines. These inventions transformed the British textile industry and made Britain into the "workshop of the world". The demand for cotton expanded. However, cotton growers in the United States could not satisfy the increased demand because they were limited by their technology to produce sufficient raw cotton to satisfy the demand.

CORN, COTTON AND CHOCOLATE: HOW THE MAYA CHANGED THE WORLD

Eli Whitney, an early American inventor, changed history with an invention for processing cotton. Eli, a 1792 Yale College graduate, was working at a Georgia cotton plantation. Mulberry Grove was the cotton plantation owned by Mrs. Nathanael Greene. Eli was employed by her as a private tutor, working to pay off his educational expenses. During his time on the plantation, Whitney observed the methodologies used for producing cotton and envisioned a machine that would simplify the process of removing seeds from the fibers of upland cotton. The cotton gin made it possible to reduce production time for processing bales of cotton and to profitably cultivate upland cotton.

The invention of the cotton gin by Eli Whitney reduced the cost of cotton production and led to increased cultivation of the plant. Before the development of the cotton gin, cotton fibers had to be tediously separated from the seeds by hand labor. The production of a single bale of cotton required over 600 hours of manpower. This massive amount of labor made large-scale cotton production uneconomical, even with the use of slave labor.

The use of the cotton gin reduced the hours required for production of a bale of cotton. Using the cotton gin, workers could produce a bale of cotton in just a dozen hours. The cotton gin was one of the first critical machines in the Industrial Revolution. This invention enabled an exponential increase in the production of cotton with a corresponding increase in the growth of cotton in the United States.

In 1791, U.S. cotton production was at only 2,000,000 pounds. Several significant factors contributed to the growth of the United States cotton industry. The increasing British demand for product due to industrial innovations, inexpensive land, a growing slave labor force and the invention of the cotton gin.

The cotton gin ("gin" is a short term for engine) enormously expanded the American cotton industry. By 1801 the annual production of cotton had reached over 50 million pounds, and by the early 1830's the United States produced the majority of the world's cotton. Cotton also exceeded the value of all other United States exports combined. The increased demand for cotton cultivation and production increased the slave population in the south from 654,121 in 1790 to 3,954,511 in 1860. Maya cotton, the cotton gin, and the wealth generated by cotton were leading the United States toward Civil War.

MAYA COTTON CREATES AND PROMOTES THE INDUSTRIAL REVOLUTION

The British Industrial Revolution, which improved technology for producing textiles, allowed British merchants to develop an international chain of commerce in which raw cotton fibers were purchased from United States cotton plantations, processed into cotton cloth in the mills of Britain, and then exported on British ships to captive colonial markets.

By the 1840's, India was no longer capable of supplying the vast quantities of cotton fibers required by the demands of the mechanized British factories. Shipping bulky, low-price cotton from India to Britain was a time-consuming and expensive effort. The emergence of American upland cotton offered a superior type of fiber, and coupled with a shorter supply line, encouraged British traders to purchase cotton from the United States. By the mid-19th century, "King Cotton" had become the backbone of the economy of the Southern United States and cultivating, harvesting and producing cotton became the leading commercial product in the United States.

CORN, COTTON AND CHOCOLATE: HOW THE MAYA CHANGED THE WORLD

Maya cotton accelerated the creation of the Industrial Revolution, a technological movement that changed the character of the modern world. The demand for cotton fabric spurred new inventions for textile manufacturing in Britain. Cotton textiles were the key industry driving innovations in all industries and enhanced production during the Industrial Revolution. Numerous new inventions went into use in the early 18th century. The inventions facilitated a tremendous increase in the output of cotton textiles. Because of these machines and improvements made to them, English weavers were producing 200 times more cotton in 1850 than they had in 1780.

The presence of large quantities of coal and iron near the British Midlands was a decisive factor in its rapid industrial growth. The presence of raw materials encouraged industrialization and made the British Midlands into an efficient and profitable manufacturing center. Manpower gave way to waterpower and then to steam power that energized the textile mills. The need for additional power sources to power the textile machines led to the invention of the steam engine. The steam engine, a key player in the Industrial Revolution, was invented by James Watt in 1763. The steam engine was used to power the new machines in British textile mills.

The Industrial Revolution may have begun in Britain but within a few decades it spread to Western Europe and the United States. New England soon developed an important textile industry. It had swift streams for power and a humid climate, which kept cotton fibers in optimal condition for spinning and weaving. The first practical power loom was installed at Waltham, Massachusetts, by Francis Cabot Lowell in 1814. New England was the first area in the United States to industrialize an industry and Maya cotton had a new domestic clientele.

As industry expanded, so did the transportation network needed to move raw materials and finished products. The main innovation in transportation of the nineteenth century was the railroad. In addition, thousands of miles of canals and all-weather roads were built in the nineteenth century.

The Industrial Revolution did not slow down in the late 19th century, it accelerated into the second wave of technology and is now in the third stage of this technological tidal wave. The first Industrial Revolution was centered on textile machinery and steam engine technology. The second Revolution was about steel, railroads, petroleum, the internal combustion engine and electricity. The third or the digital revolution was initiated with the change from analog, mechanical and electronic technology into digital technology. The third wave begat the information age, digital logic circuits and its derived technologies. These include the computer, cellular phones and the internet. The subsequent waves of technological advances were dependent on the inventions that preceded their discovery.

It is difficult to imagine what the world would be like if the effects of the first phase of the Industrial Revolution did not lead to ongoing successful phases of industrial and scientific advancement. Electric lights would be extinguished, satellites and airplanes would vanish. Mobile telephones and digital electronics would disappear. The computer typing this manuscript would not exist. Maya cotton played an important role in the changes initiated by the phases of the Industrial Revolution and its impact on the character of the world. They are all connected. Maya cotton helped invent the internet.

CORN, COTTON AND CHOCOLATE: HOW THE MAYA CHANGED THE WORLD

COTTON AND THE CIVIL WAR CHANGE AMERICAN HISTORY AND GEOGRAPHY

"There was a land of Cavaliers and Cotton Fields called the Old South. Here in this pretty world, gallantry took its last bow… It is a Civilization Gone with the Wind." These words from Margret Mitchell's classic novel summarized the philosophy of the Southern states prior to the Civil War. This was a flawed philosophy that led the south into a conflict that divided the union of the North and the South of the United States.

A historian wrote that the conflicting cultural philosophies of the North and the South could be defined by their reading choices. The gallant Southerner read *Ivanhoe* and the pragmatic northerner read the novels of Charles Dickens. This difference in attitude was an underlying contrast in the thought process of the two cultures. Antebellum life in the south fueled by the riches brought from cotton, slavery, and gallantry were the reasons that led the south into their misguided succession from the Union. Prior to the Civil War, cultivation of cotton using slave labor brought huge profits to the owners of large plantations, making them some of the wealthiest men in the U.S.

In 1860 the Confederate States produced 70 percent of total U.S. exports. Cotton was the primary export of Southern goods either shipped to northern states or exported to Europe. When the war began, cotton accounted for the largest source of cash revenue for the United States Treasury. If the Confederate States were ranked as an independent nation, in 1860, it would have been the fourth richest country in the world. The South felt rich and powerful, their fortunes in cotton and slavery moved them toward secession from the Union and Civil war. This war was the deadliest conflict in United States.

The American Civil War became the milestone that shaped America's historical consciousness. While the American Revolution created the United States, the Civil War determined the composition and character of the nation. The conflict resolved two fundamental questions left unresolved by the American Revolution: whether the United States was to be a dissolvable confederation of sovereign states or an indivisible nation with a sovereign national government; and whether this nation, born of a declaration that all men were created with equal rights, would continue to exist as the largest slaveholding country in the world.

Civil war hostilities began on April 12, 1861, when Confederate forces fired upon Fort Sumter, a Union fort in the harbor of Charleston, South Carolina. President Lincoln called for each state to provide troops to retake the fort. Consequently, four more slave states joined the Confederacy, bringing their total to eleven. The geography of the United States changed in 1863 when West Virginia, a northern state, separated from Virginia, a Confederate state. The entry of Nevada as a state was expedited in 1864. The Union soon controlled the Border States of Delaware, Kentucky, Maryland, and Missouri. In the summer of 1861, the Union blockaded Southern ports and exports of cotton all but ended and the South had to restructure itself to emphasize food production and munitions.

After losing control of its main rivers and ports, the South had to depend on a weak railroad system that, without replacement equipment and the lack of critical maintenance, had crumbled away. The financial infrastructure collapsed during the war as inflation destroyed banks and forced a move toward a barter economy. It was the first true "industrial war" where railroads, the telegraph, steamships and mass-produced weapons were utilized extensively. The massive

CORN, COTTON AND CHOCOLATE: HOW THE MAYA CHANGED THE WORLD

mobilization of civilian factories, mines, shipyards, transportation systems and food supplies foreshadowed future wars.

The results in the Eastern Theater of war were inconclusive in 1861–62. The autumn 1862 Confederate campaign into Maryland ended with the Confederate retreat at Antietam. President Lincoln issued the Emancipation Proclamation on January 1, 1863, declaring that all slaves in the Confederate states would be forever free, which made ending slavery a major goal of the war. In 1863, Confederate General Robert E. Lee's Confederate incursion northward into Pennsylvania ended with the Confederate loss at the Battle of Gettysburg.

The Confederates had assumed that European countries were so dependent on "King Cotton" that they would intervene in the conflict if cotton was withheld from them. This was referred to as Southern "cotton diplomacy". State governments and private citizens voluntarily withheld the crop from the market in hopes of causing a "cotton famine" overseas. Theoretically, widespread shortages would shut down European mills, forcing governments to recognize the Confederacy and perhaps come to the aid of the Southern military.

The "King Cotton" mentality was seriously flawed. First, a bumper cotton crop in 1860 had glutted the marketplace, lowering prices and allowing British mill owners to stockpile the fiber. Cotton prices rose sharply late in 1861, but workers, not owners, suffered from the effects of unemployment. The self-imposed embargo deprived the Confederacy of much-needed revenue. Government bonds were sold and paper money was printed to help minimize the loss, but that only devalued the market and caused prices to soar. Thus, the policy greatly harmed Southern citizens already burdened by the war.

British mills, drawing from their reserves, did not feel the pinch of the cotton shortage until late in 1862, and within a year cotton imports from India, Egypt, and Brazil sufficiently replaced the supply of Southern cotton. Furthermore, Southern society tied the production of cotton inseparably to slavery. England led the abolitionist movement in the world community. This anti-slavery attitude hardened into unassailable neutrality during the war. None of the European countries became involved and none recognized the new Confederate States of America.

The Union was concerned that the Emancipation Proclamation, being a presidential order, would not be strong enough to eliminate slavery. They pushed for a constitutional amendment and they rushed to pass the amendment before the war ended. With the war at an end, the south would be admitted back into the union, their votes would defeat the amendment. The Thirteenth Amendment to the United States Constitution, which outlaws slavery, was passed by the U.S. Senate on April 8, 1864, by the House on January 31, 1865, and adopted on December 6, 1865.

The Union had marshaled its superior resources and manpower to attack the Confederacy from all directions. The Confederate army bravely defended its homeland, but, weakened by years of warfare and a lack of resources, the army failed to defend its territory. The defeats of Southern forces lead to General Lee's surrender of the Confederacy to General Grant on April 9, 1865.

The American Civil War remains the deadliest war in American history resulting in the deaths of an estimated 620,000 soldiers and an undetermined number of civilian casualties. The toll was greater than all the deaths in all other American wars. The long, painful process of rebuilding a united nation free of slavery had begun. Maya cotton was a pawn in the civil war, a valuable commodity that drove the greed and power of Southern aristocracy.

CORN, COTTON AND CHOCOLATE: HOW THE MAYA CHANGED THE WORLD

MAYA COTTON AND THE BRITISH OCCUPATION OF EGYPT

During the American Civil War, American cotton exports slumped due to the Union blockade of Southern ports and the withholding of cotton exports due to Southern "cotton diplomacy". The shortage prompted the main purchasers of cotton, Britain and France, to turn to Egyptian cotton. British and French traders invested heavily in cotton plantations and the Egyptian government took out substantial loans from European bankers to fund the plantations.

After the American Civil War ended in 1865, British and French traders abandoned Egyptian cotton and returned to the less expensive and superior quality of American cotton, sending Egypt into a deficit spiral that led to the country declaring bankruptcy in 1876. This was a key factor leading to Egypt's occupation by the British Empire in 1882. The British army invaded Egypt to protect the interests of British Bankers. Maya Cotton was a key factor in Egypt becoming a pseudo British colony.

MAYA COTTON CREATES LAND GRANT COLLEGES AND TURNS THE USA INTO A SCIENTIFIC SUPERPOWER

The Industrial Revolution, a pivotal point in world history, was born during the 18th century in the British textile industry and has continued into the second and the third phases of the Industrial Revolution. Maya cotton fueled the textile industry and accelerated the technological advances of the first Industrial Revolution. Industrial innovations and its skills spread to other sectors and influenced every aspect of the human condition. Personal income and populations began to exhibit sustained growth and altered the character of the modern world.

The Industrial Revolution kicked off in Great Britain and within a few decades had spread to the United States. The establishment of textile mills in New England initiated industrialization in America. In the early 19th century cotton textile mills began to spring up in the American south. By the time of the American Civil war numerous textile mills populated the eastern seaboard between Massachusetts and Georgia. As the Industrial Revolution expanded in America, textile factories increased the demand for raw cotton and skilled labor, as well as the technical capabilities to design and manufacture textile producing machines and machine tools.

The demand for industrialization increased the need for education and technical skills. The demand for cotton fabric required new inventions for improving the productivity of textile manufacturing. These demands ushered in an imperative for new technical capabilities. The requisite for technological advances was an educational aptitude for enhancing of the Industrial Revolution. Deficiencies in the advancing the industrial process were identified.

Industry and government leaders recognized the growing need for trained technical professionals. Science-based trades were necessary to solve the requirements of an industrialized society. The need for college trained experts in science and engineering was apparent to America's business and government leaders. Their decision to create a college system elevated U.S. technological capabilities above the rest of the world developed the USA into a scientific superpower.

Existing American universities did not include science, engineering or agricultural sciences in their curriculum. They offered a classical or "literate" education for the wealthy elite; this privileged sector represented less than 1% of the population. With few exceptions, these "ivory

CORN, COTTON AND CHOCOLATE: HOW THE MAYA CHANGED THE WORLD

tower" institutions did not want to sully their hands with technologically based curriculums. While not requiring a classical education, the new type of technical professionals was vital for solving the real needs of an industrial society. This was a need for a new type of education, the creation of professional technical disciplines that did not exist in classical curriculums.

The lack of available technical and scientific education not only deprived the nation of essential technological talents, but the lack of an inexpensive college education deprived the children of the working-class access to a professional career and a better life. Leaders in the United States Senate determined that the nation must develop a university system that would provide technically trained professionals for the support of an industrialized society. This concept initiated the implementation of the land-grant college system. The history of the land-grant college system is interwoven with the advance of America as a technological giant. The land-grant college system is considered to be an historic breakthrough in higher education. Maya cotton created the need for technicians to design and maintain the textile industry and begat the land-grant college system.

The land-grant system began in 1862 with a piece of legislation known as the Morrill Act. This law gave the states ownership of public lands, with the proviso that the lands would be sold or used for profit with the monetary proceeds used to establish at least one college in that state. This act of congress established colleges with the intention that they would teach mechanical and agriculture engineering. Over the past 160 years these colleges and universities have become more than technical schools, they have grown and are among the leading universities in the world. The original intent of the law was to satisfy a rapidly industrializing nation's need for scientifically trained technicians. However, they grew into international giants of learning in science and engineering.

In response to the Morrill act, a new kind of university was created and the land grant-university became the most unique part of the 19th century public university movement. The land-grant university in its mature form became devoted to science and education in the service of society.

Arnold Toynbee, the British historian, once observed that the land-grant idea is the one original contribution of American higher education to the world. The fabled Mr. Toynbee, was writing in the 19th century, but if he was working today, he would now recognize additional contributions of the land grant college system to higher education.

The influence of the land-grant colleges on American higher education has been formidable. Pioneering research, has been carried out at these colleges, including advances in physics, aerospace sciences, digital sciences, medicine, bioengineering and agricultural science among other disciplines. Nearly two-thirds of all doctoral degrees are awarded by land-grant universities.

Sixty-nine land-grant colleges have been founded since the initiation of the law; these colleges include some of the world's leading centers of learning. University of California at Berkley, Georgia Institute of technology, Cornell University, Purdue University, Massachusetts Institute of Technology, Ohio State University, the University of Illinois (Urbana), and the University of Wisconsin (Madison) are among the best-known land-grant schools.

The land-grant college system was a direct result of the Industrial Revolution. This educational system has turned America into the scientific giant that put man on the moon and is leading the research for the digital revolution in the 21st century. Its graduates have become Presidents and Nobel Prize laureates; they have walked on the moon and constitute the corpus of leading scientists in the world. Maya cotton was the fuse that ignited the U.S. into a Technological giant and sustained the Industrial Revolution.

MAYA COTTON AS FASHIONISTA

Maya cotton has become king once again. It is the favorite textile of the 21st century. Denim, for instance, has become the favorite cloth for a wide range of consumers from cowboys to debutantes. The popularity of cotton denim jeans has evolved and blossomed from the mid-19th century denim work pants of Levi Strauss to the designer jeans of Calvin Klein. A pair of Levis has the status of a movie star. John Wayne would never have been the ultimate hero without his ever-present blue jeans. James Dean, a born rebel and anti-hero was attracted to this fashion. Both juvenile tough guys and altar boys emulated the cowboy way and the sale of jeans skyrocketed.

The popularity of jeans blossomed with the advent of designer jeans. The trip from Levi Strauss to Calvin Klein was a short voyage. The difference in the quality of a $20 pair of Wal-Mart jeans and a pair of $240 Calvin Klein jeans is minute. The actual difference lies in the thought process for selecting the more expensive pair. That is the difference between a label whore and a smart shopper. "Levis" said, Bill Blass "are the single best apparel item ever designed". Calvin Klein added: "Jeans are about sex".

In the 1980s, cotton soared back to claim 60% of the U.S. market. However, barely a yard is woven within the USA. Cotton is still in demand as a cultivar but it is all but defunct as an American made textile product. Blue jeans are now an international favorite as clothing, but they are all American. Conceived in the Yucatán and born in the USA.

COTTON AND COTTONSEED OIL

The by-product of cotton processing, cottonseed was considered virtually worthless before the late 19th century. Separating the seed hull from the seed meat proved difficult and most of these ventures failed within a few years. This problem was resolved in 1857, when William Fee invented a huller, which effectively separated the tough hulls from the meats of cottonseed. With this invention, cottonseed oil began to be used for illumination purposes in oil lamps as a substitute for expensive whale oil. But by 1859, this use came to end as the petroleum industry emerged and kerosene became more practical.

Through patented technology, the Procter and Gamble Company hydrogenated cottonseed oil and developed a substance that closely resembled lard. In 1911, Proctor and Gamble launched the first modern mass-marketing campaign to publicize its new product, Crisco, a solid vegetable shortening that could be used in place of lard.

In 1899 David Wesson, a food chemist, developed deodorized cottonseed oil, Wesson Oil. Wesson Oil was marketed heavily and became quite popular. Cottonseed oil has become a popular solid and liquid cooking oil.

In the mid to late 2000s, the consumer trend of avoiding trans-fats, and mandatory labeling of trans fats in some jurisdictions, sparked an increase in the consumption of cottonseed oil, with

CORN, COTTON AND CHOCOLATE: HOW THE MAYA CHANGED THE WORLD

some health experts and public health agencies recommending it as a healthy oil. Crisco and other producers have been able to reformulate cottonseed oil so it contains little to no trans-fats. In the 21st century, Cottonseed oil is considered a high-quality oil that is used as cooking oil, vegetable oil, margarine, mayonnaise, sauces, salad dressing, marinades, and biodiesel fuel. Maya cotton has produced another winner.

MAYA COTTON AND ITS PART IN CHANGING HISTORY

Maya cotton is the world's favorite fiber. This cultivar has changed history more than any other Maya cultivar. It initiated the Industrial revolution, started the Civil War and increased slavery in the US. If that was not enough it was the inspiration for the land-grant college system that made the USA into a technological superpower. It now clothes 90% of the world's population and is a fashionista leading the way as the iconic material for blue jeans.

CORN, COTTON AND CHOCOLATE: HOW THE MAYA CHANGED THE WORLD

CHAPTER 13: HENEQUEN

Botanical name: *agave sisalana* **Maya word:** *kih*.

Memories of a youth

In our neighborhood, we were familiar with ropes made from henequen. These fiber ropes were used to lash together all types of items or to tie things up. They were the typical type of ropes used in our small town. Our Boy Scout troop practiced tying multiple types of knots that was part of our bag of tricks. That that is until my grandfather brought the "mother of all ropes" to our little town. This large fiber cable set a new standard for ropes in our community.

My grandfather lived in upstate New York on the shores of Lake Erie. Before he retired, his body was worn out by working in a shipbuilding yard. After he retired, this native of Ireland would spend the winter months living with my family in the mild climate of Georgia. My grandfather traveled south on a railroad train, the train arrived at Terminal Station in downtown Atlanta. We would meet his train at the station and transport him home to our little town.

On one occasion we met him on a Sunday afternoon at Terminal Station and picked up his checked luggage. He walked with a cane because of his degraded bodily condition. Grandfather usually traveled with a single suitcase, but on this trip, he had two suitcases.

He pointed his cane at the smaller of the two. "There," he said. "Boyo, you carry that one because it contains something special for you".

Wow! I was excited. I had no idea what secret was contained in the mystery suitcase. I could not wait to get home to open the suitcase. When we finally arrived home, I could not wait to look inside the suitcase. I placed the mystery suitcase in the middle of the living room floor. I unlocked the clasps and opened the lid. The open suitcase revealed my surprise. What was it? What was I looking at? I observed what appeared to be a coiled-up fiber object that had a 2-inch thickness. I had never seen anything like the object in the suitcase.

I looked at my grandfather. "What is it, grandfather?"

He laughed and reached into the suitcase. He grabbed a section of the object and pulled it out. It was amazing. The thing in the suitcase came out rapidly and stretched out across the floor. It was a rope, a very large rope. It was 2 inches thick and very long. I'd never seen such a rope.

"It's a rope," I shouted to my grandfather," It's the biggest rope I've ever seen."

"This big rope is called a hawser, Boyo", he answered in his Irish brogue. "They are used to tow and tie down big ships. It's made from henequen grown in the Yucatán, and it's an especially strong rope."

I was amazed. I took the end of the hawser from my grandfather's hand and dragged the long rope across the floor. When the other end of the rope came out of the suitcase it was over 20 feet long. What a treasure, a 20-foot-long rope with a 2-inch diameter and it was all mine. My next thought was what I could do with such a thick long rope. Its purpose had to be something special because the hawser was special.

The solution for the use of the hawser came quickly. Our backyard was adjacent to a black-water swamp complete with pools of water and lots of black mud. An embankment at the edge

CORN, COTTON AND CHOCOLATE: HOW THE MAYA CHANGED THE WORLD

of our yard was on the border of the swamp. An oak tree growing on the embankment possessed a large limb that extended over the swamp. That was a perfect combination. A 20-foot-long Hawser, a swamp full of water and mud plus an overhanging oak limb.

The geometric arrangement was perfect. We fastened Hawser to the limb. So that when we launched ourselves from the top of the bank, we were able to cross over the swamp and swing safely back to the bank. We had created a great thrill ride and made perfect use of my grandfather's gift from Lake Erie.

The first day went well and my sisters and I enjoyed the ride, swinging over the swampy water and arcing back to the bank. On the second day, word had spread and the lineup of neighborhood kids, who were potential swamp rope riders, grew longer. We welcomed all the neighborhood kids to our amazing attraction. Before someone used this swing, we gave them a short course on hanging onto the hawser. We had tied a knot at the bottom of the rope which provided the rope rider with a foothold to hang on to during the swinging action. The rider could swing out over the swamp and then on their return, we would catch and steady them on the bank.

Well, everything was going smoothly until Bobby Wooten showed up. Bobby had a great flair for screwing things up. When his turn to came to swing, I warned him to hang on tight and to support his feet on the knot. I had a bad feeling when Bobby began his outward swing. As the swing reached the top of its arc, showing off, he swung his legs outward and let out a rebel yell.

"Bobby," I yelled. "Put your feet back on the knot!" All I got in return was a snaggle-tooted grin, and then he let out a terrified yell as his hands began to slide down the rope. The next thing we knew Bobby was falling through space and the rope was swinging back toward the bank without a rider. Bobby's legs splayed through the air and he landed smack dab in the middle of deep black swamp mud.

When the huge splash of mud and water made by Bobby's body cleared away, there was Bobby stuck up to his thighs in the black mud. The next thing we hear is Bobby crying and screaming for his mother. The sobbing was not so bad until Bobby discovered he could not move. He was completely imbedded in deep mud and was completely immobilized. Boy, that's when he really started to scream for his mother.

I knew we had to rescue Bobby in order to shut him up. I grabbed a long stick and slid down the embankment to the level of the swamp. The first thing I discovered was that the stick was a not long enough to reach Bobby's outstretched hand. Rats, I knew I had to enter the swamp mud to rescue Bobby. To make a long story short, I had to wade in ankle deep in my sneakers to reach Bobby and pull him out of the mud of the swamp.

When we finally got Bobby up on the bank he was completely covered with mud and he had lost both his shoes from the suction of the mud. He was crying hysterically about being caught in the mud, being covered in thick black mud and losing his shoes to the mud. He looked like the tar baby in the Uncle Remus story.

With Bobby rescued, dirty but unharmed, everybody relaxed. Then, somebody started laughing. The laughter was infectious, although covered in mud myself I begin to laugh. As the laughter ramped up, Bobbie cried harder. He then got up and ran, mud covered and barefoot, toward his house. I knew we were in for trouble because Mrs. Wooten was a mean woman who was vocal in her defense of her Bobby.

CORN, COTTON AND CHOCOLATE: HOW THE MAYA CHANGED THE WORLD

Well, that was the end of my marvelous swamp swing. Mrs. Wooten stormed up to our house and caught my mother unaware. Mrs. Wooten claimed that we were trying to kill her little Bobby, and that our swing was the devil's instrument and could have killed her son. Much to the chagrin of the neighborhood children, we were directed to take down the marvelous swing from the limb,

That was the end of our marvelous adventure of being able to swing over the swamp. An adventure that started in Yucatán with a cultivar created by Maya agronomists and finished with disappointed children.

THE MAYA AND HENEQUEN

The Maya have been cultivating, harvesting, and utilizing the agave plant for 9,000 years. The agave plant is the source of henequen. The earliest known evidence of henequen usage dates from 8,500 BC. Maya agronomists cultivated the henequen plant and it was used for food and for everyday uses. These plants render a strong flexible fiber that can be woven into a multitude of practical applications.

The Maya exploited the agave and discovered a myriad of purposes for all parts of the plant. The long sword shaped leaves and the stalks were used as a source of all manner of products. They ranged from an impenetrable roofing thatch for dwellings, producing thread for sewing, fiber for cloth, making strong cords for rope. Pins and needles were made from the thorns at the extremity of its leaves, and when properly cooked, the agave was converted into a nutritious food.

THE MAYA USE OF THE AGAVE AS FOOD

The agave was a major source of food for the Maya. Four major parts of the agave plant are edible: the flowers, the leaves, the stalks, and the sap. The sap is sweet and is used as a sweetener in cooking.

Each agave plant will produce several pounds of edible flowers. The stalks, which are ready to be eaten during the summer, before they blossom, weigh several pounds each. Roasted, they are sweet and can be chewed to extract the sweet sap. The leaves may be collected for eating in winter and spring, when the plants are rich in sap. The stems of the plant, when properly cooked, can be converted into a palatable and nutritious food.

AGAVE AS MEDICINE

A tea or tincture made from the leaf and taken orally is used to treat constipation, relive excess gas, treat arthritic joints and used as a diuretic. It is also used to make "*licor del henequen*", a traditional Maya alcoholic drink.

AGAVE FABRICATED INTO ROPE

The most popular use for henequen is rope making. The leaves of agave yield a strong fiber that was used in the production of rope. The agave plant was a useful cultivar that served the Maya for thousands of years and was the principal source of strong rope for construction and maritime purposes. The henequen fiber is produced by the leaves of *Agave fourcroydes.*

The archaeological record depicts the Maya using henequen rope for practical and ceremonial applications. They were creative in their use of the rope as a tool for construction, as part of a

CORN, COTTON AND CHOCOLATE: HOW THE MAYA CHANGED THE WORLD

load transporting system and as a device for self-sacrifice. The strength, durability, and resistance to deterioration in saltwater made henequen the perfect vegetable fiber for rope. Multiple applications of rope are exhibited in Maya works of art including murals, sculpture, ceramic figures and painted vases.

The raw fibers from the henequen plant are collected and shredded in order to fabricate ropes. When the plant is shredded, it is yellow and wet. After a few hours under the hot sun, it dries and it turns a white color. The fiber is pulled into alignment and then interwoven in a spiral weave and made into rope. The finished rope varies in size from fine strands used for making hammocks to large diameter ropes used in construction.

THE MAYA USE OF ROPE IN CONSTRUCTION

The Maya had multiple ways to use rope as a construction tool. It was used for its strength, durability and its elastic properties. Rope was applied to pull and to lift heavy loads and as a high strength material of construction.

Large diameter rope was used for vertical hoisting of heavy building stones and other materials during the construction process. Ropes were used for transporting construction components and stone from the quarries. Large stonework for construction use were shaped into cylinders and rolled by pulling ropes in a "come along" system.

Rope was used in the construction of the *nah*, the traditional Maya house. The structure of the house consists of timbers which were made up of diagonal roof trusses and the vertical members. The connections of the timbers consisted of thin henequen cords lashed around adjacent members to bind them together.

This rope trussing technique was also used to construct wood framed scaffolding for construction applications. The vertical and horizontal timber framing of the scaffolding is lashed together with rope at intersecting connections. A similar construction method was applied for the erection of siege towers for war. The siege towers were used by Maya Warriors in attacking a walled city. These are depicted in murals at the Temple of the Warriors at Chichen Itza.

THE MAYA USE OF NAUTICAL ROPES

The Maya were blue sea sailors. They built and sailed large sea going vessels that were the backbone of their trading network. The seagoing vessels were 80 feet long and eight feet wide. The craft was powered by thirty paddlers and carried up to 23 tons of cargo. The sailors used ropes for various nautical purposes. Rope was used to tie down the cargo and other purposes including mooring the craft and for towing lines.

Smaller craft plied the rivers and used rope for mooring stability on rivers. Boats had to be securely moored on long lines so the boats would not float away in the current. The length of ropes used by Maya canoe men probably varied from 15 feet (5 meter) lines to simple tie-offs. Ropes were used to tow the craft up rapids on rivers with swift flowing water.

THE USE OF ROPE IN MAYA RITUALS

The Maya took advantage of the flexibility and elasticity of rope in their rituals and religious ceremonies. The use of rope was a standard instrument in self-sacrifice ritual and in rituals attendant to the treatment of high-ranking prisoners of war. Prisoners were tied up with ropes

CORN, COTTON AND CHOCOLATE: HOW THE MAYA CHANGED THE WORLD

after a successful battle also provided victims for sacrifice, presumably to propitiate whatever deity had promised victory.

The Maya site of Yaxchilan offers a particularly rich gallery of images about bloodletting rituals. In a series of three door lintels from this site, a royal woman, Lady Xoc, is portrayed performing bloodletting, piercing her tongue with a rope embedded with thorns and provoking a vision serpent.

HENEQUEN FIBERS WOVEN INTO CLOTH

Agave fibers were used to fabricate a heavy fabric. Cloth can be woven from the fine fibers found at the growing tip of the bud. The fibers were woven on a back-strap loom into panels of henequen fabric. These panels were called *sakal* in Mayan.

The henequen panel can be integrated with other woven panels to develop a garment or other cloth product. The Maya used the agave to make needles, as well as thread for sewing and connecting weaving panels.

HENEQUEN AND THE TUMPLINE

The Maya used henequen rope to augment their land transportation methods. They used a device known as a *mecapal* or tumpline for transporting goods over jungle trails and roads. A tumpline consists of strap connected to a rope net. The strap, woven of henequen fibers, is placed over the forehead and the strap is then connected to a net of woven fibers to carry a heavy load. Transporting loads using the tumpline was the method for hauling a load over steep mountain trails. This type of transport is still used today by the Maya to carry many types of loads.

THE FABULOUS MAYA HAMMOCK

The Maya used henequen fiber to make their ubiquitous hammocks. Their hammock is used for sleeping and is hung from the timber structure in their houses. The Maya considered the hammock to be a gift of the gods.

These clever devices are strong and serviceable. They are perfectly suited for tropical climates. The open weave of the hammock elevated above the floor provides full body air circulation for the sleeping person. The hammock hanging from a timber support separates the sleeper from crawling insects.

A well-made matrimonial version, for a couple sleeping together, will easily hold up to 600 pounds or more due to the unique diamond-like weave. A tighter weave will give more comfort and support. Columbus brought the hammock back to Europe, and the Maya hammock has spread around the world. The navies of the world owe their famous naval hammocks to Maya inventiveness.

THE MAYA BUILD THE LONGEST BRIDGE IN THE ANCIENT WORLD

The Maya pulled off one the most significant feats of engineering in ancient history. They constructed the long span suspension bridge at the ancient City of Yaxchilan using their rope fiber technology.

The ancient Maya city of Yaxchilan is situated within an omega shaped oxbow formed by the powerful Usumacinta River. The omega shaped bend in the river is so severe that only a narrow

CORN, COTTON AND CHOCOLATE: HOW THE MAYA CHANGED THE WORLD

strip of land stands between the two banks of the river at the narrow neck. Six months a year the river is in a wildly surging flood stage creating a 200-meter-wide turbulent barrier around the city. The broad swirling river embraces the oxbow and converts this magnificent city into an isolated "island", its perimeter almost entirely bounded by water.

The Maya built a three-span suspension bridge across the mighty Usumacinta River at the ancient city of Yaxchilan. This bridge was the lifeline for that city and assured a year-round method of traversing the broad river.

This lifeline was an ingenious feat of Maya technology and engineering that may prove to be their most creative engineering project. This was a structure that was destined to be recognized as the longest bridge in the ancient world.

Engineering historian Dr. Neil Fitzsimmons researched and developed a record of the construction of bridges throughout history. A review of Dr. Fitzsimons records indicates that the Maya bridge at Yaxchilan, constructed in the seventh century, was the longest bridge in the world until 1377, when Italians built a stone bridge over the Adda River at Trezzo Italy.

HENEQUEN SPREADS ACROSS THE PLANET

Spaniards introduced the *henequen* fiber to Europe before 1560. The fiber became popular and was a mainstay with navies across the world. The strength of henequen ropes made them invaluable as mooring lines and sheets for sailing ships. In addition, the ropes were resistant to deterioration from microorganisms found in saltwater. The agave plant was considered by the Spanish to be too valuable to share with other countries. Their ability to plant and grow the Maya cultivar was not shared with the world.

Keeping the plant safe at home had the blessing of the Spanish colonial government. However, their plans were foiled and the protected agave plant was purloined and spirited away during the colonial period. The plant was taken from the Yucatán to the state of Florida in 1836. The plants growing in Florida were the basis of the agave that has spread to tropical areas around the world. The smuggled plants were the start of all agave plantations in Africa, South America, the Caribbean, and Asia.

Henequen was an important export of the Yucatán as early as the colonial period, but was never exported on a large-scale due to the lack of shredding machinery. The invention of shredding machines in the late 19th century revolutionized henequen processing and led to a boom of prosperity in the region. Commercial interest in henequen was stimulated by the development of the mechanical grain binder in the 1800s and the grain binder required a low-cost twine. The sales of henequen soared.

In the 19th century, cultivation of the agave started in the Caribbean islands and Brazil, as well as to countries in Africa and Asia. The first commercial plantings in Brazil were made in the late 1930s and the first fiber exports from there were made in 1948. It was not until the 1960s that Brazilian production accelerated and the first of many spinning mills was established. Today, Brazil is the major world producer of henequen.

WORLD PRODUCTION OF HENEQUEN

CORN, COTTON AND CHOCOLATE: HOW THE MAYA CHANGED THE WORLD

The Yucatán may be the home of the agave, a Maya cultivar, but the species has spread to many tropical countries. The species is now grown in Mexico, as well as in Brazil, Ecuador, Spain, Libya, Morocco, Madagascar, China, India, Pakistan, Nepal, Burma, Cambodia, Thailand, Queensland, Hawaii, Florida, Central America, and the West Indies.

Global production of the fiber amounts to 240 thousand tons. Brazil is the largest producing country. Henequen occupies 6th place in the world among fiber plants, cotton is in first place, representing 2% of world production. Following is the listing of producing countries and metric tonnage produced in that country.

TOP HENEQUEN PRODUCING COUNTRIES IN THE WORLD

THOUSANDS OF METRIC TONS

RANK	COUNTRY	PRODUCTION
1	Brazil	113.3
2	Tanzania	36.9
3	People's Republic of China	34.0
4	Kenya	27.6
5	Madagascar	9.1
6	Haiti	2.2
7	South Africa	1.6
	WORLD TOTAL	**240.7**

GREEN GOLD MAKES THE YUCATAN RICH AND POWERFUL

Henequen created an amazing boom for the Yucatán, Yucatán became similar to Camelot. It changed the wealth of the area, then the bubble burst and everything new was old again.

Henequen was always an important export for the Yucatán, but its demand exploded in the 19th century. At that time, the International Harvester company developed a mechanical harvester that revolutionized wheat production in the United States. They found that twine made from henequen was ideal for mechanically bundling wheat. Demand for Yucatán's henequen exploded, the export of henequen made millionaires of the hacienda owners.

Wealth from the fiber became known as "Green Gold". In the late 19th century and the early 20th century, the area surrounding Mérida prospered from the production of henequen. For a brief period, around the turn of the 20th century, Mérida was said to be the home to more millionaires than any other city in the world.

Prior to the boom in green gold, the old haciendas in the Yucatán were devoting their efforts to the cultivation of sugar cane, maize, and cattle ranching. When they discovered the potential of henequen as a versatile fiber, they became very rich and their lifestyle changed dramatically.

The exploitation of the fiber brought wealth and splendor to the Yucatán. The arrival of this new wealth saw a notorious growth of the city. Rich citizens of Mérida became Eurocentric, leaving behind their dusty and neglected buildings and overseeing the construction of luxurious mansions. The architects of the buildings were from Europe. The ladies sent their dry cleaning to Europe and the money kept flowing until the boom ran out.

CORN, COTTON AND CHOCOLATE: HOW THE MAYA CHANGED THE WORLD

Once the time of the green gold passed into history, life in Mérida returned to its provincial tranquility. Slowly Mérida grew into a small and picturesque city, it lost the desire for universality. Now, Mérida is a destination for tourists as a Colonial City. The result of this fleeting concentration of wealth can still be seen today. Many large and elaborate homes line the main avenue called Paseo de Montejo, though few are occupied today by individual families. Many of these homes have been restored and now serve as office buildings for banks and insurance companies. Today, this area, once the home of millionaires, is home to restaurants, trendy dance clubs, and expensive hotels.

YUCATAN GREEN GOLD HIRES THE TEXAS NAVY TO FIGHT OFF MEXICO

The Yucatán was a Mexican territory in 1841. While it was a part of the Mexican Republic it still did not have the status of a state. Mexico's Yucatán Territory and the Texas Territory conspired to succeed from Mexico. The Yucatán had several reasons to be an independent country. It felt like a red headed stepchild, it was the most southern part of Mexico and more than 1000 miles distant from Mexico City. Thus, it received little support from the capital. It was unconnected to the major body of Mexico. Reaching the Yucatán by land was nearly impossible due to the dense jungles. Sailing ships were the only method of communication and contact with the nation's capital.

The Yucatán had a great amount of wealth from the cultivation and sale of the product known as "green gold". This was the name given to henequen, the invaluable Maya cultivar. Henequen provided of 90% of the world's supply of the high strength fiber that wove strong rope for mooring ocean ships, cordage for rigging ships, and burlap sacks for agriculture. Most important, the Yucatán with its Maya cultural heritage was fiercely independent.

Texas succeeded from Mexico in 1836 and was followed by the Yucatán in 1841. The Yucatán fortified its defensive position by retaining the Republic of Texas navy to patrol its coast. In September 1841, Texas made a deal with the Republic of the Yucatán. The Republic of Yucatán would pay $8000 a month for the services of three Texas warships to defend the Yucatán against raids from the Mexican navy. It was determined that the Republic of Texas and the Republic of Yucatán would split the proceeds from any prizes seized in the naval battles. Records indicate that the Texas navy wreaked havoc upon Mexican shipping and warships.

During the period of independence, the Republic of the Yucatán considered annexation by the United States. The bill approving the annexation passed the U.S. House but was defeated by the U.S. Senate.

In 1847, a Maya rebellion, known as the War of the Castes, was successfully challenging the internal security of the Republic of the Yucatán. The Republic of Yucatán required assistance in controlling the war and contacted several countries for armed assistance. Unsuccessful with assistance from foreign countries the Republic turned to Mexico. They committed to rejoining Mexico, if Mexico sent armed reinforcement in the War of the Castes.

In August 1848, the Mexican Army assisted the Yucatán in putting down the Maya revolt and ended the caste war. With the caste war over and the Yucatán back in the folds of Mexico. The Texas navy retired from the field. Henequen, the Maya cultivar that made the Yucatán immensely rich had also provided the funds to hire the Texas navy for its defense. Henequen and its riches, plus the Lone Star of Texas, achieved a place in history.

CORN, COTTON AND CHOCOLATE: HOW THE MAYA CHANGED THE WORLD

THE WORLD INNOVATES AND FINDS NEW USES FOR HENEQUEN

Once the fiber from the Maya cultivar spread across the globe its uses have greatly expanded. Applications grew from making rope and general cordage to a multitude of other uses. Henequen is used in low-cost and specialty paper, dartboards, filters, geotextiles, mattresses, carpets, handicrafts, and wire rope cores. The fiber is utilized as a strengthening agent in composite materials for applications including the automobile industry.

Three grades of henequen are utilized for various purposes. The lower-grade fiber is used by the paper industry due to its high content of cellulose. The medium-grade fiber is used for making ropes, baler and binder twine. The higher-grade fiber is converted into yarns and used by the carpet industry.

Agave nectar (agave syrup) is a sweetener commercially produced from agave. Agave syrup is sweeter than honey and tends to be less viscous than honey.

YOU WANT YOUR LIQUOR WHERE?

The ancient Maya loved their alcohol. However, available booze drinks made from agave were so harsh on the stomach that they infused them into their bodies by using enemas. Archaeological iconography has verified that the Maya were consumers of pulque, an alcoholic drink made from agave plants. The Maya even had a god for pulque, the Maya deity *Akan*.

The Classic Maya drink called pulque or *chih*. Translated Maya codices reference that agave plants were well-known and familiar to the Maya. This was in addition to their use of the plant as fiber.

The flavor of pulque is sweet and slightly astringent. Allowed to age, it starts to ferment and changes into a milky white color with low alcohol content. In moderate amounts pulque is nutritional and stimulating, but in larger amounts can cause the same havoc produced by any alcoholic drink.

TEQUILA, THE SON OF PULQUE

Pulque was the precursor of tequila. The Maya or other pre-Columbian culture did know of tequila because tequila is the product of the distillation of pulque. Tequila was first produced in the 16th century, when Spanish conquistadors ran out of their own brandy and began to distill agave to produce North America's first indigenous distilled spirits.

Why is tequila not known as a product of the Yucatán? Mexican laws state that tequila can only be produced in the state of Jalisco and some towns in nearby states. Tequila has been granted a pedigree by the European Union. It has been a protected designation of origin product in the European Union since 1997.

TEQUILA IS USUALLY BOTTLED IN ONE OF FIVE CATEGORIES

In recent years, tequila has become a gentleman's drink. The old days of tossing back a shot of the old-style *Blanco* tequila, followed by a pinch of salt and a squeeze of lime are gone with the wind. Now, aged in wood barrels, that were once used to age bourbon, tequila has become a smooth tasteful drink but it still has its famous kick. Tequila is now produced in five categories:

CORN, COTTON AND CHOCOLATE: HOW THE MAYA CHANGED THE WORLD

Blanco (white): White spirits, un-aged and bottled or stored immediately after distillation or aged less than two months in stainless steel or neutral oak barrels

Joven (gold): Un-aged silver tequila that may be flavored with caramel coloring, oak extractor sugar-based syrup or could also be the result of blending silver tequila with aged or extra-aged tequila.

Reposado (rested): Aged a minimum of two months, but less than a year in oak barrels.

Añejo (aged) Aged a minimum of one year, but less than three years in small oak barrels

Extra Añejo (extra aged): Aged a minimum of three years in oak barrels.

THE POPULARITY OF TEQUILA

Over 100 Mexican distilleries distill over 900 brands of tequila and over 2,000 brand names have been registered. The production of tequila was 235 million liters in 2015. The USA is the largest consumer of the elixir, with 156 million liters followed by Spain with 4 million drinkers. Looks like the USA loves their margaritas. The Maya cultivar has changed the drinking habits of the world.

HOW HENEQUEN HELPED CHANGE WORLD HISTORY

Henequen was a mainstay with navies across the world. During the day of sailing ships, it was the most popular fiber for ropes used on ships. The strength of Henequen ropes made them invaluable as mooring lines and cordage for sailing ships. The fiber of the agave plant made the Yucatán rich as "Green Gold" and hired the Texas Navy to guard its shores. Tequila is produced from agave, and is a favorite liquor of people around the world.

CORN, COTTON AND CHOCOLATE: HOW THE MAYA CHANGED THE WORLD

CHAPTER 14: MAIZE

Botanical name: *Zea mays* **Maya name:** *ixi im*

Memories of a youth

Summer days seemed to last forever. Each day contained 24 hours just like other days of the year, but daylight hours in the summer seemed to last much longer. I magnified the potential of summer time by spending each day with a group of my best friends. We got out early in the morning, because we knew we were bound to be home by dark.

Our system of time management produced long summer days of fun and companionship. We were four close friends, bonded by personal friendships and by being fellow Boy Scouts. We were a true band of brothers. Our summer days were spent as a team. There was John, Murray and two Jimmy's, of which I was one.

Our greatest adventures seemed to be during our hikes up to Black Jack Mountain. This was a 5-mile trek from our little town to the summit of the mountain. We would rise early and be on the road by eight in the morning. Traveling light, all we all wore surplus WWII army equipment.

Everything was war surplus, our basic equipment included a utility belt with grommet holes for connecting our canteens, sheath knives and pouches. Our provisions for the day would include water in our canteens, Irish potatoes and if someone had a nickel we would buy a can of pork and beans. We also knew that we would supplement our provisions along our line of march.

We were quite familiar with our route. If we had to fill our canteens, there was a farmhouse near the four-lane highway with a wonderfully cool spring. We knew the family in the house, but we would always knock on the door to ask permission to fill our canteens at their springhouse. We asked because that was the accepted and polite procedure. Besides, as Boy Scouts and young Southern gentleman, we were conditioned to conduct ourselves in a courteous manner.

After crossing the paved four-lane highway, we entered a landscape of farms and heavily wooded pine forests. Our treks lead eastward to our mountain destination. We walked along the dirt road, passing farms growing corn and other vegetables. Our only stop along the way was to supplement our provisions. One of the farms along the route was bisected by a small creek. The stream crossed the dirt road by passing under a small bridge.

Our maneuver used to supplement our provisions was what we thought was a clever bit of deflection and misdirection. The farm raised sweet corn. Our goal was to collect four ears of that delicious yellow corn for our lunch. Our proven routine for collection of the corn was what we thought was a brilliant methodology. My band of brothers would dawdle on the bridge appearing to be interested in something in the water below. While I, being the swiftest afoot, would pull off an end run for our "corn caper". I would slip into the depressed creek bed and make a speedy run to the nearest stand of the sweetest and juiciest corn.

This was a small creek with a flow of water that was a mere three feet in width, it meandered between sand bars bordering the flow. I would jump down onto a sand bar and use the sandbars to speed along the creek. Of course, like all boys of that time, I was equipped with high top black canvas sneakers. They were my treasured PF Flyers. I had a great advantage with these magic shoes, they were guaranteed "to make a kid run faster and jump higher". My dash carried me past the watermelon patch and toward the tall stand of sweet yellow corn.

CORN, COTTON AND CHOCOLATE: HOW THE MAYA CHANGED THE WORLD

As I made the run, I bent over to keep a low profile. I did not want to alert the farmer working in the adjacent field. Leaping from sandbar to sandbar, I literally sailed over the water of the stream. It was important to keep my PF Flyers as dry as possible. The tall stand of corn gave me excellent cover from the farmers' view and an opportunity to climb out of the creek bed. I would slither along the ground between the corn stalks until, I spied some excellent prospects for "roastin' ears", as the delicious grain was called in my Southern patois.

I would then quickly reach up and collect four succulent ears of corn for our lunch. Securing the corn in my rucksack, I would retrace my route. Slithering back into the creek and repeat my acrobatic run. Running and jumping on my incoming footprints, I returned to the bridge and my waiting team who were casually working their misdirection techniques. Arriving at the bridge I casually climbed up into the center of my cohorts. We, then, casually strolled away and continued our trek to the mountain, now supplied with delicious sweet corn.

The total hike took less than 2 hours and it was well before noon when we arrived at the summit. Black Jack Mountain was not a tall mountain. The geologic formation was a mere 300 feet above the surrounding flat lands. However, the summit boasted a clear spring fed pond, heavy pine forests, and a 360° view of the surrounding countryside. This was a grand place to spend a summer day.

Arriving at the summit, we would make camp and start a cooking fire. We would while away the time while the fire burned down to coals. We would swim in the pond, try our luck at catching frogs, played mumblety-peg, and pick a canteen cup full of sweet black berries for our lunch. It would take an hour or so for the fire to burn down to the coals. We would then place our ears of corn and potatoes onto the hot coals for the appropriate cooking time. We would warm up the pork and beans in a canteen cup.

When dinnertime arrived (lunch was called dinner in the day), the corn and potatoes were properly charred and the pork and beans were ready. The band of brothers would then share our wonderful meal. Back in those blissful summer days as a youth doing things that other boys could only dream about, lunch conversation would be minimal and a consist of thought provoking comments like, "it doesn't get any better than this" and "I'm just glad to be here".

However, my most memorable thought about our adventures was crunching down on that first juicy bite on the plump kernels of the sweet yellow corn and enjoying the sugary juice of the kernels. I often think of those long summer days of my youth and the sweet unforgettable taste of Maya maize. Little did I know how maize had changed the world as well as my life.

MAYA AND MAIZE: THEIR GREATEST INVENTION

Maya agronomists performed a feat of genetic magic when they developed a native grass, *tenosinte*, into a high-yielding grain. This transformation from an inconspicuous grass to a highly evolved and productive food plant is a story of co-evolution and interdependence between humans and maize that spans thousands of years. The transformation of the grass into maize, which we call corn, was the most significant feat of Maya agronomy and arguably the greatest feat of agronomy in history. The ancient Maya husbanded a native grass into the highest yielding grain in agriculture history.

The practice of genetic alteration probably started as a conscious effort to alter a single type of plant into a more advanced specimen that produced a higher yield. *Teosinte's* alteration into maize is the classic example of genetic modification. *Teosinte* is a tall, drought-tolerant grass

CORN, COTTON AND CHOCOLATE: HOW THE MAYA CHANGED THE WORLD

that produces fruiting spikes that are filled with rows of small seeds. A hard shell around each seed protects them once they fall to the ground prior to their sprouting. Maya farmers discovered that *teosinte* seeds were edible and began selecting promising seeds from *teosinte* spikes to plant in cultivated plots. These selected plants were grown in an isolated plot away from wild *teosinte* growing in the surrounding forests. This isolation was required to avoid cross-pollination.

It was a long and patient voyage through thousands of planting cycles for the Maya to evolve *teosinte*, converting its grain spikes into the familiar cylindrical cobs of maize. The firm attachment of kernels to a central cylinder cob has inextricably bound maize to human involvement. The ears must be harvested and the kernels manually removed from the cob to successfully reproduce maize. When maize was created by Maya agronomists this process guaranteed that humans would not let the species die out. The Maya developed a powerful symbiosis with maize that has continued into the 21st century.

Yale archaeologist, Dr. Michael Coe, has labeled maize the key to understanding how the Maya advanced into a scientific society: *"Where maize flourished, so did high culture."* Coe's research has led him to the conclusion that the harvest of maize become an economical asset between 2000 BC and 1500 BC. Science has detected little change in the ear form of maize until 1100 BC, when great changes began to appear in the maize cobs. The diversity of maize varieties rapidly increased as well as its productivity. Maize has been a necessity in the Maya diet for millennia, and became the most popular planted crop in Mesoamerica. The rest is history since maize has become the most productive grain in the world.

NIXTAMALIZATION

The amazing grain cultivated by the Maya had one serious flaw. Unprocessed maize is deficient in niacin and a diet of too much untreated maize is bad. Any population that depends on untreated maize as a staple food will become malnourished and tend to develop deficiency diseases such as pellagra. Malnutrition and disease impede the progress of a civilization.

Long ago the Maya invented a very simple solution to reverse the nutritional failing of maize. It is a process known as "nixtamalization". This is a process of preparing corn in which the grain is soaked or cooked in an alkaline solution (lime) so that it is more easily ground. The alkalinity helps dissolve the cellulose of the maize cell walls, loosens the hulls from the kernels and softens the corn which makes it easier to grind and use.

Maize prepared with lime thus introduces niacin into the diet. The major contribution of nixtamalization to human nutrition is the enhancement of the protein value of maize. Nixtamalized maize induces a chemical change in processed maize, and is so superior to the unprocessed version that the rise of the Maya civilization was created because of this invention. Without nixtamalization the Maya culture would have remained forever on the village level. When and where this discovery was made is unknown, however, between 1500 B.C. and 1200 B.C. the process was being utilized by Maya cooks.

THE MAYA SYMBIOSIS WITH MAIZE

Maize was the central component in the diet of the ancient Maya. The significance of maize and its influence on their culture was not lost on the Maya and maize figured prominently in their mythology and ideology. The Maya viewed maize as the foundation of humanity, and it is

CORN, COTTON AND CHOCOLATE: HOW THE MAYA CHANGED THE WORLD

revered as the seed of life. This reverence is clearly shown by their mythological traditions. In mythology, the gods used maize to create man. They believed that their flesh was made of white and yellow maize.

Maize shaped the cultural identity of the Maya and their civilization was reinforced upon the cultivation of maize, through its harvesting, how it impacted their diet and its religious and spiritual significance. In Mayan hieroglyphics, the ear of maize became equivalent with the highest royal title.

MAYA CUISINE BASED ON MAIZE

Maize was the central component to the Maya diet. The Maya relied on maize as their major source of subsistence and they consumed maize as part of all their meals. Maize would be combined with other foods and flavorings and consumed in various liquid and solid dishes.

For breakfast in the mornings Maya ate a porridge made of maize and chilies. For the mid-day meal Mayas, would eat maize gruel of water that they sometimes flavored with chocolate, honey, chili peppers or herbs. This gruel, known as *atole*, is a liquid based meal that was made by mixing ground maize with water. *Atole* was easily transportable in a gourd for farmers working in the fields and individuals traveling away from home. *Atole* is also reported to have combated dehydration.

The third meal of the day was a more substantial offering which included preparing a stew and tortillas or tamales. Tamales or *"Tamali"* in Mayan, consisted of maize dough mixed with ground chili and black beans, wrapped inside of a maize husk. Tortillas or *"waaj"* in Mayan are flat maize "pancakes" that were used to wrap around other foods such as meat, or beans. The tortilla served as a plate and utensils for the Maya diner. Tortillas are perhaps the best-known Maya food in the world.

THE MAYA KITCHEN

The Maya kitchen consisted of a cooking hearth and several other basic kitchen implements. Maya cooks used a classic fireplace surrounded with three equidistant stones in a triangle supporting a flat earthenware surface. This triangle of three supporting stones was the most sacred part of the home. The hearth is the center of every traditional Maya dwelling. These versatile cooking components are still in use in rural Maya kitchens during the 21st century.

When preparing a meal, the first step, involved boiling the dried corn kernels, in a *cazuela,* a classic round earthenware pot. The *cazuela* was the all-purpose cooking pot for making stews, soups, and beans. The maize was cooked in the *cazuela* with mineral lime which loosened the husks covering the kernels

After boiling, the expanded maize was then placed upon a stone implement called a *metate*, which resembles a small, sloped three-legged table. The maize was then ground up on the *metate* using a cilyndridal *mano* as a grinding stone. Then the maize was patted by hand and shaped into flat cakes forming tortillas. The tortillas were then baked on the *comal*, the flat circular earthenware utensil that rested on the three-stone hearth. The *comal* has served Maya cooks for millennia as a cooking surface for the preparation of various types of food. The *comal* was used to cook not only tortillas but chilies, tomatoes, meats and other vegetables.

CORN, COTTON AND CHOCOLATE: HOW THE MAYA CHANGED THE WORLD

MAIZE IN MAYA ART

The art of the Maya has a rich tradition and is diverse in media and style. The subject matter of art reflects their lifestyle, religion and culture. Maya art consisted of a multitude of media including drawing on paper in their books, painted scenes on vases, colorful murals on stucco walls, carvings in wood and stone, and sculptures molded in clay and stucco.

Many art subjects were related to the lives of the elite and includes great variation: palace scenes, courtly ritual, mythology, divinatory glyphs, and dynastical texts. Maya beliefs including representations of maize and the Maize god figured prominently in their art. Recognized as young and beautiful, the image of the Maize god was the image emulated by Maya lords.

Mural scenes of maize depict rows of maize plants with human heads in the place of the ears of maize. Murals discovered at the ancient Maya city of Calakmul are unusual in that they depict scenes of common people doing everyday activities involving maize. The images on the murals show people engaged in activities including the preparation of food.

HUITLACOCHE: THE TRUFFLE OF THE MAYA

Huitlacoche is a fungus that is considered a food delicacy for Maya gourmets. The fungus is a parasite that grows on ears of maize and can infect any part of the plant. It replaces the normal kernels of the cobs with large, distorted tumors analogous to mushrooms. This fungus is eaten, usually as a filling, in quesadillas and other tortilla-based foods. Another Maya favorite is adding *huitlacoche* to omelets and to soups. Its earthy flavors bond with the fats that cook the eggs to mellow the flavors into a truffle-like taste.

In 1989, the James Beard Foundation held a high-profile *huitlacoche* dinner, prepared by Josefina Howard, chef at Rosa Mexicano restaurant in New York city. This dinner was to encourage Americans to eat more huitlacoche by renaming it the Mexican truffle.

MAIZE, A WORLD TRAVELER, STARTS ITS INFLUENCE ON HISTORY

At the time of European contact in 1492, the Maya trading network had disseminated maize throughout Mesoamerica, the Caribbean, North America, and South America. The Maya cultivar had been adopted by numerous cultures and was the prime source of grain for populations extending from North America, to the Aztec Empire in Mesoamerica and south to the Inka Empire. The people of the New World were being nourished by maize, the miracle grain of the Maya. Greater success for maize was yet to come when the remainder of the world became converts of the Maya invention and maize became the agricultural conqueror of the world.

The word for maize used in many Maya languages is "*ixim*". The word "maize" is not of Mayan origin but has its basis in a native language of the Caribbean islands. The indigenous Taino name for maize is "maiz". Christopher Columbus saw maize growing on the Caribbean islands where he learned the name as "maiz". The name "maize" was the corrupted Spanish form of the Taino word brought back to the Old World by the great navigator. Based on this common name, Carl Linnaeus included the name, *Zea mays* as the species label for the botanical classification of maize in his 1715 book, *Systema Naturae*, the hierarchical classification of the natural world.

Maize was introduced to Europe by Christopher Columbus on his early voyages. It was being grown in Spain as early as 1496. Initially, maize was a garden curiosity in Europe, but it then

CORN, COTTON AND CHOCOLATE: HOW THE MAYA CHANGED THE WORLD

began to be recognized as a valuable food crop. Within a few years, it spread throughout France, Italy, southeastern Europe and northern Africa. Portuguese colonists grew maize in the Congo as early as 1560, and become a major food crop in Africa. By 1575, it made its way into western China, and became an important crop in the Philippines and the East Indies. Maize was adopted by cultures around the world because of its food value and the ability of the cultivar to grow in diverse climates.

Maize is known by many names around the world. In Canada and the United States, the term "corn" primarily means maize. The term corn outside of Canada and the United States means any grain or cereal crop including wheat, rye and barley. Corn in England means wheat, in Scotland and Ireland it refers to oats. Corn mentioned in the Bible probably refers to wheat or barley. Maize is preferred in formal, scientific, and international usage because it refers specifically to this one grain, unlike corn, which has a complex variety of meanings that vary by context and geographic region.

MAYA MAIZE INCITES THE WHISKEY REBELLION, AND PROVES THE STABILITY OF THE U.S. GOVERNMENT

The American farmer has embraced the production of corn whiskey since colonial history. However, the farmers thought that making Maya corn whiskey was a God given right and should not be a government issue. In 1791, an excise tax was imposed on corn whiskey by the federal government. Angry farmers in the western counties of Pennsylvania carried out a series of armed attacks on federal tax agents.

Corn whiskey was an important cash crop and the tariff eliminated any profit from its sale. The tariff became the lightning rod for a wide variety of grievances by the settlers of the region. The rebel farmers continued their attacks, rioting in river towns and roughing up tax collectors until the so-called "insurrection" flared into the open. In July of 1794, a federal marshal was attacked in Allegheny County, Pennsylvania. At the same time, several hundred men attacked the residence of the regional tax inspector, burning his home and barn.

On August 7, 1794, President George Washington called out the militia. Washington's order mobilized an army of approximately 13,000 soldiers, a force which was as large as the army that had defeated the British in the Revolutionary War. The force was under the command of General "Light Horse" Harry Lee, the father of General Robert E. Lee.

Washington himself, in a show of presidential authority, set out at the head of the troops to suppress the uprising. This is the first and only time that a standing U.S. president led an army.

By the time the federal force arrived, the rebellion had collapsed and most of the rebels had fled. Two men were convicted of treason and later pardoned by Washington. Alexander Hamilton was elated. The fledgling federal government had proven it could keep order, which was a necessity if the U.S. was to avoid instability. Maya maize was part of the only armed rebellion in the United States involving whiskey and helped the young country prove its stability.

CHARACTERISTICS OF MAIZE: *THE CORN IS AS HIGH AS AN ELEPHANTS EYE*

Maize stalks can vary in height, from as little as 2-3 feet at maturity to a world record height of over 34 feet. Most common varieties are 6-8 feet tall, when ready to harvest, though some maize grown for animal feed may be 14-16 feet tall.

CORN, COTTON AND CHOCOLATE: HOW THE MAYA CHANGED THE WORLD

Unlike all other major grain crops, the maize plant has separate male and female flowering parts. Tassels are the male flower of the maize and silk on the ears is the female part. Ears develop above a few of the leaves in the midsection of the plant, between the stem and leaf female inflorescences. The husk is tightly enveloped by several layers of ear leaves commonly called husks.

The numbers of ears on a single stalk vary with the variety of maize. The kernels of maize on the cob are referred to as the "seed". The cob is similar to a multiple fruit in structure, except that the individual fruits (the kernels) never fuse into a single mass. The grains are approximately the size of peas, and adhere to the cob in regular rows of two kernels in each row; however, the rows are vertically staggered a half space, providing a complex geometry that had great significance to the Maya. The kernels surround a white, pithy substance, which forms the ear; an ear commonly holds 600 kernels. Maize can be grown in various colors: blackish, bluish-gray, purple, green, red, white and yellow.

MAIZE DIVERSITY AND THE ONGOING EVOLUTION OF MAIZE IN THE MAYA TRADITION

Modern agronomists are constantly developing new varieties of maize which adds to the staggering diversity that exists in contemporary maize agriculture. Varieties of maize including heirloom, traditional, and newly developed corn varieties constantly expand the list of modern cultivars. The familiar types of yellow and white sweet maize might resemble what one may think of as the classic corn on the cob. The most familiar types of maize include:

Sweet Corn: Is the newest type of corn; it was developed about 200–250 years ago. It can be distinguished from corn by its high sugar content during the earlier stages of maturity and its wrinkled, translucent kernels when dried. Sweet corn is eaten fresh served a vegetable dish, on the cob or it is canned. This type of corn that is commonly grown in home gardens and found in grocery stores for "corn on the cob".

Popcorn: Is perhaps the most ancient type of corn that extends back to Maya cultivation. It has a kernel with an extremely hard endosperm, the interior of the seed containing stored food which, when heated, the explodes with the familiar popping sound. Archaeologists have found these kernels in popped form that are at least 1000 years old. In this respect, the Maya were considerably lucky, they got to enjoy popcorn much sooner than the rest of the world. Too bad the movie theatre had not yet been invented.

Dent Corn: Has a distinct indentation on the top of the kernel caused by the softer inner endosperm shrinking more than the harder, translucent outer portion of the kernel. This type is the most widely grown commercial type in the U.S. and is an ancient variety of maize. it produces nutty, green flour, which makes delicious cornbread. Dent corn is the work-a-day corn that's used for animal feed, for making corn syrup, and for everything from alternative fuel to biodegradable plastics.

Flint corn: Has a very hard, translucent endosperm, and unlike dent types, it lacks the softer interior. It is known for its gorgeous array of colors and its versatility as a high-quality forage grain for livestock.

Flour Corn: Has a soft endosperm, which is easier to mill than the harder dent and flint types. It is the only corn that can be ground into a fine flour that is less course than cornmeal.

CORN, COTTON AND CHOCOLATE: HOW THE MAYA CHANGED THE WORLD

THE CURSE OF MAIZE AS A PRIMARY FOOD

When maize was first introduced into global populations, it was welcomed with enthusiasm for its agricultural productivity and food value. In locations where maize was employed as a staple food, the preparation of maize as food did not include vital information relative to additives required to enhance B-vitamin and niacin. This method of maize preparation method was solved by the Maya before 2500 BC. Widespread epidemics of malnutrition became apparent in locations of high maize consumption.

Maize had been introduced into the diet of consumers around the world without the necessary cultural knowledge for safely preparing the grain. The Maya and other Native American cultures consumed maize as a food staple, but they knew the appropriate process for solving the lack of B-vitamin niacin. The solution for healthy maize preparation was hidden in plain sight.

During the late 19th century, Pellagra reached epidemic proportions in parts of the southern U.S., Europe and Africa. The cause of the epidemic was a mystery. At least two theories were considered for the cause of pellagra: one theory said that pellagra was due to a deficiency of an unknown nutrient, and the germ theory said that pellagra was caused by a germ transmitted by stable flies.

For several decades, U.S. government medical teams overlooked the obvious solution. Instead they choose the wrong track, while pellagra victims suffered and died. In 1914, the U.S. government erroneously endorsed the germ theory as a cause of pellagra. However, by the mid-1920 s, the nutritional deficiency theory of pellagra was becoming a scientific consensus. The theory was validated in 1937, when niacin deficiency was determined to be the cause of the illness. It took decades for the U.S. medical teams to discover what the Maya knew in 2500 B.C.

MAYA MAIZE CONQUERS THE WORLD AND BECOMES THE LARGEST PRODUCER OF GRAIN

The Maya cultivar has become the most productive grain on the planet. Maize is widely cultivated throughout the world, and a greater quantity of maize is produced each year than any other type of grain. The United States leads the pack and produces 40% of the entire world's maize harvest; other top producing countries include China, Brazil, Mexico, Indonesia, India, France and Argentina. Worldwide production of maize in 2016 was 1018 million metric tons , which is more than rice which produced 741 million metric tons or wheat which produced 716 million metric tons.

Production of maize per acre is significantly different in different regions of the world. In the United States the average yield is 154 bushels per acre, while the average yield in China is 82 bushels per acre. The Chinese have a lower production rate because of sowing fewer plants per acre, using outdated hybrid seeds and manual harvesting. However, they are changing their techniques and increasing the yield. To meet future food needs of growing world populations, the goal of agronomists is to produce an average of 300 bushels per acre of corn. This goal has been surpassed by farmers in the United States with a yield of 307.37 bushels per acre achieved by a champion farmer in 2012.

CORN, COTTON AND CHOCOLATE: HOW THE MAYA CHANGED THE WORLD

The top ten maize producing countries are wide ranging in their geographical locations, indicating the diverse climatic conditions which successfully support the growth of the Maya cultivar.

TOP 20 MAIZE PRODUCING COUNTRIES IN METRIC TONS

RANK	COUNTRY	PRODUCTION
1	United States:	366,539,000
2	China:	218,000,000
3	Brazil:	82,000,000
4	EU-27:	64,275,000
5	Argentina:	34,000,000
6	Ukraine:	26,000,000
7	Mexico:	23,500,000
8	India:	23,000,000
9	Russia:	14,000,000
10	Canada:	13,750,000
11	Indonesia:	9,600,000
12	Philippines:	8,000,000
13	Nigeria:	7,200,000
14	South Africa:	7,000,000
15	Serbia:	7,000,000
16	Nigeria	7,000,000
17	Turkey	6,000,000
18	Viet Nam	6,000,000
19	Ethiopia	6,000,000
20	Egypt	6,000,000

THE CORNUCOPIA OF APPLICATIONS OF THE MAYA CONSUMMATE CULTIVAR

The superlative chemical and nutritional characteristics of the grain have produced a cornucopia of uses for food and industrial purposes. The unique properties of maize have been capitalized upon for its value across the globe.

One reference lists over 500 different uses for maize. Maize can be fermented and distilled to produce grain alcohol and is sometimes used as the starch source for beer. Maize is the major component of cooking oil, cornstarch, corn syrup, baby food, hominy, mush, puddings, tamales, and many more human foods.

Some industrial uses of corn include filler for plastics, packing materials, insulating materials, adhesives, chemicals, explosives, paint, paste, abrasives, dyes, insecticides, pharmaceuticals, organic acids, solvents, rayon, antifreeze, soaps, and many more products. Corn meal is also a significant ingredient of some commercial animal food products.

CORN, COTTON AND CHOCOLATE: HOW THE MAYA CHANGED THE WORLD

MAYA MAIZE CHANGES THE SOURCE OF WORLD CUISINE

As the cultivation of maize spread throughout the world, the consumption of maize became a staple food for the lower classes of society. Maize was plentiful and had a high nutritional value. For the first-time people did not go hungry because maize production enabled a steady supply of sufficient food for millions of people. Maize based cuisine has become a symbol of quality food in modern society. Maize is more than just a source of energy, it has become a key ingredient in the cuisine of countries all across the face of the earth.

During the time when maize was mostly consumed as peasant food it was developed into tasty regional dishes, these dishes have become popular and are now part of world cuisine. Maize-based dishes from Mexico, the Southern United States and Italy have crossed borders and are now a part of international cuisine. Popular examples include tortillas, cornbread, and polenta.

Sweet corn, the favorite of cooks, has handsome rounded kernels that have become a popular food in countries across the globe. Mexican food is a front-runner in fast food restaurants with their spicy maize based foods. The Southern United States has been a leader in maize based foods with its corn bread, corn battered chicken and other maize foods.

Maize has changed the cuisine as well as the tastes of cultures across the world. The change has occurred in diverse cultures including French cuisine, Italian menus and in the porridge eaten daily by Africans. The following are representative of the changes maize has induced in the cuisine of the world:

ITALIAN CUISINE

When maize was introduced to Italy, Italians were not aware of the nixtamalization process, and cooks skipped this stage of the cooking process. Maize was simply grown, dried and then ground into flour to make polenta. Because the Europeans already had a more efficient milling process for hulling grain mechanically, this vital process was skipped. Without alkaline processing, malnutrition struck many areas where maize became a dominant food crop.

Early in the 18th century, some Italians began to fall victim to pellagra. The symptoms included nervousness, sore joints, mental illness and people looking pallid and unhealthy. At first maize was blamed and the grain was actually banned as a cause of the disease. With little else to eat, many peasants had no choice but to continue cooking polenta as they had in the past. Early in the 20th century medical advancement made clear that a nutrient-deficient diet, not maize itself, was the cause of pellagra.

Polenta is now one of the most important dishes in northern Italian cuisine. One would think that maize is a popular grain throughout Italy but is not, except for polenta. In most of Italy, maize as we know it is fed to animals.

Polenta derives from earlier forms of grain mush, known as puls or *pulmentum* in Latin. Gruel or porridge, has been eaten since Roman times. Before the introduction of maize in the 16th century, polenta was made with starchy ingredients including chestnut flour, millet, spelt, or chickpeas. However, the Maya grain changed the way that Italians made polenta.

CORN, COTTON AND CHOCOLATE: HOW THE MAYA CHANGED THE WORLD

The popularity of polenta made with maize in Italy was contagious and the cuisine spread across Italian boarders into European countries around the Mediterranean and Adriatic countries from the former Yugoslavia, Eastern Europe and as far to the east as Russia. Maize based polenta is popular in these countries and goes by many names. Maya agronomists would be proud.

FRENCH CUISINE

In France, maize has long been a staple food for poorer communities because of its nutritional value. Over time, maize has gradually become a symbol of quality food. and; is an ingredient in French cuisine. It can be served moist and tasty as a salad vegetable or prepared in different dishes. As feed for animals, maize is known to produce tasty meat.

France discovered maize in 1493. The Maya grain remained a food for peasants for centuries. Some of today's traditional French dishes were developed in the provinces using maize, for example, yellow root soup made in the Burgundy region. These cooks use grilled maize meal. Polenta, the delicious, smooth cornmeal from Italy is a long-time favorite in southern France.

In the last twenty-five years, sweet corn has become a popular part of French meals. It is now the number five vegetable in the French shopping basket. Whether as corn on the cob or as a salad, it is always served fresh, with a fine, crisp texture and a sweet flavor that is quite unique. Sweet corn has even become popular with leading chefs devising new flavors and attractive dishes.

BRITISH CUISINE

British cuisine is the specific set of cooking traditions and practices that are associated with the United Kingdom. British cuisine has been described as "unfussy dishes made with quality local ingredients, matched with simple sauces to accentuate flavor, rather than disguise it." However, British cuisine has changed through the years and has absorbed the cultural influence of people that have immigrated and settled in Britain.

The British have an affinity for maize as an ingredient both in traditional British foods and the adopted food from other countries. A traditional British recipe for classic maize flour biscuits is made with lightly sweetened milk dough that contains maize flour as an ingredient.

Traditional British dishes include the maize based haddock and corn chowder that is a classic British favorite, and of course, the always-popular corn on the cob, creamed corn and kettle corn, similar to popcorn.

The British are quite fond of Italian polenta and the cuisine of Mexico. For home cooks, there are popular maize based foods including tortilla chips, tacos, tamales and quesadillas. The popularity of maize based food is reflected by the hundreds of Mexican restaurants in Britain.

AFRICAN CUISINE

Maize was introduced into Africa by the Portuguese in the 16th century. Prior to this; sorghum and millet were the principal grains in most of Sub-Saharan Africa. Maize was readily accepted by African farmers. Eventually maize displaced sorghum as Africa's primary grain and has become its most important staple food crop.

CORN, COTTON AND CHOCOLATE: HOW THE MAYA CHANGED THE WORLD

By the end of the nineteenth century, a maize meal called *posho* was among the most popular foods of eastern Africa. The primary African use of maize as a food is in the form of mush or porridge. Ground maize meal is made into a thick porridge in many African cultures. In other parts of Africa, maize meal is also used as a replacement for wheat flour, to make cornbread and other baked products.

THE MAYA ROLE IN DEFINING THE CUISINE OF THE AMERICAN SOUTH

The cuisine of the Southern United States is defined as the historical culinary style of states that are located south of the Mason Dixon Line. This 1767 colonial-era land survey extends east to west along the state lines dividing Pennsylvania from West Virginia and Maryland. The line then extends southward separating the states of Maryland and Delaware. The phrase "south of the Mason-Dixon line" has been customarily used as the political divide between the North and the South. However, Maryland, West Virginia and the District of Columbia are south of this line and were part of the Union. Some of these states consider themselves as Southern, if not politically, then as cultural Southerners.

The most notable influences on Southern food come from European, Native American and African American cuisines. In recent history, elements of Southern cuisine have spread north, having a fusion effect on the development of other types of American cuisine.

Many foods such as maize, squash, and beans were always a part of Southern cuisine. These cultivars were consumed in the south before European contact and were inherited from southeastern Native American cultures such as the Caddo, Cherokee, Choctaw, and Seminole. These cultures, in turn, owe their agriculture heritage to Maya agronomy and its bountiful cultivars. African slaves were familiar with maize before their arrival in America. Maize had been introduced to Africa by Europeans in the 16th century and by the 18th century it was an African food staple. Most Southern cooking is based on maize derived ingredients. However, the names of the foods are American, wherein maize is referred to as "corn", therefore the names of the dishes will be referred to as "corn".

Southern cooking includes a wide variety of corn-based dishes. These foods include corn breads, creamed corn, corn soups, corn chowder, corn casserole and corn on the cob. Favorite Southern dishes, however, are breads or porridge made with corn including: cornbread, cornpone, hominy grits, mush, cornbread pudding and hominy stew.

CORN BREAD

Skillet-fried or skillet-baked cornbread is a traditional staple in the rural Southern United States. The preparation of cornbread involves heating bacon drippings or another oil in a heavy, cast iron skillet in an oven. Then a batter composed from cornmeal, egg, and milk is poured directly into the skillet and onto the hot grease. The mixture is returned to the oven to bake into a large, crumbly and sometimes moist cake with a crunchy crust. This cornbread tends to be dense and is usually served as an accompaniment to the meal.

Cornbread also may be made in sticks, muffins, or loaves. In some parts of the South it is crumbled into a glass of cold milk or buttermilk and eaten with a spoon. Another Southern staple is "Beans and Cornbread," consisting of pinto beans, stewed with ham or bacon, and cornbread. This is served sometimes with collard or turnip greens. Cornbread was popular during the

CORN, COTTON AND CHOCOLATE: HOW THE MAYA CHANGED THE WORLD

American Civil War because it was very cheap and could be made in many different forms: high-rising, fluffy loaves or simply fried, as unleavened pone, corn fritters, and hoecakes.

GRITS

Grits are a coarse meal made from corn. They are made by soaking raw corn grains in hot water containing calcium hydroxide, just the way the Maya did. The mixture loosens the grain hulls and increases the nutritional value. You can make grits fancy or you can make them plain. What plain means is stone ground grits cooked with water. Seasoning would only be salt and maybe a little black pepper. This favorite of Southern cooks is not just served for breakfast! Grits may be made fancy and added to dinner menus in the form of cheese grits, shrimp and grits, or fried grits.

The word "grits" is derived from the Old English "Grytt" for "bran". Americans have been using the term grits since at least the end of the 18th century. The word, "grits", may be used as either singular or plural. Historically, in the American South the word was invariably singular not withstanding its plural form. The state of Georgia declared grits its official prepared food in 2002.

CORN FRITTERS

Corn fritters are a savory snack that is a traditional Southern favorite. Corn fritters are a mixture of corn kernels, egg, flour, milk, and melted butter. They can be deep-fried, shallow fried, or baked, and may be served with jam, fruit, honey, or cream. They may also be made with creamed corn, baked, and served with syrup.

HOMINY

Hominy consists of dried maize kernels which have been treated with a limewater solution as with grits. Hulls are separated from the kernels by washing in water, grains become softened and swelled. The kernels are not ground for hominy dishes; they remain moist and full size and are used in a variety of Southern dishes combined with meats and vegetables including soups, stews and casseroles.

The English term "hominy" is derived from the Native American Powhatan language word for maize. The Cherokees, for example, made hominy that was used to make a traditional hominy soup, in post contact times, Hominy was fried with bacon and green onions.

CORN PONE

Corn pone is a type of cornbread made from thick, malleable cornmeal dough and baked in a specific type of iron pan. The pans have indentations shaped like a corn cob that shapes the corn pone. The pone is cooked over an open fire using butter, margarine, or cooking oil. Corn pones have been a staple of Southern U.S. cuisine, and have been discussed by many

CORN, COTTON AND CHOCOLATE: HOW THE MAYA CHANGED THE WORLD

American writers, including Mark Twain. The term has found its way into American slang to refer to a rural, unsophisticated person.

HUSHPUPPIES

A hushpuppy is a savory buttermilk-based batter which is deep-fried or baked in small ball, sphere shapes, or occasionally oblong shapes. Hushpuppies are frequently served as a side dish, usually with seafood. Hushpuppy recipes vary from state to state; variations include onion seasoning, chopped onions, beer, or jalapeños. Fried properly, the hushpuppy will be moist and yellow or white on the inside, while crunchy and medium-dark golden brown on the outside.

The first recorded reference to the word "hush-puppy" dates to 1899. The name "hushpuppy" has legendary roots. The term was originally attributed to cooks on Southern plantations who would prepare the treat to appease the barking dogs hanging around the kitchen. The cooks would toss the cornbread treats to the dogs with the admonition: "hush puppies." Other hush puppy legends purport to date the etymology of the term "hushpuppies" to the Civil War, in which soldiers are claimed to have tossed fried cornbread to quell the barking of Confederate dogs.

CORN PUDDING

Corn pudding is a gelatinous food product made from stewed corn, water, any of various thickening agents, and optional additional flavoring or texturing ingredients, typically used as a food staple in rural communities in the southern parts of the United States, especially in Appalachia.

SLOOSH

Sloosh was a form of cornbread that was popular during the American Civil War, especially among Confederate soldiers. Civil war historian Shelby Foote described it as a mixture of cornmeal, lard or bacon, water and egg formed around a rifle ramrod and cooked over a campfire.

SPOON BREAD

Spoon bread is a moist cornmeal-based dish prevalent in parts of the southern United States. Although named bread, spoon bread is closer in consistency and taste to many savory puddings. In some recipes, spoon bread is similar to a cornmeal soufflé, although typical Southern recipes do not involve whipping the eggs to incorporate air.

The first print recipe for spoon bread appeared in a cookbook by Sarah Rutledge in 1847. Spoon breads became popular around the turn of the 20th century, as cornmeal replaced yeast in Southern cooking.

CORN SYRUP

Corn syrup is made from the starch of maize and contains varying amounts of maltose and higher saccharides, depending on the grade. Corn syrup is used in foods to soften texture, add volume, prevent crystallization of sugar, and enhance flavor. Corn syrup is distinct from high-

CORN, COTTON AND CHOCOLATE: HOW THE MAYA CHANGED THE WORLD

fructose corn syrup (HFCS), which is created when corn syrup undergoes enzymatic processing, producing a sweeter compound that contains higher levels of fructose. The more general term glucose syrup is often used synonymously with corn syrup, since glucose syrup is in the United States most commonly made from corn starch..

CORN WHISKEY

The Maya liked their booze and Americans have followed in their footsteps. The Maya cultivar led the way in producing a favored whiskey. Corn whiskey is an American alcoholic liquor made from corn mash. Mash is a slurry composed of crushed corn stirred with boiling water, sugar and barley malt. The liquid that drains from the mash is fermented and then distilled to make corn whiskey. The whiskey is distilled in copper pot stills. The process is based on traditional methods for making homemade American corn whiskey which was the predecessor of Bourbon whiskey and moonshine whiskey.

The whiskey is typically distilled to greater than 160 proof, the distilled corn whiskey is then diluted with water to a 40 percent or greater alcohol content by volume. The whiskey can be aged in oak barrels. Aging usually is a brief period, six months or less, during this time the whiskey absorbs color and flavor from the charred barrel. Aging mellows the taste of the whiskey and makes the drink more palatable. However, illegal corn whiskey made in the mountains of Appalachia is traditionally un-aged whiskey, and was made in copper pot stills. This type of illegal whiskey is consumed without the aging process.

Thanks to Maya maize, American history includes a long tradition of making whiskey. The process was a simplistic way of earning money for early American farmers. They found that fresh corn which sold for a few dollars a bushel at market could yield a few hundred dollars after it was distilled into whiskey. Using a copper pot still and wooden barrels for mixing the mash and storing whiskey, a farmer could produce enough liquor to meet the needs of his family and local community. Three bushels of dried corn could be distilled into about two gallons of alcohol.

From the time of early settlement, small farm and community distilleries were a natural complement to the agricultural character of the American south. Roads were rough in rural areas, and farmers often faced difficulties delivering crops to market in a timely manner. In addition to being a money maker, distilling of corn whiskey was a way to condense and preserve grains and an easy way to transport their corn to market.

Therefore, an American tradition was born, mashing corn and turning it into alcohol became the standard method of alcohol production on American farms. Even George Washington made liquor commercially at Mount Vernon. The craft of distilling alcohol from Maya maize became part of an all-American tradition, and "corn whiskey" was born.

BOURBON, THE ALL-AMERICAN MAYA WHISKEY

Little did Maya agronomists know, as they toiled to perfect the characteristics of maize, that the cultivar would conquer the world as a highly-valued grain and their amazing grain would also be basis of one of the legendary alcoholic beverages in world history.

The legal distilled form of the corn-based drink is known as Bourbon whiskey. Before it became a gentleman's drink, this alcoholic beverage evolved from the illegal rough and tumble corn

CORN, COTTON AND CHOCOLATE: HOW THE MAYA CHANGED THE WORLD

whiskey made in the backwoods. The now famous refined and aged Bourbon started its existence as the working man's alcoholic drink known as corn whiskey. It was born as the product of illegal whiskey distilling. It did not come quietly and it left an impressive footprint on history, it has caused armed rebellions, became the product of rouges known as bootleggers, and paved the way for NASCAR, the most popular motor racing sport in the world.

Bourbon whiskey is a barrel-aged distilled spirit made from corn. The name of the spirit derives belies it rough and tumble beginnings. The name was derived from the French House of Bourbon royal family and its historical association with what is now Bourbon County, Kentucky. It has been legally produced since the 18th century and is strongly associated with the American south in general and the states of Tennessee and Kentucky in particular.

The origin of bourbon is one of legend; there are many yarns about its invention. One is attributed to a Reverend Craig is said to be the first to age the distillation in charred oak casks, a process that gives the bourbon its reddish color and unique taste. There was probably no single "inventor" of bourbon, which developed into its present sophisticated form during the late 19th century. The use of American corn for the mash and oak for forming the barrels was a logical combination. The creative use of native materials was part of the cognitive genius of Scotch-Irish settlers in America.

By an act of Congress Bourbon became an all-American product. In 1964, a resolution of the U.S. Congress declared bourbon to be a "distinctive product of the United States". That resolution asked, "the appropriate agencies of the United States Government ... to take action to prohibit importation into the United States of whiskey designated as "Bourbon Whiskey." Federal regulation now defines a whiskey labeled "bourbon whisky" to only include "bourbon" produced in the United States.

Presently, the beverage produced from the Maya cultivar has a pedigree protected by law. Earning the pedigree does not come easy, the preparation of bourbon making is exceedingly technical and Federal Standards requires that the whiskey meet a rigid set of criteria. To identity a whisky as Bourbon, the standards stipulate a finite set of rules to determine its composition. To call itself bourbon, the mash, which is the mixture of grains from which the product is distilled, must contain at least 51% corn. The remanding 49% of the mash is other grains, wheat, rye, or malted barley.

The prepared mash must then be distilled into a clear liquid that is at least 160 proof (80% alcohol) or less. Distillation was historically performed using an pot still, although in modern production, the use of a continuous still is much more common.

The distillate is then placed in the aging barrels at 125 proof (62.5 % alcohol) or less, and it must not contain any additives. The clear distillate must be aged in a new charred oak barrel, usually made of white American oak. During aging, bourbon gains color and flavor from the caramelized sugars in the charred wood.

The longer bourbons are permitted to mature, the more they gain color and flavor. Maturity, not a particular numerical age, is the goal. Bourbon can age too long and become woody and unbalanced. Products aged for as little as three months are sold as bourbon. After the bourbon, has aged, it is placed in bottles at no less than 80 proof.

CORN, COTTON AND CHOCOLATE: HOW THE MAYA CHANGED THE WORLD

When they are emptied the barrels still contain 20 pounds of bourbon absorbed within the matrix of the wood. This known as the "devil's share". By law, they cannot be re-used for ageing bourbon. They are sold to tequila distillers in Mexico. The Maya made alcoholic beverages from the agave plant, which is the basis for tequila. The Maya maze based bourbon from the U.S. blends with the aging tequila from Mexico to develop its smooth flavor and gold color. The Maya legacy of maize returned home to Mexico in the form of bourbon barrels to improve the pedigree of the famous Tequila.

Bourbon is served straight, diluted with water, over ice cubes, or mixed with soda into cocktails, including the Manhattan, the Old Fashioned, and the mint julep. American whiskey made from Maya maize is now sold in more than 100 countries, and has changed the taste of cocktails around the world

MOONSHINE WHISKEY

"Moonshine" is the legendary name given to illegal corn whiskey. The term was coined because illegal distillers made their whiskey in the middle of the night. *Ixchel*, the Maya goddess of the moon, must have been smiling down upon the country artisans' making corn whiskey in their secret backwoods stills. Avoiding detection from prying eyes, they carried out their work while bathed in the illumination of her moonlight. Does this make the Maya goddess a partner in their crime of illegal whiskey making? After all, she supplied the light which illuminated the clandestine operations, converting Maya maize into corn whiskey, and was honored for providing the nickname for the legendary rogues: Moonshiner.

The legends surrounding the production and delivery of the illicit whiskey are replete with tales of derring-do, risky escapades, fast cars and bad company. Their history began in the 18th century, during the colonial and antebellum periods, its production played an important role in the economy of the fledging colonies. The distillation of whiskey became a cottage industry that allowed small farmers to earn cash money. While whiskey production was mostly associated with the Appalachian Mountains, the skill was practiced by farmers throughout the Southern states.

Scots-Irish immigrants brought the skills of distilling alcohol to the American colonies. The production of corn whiskey may be an involved process, but it was not so difficult that the average farmer could not became a master of successfully completing the major steps in the process of making corn whiskey: fermentation and distillation

Antebellum citizens viewed distillers as well-respected members of the community and denounced the federal government's attempt to impose a tax on liquor manufacturing in the 1790s. A rebellion against the Federal Government grew out of the unpopular taxation.

During the Civil War, the U.S. Congress attempted to balance the national budget by creating the Internal Revenue Service to collect taxes on liquor and other luxuries. After the war, when the Southern states were readmitted to the Union, Southerners found themselves subject to the Yankee federal liquor tax. Many corn whiskey producers, mostly small farmers, refused to either pay the tax or terminate their distilling operations. The actual production of corn whiskey was not illegal, but refusal to pay the federal tax was a crime. The tax-resisting distillers became known by the trademark name of "moonshiners" because of their nocturnal operations. Maya maize assumed a negative role in American history.

This resistance to the liquor tax sparked a war between moonshiners and revenuers, who were federal agents who sought to enforce the liquor law. The once peaceful whiskey distillers turned

CORN, COTTON AND CHOCOLATE: HOW THE MAYA CHANGED THE WORLD

violent and became outlaws. Moonshiners attacked revenuers and intimidated local residents who might be tempted to help revenuers identify the rouge distillers. In the early 1870s the Ku Klux Klan joined forces with the moonshiners, now known as bootleggers, to combat the Federal Tax agents. Things went from bad to worst.

The brutal tactics used by the moonshiners resisting revenuers led to a shift in the public's attitude toward moonshiners. The public in the Southern states began to support the federal government's efforts. During the 1880s, public sentiment fueled the temperance movement, which was an emotional anti-alcohol force led primarily by preachers, evangelicals, and women. The movement encouraged citizens to abstain from drinking alcohol and accepted federal liquor taxation as a device to reduce alcohol consumption. Moonshiners were increasingly portrayed as violent criminals. By 1900 many communities ceased supporting the activity of illegal distilling in their areas. Business began to slow for the moonshine business.

During the twentieth century, the bootlegging game changed when national prohibition became law and the moonshiner degenerated from a skilled whiskey artisan to a ruthless and greedy gangster. The Eighteenth Amendment to the United States Constitution was passed in 1919 and enacted in 1920 through the Volstead Act. By passing the act, Congress declared the consumption of alcohol and alcohol manufacturing to be illegal. Thus began the period in American history known as prohibition. Prohibition greatly escalated the demand for moonshine whiskey.

Gangsters turned the small business enterprise of producing moonshine into big business. They created elaborate production and distribution networks and forced distillers to operate sills to supply their illicit operations. Moonshiners transported millions of gallons of whiskey from their clandestine stills in the Appalachian Mountains down into the big Southern cities. Their clientele had expanded greatly from the working class and now catered to all social classes and supplying the ubiquitous speakeasies.

Moonshiners played a dangerous game of cat and mouse with revenuers. Moonshine was transported from the mountains into the cities by skilled drivers called "trippers" These were men who shouldered the responsibilities of driving loads of moonshine whisky down twisting mountain roads into urban markets.

Trippers were the true daredevils and the heroes of the moonshine era. Everything hinged on their ability to deliver the liquor and return home with the much-needed money that kept their families fed and clothed. Everyone had respect for the tripper, even the revenuers who chased them, tried to catch them and put them in prison.

However, this real-life drama was a serious game played by both sides. To evade revenuers, trippers drove specially designed high-performance automobiles, called "tanker cars." The fast and furious car chases over mountain roads often ended in the death of the moonshiner or the revenuer. In the process of blockade running, moonshiners had become reckless outlaws who were concerned only with making money rather than manufacturing quality whiskey. However, the experienced drivers of these powerful cars and veterans of high-speed chases became skilled automobile racers and grew the popular sport known today as stock car racing.

Since the 1960s, moonshining activity has slowed considerably, and much of it has migrated from the mountains to metropolitan areas, where producers have found it easier to evade the

CORN, COTTON AND CHOCOLATE: HOW THE MAYA CHANGED THE WORLD

federal liquor tax. They place their illicit stills in homes and barns, which revenuers who now work under the federal Bureau of Alcohol, Tobacco, Firearms, and Explosives, must have a search warrant to enter.

Today, lost tax revenue from the sale of illegal liquor is of less concern to officials than the health threat posed by moonshine. Because moonshine whiskey is not the quality product of old and contains impurities and toxins, especially lead, moonshine consumption can be deadly. Poor people have suffered most, since moonshine is extremely inexpensive, and illegal distributors may target poor neighborhoods in which to sell their products.

THE MAYA INVENT NASCAR, THE POPULAR SPORT OF STOCK CAR RACING

The fabled craft of producing moonshine whiskey spun off an even greater legend, one that was based on the feats of the bold and skillful trippers cruising in their high-octane cars. These daredevils functioned as the supply line that negotiated treacherous mountain roads and evaded government blockades while delivering moonshine down into the cities.

The battle between the trippers and the revenuers basically came down to a deadly car race. Historically, it comes as no surprise that the greatest stock car drivers, racecar builders, and mechanics came from rural areas in the south. Much of early stock car racing is associated with the great legends in moonshine running and one that has been heavily romanticized by literature and the media.

A traditional moonshine-running car had certain standard automotive components. The exterior of the car, had to look as much like a "stock car" as possible. However, under the hood the cars were anything but "stock". In addition to a supercharged engine, moonshiner's mechanics installed heavy shocks and springs. The reinforced suspension system was so designed that when the car was carrying a heavy load the chassis did not deflect and reveal the weight of the load being transporting. This was a sure sign of a moonshine tanker for the police. If you were spotted by the law, the driver of the innocent looking car had to change into the "king of the road" and the driver had to really know how to handle that high-octane horsepower on the twisty mountain roads.

The trippers raced their cars on the weekends and on Sunday they hauled sugar back up into the hills to supply their illegal stills. If they were lucky and skilled, they'd come away with a purse of cash and a case of beer. If not, reckless driving might toss them off the road with their cars smashing into whatever solid object they first encountered.

The runners loved to race and they wound up racing each other on the local highways and byways. Then, somebody had the bright idea to excavate a crude oval racetrack out of a cow pasture and the rest is history. The performance of these racing cars continued to improve, and by the late 1940s, races featuring these souped-up cars were being run for pride and profit. These races became popular entertainment for audiences in the Southern states. Junior Johnson was the most famous bootleg runner to make a name for himself, but he wasn't the only tripper who raced in the big time.

William France, Sr, who was also a stock car racer, knew the other racers and they trusted him. This trusting relationship enabled him to convince these racers to participate in his racing events. France decided that organized auto racing would not grow without a formal sanctioning

CORN, COTTON AND CHOCOLATE: HOW THE MAYA CHANGED THE WORLD

organization, standardized rules, regular schedule, and an organized championship. The National Association for Stock Car Auto Racing, or NASCAR was founded by France in 1948.

Bill France took over the running the Daytona race course in 1938. France had the notion that people would enjoy watching "stock cars" race. The added attraction of "bootleg runners" racing in the events added to the thrill of the chase. However, drivers were frequently victimized by unscrupulous promoters who would slip out of town with the prize money before the drivers were paid.

The organization that Bill France founded has grown bigger than his dreams. NASCAR is second only to the National Football League among professional sports franchises in terms of television ratings in the United States. NASCAR has 75 million fans that purchase over $3 billion annually in licensed products.

It's not uncommon for people from the Northern U.S. and fans of Grand Prix racing to think of NASCAR as vulgar and common. But like so many elements of American heritage, its roots extend back to a culture that embraced American values of independence, self-sufficiency and mastery of craft, not to mention a love of corn whiskey and the raw mechanical power of the internal combustion engine. NASCAR's roots are soaked in Americana and moonshine. No trophy in the fabled Junior Johnson's palatial country home, and no victory in his 50 triumphs in NASCAR racing means more to him than his pride expressed in his eloquent quote, "*They never caught me a-haulin'.*"

However you may feel about moonshine whiskey, it is a part of America's history. NASCAR is a sport of the American masses. Maya maize can be proud of being part of this American heritage.

MAYA MAIZE AND ITS PART IN CHANGING HISTORY

Maize is now the most favorite grain in the world. Maya agronomists never envisioned that maize would become the most productive grain in the world and feed billions of people each day. The Maya cultivar has made significant changes in history including changing the food tastes of the world, the creation of a whiskey that has earned both a pedigreed and a gangster reputation. Furthermore, maize whiskey ignited a rebellion and started NASCAR, a sports empire.

CORN, COTTON AND CHOCOLATE: HOW THE MAYA CHANGED THE WORLD

CHAPTER 15: PAPAYA

Papaya Botanical name: *Carica papaya*   Maya name: *puut*

Memories of a youth

My knowledge of the papaya did not come as a youth since the fruit did not make inroads into the Southern U.S. until the 1970s. I was not familiar with the papaya until I spent a year in Mexico during the 1960s. While there, I indulged myself by enjoying the fruit in every form possible.

The papaya is a tropical fruit that is popular worldwide for its delicious flesh and juice. Its popularity as a delicious fruit is sufficient to love the papaya, however, it was its curative powers that caused me to become a disciple of the medical benefits of the papaya. My medical knowledge the papaya began after I read an article in Time Magazine about the beneficial aspects of papaya enzyme Injected into herniated discs in the human spinal cord.

I knew that papaya juice was used in cooking by the Maya and as a commercial meat tenderizer available in grocery stores. So it seemed logical that chymopapain, the principle enzyme in the papaya, could reduce the size of herniated disks. I stored this medical information in one of the boxes in my brain, titled miscellaneous.

A few weeks later I had a luncheon appointment with an old friend, an architect of some note. We met at his office and sat for a few minutes discussing an unusual type of dog he had just seen.

Henri described the dog, "It's a rare Hungarian hunting dog. I can't even pronounce the name, I really want one, but the owner would not give me information about where to buy them."

He held up a business card with the name of the dog hand written on the back. It said "*Visla*".

I responded, "That's a "*Visla*." It's a Hungarian hunting dog. I know someone who breeds this type of dog, I can give him a call and see if he has a puppy for you."

"Great", Henri said. He tried to stand up but had to use the arms of his chair to steady himself. "Rats," He remarked. "I'm sorry, but I've got herniated disks in my back and the Doc doesn't seem to have a cure."

"Well," I said, "I think I may be of more help to you than just finding that dog".

Over lunch I told Henry about the Time Magazine article concerning the use of papaya enzyme to cure spinal issues. I thought it might be a good idea to alert his doctor to the technique. When we parted after lunch, I told him I would contact my friend, the breeder, and check if he had a puppy available for Henri.

When I next spoke with Henri, it was good news all around. His doctor had researched the papaya enzyme treatment and had started to apply the enzyme to his herniated disks. He had immediate results. The pain was ceasing and his freedom of movement became almost normal.

CORN, COTTON AND CHOCOLATE: HOW THE MAYA CHANGED THE WORLD

To top off the good news, I had contacted the breeder and he said that he had a female Visla available for Henri. To sum up our adventures, Henri was cured of his disk problems with the papaya enzyme, and he received the dog without charge as a professional courtesy. He named the dog, *Schotte*, and later I received the pick of Henri's dog's litter. I named my dog *Urchi*, which means little brother in Hungarian.

Little did Maya agronomists know that their papaya cultivar would travel from their forest gardens and would wind up in modern surgical suites helping to cure spinal cord injuries.

MAYA AND THE PAPAYA

Ancient Maya agronomists worked their agricultural wizardry over 4,000 years ago when they cultivated the papaya. During the long period of cultivation, the Maya discovered uses for the papaya as a food and for its valuable health-giving properties. These amazing properties were the reason the Maya held this miraculous tree in such high esteem.

The papaya tree was known as the "Tree of Life" in the Maya culture, was a gift from the gods to them. The ancient Maya venerated the papaya as their sacred tree because every part of the tree can be used to nourish and heal the human body. They cultivated the papaya tree in their forest gardens where they developed their tree-borne fruit like papaya, cocoa, avocado and the vanilla orchid.

MAYA USE OF THE PAPAYA IN COOKING

When ripe, the flesh of the papaya fruit turns orange, and it can be eaten raw. The Maya ate the fruit in the morning, at midday or the evening meal with a main course. The green papaya can be sliced, steamed like a squash or added to stews.

When making a soup or stew, the Maya cooks cut up the green leaves, the flesh of the green papaya, or dried papaya leaves and added them to the mix. The Maya used the papaya for a meat tenderizer. Its ability to break down tough meat fibers was used by Maya cooks for thousands of years, and is still used in products in today's kitchens.

THE PAPAYA IN MAYA MEDICINE

The Maya have used papaya in ethno-medicine for centuries to treat diseases and digestive symptoms. Papaya is one of the best foods for digestion and helps to maintain the human body's health. It contains the digestive enzyme papain, which the enables balancing of stomach acid levels. The Maya believe that after digesting papain people are revitalized and begin to experience more energy and vitality.

The Maya used papaya peel ointments as a treatment for skin wounds that don't heal quickly. Papaya encourages the renewal of muscle tissue. Mature, ripe papayas have been used as an effective remedy against ringworm. The raw seeds are used to treat or prevent intestinal parasites.

THE PAPAYA IS INTRODUCED TO THE WORLD

The papaya was one of the New World foods that was enjoyed by the great explorer, Christopher Columbus, who reputedly referred to the papaya as "fruit of the angels" when he

CORN, COTTON AND CHOCOLATE: HOW THE MAYA CHANGED THE WORLD

first tasted the sweet orange fruit. Lore has it that when the natives greeted the crew of Columbus' ships they offered them a surfeit of food, which was way too much when compared with the meager fare served at sea, and some of the sailors experienced digestive pains. To cure this condition, the natives fed them papayas, which brought relief.

In historical literature, papayas were first mentioned by the Spanish explorer Oviedo in 1526 who observed the tree growing along the Caribbean coasts of Panama and Colombia. Before 1525 papaya seeds were taken to Panama and then to the Dominican Republic. From there cultivation spread throughout South America, the West Indies, the Bahamas, and to Bermuda. Spaniards carried seeds to the Philippines about 1550 and the papaya traveled from there to Malaysia and India. By the mid-17th century, the papaya was distributed all over the tropical regions of the world. Papaya was introduced to Hawaii in the 1800s, and has become naturalized in many areas.

WORLD PRODUCTION OF PAPAYA

Papaya is now produced in about 60 countries, with the clear majority grown in developing economies. Global papaya production has grown significantly over the last few years, The United States is currently the largest importer of papaya because of its high per-capita income, and sizable Asian and Hispanic populations.

Papaya has become an important agricultural export for developing countries, where export revenues from the fruit provide a livelihood for thousands of people, especially in Asia and Latin America. The world production of papaya as a fruit ranks fourth behind the banana, the pineapple, and the mango. Papaya exports contribute to the growing supply of healthy food products on international markets. World production exceeded 12,000,000 metric tons in 2015.

TOP 10 PRODUCERS OF PAPAYA IN METRIC TONS

RANK	COUNTRY	PRODUCTION
1	India	5,160,390
2	Brazil	1,517,696
3	Indonesia	906,312
4	Dominican Republic	815,499
5	Nigeria	775,000
6	Mexico	712,917
7	Democratic Republic of the Congo	230,000
8	China, Taiwan Province of	222,000
9	Thailand	215,000
10	Guatemala	206,500

THE BIOLOGY OF THE PAPAYA

Papaya is the fruit of the *Carica papaya tree*. The fruit grows on a tree that comes in one of three sexes, male, female, or hermaphrodite. Only the hermaphrodite version produces the large yields preferred by commercial growers. Farmers can't tell which papaya seeds will grow into the desired plant of the hermaphrodite sex. So, they plant a bunch of seeds in the ground, wait for

CORN, COTTON AND CHOCOLATE: HOW THE MAYA CHANGED THE WORLD

them to grow and then chop down the one-third to one-half of the plants that aren't the hermaphrodite variety.

There are two types of papayas, Hawaiian and Mexican. Mexican papayas are much larger than the Hawaiian types and may weigh up to 10 pounds and be more than 15 inches long. The papaya tree is a large woody herb that grows to 10 or 12 feet in height and is a short-lived and fast-growing. The hollow green or deep purple trunk is straight and cylindrical with prominent leaf scars. Its diameter may be from 2 or 3 inches to over a foot at the base.

THE PAPAYA AS FOOD FOR THE WORLD

The ripe papaya is popular when eaten raw and its juice is a favorite drink. The fruit is the ingredient in a multitude of cuisines throughout the world. The unripe green fruit can be eaten cooked or served in salads and stews.

The black seeds of the papaya are edible and possess a sharp, spicy taste. They are sometimes ground and used as a substitute for pepper. In some parts of Asia, the young leaves of the papaya are steamed and eaten like spinach.

American cuisine: The United States is the largest importer of papayas in the world. Recipes include salads where papaya is paired with chicken, shrimp, cheese, and cucumbers. Papayas are enjoyed as soup and in smoothies.

Mexican cuisine: The original home of the papaya features numerous recipes ranging from quesadillas, bread, paletas, and coolers. Have you tried a papaya margarita or papaya ice cream?

Caribbean cuisine: The melting pot of the Americas features papaya recipes using raw, stuffed and baked fruit. Recipes include papaya chutney, relish and shrimp.

Thai cuisine: Green papaya is used in Thai cooking, both raw and cooked. In Thai cuisine, unripe papaya is used to make salads such as *som tam* and curries such as *kaeng som* when still not fully ripe.

Indonesian cuisine: The unripe papaya and it's young leaves are boiled for use as part of *lalab* salad, the flower buds are sautéed and stir-fried with chilies and green tomatoes as the *Minahasan* papaya flower vegetable dish.

PAPAYA A MEAT TENDERIZER

The papaya has achieved worldwide fame as an efficient meat tenderizer. The papain contained in the papaya is the active ingredient that breaks down tough cuts of meats. The Maya knew the secret of papaya as a meat tenderizer for thousands of years.

You can thank collagen for tough steaks. Collagen is the primary component of tendons, ligaments and other connective tissues. These long strands of protein bind the meat in steaks together. The papain tenderizer breaks down this structural binding of the muscle tissue and reduces the meats toughness to increase your eating enjoyment. Much in the same way enzymes in the human body help digest food.

CORN, COTTON AND CHOCOLATE: HOW THE MAYA CHANGED THE WORLD

THE PAPAYA SAVES INDIANA JONES

The Maya cultivar played a key role in the making of a classic adventure film. During the filming of the movie classic, *Indiana Jones and the Raiders of the Lost Ark,* Harrison Ford, who played the Indiana Jones character, injured his back while performing stunts. The injury caused the movie to shut down. Back surgery for Harrison Ford was planned. It appeared that the surgery and recovery period would delay the movie for months.

Director Stephen Spielberg, then learned of the curative powers of an enzyme derived from the papaya fruit. He learned that the enzyme papain, when injected into the disc space of the vertebra, cured back injuries. He consulted with a doctor who applied the enzyme to the ruptured disc in the spine of Harrison Ford. The enzyme worked like a charm. In a few days, Harrison was back working in front of the cameras.

The papaya enzyme came to the rescue and saved the show. Just like something out of an Indiana Jones movie, the production was saved by a fruit from the rainforest. The injections healed Indie's problems and the movie became a worldwide blockbuster and is now a classic cult movie.

CHEMONUCLEOLYSIS AND THE PAPAYA

How did the papaya enzyme cure the spinal injuries of Indiana Jones? Chemonucleolysis is name for the injection of an enzyme into a bulging spinal disc, with the goal of reducing the size of the disc. Doctors have learned that chemonucleolysis is an alternative to surgical excision in curing back injuries. Chymopapain, a purified enzyme from the papaya plant, can be injected into the disk space to reduce the size of the herniated disks. Chymopapain speeds up the breakdown of the jellylike substance inside the disc by releasing water. Thus, the bulging disc will shrink and relieve pressure on the nerve root and the healing is complete.

PAPAYA AND THE ABUSE OF PAPAIN IN DRUG TESTING

Papaya has a multitude of beneficial properties, but a singular property of the Maya cultivar can be applied by users of illicit drugs to cloak their use of banned substances. Each year approximately 20 million employees in the United Stated are screened for illicit drugs.

Marijuana is the most frequently abused drug. Urine adulterants provide an opportunity for drug users to obtain a false-negative result on commonly used drug screening methods. Papain, the papaya enzyme, is popular as an adulterant that can alter the results of a drug test.

Papain can interfere with urine drug tests for cannabinoids. Papain is an antibody to tetrahydrocannabinol, or THC, and will destroy THC when added to the urine sample. Positive urine contains THC byproducts. The papain attacks and destroys the THC byproducts and will result in a false negative in most tests and can't be detected by most labs. Papain is found in some drug detox products but for the drug users it is easier to obtain papain from commercial meat tenderizers purchased in the supermarket.

THE PAPAYA AS MEDICINE

The papaya has components with unique curative characteristics. The fruit contains multiple nutrients that cure a range of ailments. Papaya seeds contain vital nutrients that are thought to

CORN, COTTON AND CHOCOLATE: HOW THE MAYA CHANGED THE WORLD

produce results in the healing of cirrhosis of the liver. Papaya seeds have also been used for treating kidney disease and preventing renal failure.

The papaya seed has antibacterial capabilities. A small amount of papaya seeds can kill bacteria such as staph, E. coli, and salmonella. Thus, the papaya seeds can cure many causes of food poisoning. Papaya seeds also work as an anti-viral agent helping to heal viral infections. They contain the alkaloid "carpaine" that kills intestinal worms and ameba parasites.

Papaya seeds contain agents that are thought to stop the growth of cancer cells and tumors and they contain isothiocyanate which works to treat colon, breast, lung, prostate cancer and leukemia.

Papain is useful in combating dyspepsia, or upset stomach, and other digestive orders. Papaya preparations are marketed in tablet and liquid form to remedy digestive problems.

Papain is also applied topically for the treatment of cuts, rashes, stings and burns. Papain ointment is commonly made from fermented papaya flesh, and is applied as a gel-like paste. The unique protein-digesting enzymes, papain and chymopapain, have been shown to help lower inflammation and to improve healing from burns. The juice is used for warts, tumors, corns, and abrasions of the skin.

Women in India, Bangladesh, Pakistan, Sri Lanka, and other tropical countries have long used green papaya as an herbal medicine for contraception and abortion.

PAPAIN AS A WORKHORSE IN INDUSTRY

Papain, the enzyme in the papaya, has applications for industrial and cooking purposes. Most of the papain imported in the U.S. is used for meat-tenderizers. Nearly 80% of American beer is treated with papain, which digests the protein fragments allowing the beer to remain clear upon cooling. Cosmetically it is used in some toothpaste, shampoos, and face-lifting preparations. Papain is used to clean silks and wools before dying, and to remove hair from hides during tanning.

THE PAPAYA IN POPULAR CULTURE

The papaya appears in the lyrics of the song *The Bare Necessities* from Disney's animated film, *The Jungle Book*. Baloo the Bear, with the voice of comedian Phil Harris, sings the song which contrasts the smooth fruit of the papaya with the spiny, prickly pear.

Jazz vocalist Urszula Dudziak sings a playful song entitled *Papaya* (1976).

Poems about the pleasures of the papaya are plentiful. "Under the Papaya Tree: A Book of Love Poems ", by poet Tina S Karagulian is a book of love poems.

HOW THE PAPAYA HELPED CHANGE WORLD HISTORY

The Maya papaya is a tropical fruit that is enjoyed around the world for it delicious taste. Over 12,000,000 metric tons are grown each year in the tropics. The juice of the papaya is a great meat tenderizer and is used in medicines. The Maya cultivar saved an epic movie from failure when it cured a spinal injury to Indiana Jones.

CORN, COTTON AND CHOCOLATE: HOW THE MAYA CHANGED THE WORLD

CHAPTER 16: THE PEANUT

Botanical name: *Arachis hypogaea* **Maya name:** *mani*

Memories of a youth

A springtime visit to the city of Atlanta from our small town of Marietta was always exciting. The trip was 18 miles, which may have been a long jaunt by automobile in those days, but was a breeze riding on the trolley car. The trolley operated on a dedicated track that allowed the vehicle to reach speeds of 65 miles an hour. The railed vehicle made 42 stops along its route. The stops included hamlets and major junctions along the route: Fair Oaks, Smyrna, Windy Hill, Bolton, and then the eastern turn down Marietta Street in downtown Atlanta.

From there it would continue on to our stop on the corner of Marietta Street and Peachtree Street. This was in the center of what was then called "The Gem City of the South" a long time before the city burgeoned and became known as "Hotlanta". Our primary mission was to purchase baby chicks or "biddies" for our chicken house. We always made the purchase of chicks at Hastings Seed and Feed.

During this time, World War II was raging in two theatres and by raising chickens we supplemented the crops growing in our victory garden. I was permitted to accompany my dad on this adventure because I was responsible for taking care of the chickens. We rode the trolley into the big city to make our purchases from Hastings and then returned by the same trolley carrying a perforated box, alive with the peeping of my new friends.

Before visiting Hastings we would stroll up the original Peachtree Street, Atlanta's main street, have our lunch at Leb's Restaurant and then widow shop in the lavish displays of the big department stores. It was Saturday and the sidewalks were crowded with shoppers. At seven years of age I was short, not short for my age, but seven years old short. The hustle and bustle of the crowds caused me to keep close to my father. He was running interference for me.

I smelled the fragrance of the giant before I saw him. The aroma that wafted from his direction was toasty and delicious. This was a new food perfume to my novice olfactory senses.

Then, the crowd opened up and this giant figure loomed up over me! He was eight feet tall, wore a monocle, a top hat and his body was in the shape of a giant yellow peanut. I quickly slid behind my father for protection. However, it was too late, the giant peanut had made eye contact with me and was extending his white-gloved hand toward me. I stepped back, not in fear, but in shyness. He opened his hand and the large white-gloved hand held two roasted peanuts in its palm. He beckoned for me to take them. I reached forward and took the warm toasty peanuts in my fingers. The giant gracefully nodded and turned to others in the crowd, also offering them roasted peanuts. I was astounded. I had scored a double first, meeting Mr. Peanut and tasting my first roasted peanuts.

This was true wonderment, warm delicious Maya peanuts that crunched as I chewed. I did not have a clue in my seven-year-old head what this delicious legume would mean to my future, to Georgia, to American and to world history.

CORN, COTTON AND CHOCOLATE: HOW THE MAYA CHANGED THE WORLD

THE MAYA AND THE PEANUT

The wild peanut is indigenous to the northern part of South America. Somehow the peanut found its way to Mesoamerica and into the resourceful hands of Maya agronomists. They adopted the legume and cultivated the plant early in the Maya Pre-Classic Period, from 2000 BC to 100 AD. During three millennia of cultivation the Maya improved the quality of the wild nut.

The Maya also used the peanut for medicinal purposes for a variety of cures. Maya shamans used ground peanuts mixed with water to cure fever and applied peanut paste to soothe aching gums.

The Maya used the peanut in their cuisine as a food and as a flavoring. It was consumed raw, toasted on a Maya griddle, *comal*, or added to stews whole, or ground up, reduced to paste, and used to thicken soups and stews. Peanut oil was also used in their cooking and the peanut is still used today in Maya recipes.

The Maya were well ahead of their time in combining the tastes of their cultivars. They mixed peanuts into their chocolate drink for a combined flavor. Modern confectioners have followed the Maya lead and combined the two flavorful ingredients into a wide variety of chocolate and peanut candies.

THE PEANUT MEETS THE WORLD AND CHANGES HISTORY

Columbus encountered the peanut during his voyages of discovery. The conquistadors found peanuts being sold in the marketplace of Tenochtitlan, the capital city of the Aztecs. The existence of the peanut was first recorded by Bartolome de las Casas in 1502. He wrote that peanuts, called a "*mani*", were being grown to by indigenous people.

The delicious legume was subsequently transported to Europe, Africa, Asia, and the Pacific Islands by European traders. Cultivation is now widespread in tropical and subtropical regions. In West Africa, it replaced a traditional plant, the *bambara* groundnut.

During colonial times, the peanut was introduced to the Southern United States by slave traders. Slave traders found that the peanut could provide cheap, nutritious food for Africans being transported on slave ships across the Atlantic. Peanuts from Africa were re-introduced to the New World when Africans were transported to America as slaves, and peanuts came with them. Slaves planted peanuts throughout the Southern United States. Most Southerners recognize the terms goober and goober pea as another name for the peanut. The word goober comes from *nguba*, the Congo name for peanuts.

In the 1700s, peanuts, then called groundnuts or ground peas, were studied by botanists and were regarded as an excellent food for pigs. Records show that peanuts were grown commercially in South Carolina around 1800 and used for oil, food, and a substitute for cocoa. However, until 1900 peanuts were not extensively grown, partially because they were regarded as food for the poor.

The first notable increase in U.S. peanut consumption came in 1860 with the outbreak of the Civil War. Southern soldiers, as well as Northern soldiers, used the peanut as food. After the

CORN, COTTON AND CHOCOLATE: HOW THE MAYA CHANGED THE WORLD

war, peanut consumption increased because when Northern soldiers returned from the South, they had learned to eat peanuts and the importation of peanuts to the North increased.

During the last half of the 19th century, peanuts were eaten as a snack, sold freshly roasted by street vendors and at baseball games, county fairs and circuses. It is now traditional at modern sports events to see a peanut vendor tossing bags of peanuts to patrons in the grandstand.

While peanut production rose during this time, peanuts were still being harvested by hand. Hand harvesting left stems and trash in the harvested peanuts. Poor quality and lack of uniformity kept down the public demand for peanuts. Around 1900, on the peanut farms, equipment was invented for planting, cultivating, and harvesting peanuts. In the processing plant, machines were developed for shelling and cleaning the kernels. With these mechanical aids, peanuts rapidly came into demand for roasted and salted nuts, peanut butter, oil and candy.

At the turn of the century the popularity of the peanut changed. Previously, the peanut was considered a "low class" food. This attitude changed at the turn of the 20th century. In 1906, a magazine article stated: *"The patrician palette has generally tabooed the peanut. It has shown a preference for the sawdust of in the circus. Scientific investigation combined with commercial instincts has finally placed the products of the American peanut on the home table of all Americans."*

By 1923, peanut oil was used in the manufacture of margarine. One of the attractive features of using peanut oil was that it produced a yellow a color in margarine. Previously, color had to be added by the consumer and there was a tax for added color. Using peanut oil eliminated the tax.

Peanut production rose rapidly during and after World Wars I and II because of the peanut's popularity with Allied Forces for its use in explosives and because of the post-war baby boom. Procter & Gamble entered the peanut butter business and introduced Jif in 1958. Jif still operates the world's largest peanut butter plant, producing 250,000 jars every day.

During the early 1990s, the demand for peanuts was reduced. Weight conscious Americans stopped buying peanuts and allergy-conscious schools eliminated peanuts from their menus. However, reports of the peanuts demise have been greatly exaggerated.

In the 21st century, the peanut has graduated into the broader culture and has become an American icon. The peanut is a well-traveled Maya cultivar. It had a round trip ticket from America to Africa and back again. Today, peanuts contribute over four billion dollars to the U.S. economy each year.

WHAT'S IN A NAME? WHAT ARE PEANUTS CALLED AROUND THE WORLD?

An actual name for the peanut was uncertain for many years. People who wrote about the legume in books and newspapers did not pick a standardized name for the plant. Names for the peanut varied. In 1848, one patent application referred to the peanut as: "the ground pea of the South, the goober, or Pindar pea." The Department of Agriculture called it "the earthnut, groundnut, goober, Pindar, or pea-nut". An 1884 guide referred to the peanut as "mandubi, pea-nut and monkey nut".

CORN, COTTON AND CHOCOLATE: HOW THE MAYA CHANGED THE WORLD

By the 20th century, despite its horticultural confusion, the name "peanut" won out. As the peanut went from being an unappreciated slave food to a multibillion-dollar crop, the other words for peanut fell out of use. "Pindar" lingers in only a few corners of the South. Earthnut, ground-pea and other variants have also disappeared. But how about "goober"? The familiar term, goober hangs on. Throughout the South, you might eat goober pie, goober cake or plain old roadside goobers, freshly boiled.

When the conquistadors visited Tenochtitlan, the Aztec capital, they saw peanuts for sale in the markets. The peanut's Aztec or Nahuatl name was *tlalcacahuatl*. This word was the basis for *cacahuate*, the Mexican Spanish name for peanuts and French name *cacahuete*.

The term m*ani* for peanuts was used in the Mayan language. This is the name for the peanut that is still used in Cuba and parts of South America. *manobi* is used in Brazil, and the peanut is called *inche* in Peru, and *amendoin* is the name in Portugal.

THE MAYA CULTIVAR CAPTURES A WORLD MARKET

This Maya cultivar has captured a world market. The peanut, is currently grown in over 100 countries and produces 34,430,000 metric tons a year. That's about 9 pounds of peanuts for every person on the planet. China, India and Nigeria have been the leading producers.

TOP TEN PRODUCERS OF PEANUTS IN METRIC TONS PER YEAR

RANK	COUNTRY	PRODUCTION
1	CHINA	17.00
2	INDIA	9.50
3	NIGERIA	3.00
4	UNITED STATES	1.90
5	MYANMAR	1.70
6	INDONESIA	1.25
7	SUDAN	0.85
8	SENEGAL	0.71
9	ARGENTINA	0.58
10	VIETNAM	0.05

THE PEANUT AND ITS PECULIAR GROWTH PATTERN

The peanut is not actually a nut but is a species in the legume or bean family. The peanut follows an unusual pattern of growth. The fruit of the peanut starts life above ground and then it dives beneath the surface of the soil to complete maturation. The orange-veined, yellow-petal, pea-like flower appears in clusters above ground. Following self-pollination, the flowers fade and wither. The stalk of the plant at the base of the ovary elongates rapidly, develops a point, turns downward and penetrates the soil to a depth of several inches. This is where the subterranean peanuts complete their development and ripen. The fruit is called a pod and contains 1 to 4 seeds or nuts.

CORN, COTTON AND CHOCOLATE: HOW THE MAYA CHANGED THE WORLD

THE PEANUT SERVED AS FOOD

For centuries peanuts have been enjoyed in many culinary applications from Chinese to African and Western cooking. Whether used in stews, soups, sauces, porridge, mixed dishes, boiled, or eaten out of hand, peanuts have continually nourished different cultures while providing an enjoyable flavor. Peanuts and peanut butter are an affordable and readily available food option. Hundreds of Millions of tons of peanuts are grown and consumed around the world.

There are over 5000 recipes for peanut-based dishes. The choice of dishes includes: peanut coffee, peanut bread, boiled and roasted peanuts, peanut butter, peanut candies, peanut cakes and cookies, peanut ice cream and peanut dishes as a main course. However, peanuts and peanut butter comprise over two-thirds of all nut consumption.

NUMEROUS USES OTHER THAN FOOD ACHIEVED BY THE TALENTED MAYA LEGUME

Approximately two-thirds of all United States peanuts are used for food products, including peanut butter, roasted and shelled peanuts, boiled peanuts, candy, and roasted-in-shell peanuts, which differs from its popular use as cooking oil elsewhere in the world. The remaining one-third of annual production of this Maya cultivar is used for seed, feed, production of oil, and nonfood products including a diverse variety of soaps, medicines, cosmetics, paints, varnishes, furniture polishes, insecticides, lubricating oils, leather dressing and lubricants and nitroglycerine. The shells of peanuts are used in the manufacture of plastic, fuel, abrasives, wallboard, mucilage, cellulose, fireplace logs, livestock feed and fertilizer.

THE PEANUT AND GEORGE WASHINGTON CARVER

In the United States, peanuts were considered a regional food of the South until after the Civil War. Scientist George Washington Carver identified numerous nonfood uses for the peanut and other parts of the plant and encouraged plantings of peanuts as a rotational crop for cotton production.

George Washington Carver discovered over three hundred uses for peanuts. His research and promotion of numerous peanut products and additives include adhesives, axle grease, bleach, buttermilk, chili sauce, fuel briquettes, ink, instant coffee, linoleum, mayonnaise, meat tenderizer, metal polish, paper, plastic, pavement, shaving cream, shoe polish, synthetic rubber, talcum powder, wood stain, peanut soap, biodiesel fuel, peanut laxative, peanut dye, peanut shampoo, peanut insecticide, peanut grease, peanut explosive, peanut shell seat cushion, peanut fertilizer and peanut glue.

CIVIL WAR FOOD: THE PEANUT CHANGES THE WAY AMERICANS EAT

Napoleon aptly stated, "an army travels on its stomach". This was still true 50 years later during the American Civil War. The morale of the soldiers, as well as the physical stamina of each combatant, was directly dependent on the food that a soldier put into his stomach. The quartermasters who oversaw the food supply, for both the Union and Confederate armies, were among the most important officers because if they failed in their duties, the entire army could literally collapse from hunger.

CORN, COTTON AND CHOCOLATE: HOW THE MAYA CHANGED THE WORLD

The duties of the quartermaster were among the military's most complex tasks. Tons of food and other supplies had to be collected, secured, and moved in a highly organized manner under the most chaotic and harrowing of conditions. The job required particularly talented and driven individuals armed with resourcefulness in maintaining the food supply. Prior to the Civil War, peanuts were not a widely-cultivated crop and were generally viewed as a foodstuff fit only for the lowest social classes and for livestock.

The status of the peanut or goober pea in the Southern diet changed during the war as other foods became scarce. Excellent sources of protein, peanuts were a means of fighting malnutrition. The army and civilians turned to the peanut as a new food supply. In addition to their prewar consumption, peanuts were used as a substitute for items that were no longer readily available, such as coffee.

Peanut oil had the advantage of not gumming up machinery and peanut oil was used to lubricate locomotives when whale oil could not be obtained. On the home front housewives saw peanut oil as a sound substitute for lard and shortening as well as lamp fuel. Georgia soldiers in the Civil War were commonly called "goober grabbers".

Northern soldiers were introduced to the peanut during the Civil War. They consumed peanuts when occupying Southern states. When the soldiers returned home, they came home with a taste for peanuts. These new consumers increased the Northern demand for imported peanuts from Africa and the Caribbean. Peanut imports from Africa and the Caribbean increased from 4.8 million pounds in 1865 to 11.5 million pounds in 1868.

THE PEANUT IN SONG AND LANGUAGE

The Maya cultivar has changed the English language and has won fame in songs and music. There is a long list of slang verbiages and songs that are attributed to the peanut.

The interjection of the word in peanut in the language has different meanings including, a cute person, an obnoxious person, a small annoying person, an affectionate name for a child, an insignificant amount of money, and the cheapest seats in the balcony.

The peanut has been honored in song and music in several countries. Several are children's songs including: "Found a Peanut" and "A Peanut Sat on a Railroad Track". A Cuban song, "The Peanut Vendor" sold more than a million records.

The lyrics of a Civil War song about peanuts are called an American legend. The lyrics of "Goober Peas" are an accurate description of daily life during the last years of the Civil War for Southerners. The South had little to eat aside from boiled peanuts, or "goober peas", which often served as an emergency rations. "Goober Peas" is a traditional folk song originating with Confederate soldiers during the American Civil War.

Verse 1

>Sitting by the roadside on a summer's day
>Chatting with my mess-mates, passing time away
>Lying in the shadows underneath the trees
>Goodness, how delicious, eating goober peas.

CORN, COTTON AND CHOCOLATE: HOW THE MAYA CHANGED THE WORLD

Chorus
>Peas, peas, peas, peas
>Eating goober peas
>Goodness, how delicious,
>Eating goober peas.

Verse 2

>When a horse-man passes, the soldiers have a rule
>To cry out their loudest, "Mister, here's your mule!"
>But another custom, enchanting-er than these
>Is wearing out your grinders, eating goober peas.
>*Chorus*

Verse 3

>Just before the battle, the General hears a row
>He says, "The Yanks are coming; I hear their rifles now."
>He turns around in wonder, and what d'ya think he sees?
>The Georgia Militia, eating goober peas.
>*Chorus*

BOILED PEANUTS

The boiled peanut is a tasty snack that is a Southern treat. Unlike fried green tomatoes or pimento cheese, boiled peanuts have been a Southern staple for a very long time, extending back to the colonial era. In other parts of the country, millions of people snack on roasted peanuts and spread peanut butter on their sandwiches. But, after all these years, boiled peanuts remain almost exclusively a Southern thing.

Boiled peanuts are boiled in their shell with salt or with a piquant spice mixture and sold while still in their hull. Fully mature peanuts do not make good quality boiled peanuts; raw or "green" peanuts are preferred. "Raw" denotes peanuts in a semi-mature state, having achieved full size, but not being fully dried. After boiling in salt water the peanuts have a strong salty taste and become softer with the length of cooking.

Boiled peanuts were probably introduced to America by African slaves, but it was not until 1899 that a recipe for boiled peanuts was published. Boiling peanuts has been a folk cultural practice in the Southern United States since at least the 19th century, where they were originally called "goober peas".

Peanut boils were organized principally for social gatherings and were compared in popularity with watermelon cuttings and fish fry's, where extended families and neighbors would gather to share conversation and food. At peanut boilings, bushels of peanuts were cooked in big black cast iron pots. Like okra, black-eyed peas, collard greens and pork barbecue, the boiled peanut has become a symbol of Southern culture and cuisine.

CORN, COTTON AND CHOCOLATE: HOW THE MAYA CHANGED THE WORLD

ROASTED PEANUTS

Roasted peanuts are available in several different packaging and roasting variations. The roasted peanut may be plain, salted or coated with different flavors including honey, sweet, hot and spicy, and salty. Beer Nuts snack brand are peanuts coated with "sweet-and-salty glazing".

Roasted peanuts may also be sold while still in the shell, plain or salted. Summertime in America just would not be the same without attending a baseball game with bags of roasted peanuts sailing through the air and into the hands of delighted fans. This iconic American scene is played with background music set to the classic tune of: *"Take me out to the ballgame. Buy me some peanuts and Cracker Jacks. I don't care if we never get back."*

PEANUT BUTTER IS EVERYBODY'S FAVORITE

Like other all-American foods such as the hamburger, the hot dog, and the ice-cream cone, peanut butter first emerged at the end of the nineteenth century. A physician in St. Louis, Missouri started manufacturing peanut butter commercially in 1890. Featured at the St. Louis World's Fair as a health food, peanut butter was recommended for infants and invalids because of its high nutritional value and its ease of digestion.

John Harvey Kellogg, known for his line of prepared breakfast cereals, patented the process of preparing peanut butter with steamed nuts in 1895. He reportedly served peanut butter to the patients at his Battle Creek Sanitarium.

Joseph Lambert, who had worked at Battle Creek Sanitarium, and Dr. Ambrose Straub obtained a patent for a peanut-butter-making machine in 1903. Chemist Joseph Rosefield invented a process for making smooth peanut butter in 1922. He licensed his invention to the company that created "Peter Pan" peanut butter in 1928 and in 1932 he began producing his own peanut butter under the name "Skippy" peanut butter. Peanuts prepared for peanut butter are roasted, blanched and sorted before grinding into a creamy consistency. Peanut butter produced in the U.S. must contain a minimum of 90 percent peanuts.

There are plenty of other countries that adore the crushed goober pea. Canadians eat it for breakfast; Haitians call it *mamba* and buy it from street vendors; it is quite popular in the Netherlands where it is known as peanut cheese, and the people of Australia, France, Ireland, England and China enjoy peanut butter. Peanut butter was transformed into a billion-dollar business by the middle of the twentieth century.

AN AMERICAN CLASSIC: PB&J, THE PEANUT BUTTER AND JELLY SANDWICH

A classic American food, the peanut butter and jelly sandwich or the PB&J lives in fame across American culture. It is a favorite food that can be found in kitchens, on the menus of diners as well as high scale restaurants. The sandwich, popular in North America, includes a layer of peanut butter and either jelly or jam spread on bread, commonly between two slices, but sometimes eaten open-faced or with one slice folded over. It is a nutritional sandwich that children can make for themselves. A national survey showed the average American will have eaten 2,500 PB&J sandwiches before graduating from high school.

In the early 1900s, peanut butter was considered a delicacy that was only served to the elite. Peanut butter was first paired with a diverse set of foods such as pimento cheese, celery,

CORN, COTTON AND CHOCOLATE: HOW THE MAYA CHANGED THE WORLD

watercress, and spread on toasted crackers. By the late 1920s, preparation of the iconic sandwich became much easier and the PB&J sandwich moved down the class ladder with the advent of sliced bread and the lower price of peanut butter. During World War II, peanut butter and jelly were found on U.S. soldier's military ration list.

PEANUTS AS SNACK FOODS, PEANUTS AND CHOCOLATE: THE MAYA COMBO

The rising demand for peanuts in the early 20th century was partly due to a demand for peanut oil during World War I, combined with the growing popularity of peanut butter, roasted peanuts and peanut candies. Peanut candy products originating in the early 20th century included many brands that are still sold today such as Cracker Jacks (1893), Planters Peanuts (1906), Oh Henry! candy bar (1920), Baby Ruth candy bar (1920), Goobers chocolate covered peanuts (1920), Butterfinger candy bar (1923) and Mr. Goodbar candy bar (1925). M&M's candy, a chocolate covered peanut, originated in the United States in 1941, and is now sold in as many as 100 countries.

Reese's Peanut Pieces manufactured by The Hershey Company, are peanut butter covered in candy shells that are colored yellow, orange, or brown. The relatively new product became very popular with the 1982 release of the cult movie *E.T. the Extra-Terrestrial,* in which the candy is featured.

A little over a century ago many Americans considered between meal snacking to be unhealthy. Peanut candies broke down the attitude popular against eating between meals by catering to America's sweet tooth.

In the 21st century, peanuts, cracker jacks, and peanut candy bars remain the stars in the snack food industry. Popularity of these treats grew until, America and the peanut supported a multi-billion dollar snack food industry. Snickers are the best-selling candy bar in the world, selling $3.6 billion worth of candy bars each year. Reese's peanut butter cups are second with $2.7 billion in world sales.

PEANUT ALLERGIES

Everything is not pleasant with the popularity of the peanut. Certain people, perhaps 1-2% of the United States population, have mild to severe allergic reactions to peanut exposure. Their symptoms can range from watery eyes to anaphylactic shock, which can be fatal if untreated. For these individuals, eating a small number of peanuts or even inhaling peanut dust can cause a reaction. Because of their widespread use in prepared and packaged foods, the avoidance of peanuts is difficult. Peanut products may carry warnings on their labels indicating the presence of peanut products.

PEANUT OIL: AN IMPORTANT VEGETABLE OIL

Peanut oil was used by the Maya in their cooking and the use of peanut oil continues today across the globe. Because refined peanut oil does not absorb food flavors and has a high smoke point, it is the frying oil preferred by many nations. Unrefined peanut oil is a popular choice for salad dressings, roasting vegetables and other uses where healthy but flavorful oil is desired.

CORN, COTTON AND CHOCOLATE: HOW THE MAYA CHANGED THE WORLD

The oil is available in refined, unrefined, cold pressed and roasted varieties. Peanut oil is the third most popular cooking oil in the world. Although India and China are the world's largest producers of peanuts, they account for a small part of international trade in peanuts because most of their production is consumed domestically as peanut oil.

BIODIESEL FUEL

The use of peanut oil may help replace petroleum based diesel fuel by converting crops into fuel. Since peanuts are 50% oil, they are excellent sources of biodiesel fuel. Rudolph Diesel, the inventor of the diesel engine, used peanut oil as fuel for his first diesel engines in 1886.

Under heat and pressure, peanuts release their oil, leaving a dry cake that can be used for animal feed. A ton of peanuts yields about 800 lbs. of animal meal, and about 100 gallons of crude oil. With a yield of 3,000 pounds per acre, a 70 grade (70% of the weight of the peanut in shell) and 50 percent oil content, peanuts could potentially produce 120 to 150 gallons of biodiesel per acre. Biodiesel production in the USA exceeded 1 billion gallons in 2011 with a projected production level of 12 billion gallons in 2020.

PEANUT FLOUR

Defatted roasted peanut flour is a gluten-free source of protein. The flour can be used to thicken soups, fortify breads and pastries and coat meats and fish. Made from raw peanuts which have been blanched, and electronically sorted to select the highest quality nuts, they are roasted and processed to obtain a lower fat flour with a strong roasted peanut flavor. Peanut flour is used in confectionery products, seasoning blends, bakery mixes, frostings, fillings, cereal bars, and nutritional bars.

THE PEANUT, THE PEANUT BRIGADE, AND THE AMERICAN PRESIDENT

Fate played a hand in the interplay between a Maya cultivar and American history. The peanut produced a change in world history when a rising young American Naval Officer was forced to return to his family's peanut farm in Georgia. This was the first step in the young man becoming American's 39th President.

James Earl Carter, Jr. was the first American president to be born in a hospital. His family had lived in America for 300 years, and his ancestors had fought in the revolutionary and Civil War. Jimmy grew up on his family peanut farm in Plains, Georgia.

However, Jimmy Carter had his sights set on a higher goal than farming. He attended Georgia Tech and graduated from the Naval Academy. Carter intended to make the Navy his career. He served on submarines and was selected to be a part of the new nuclear program for the Navy. The program was commanded by the famed Admiral Richtover.

His star was quickly rising in the Navy, when his father passed away and he was called home to run the family peanut business. The Maya peanut called the future president back to his roots. Carter made the family peanut business very successful and began his involvement in politics. First as a school board member, a Georgia state senator and then in 1970 he was elected the Governor of Georgia.

CORN, COTTON AND CHOCOLATE: HOW THE MAYA CHANGED THE WORLD

In 1976, he ran as a candidate for the president of the United States. He was swept into office by groups of volunteers from Georgia and across the nation. These devoted volunteers went from door to door, met early morning workers at industrial plants, and set up tables in shopping malls to campaign for Carter. This group became known as the "Peanut Brigade". This was a band of brothers that made lifelong relationships during that campaign. They surprised the world when their efforts paid off and Jimmy Carter was elected President of the United States.

President Carter served one term and made significant advances in peacekeeping efforts including the Camp David Accord Treaty and the SALT II Nuclear Arms Treaty. His peace keeping and humanitarian efforts after his presidency make Jimmy Carter renowned as the most successful ex-president in history. Jimmy Carter was awarded the Nobel Peace Prize in 2002 for his efforts to find peaceful solutions in international conflicts. All this thanks to the Maya peanut.

PEANUTS, THE COMIC STRIP

Peanuts is an American comic strip that was created, written, and illustrated by Charles M Schultz for nearly 50 years. *Peanuts* was the most popular and influential strip in the history of the comic strip and altered the culture of the United States. Schulz drew more than 17,897 strips that were published, making it arguably the longest story ever told by one human being. *Peanuts* has been termed the most shining example of the American success story in the comic strip field.

The comic strip had a small cast of characters, but they made a large impression on its readers. The cast of *Peanuts* featured Charlie Brown, Lucy, Linus, Schroeder, Shermy, Pig-Pen, Patty and a beagle named Snoopy. The script and characters created socio-psychological cerebral comments and situations that became part of Americana. These include Snoopy as the Red Baron and the ongoing situation of Lucy holding a football, only to pull it away at the last second causing Charlie Brown to slip and fall. The characters were immortalized in hit songs including, "Charley Brown" and "Snoopy vs. The Red Baron", and Charlie Brown's periodic television specials.

The comic strips themselves, plus movies, musicals, television shows, merchandise and product endorsements, produced revenues of more than $1 billion per year, with Schulz earning an estimated $30 million to $40 million annually. Schultz retired the "Peanuts" comic strip in 2000.

MR. PEANUT

Mr. Peanut is the advertising logo, mascot and a television spokes-peanut of Planters, an American peanut producing company. He is depicted as an anthropomorphic peanut in its shell, dressed in the formal clothing of an old-fashioned gentleman with a top hat, monocle, white gloves, spats, tights, and a cane.

Planters Peanuts was founded in 1906, in Wilkes-Barre, Pennsylvania. In 1916 the company held a contest to create a company logo. A fourteen-year-old schoolboy named Antonio Gentile won the contest with his drawing of a Peanut Man. An artist later added the spats, top hat, monocle, and a cane to the drawing and Mr. Peanut, the icon, was born.

By the mid-1930s, the raffish figure had come to symbolize the entire peanut industry. Mr. Peanut has appeared on almost every Planters package and advertisement. He is now one of

CORN, COTTON AND CHOCOLATE: HOW THE MAYA CHANGED THE WORLD

the best-known icons in advertising history. He has renewed following in current television comercials.

THE PEANUT GALLERY

In the days of vaudeville, the peanut gallery was a nickname for the cheapest and rowdiest seats in the theater, the occupants of which were all too willing to heckle the performer.

The least expensive snack served at the theater would be peanuts, which the patrons would sometimes throw at the performers on stage to show their disapproval. The phrases "no comments from the peanut gallery" or "quiet in the peanut gallery" are extensions of that name.

THE PEANUT GALLERY AND HOWDY DOODY

In the late 1940s, the "Howdy Doody" children's television show had on-stage bleachers seating about 40 kids that was called the "Peanut Gallery". Each show began with Buffalo Bob asking, "Say kids, what time it is?" and the kids would yell in unison, "Howdy Doody Time!" Then the kids all sang the show's theme song. It was one of the first television shows with audience participation as a major component.

THE PEANUT AND ITS CHANGES TO HISTORY

The Maya peanut took a round trip to Africa and back to America as it began its history-changing career. The peanut has become a worldwide favorite as oil and as a food. It changed African cultivation practices by replacing traditional plants with the peanut. Peanuts are part of America's favorite snacks and candies, and the Maya peanut played key role in electing America's 39th president. George Washington Carver, a famed botanist arose to develop new and wonderful uses for the legume. *Peanuts* will go down in history as its most popular comic strip and a folk song. The world produces 34 million tons of peanuts per year.

CORN, COTTON AND CHOCOLATE: HOW THE MAYA CHANGED THE WORLD

CHAPTER 17: PINEAPPLE:

Latin name: *Ananas comosus.*   **Maya name**: *anana*

Memories of a youth

The sky was always bluer, the sun was always more golden and the trees were always much greener in my childhood memories of that September afternoon. I was six years old and everything was right with the world. Walking home from school, a roaring sound attracted my attention. I looked up, the sound came from the roar of four powerful rotary engines of a B-29 Super fortress sweeping low overhead. The ship was on its downwind leg for landing and would be touching down on the runway at the Bell Bomber plant. Its silver skin was sleek and unblemished. Its livery would not be painted onto the aircraft until it was ferried off to its first mission in World War II.

The sound of the aircraft engines faded away as I turned toward our house. A white bungalow with wide open windows and doors that were covered with screens. The open windows provided an airy respite from the torrid summer heat and the screens were a barrier against the swarms of flying insects that filled the humid air.

Turning toward the house, I was stopped in my tracks by a luscious and almost unbelievable aroma. Wafting toward me on the air, the aroma flowing from our kitchen was a perfect combination of sweet and delicious flavors. My pace quickened as I slid through the front door. The screen door slammed behind me as I made straightaway toward the source of that magical scent. However, the slamming of the screen door had given me away.

My mother called out from the rear of the house, "Jimmy, do not touch that cake". Rats! I was caught.

By this time, I had spied the object of my affection. I was orbiting the table, circling slowly, despite being deprived of a tasteful feast, I was enjoying a visual and olfactory delight of its savory perfume. There it was, a baked rectangle adorned with eight perfect golden circles of pineapple, each punctuated in the center by a bright red maraschino cherry. Behold the perfect food, the pineapple upside-down cake.

Little did I know that the delightful object before me on the table had its baking techniques born in medieval ovens, and the luscious pineapple was invented in the Yucatán as a Maya cultivar. However, I was only six years old and I was far distant from a time when I would know the history of the world and how the pineapple contributed to historic changes.

THE MAYA AND THE PINEAPPLE

The pineapple is indigenous to the Orinoco Basin in southern Brazil, where its wild relatives may still be found. However, the barely edible wild pineapple somehow migrated north to Mesoamerica and into the Maya domain. The wild ancestor of today's sweet and luscious fruit is inedible. The raw fruit of the ancestor plant is extremely acidic and can burn the lip, tongue and throat. Despite its shortcomings, Maya agronomists recognized the potential of the primitive pineapple as a valuable cultivar and converted the fruit into a treasure. The Maya seized an opportunity and the process of genetic alteration began, the pineapple was domesticated by Maya agronomists, who converted the cultivar into one of the most popular tropical fruits in the world.

CORN, COTTON AND CHOCOLATE: HOW THE MAYA CHANGED THE WORLD

Archeological records indicate that the pineapple was cultivated early in the Maya culture, so early that a Maya word for the fruit existed in the 5,000-year-old proto-Maya language. The Maya recognized the pineapple as a valuable source of nutrition and added them it their everyday maize based diet. The addition of the pineapple helped create a balanced diet.

The Maya disseminated the valuable fruit throughout its wide-ranging trade network. Maya sea traders carried the fruit to the islands of the Caribbean, Mesoamerica and Central America where the pineapple became part of the local diets.

At the time of European contact, the domesticated pineapple had become part of the tropical diet. They grew in tropical areas of Mesoamerica as well as the hot, humid parts of South America.

THE PINEAPPLE MEETS THE WORLD

The first European known to eat a pineapple was the Great Navigator, Christopher Columbus. Most culinary historians agree that this took place on November 4, 1493, when he landed on the Caribbean island of Guadeloupe. Even though he found the pineapple to be unusual looking, he liked the sweet taste and enjoyed the curious new fruit. While having an abrasive, segmented exterior like a pinecone, it possessed a firm succulent flesh. Nothing about the fruit resembled an apple, however, to enhance its appeal Columbus added "apple" to the name, thus the name "pineapple" became a part of our vocabulary.

In 1516, King Ferdinand II, upon being presented with the only unspoiled pineapple that made the journey back to Spain, declared it was the best thing he had ever tasted. Other Europeans agreed and by the 17th century, pineapples had become a major status symbol in many parts of Europe. *"The pineapple,"* wrote Fernandez de Oviedo in the 16th century, *"appeals to every sense, but that of hearing."* This chief to the royal family of Spain may have seemed somewhat extravagant in his praise of the fruit, but history reveals that the Maya cultivar did indeed take Europe by storm. It became a symbol of all things exotic, available only to the wealthy and privileged.

By the end of the 16th century, Portuguese and Spanish explorers introduced pineapples into many of their Asian, African and South Pacific colonies, countries in which the pineapple is still grown today. Spaniards introduced the pineapple to the Philippines early in the 16th Century. Portuguese traders are said to have taken the plant to India from Indonesia in 1548 and they also introduced the pineapple to the east and west coasts of Africa. The plant was growing in China in 1594 and in South Africa by 1655.

When Columbus initially brought pineapples back to Europe, attempts were made to cultivate the fruit. The growers realized that the fruit needed a tropical climate to survive. The pineapple reached England in 1660 and around 1720 growers began to try to cultivate them in greenhouses. Greenhouse agriculture flourished in England and France in the late 1700s.

The desire to cultivate the pineapple in Europe led to a continental competition to grow the first European pineapple. The competition accelerated advances in greenhouse design technology. The Maya fruit changed the way Europe cultivated exotic fruits that could not be grown without the artificial tropical environment created by the greenhouse. Thanks to the pineapple, the use of greenhouse agriculture has become sophisticated and is now practiced on a large scale growing numerous cultivars in Northern European countries.

CORN, COTTON AND CHOCOLATE: HOW THE MAYA CHANGED THE WORLD

Pineapples soon became a symbol of wealth. The raw fruit was initially used for display at dinner parties, rather than being eaten, and were used again and again until they began to rot. By the second half of the 18th century, the production of the fruit on British estates had become the subject of great rivalry between wealthy aristocrats.

In the 18th century, pineapples began to be cultivated in Hawaii. If you wanted a fresh Hawaiian pineapple, you had to go there to get one. Picked ripe, a fresh pineapple simply could not survive the long journey by ship. It was only when air cargo became available that fresh Hawaiian pineapple began to arrive in mainland markets.

THE PINEAPPLE IS A MEMBER OF THE BROMELIAD FAMILY

The pineapple is the leading edible member of the family *bromeliaceae* which embraces about 2,000 species. The fruit of the pineapple starts out as a stalk with a hundred or more-small purple or red flowers shooting up from a three-foot tall plant. Each flower develops a small fruit that eventually close ranks and join together into a single barrel-shaped fruit. These flower elements also form the scales on the outside of the pineapple. The more scales on a pineapple, the stronger the tropical taste will be. A pineapple with fewer and larger scales will have a milder but sweeter flavor and more juice. The tough waxy rind, made up of hexagonal units, may be dark-green, yellow, orange-yellow or reddish when the fruit is ripe. The flesh ranges from nearly white to bright yellow.

WHAT'S IN A NAME?

The fruit has acquired a few vernacular names in places around the world. It is widely called *piña* by Spanish-speaking people and *abacaxi* in the Portuguese tongue. The word is used by the rest of the world is pineapple, with the exception of the name *nanas* in southern Asia and the East Indies.

ALL THE WORLD LOVES THE PINEAPPLE

The pineapple has created a global market. It is grown in most tropical countries in Latin America, Asia, and Africa. The Philippines, Thailand, and Costa Rica lead the world production of Pineapples. In 2015, 24,400,000 metric tons of pineapple were produced.

TOP 10 COUNTRIES PRODUCING PINEAPPLE IN METRIC TONS

RANK	COUNTRY	PRODUCTION
1	Thailand	2,650,000
2	Costa Rica	2,484,729
3	Brazil	2,478,178
4	Philippines	2,397,628
5	Indonesia	1,780,889
6	India	1,456,000
7	Nigeria	1,420,000
8	China	1,000,000
9	Mexico	759,976
10	Colombia	157,098

CORN, COTTON AND CHOCOLATE: HOW THE MAYA CHANGED THE WORLD

THE PINEAPPLE INVENTS THE GREENHOUSE AND CHANGES WORLD ARCHITECTURE

Once Christopher Columbus returned to Spain, he was fortunate to offer a surviving example of the fruit to the King. When the pineapple was introduced to Europe it created a sensation with its juicy sweet taste and overnight the pineapple became a sensational item of celebrity and curiosity for the aristocracy, gourmets, and professional horticulturists.

An unfortunate factor in the acceptance of pineapples was that obtaining the fresh fruit was almost impossible. The lengthy sea voyage from the Caribbean and a notoriously short shelf life combined to make the delivery of a viable fruit for European consumption an impossible task. A flurry of attempts was made by horticulturists to grow the cultivar and share its exotic flavor with wealthy Europeans. It was not as easy as it appeared. Nearly two centuries would pass after King Ferdinand enjoyed the pineapple before European horticultural technology was able emulate the tropical environment to grow the fruit.

Developing an artificially controlled environment to promote the growth of plants was not a new concept. In 50AD, the Roman emperor, Tiberius (42 BC-37 AD) used artificial environmental methods of successfully growing a cucumber like vegetable on a year-around basis. He used a proto-greenhouse called a *specularia*. The vegetables were planted in wheeled carts which would be rolled outside during the day to be placed in sunlight, and at night the carts would be rolled inside the *specularia* to a heated environment. In winter, the carts would remain inside the *specularia* which was had a roof covered with oilcloth or transparent stone to get available sunlight.

Early greenhouses were constructed in 13th century Italy to house exotic and medicinal plants. These first greenhouses, sited mainly on the estates of the rich, were used to protect orange trees from freezing during the winter. These first greenhouses were called *orangeries* and were constructed by the Italians in 1545.

Most *orangeries* were little more than a typical house structure with a small number of windows near the roof and primitive heating. They were appropriate for growing the undemanding citrus fruit, but they proved to be totally unsuitable for the raising of pineapples.

With horticultural technological capabilities lagging, the quest to grow this luxury tropical fruit became the major catalyst for a series of technological breakthroughs in greenhouse design. The competition to grow a European-bred pineapple swept across the Continent. The greatest criterion for success was the ability to simulate an artificial environment suitable for the growth of the fruit. Horticulturists realized that the pineapple could only mature and bear fruit in a truly tropical environment. Environmental control did not only mean a suitable ambient temperature but appropriate soil temperatures, proper light levels, high humidity, and nutrient rich soils.

Assuring appropriate heating levels was the first criteria and this challenge was satisfied when a reliable source of heat was developed by using the proper a mixture of maturing compost. With an adequate heat source solved, the gardeners began to seek an appropriate environmental envelope or greenhouse building design. They needed a design that would synergistically integrate the required humidity, lighting levels, ventilation and ambient temperature.

Once the criteria were established for building systems that would achieve the appropriate environmental factors to grow the luscious fruit, the quest for the answer accelerated greenhouse design technology to include the combination of architectural, structural, and environmental elements that would achieve the optimum design for growth of the pineapple.

CORN, COTTON AND CHOCOLATE: HOW THE MAYA CHANGED THE WORLD

An important development in the technological process was the introduction of a sunken compost hot bed enclosed with large glass frames. This was the first step toward developing the classic transparent envelope for a greenhouse. This type of greenhouse came to be called a "pinery" as an abbreviated term for "pineapple nursery".

The first pineapple to be grown in Europe was produced by Agnes Block, a Dutch woman, who successfully matured a pineapple in 1687, on her estate at Vijerhof near Leiden, Holland. This was 183 years after the first pineapple was introduced to Europe by Christopher Columbus.

In 1773, William Parker, an English gardener, elevated greenhouse technology to a higher level by combining the heat generating compost pit with hot air flow. This heating system was installed in glass greenhouses. This was the first time a building system was created that enabled controlled environmental conditions throughout the entire year. This development is considered to be the first real "pinery" or greenhouse. The technical sophistication of the pinery was enhanced from 1760 to 1810 when glass sidewalls and front hot air flues were added to the building systems.

In 1803, Joseph Paxton was born as the seventh son of an English farmer. Paxton would become a renaissance man who developed the technology that revolutionized greenhouse design that would be extrapolated to change the architectural and agricultural practices of Europe and the world. Working as a gardener, he began his homegrown greenhouse design while employed as the head gardener at Chatsworth, England for the Duke of Devonshire.

His innovations include the optimization of the geometry of the greenhouse envelope by using the ridge and furrow roof and innovative structural support systems for glazing. His designs enabled the greenhouse to admit maximum light with a watertight roof. These structures were the precursors of modern greenhouse design. Paxton became a master gardener and one of the most successful pineapple gardeners in Europe.

Paxton was not an architect or engineer but a creative and intuitive master gardener. His creative mind became fascinated with the organic structure of plants including the leaf of the gigantic Amazonian water lily. The inspiration from the organic structure of the water lily lead to the development of innovative structural systems for greenhouses, then to larger structures, including the development of the design for the Crystal Palace in London. This masterpiece was the major structure for the Great Exhibition of 1851 and became the quintessential design for glass-clad structures in the 19th century and the forbearer of 20th century architectural glass buildings.

For the exhibition structure, Paxton was given only 14 months to plan, design and construct the building. The structure was required to be temporary requiring a simple and economical design. Paxton's simplistic design was selected because it could be constructed with speed, efficiency and innovation. The design consisted of a structure that was 1851 feet long and rose to 128 feet in height.

The hierarchical design reflected his practical brilliance as a designer. Paxton required only 10 days for the design process and the structure was erected in six months. Paxton's advanced building technology included modular structural iron frames, glass panes, cast iron glazing bars, and cast-iron water channel drains flowing into hollow columns for downspouts.

The Crystal Palace was the largest glass building in the world until the early 20th century. The structure revolutionized the construction and design technology of all future buildings with its

CORN, COTTON AND CHOCOLATE: HOW THE MAYA CHANGED THE WORLD

innovative construction methodology. The Crystal Palace was the epitome not only of greenhouse design but of monumental glass architecture buildings and became the historic pivot point where the greenhouse was changed forever from an aristocratic garden building into the new focus of European commercial agriculture.

Commercial pineapple cultivation in greenhouses came to an end with the introduction of fast moving steam ships and air transportation. However, the pineapple did change European and world architecture with environmental designs using innovations of glass and iron. Commercial agriculture was altered by the invention of large-scale greenhouses in northern latitude countries where large varieties of fruits and vegetables are now grown. Maya agronomists would be proud.

THE PINEAPPLE BECOMES THE SYMBOL OF HOSPITALITY FOR THE WORLD

On Guadeloupe, where Columbus first encountered the fruit, the pineapple was used to make wine and was a staple at feasts and rituals. The indigenous culture revered the excellent fruit. The natives of Guadeloupe had a custom of placing pineapples or pineapple crowns outside the entrances to their dwellings as symbols of welcome, friendship and hospitality.

This practice was adopted by the American colonies and later by Europeans. A sea captain would impale the fruit on his front door or fence post to subtly communicate to neighbors that he had safely returned from some distant, tropical destination. It was a notice to friends that the man of the house was home and receiving visitors.

The sea voyage from the Caribbean Sea to the American colonies was short compared with the long voyage to Europe. The shorter voyage to the mainland colonies made the pineapple readily available to the consumer. However, while more readily available, the tropical fruit was still a rarity and cost a pretty penny. Only the speediest ships and most fortuitous weather conditions could assure the delivery of ripe, wholesome pineapples to the confectionery shops of colonial cities.

The sweetness and unusual appearance of the pineapple made it a sought-after delicacy in colonial America. When it was served to guests, they were naturally flattered at the honor, and this evolved into the concept of the pineapple being considered to be a symbol of the highest form of hospitality.

In colonial America, hosting friends for home dinners was the primary means of entertainment. The prime source of amusement during a formal home dinner was a creative display of exotic foods. This was the way a woman presented her personality, hospitality and communicated her family's social status. The dinners were extravaganzas of visual delights, novel tastes, new discoveries and congenial conversation that went on for hours. While fruits in general were the major attractions of the sophisticated appetites and dining practices, the pineapple was the star celebrity. Its rarity, expense, and striking visual attractiveness made it the ultimate exotic fruit.

All a party hostess had to do was to display the fresh fruit as part of her decorative centerpiece and the hostess would be awarded the highest social recognition. The competition for acquiring a pineapple was so keen, that colonial confectioners sometimes rented them to households. Later, the same fruit would be sold to other, more affluent clients who actually ate it. As you might imagine, hostesses would have gone to great lengths to conceal the fact that the exotic topic of the evenings conversation was from the "rent a pineapple" store.

CORN, COTTON AND CHOCOLATE: HOW THE MAYA CHANGED THE WORLD

The rarity and expense of the pineapple as a symbol of wealth, hospitality, and luxury also became an iconic image of success and the pineapple became a design element for architects, designers and craftsman throughout the colonies, and in Europe. It was used by architects to decorate gateways, door lintels and other design details on their buildings. They stenciled pineapples on walls and canvas rugs and wove pineapples into tablecloths, napkins; carpets and draperies. There were whole pineapples of all sizes carved of wood or stone, pineapple graphics on the finest china and its image was painted or carved onto all manner of furniture.

The form of the pineapple has been replicated in landscape garden architecture and fountains throughout Europe and the United States. Pineapple shaped finials and pineapple motif fountains are still popular in the 21st century. The shape may be chiseled in stone, pressed in concrete, or cast in iron, but invariably, you will find yourself looking at the same tropical fruit. An observer will note that neither grapes, strawberries, apples, nor bananas have made themselves such a prevalent motif. In the built environment, the pineapple is king. The Maya cultivar changed the world's method of expressing welcome.

THE PINEAPPLE OVERTHROWS THE HAWAIIAN MONARCHY

The pineapple was once the king of Hawaiian tropical fruits. The earliest migrants to the Hawaiian Islands were Polynesians who traversed the Pacific Ocean using large double-hulled canoes. They arrived between 1000 AD and 1400 AD. Hawaii was established by the chiefdom of Hawaii during the years 1795 to 1810 by the subjugation of the independent chiefdoms of smaller islands into one unified monarchy.

The Hawaiians possessed a strong army and navy that was developed under King Kamehameha I, who unified Hawaii in 1810. The army and navy used a combination of traditional and western armaments including canoes, helmets and uniforms made of natural materials as well as cannons, muskets, and European ships. When Kamehameha died in 1819 he left his son Liholiho a large arsenal with tens of thousands of men and many warships.

In 1820, the first Protestant missionaries arrived on Hawaii. By then, Hawaii had become a port for seamen, traders and whalers. The whaling industry boom flourished on Maui. Following the arrival of the outsiders, the population in Hawaii was ravaged by epidemics and western crowd diseases. The military shrank along with the population and by the end of the dynasty the Hawaiian navy had been disbanded and the army numbered only a few hundred troops.

The pineapple finally made its way to Hawaii 300 years after Columbus first saw the fruit. The first noted appearance of the fruit was in 1813, when Don Francisco de Paula y Marin, a Spanish advisor to the Hawaiian King, brought the famous fruit with him. That year the first pineapple was planted in Hawaii. But, it would be over 70 years before the pineapple really took off. The mass production of pineapples in Hawaii didn't start until 1885 when an English Captain, named John Kidwell, opened his commercial plantation in 1885. The pineapple was sold only in its raw form until captain Kidwell decided to build a pineapple cannery in Hawaii and shipped the canned fruit to the U.S. mainland.

Queen Liliuokalani was the last reigning monarch of the Hawaiian Islands. She felt her mission was to preserve the islands for the native residents. In 1893, however, local businessmen and politicians, composed primarily of American and European residents with interests in the pineapple and sugar cane production, carried out a coupe d'état. They were able to overthrow the queen and take over the government of the Kingdom of Hawaii.

CORN, COTTON AND CHOCOLATE: HOW THE MAYA CHANGED THE WORLD

Historians suggest that the businessmen were in favor of overthrow of the monarchy and annexation to the U.S. in order to benefit from more favorable trade conditions for fruit and sugar exports to markets in the U.S. The delicious pineapple was a part of the scheme to overthrow the monarchy of Hawaii. The change in governments was a product of greed perpetrated by pineapple growers who wanted to increase their profits by reducing tariffs.

In March 1897, President McKinley was inaugurated and negotiations between the U.S. and Hawaii resumed. Shortly after, Hawaii was annexed as a part of the U.S. by a joint resolution of Congress. The U.S. flag was raised over the executive building in August 1898, and in 1900, Hawaii became an official territory of the United States. Queen Liliuokalani was forced to give up her throne and was arrested and forced to reside in 'Iolani Palace. In 1896, she was released and returned to her home at Washington Place in Honolulu where she lived for the next two decades.

The high tariff was, of course, lifted. The goals of the powerful pineapple growers had been achieved. Those who profited from the annexation of Hawaii had committed an act that The New York Times headline called "the political crime of the century" The actors in the scheme remain some of the Hawaii's wealthiest and most influential landholders. The overthrow of the Kingdom of Hawaii and the subsequent annexation of Hawaii have recently been cited as the first major instance of American Imperialism.

DOLE PINEAPPLE, AIR TRAVEL AND TOURISM

James Drummond Dole, a Harvard graduate, had a dream of growing pineapples. In 1901, Dole began growing Pineapples on sixty acres on Wahiawa District, in north Oahu. He named his business the "Hawaiian Pineapple Company." Dole constructed a cannery and packing plant in the town of Wahiawa. Soon, yields and popularity of his product proved greater than he expected and he became very wealthy.

By 1922, Dole had purchased the island of Lāna'i, the sixth largest island in the chain and developed it into the largest pineapple plantation in the world with over 20,000 acres. Dole was so successful in his endeavors to place fresh and canned pineapple in grocery stores that he was dubbed, "The Pineapple King".

Inspired by Charles Lindbergh's successful transatlantic flight in 1927, James Dole saw the potential role that air transportation could play in delivering his fresh fruit to the American mainland. He also considered that air transport service to the islands would encourage tourism to Hawaii. He could not see into the future when tourism would be all important and the pineapple plantation would be no more.

Dole sponsored the Dole Air Race, also known as the Dole Derby, and the race was a disaster. Of the 15 aircraft that started the race on August 16, 1927, only two finished, and ten aviators died in their attempt to complete the flight. However, the notoriety and interest in the race elevated public interest in Hawaii and opened the air-travel business to Hawaii and Dole quickly developed his network of commercial flights for the delivery of fresh pineapples and tourists.

Pan American Airways began regular air passenger service to Hawaii in November 1935. The flight took only 21 hours and 33 minutes. Steamship travel to the island required 4 1/2 days. Air traffic swept the field.

CORN, COTTON AND CHOCOLATE: HOW THE MAYA CHANGED THE WORLD

Tourism was a small industry when the knowledge of the islands and their exotic allure became known. Hawaii became an exciting destination. Tourists numbered only 2000 in 1903 and grew to 31,846 in 1941 and passed the million mark in 1967. The booming tourist industry, spurred by the pineapple, totaled over 8,000,000 people in 2015.

The Maya pineapple changed the history and economics of Hawaii by creating the pineapple industry, overthrowing the monarchy, participating in the opening of air service and birthing the booming tourist industry.

THE PINEAPPLE CHANGES THE TASTES OF THE WORLD

After being introduced into Europe, the pineapple modified the methods that fruit was consumed as food and drink. Europeans initially consumed the pineapple as a raw fresh fruit.

But the popularity of the pineapple continued to soar into the 21st century. The methodologies of preparing the pineapple for consumption have been transformed along with new technologies for transport and processing of the fruit.

The Maya cultivar was so popular that the pineapple's conspicuous profile was used to create whimsical designs and became a ubiquitous form for shaping amusing food creations. There were pineapple-shaped cakes, pineapple-shaped gelatin molds, candies pressed out like small pineapples, pineapples molded of gum and sugar, pineapples made of creamed ice, cookies cut like pineapples and pineapple shapes created by arrangements of other attractive fruits.

As the pineapple became more accessible to the market, recipes for new pineapple dishes begin to emerge. Their numbers accelerated at the turn of the 20th century when canned pineapple hit the shelves of grocery stores. Canned pineapple made the fruit easily available. The home kitchen then became a laboratory for experimentation and development of new recipes for the popular fruit. The attractive golden circles of sliced pineapple became a luscious ingredient and soon became a visual and tasty treat for sensational culinary delights.

The pineapple is now consumed fresh and cooked, canned or juiced and the fruit has found its way into a wide array of international cuisines including American, Mexican, Hawaiian, Chinese and many others. They are used to complement meat dishes, salsas, desserts, fresh fruit salads, jam, yogurt, ice cream and candy.

The recipes for pineapple based culinary delights now number in the thousands. Some pineapple dishes and drinks are iconic while other recipes are slightly bizarre including the popular Hawaiian dish, combining pineapple and spam. Who can imagine a world without piña coladas or mai tais?

THE PINEAPPLE UPSIDE-DOWN CAKE

When did people get the idea of putting fruit at the bottom of a cake? The "upside down" technique has been around since the Middle Ages and was a natural development of ancient cooking technology. Traditionally, upside down cakes were made with seasonal fruit including apples and cherries. Cakes were made in cast-iron skillets and cooked on top of the fire or stove. The flavorful fruit ingredients were placed at the bottom of the skillet prior to placing the cake batter. When the cake was finished cooking, the skillet would be turned upside down and the finished product would pop out onto a plate. Presto, you had a delicious delight with the fruit exposed to the view of the hungry gathering. This was the advent of the "upside down" cake.

CORN, COTTON AND CHOCOLATE: HOW THE MAYA CHANGED THE WORLD

It seems hard to believe that the pineapple upside down cake has not always been a part of American cooking culture. Since it could be used with any type of fruit. It was not until 1903, when the Hawaiian Pineapple Company introduced the canned delight to the public. When the canned pineapple was introduced the delicious golden rings became the perfect partner for the visual and luscious upside down baking technique and the company introduced the recipe for upside down cake. The use of pineapple on the bottom and a cake baked in an oven was the newest and novel twist on the medieval favorite. Indeed, it did not take long for the recipe to work its way into the American housewife's cooking repertoire.

PINEAPPLE AND SPAM BECOME A MAGICAL LURE OF HAWAIIANS

The team of Span and pineapple became popular during World War II. Surpluses of the canned spiced meat, obtained from C rations of soldiers, found their way into native Hawaiian diets. After the war, spam became a favorite food of Hawaii. Consequently, Spam has become part of the history of the Islands. Hawaiians have a unique love affair with Spam and the pineapple. They treat it as a dietary staple, adding it to soups and stews, eating it as a side dish for breakfast, and enjoying it as the main event for lunch and dinner, it is usually paired with the luscious pineapple.

Residents of Hawaii consume more Spam than any other population in the world, seven million cans, or an average of 12 cans of Spam per person per year are consumed in the Aloha State. The number of recipes combining spam and pineapple are numerous and the names of the dishes are as just as exotic as the unique combo: Hawaiian Spamburger, barbecued Spam kabobs, Hawaiian Spam loaf, Spam and Pineapple casserole, pineapple Spam upside down cake and many more.

PINEAPPLE PIZZA

Pizza has a long and illustrious history. The name pizza extends back to the year 997 in Italy. The legendary dish has changed over the centuries. The biggest change came when the tomato, also a Maya cultivar, was introduced in Italy and was added as a topping. In the late 18th century, pizza made with mozzarella, basil and tomatoes were added as a topping. The white green and red were the colors of Italian flag. This pizza was presented to queen Margarita and it became her favorite. Thus, the first named pizza was coined the Pizza Marguerite.

Pizza took America by storm, and became the quintessential New York Food. The number of toppings and combinations of toppings have reached a gourmet level. The world of the pizza gourmet was turned upside down when the Hawaiian pineapple pizza was added to the pizza lineup. The Hawaiian pineapple pizza was introduced in 1962. It was not invented in Hawaii but in Ontario, Canada. The pizza world was up in arms.

Traditional Pizza aficionados consider that a pineapple pizza to be an insult to all pizzas. Hawaiians do not favor pineapple pizza any more than other American pizza lovers. They either love it or hate it. Australians are the exception; this maverick pizza is a favorite of 17% of Aussie pizza lovers.

The American attitude regarding the pineapple pizza can be summed up by an old joke. An individual was being asked, "What is a pineapple?" He answered, "A pineapple is something that you should not put on a pizza."

CORN, COTTON AND CHOCOLATE: HOW THE MAYA CHANGED THE WORLD

THE APPEAL OF THE RAW FLESH AND THE JUICE OF THE PINE APPLE

The flesh and juice of pineapples are used in cuisines around the world. In many tropical countries where pineapple is grown, pineapple is prepared, and sold on roadsides as a snack. They are sold whole, or in halves with a stick inserted into the flesh. Pineapple recipes in tropical countries tend to use the raw rather than a cooked pineapple as part of the dish. It is used in salsas, cored slices with a cherry in the middle are a common garnish on hams. Chunks of raw pineapple are not only used in such dishes as fruit salad, but also as a main ingredient in savory dishes. Crushed pineapple is used in yogurt, jam, sweets, and ice cream. The juice of the pineapple is served as a beverage, and is also as a main ingredient in cocktails.

THE LONG-TERM MEXICAN AFFAIR WITH THEIR LOCAL FRUIT

Mexico is the homeland of the pineapple. The country produces 500,000 metric tons of pineapple each year, only a small fraction of this yield is exported because most of the crop is consumed by Mexicans. Mexican cuisine makes great use of the pineapple for both savory foods, such as Oaxaca's pineapple chicken, pineapple-filled sweet tamales and sweet foods like the candied fruit found at Mexican fairs.

The pineapple is cooked with lentils and spices to make a savory Lenten dish and fermented to make the slightly alcoholic and very refreshing drink called *tepache*. It is used in fruit salsas, in *aguas frescas*, and is great on the grill as an accompaniment to chicken, pork or fish. It can be cut into a "boat" to shape an elegant salad presentation, cut into chunks for fruit salad or into slices for garnishes and cakes.

The fruit was an ancient Maya cultivar and was used as an everyday food. How the Maya would be surprised at the sensation and expense that the world has expended on their cultivar.

THE PINEAPPLE AS FUNCTIONAL MEXICAN FOLK ART

The form of the pineapple that was nurtured by Maya agronomists has been an object of art for hundreds of years, back to the Classic Maya culture. Pineapple designs appear everywhere in traditional Mexican folk art and decorative accessories. The *piña*, pineapple in Spanish, has served as the principal geometric form for specific art figures that are unique to artisanal objects in central Mexico. The characteristic green glaze on these oversized examples of the pineapple is made from the copper derived from deposits in the state of Michoacán. The lustrous glaze coating of jewel-like colors give a glass-like sheen to the artwork. These examples of Mexican art are treasured by collectors, but are seldom seen outside of central Mexico. The eloquent ceramic pineapple conveys true hospitality.

THE PINEAPPLE IN CARTOON LIFE

SpongeBob Square Pants is a popular American animated character on children's television and has a worldwide audience in dozens of languages. SpongeBob is a sea sponge employed in a restaurant named the Krusty Krab. Sponge Bob's house is a classic pineapple shape situated on the sea bottom. The creatures living in the house are SpongeBob and Gary, SpongeBob's pet snail. The house did not originate on the sea bottom, but feel off ship navigating the sea above Bikini Bottom. The house is a symbol of friendship and stands out against the vernacular sea bottom architecture on Conch

CORN, COTTON AND CHOCOLATE: HOW THE MAYA CHANGED THE WORLD

CLASSIC PINEAPPLE BASED DRINKS AND COCKTAILS

The pineapple is the basic component and main ingredient in many famous and infamous alcoholic drinks and cocktails. Not only the juice but the flesh is used in drinks and cocktails. The pineapple based drinks all seem to have a tropical or beach ambiance and are popular at beach bars or functions where one may find a little paper umbrella in the drink. There are dozens of drink formulas that use pineapple as the basis for their flavor. A flavored vodka is produced that combines the essence of the pineapple and mint.

The most popular pineapple drinks have an affinity to the tropics and their name reflects its association. Even the liquor used in these "boat drinks" has a tropical origin and some have legends that reflect their beginnings. Examples include the Piña Colada, the Rum Punch, the Mai Thai, The Bahama Mama, The Pineapple margarita, The Pineapple Mojito, and the Pineapple Cilantro Serrano Cocktail. The winner of the best name for a pineapple drink goes to the, "Don't pine for me Argentina". Be cautious when consuming these tropical libations, they are generally formulated with rum, tequila or vodka or combinations and they will sneak up on you.

THE MAYA PINEAPPLE AND ITS PART IN CHANGING HISTORY

The luscious Maya cultivar has made a significant mark on history. The quest to grow the pineapple in Europe produced building technology that advanced the capabilities for creating the tropical climate required for cultivation of the plant. The technology for greenhouse building systems that produced architectural glass buildings was created from these efforts. Pineapple greenhouse technology also changed the agriculture systems used in northern climates. The image of the pineapple has become the symbol of world hospitality. The monarchy of the Hawaiian Islands was overthrown by the greed of pineapple planters in the first act of American Imperialism. The delicious Maya cultivar has altered the tastes of the world in food and drink. 24,4000,000 metric tons of pineapple are produced each year.

CORN, COTTON AND CHOCOLATE: HOW THE MAYA CHANGED THE WORLD

CHAPTER 18: SQUASH

Botanical name: *Cucurbita* **Maya name:** kuum

Memories of a youth

Halloween was always an exciting event in our little town. The town people followed time proven customs of dressing up in scary costumes, carving pumpkins into frightening candle lit heads, trick or treating (mostly treating), telling ghost stories, attending costume parties and visits to haunted places. The occasional vandalism was mostly preplanned tricks. Our town was surrounded by Civil War battlefields lending themselves to haunting. Spectral viewings were commonplace with sightings of phantom armies and ghostly Confederate generals strolling around the Confederate cemetery.

Of course, there were witches, vampires, mummies, and ghosts. On that hallowed night, I was visiting Mickey, a friend living on a nearby street. Our streets were separated by a wooded area transected by a small creek. At 12 years of age we considered ourselves too old for dressing up in costumes or playing trick or treat. We had visited the usual haunted places in our town on past Halloweens and to our horror and delight the haunted places turned out to be the real thing. We surely were not going back to those scary places.

We took the old warning seriously, that ghosts will not hurt you, but they sure will make you hurt yourself. Our terrorized flight away from the imagined ghouls resulted in injuries due to stepping in unseen holes, tripping over logs, and running into trees. The spirits did not hurt us, but we sure hurt ourselves.

That Halloween night, we enjoyed strolling around the neighborhood, watching the little kids parading in their costumes and playing trick or treat. In our little town, it was unnecessary for parents to escort the young ghosts and goblins. Sexual predators were unheard of in the day.

The sun set around 6:00 PM at the end of October, so when darkness fell we went to Mickey's house and visited with his parents. We discussed the recent Walt Disney movie, *Ichabod Crane and The Headless Horseman*. This was the animated version of the popular short story written by Washington Irving in 1820, *The Legend of Sleepy Hollow*.

The story is known by every child who has read the story. Ichabod Crane, a timid schoolteacher, is pursued by a headless ghoul mounted on a fire-breathing horse. The ghoul has a horrible carved fiery pumpkin head in his hand. The chase continues through a wooded hollow replete with fog and obstacles. Just when the reader thinks that Ichabod is safe over a bridge, the headless horsemen hurls the pumpkin with unerring accuracy. The horrid pumpkin strikes Ichabod and he vanishes.

Discussing the headless horsemen and the dispatching of Ichabod, gave me the chills, but I really got goosebumps when Mickey's dad, Mr. Griffin, began telling Irish ghost stories. Mr. Griffin was from the old sod and he spun the chilling yarns in a classic Irish brogue. There are no more terrifying ghost stories than Irish ghost stories. When it came time for me to leave for home I was scared stiff and I knew I had to cross the dark wooded patch between our streets.

Leaving their house and after saying my goodbyes I still had goose bumps from listening to Mr. Griffin's ghost stories. Walking down their street I came to the pathway connecting our streets. Looking down into the dark woods, I was surprised to see a thick fog flowing over the creek and enveloping the woods. The fog was so thick that it was impossible to see my hand in front of your face.

In my state of fright, I envisioned that the fog-shrouded wooded setting was like that which confronted Ichabod Crane on that fateful night. But there was no other way to reach my home without passing through the woods, crossing the creek and then up the trail onto my street.

Taking a deep breath, I started my journey into the unknown. I began at a trot, then when I reached the dense fog, I broke into a dead run. I was a fast runner and I knew that I could get through the fog in a matter of seconds. When I entered the fog, all was well for a few heartbeats. Relieved, I thought that I was silly to be frightened. Then, I heard the hoof beats of a horse. I knew my ears were deceiving me, but the sound seemed to grow louder. I imagined that racing up behind me was a headless ghoul mounted on his fire-breathing steed with a fiery pumpkin in his hand ready to hurl at me.

I put my hands over my ears, increased my speed, and shouted," La, la, la, la." I made the sound to drown out the sound of my pursuer, who was hidden in the fog. I knew that at any second he would hurl the pumpkin at my head. I remember requesting additional speed from my legs: "feet do your stuff."

Just as I expected life-threatening contact with the feared pumpkin, I broke out of the fog and into clear air. I couldn't believe it, I escaped the headless horsemen and all was well. I scurried up the trail onto my street and celebrated with a big rebel yell. I was soaked in sweat, and I felt that I did have a close call.

Looking back on that night, with the ghost stories, the darkened woods, the dense fog, and my overactive imagination, it is humorous to think of my fear of the Maya squash we call a pumpkin and the terror in my young heart. Fear that was conjured up by a movie and some Irish ghost stories. Little did Maya agronomists envision when they developed their great variety of squashes, that one of their largest creations would become famous as a thing of terror at Halloween.

MAYA AND THE PUMPKIN

Squash was the firstborn of Maya cultivars. The basic Maya foods were composed of the triad of maize, beans and squash. They became the foundation of Maya agriculture and the foods that empowered the civilization. Despite the fame that is heaped on maize, squash was the first of the triad to be cultivated. Squash was born about 10,000 BC and maize was cultivated around 8,000 BC.

MAYA AGRONOMISTS CULTIVATE THE WORLDS FAVORITE SQUASH

The squash genus developed by Maya agronomists was *Cucurbita*. Centuries of cultivation transformed the wild squash from an inedible stringy fruit into a delicious pulpy vegetable. Maya agronomists cultivated the five species of squash that still exist and are popular throughout the world.

Cucurbita maxima: Includes winter squash, hubbard squash, buttercup squash, banana squash, and the pumpkin.

CORN, COTTON AND CHOCOLATE: HOW THE MAYA CHANGED THE WORLD

Cucurbita mixta: Includes pipian and cushaw pumpkin.

Cucurbita moschata: Includes butternut squash.

Cucurbita pepo: includes acorn squash, yellow summer squash, spaghetti squash, patty pan and zucchini.

Cucurbita radicans: Includes calabacilla, calabaza de coyote.

HOW THE MAYA CONSUMED THE SQUASH.

The Maya ate all parts of the squash, including the flesh, the young leaves, young shoot tips, the flowers and even the runners. Squash was a favorite vegetable in stews, soups and other dishes. A soup made with the young flowers was a delicacy. Squash was a Maya favorite dish when mixed with maize and beans.

However, the preferred part of the squash was the seed. Squash seeds, usually pumpkins seeds, were toasted lightly on a *comal* prior to eating. Eating a handful of crunchy, toasted pumpkin seeds may be enough to prove why the Maya consumed them in such quantity. The oils from seeds were the main source of fat in the diet of the Maya and the seeds of the pumpkin are full of protein.

Although delicious in their unadulterated state, squash seeds were so ubiquitous in Maya life that they found their way into a wide array of early recipes, both humble and complex. Toasted, ground seeds were included in the maize porridge *atolli* to give it flavor and texture. *Tamales* were filled with toasted, ground squash seeds; *tortillas* were stuffed with eggs and covered with squash seed sauce. Toasted or green seeds were boiled in honey, which was then poured into small puddles and allowed to cool. This made for a sweet treat.

The most unique of Maya squash seed recipes was the sauce that is now known as *pipián*. The term for *pipián* in Mayan is *óom sikil*, which translates roughly to "squash seed foam". This describes the ancient Maya custom of using ground squash seeds mixed with chilies, achiote, salt and liquid to make a sauce for fish or venison. The red coloring does not come from the chilies, but from achiote, or annatto, the ubiquitous Maya condiment.

THE SQUASH AS A WEAPON OF WAR

The Maya combined cultivars into a toxic weapon that was quite effective in close combat. They invented an effective hand grenade. Maya warriors would hollow out the inside of a pumpkin and fill the interior with hot ashes and a mixture of ground dried chili peppers.

They would seal the top of the pumpkin and then launch the hot chili grenade into the midst of the enemy. The pumpkin would burst upon contact with the ground and the contents would explode upward. The toxic smoke from the hot chilies would fill the air and cause blindness and choking among the enemy. The enemy warriors would become incapacitated and they would become easy prey to Maya weapons.

THE SQUASH AS MAYA MEDICINE

Squash was used as a medicine by Maya healers. It was used to treat a range of ailments from wounds to prostate problems and the infestation of parasites. The pulp from the pumpkin, when

CORN, COTTON AND CHOCOLATE: HOW THE MAYA CHANGED THE WORLD

applied to a wound, would assist in healing. Maya healers recommended that eating pumpkin seeds alleviated prostate complaints including urinating difficulties. Healers recommended pumpkin seeds to kill tapeworms and other intestinal parasites. This technique is still in use as a folk remedy. Pumpkin seeds help cut the frequency of cold sore infections. They contain lysine which prevents cold sores.

THE MAYA, THE SQUASH, AND THE THREE SISTERS

Squash was one of the "Three Sisters" planted by the Maya. The Three Sisters were composed of the three main Maya crop plants: maize, beans, and squash. This combination of plants was not only the basis of the Maya diet, but were developed by Maya agronomists as a self-supporting team of companion plants. They had a truly symbiotic relationship.

Companion planting in agriculture is the planting of different crops in close proximity for pest control, pollination, creating a self-contained habitat for beneficial cultivars, maximizing use of space, and otherwise increase crop productivity.

The three crops benefited from each other's strengths. The maize stalk provides a vertical structure for the beans to climb, eliminating the need for a trellis. The beans grow up through the tangle of squash vines, climb the cornstalks, and wind their way into the sunlight, their vines holding the sisters close together.

Beans extract nitrogen from the air and transfer it into the soil for the benefit of all three plants. The large leaves of the sprawling squash plant spread along the ground, blocking the sunlight, helping prevent the growth of weeds. The squash leaves also act as a "living mulch", creating a microclimate to retain moisture in the soil, and the prickly hairs of the vine deter pests.

The sisters went even farther than their symbiotic benefits during cultivation. The introduction of the trio into the Maya diet made the sisters extremely important to Maya health. Maize lacks the amino acids lysine and tryptophan, which the human body needs to make proteins and niacin, but beans contain both nutrients. Therefore, maize and beans together provide a balanced diet.

It was pure agricultural brilliance, and is the reason that these three humble plants play such a large part in so many Native American legends. The Maya believed that since they were so magical when grown together, that they should also be eaten together. They also believed that since they protected each other while growing, that they would protect whoever ate them together.

The three sisters were an attractive asset to Maya agronomy and were transported into North America where they were the foundation of Native American agriculture.

SQUASH MAKES A NAME ACROSS THE WORLD

Christopher Columbus brought squash back to Europe from the New World but cultivation of squash did not catch on in Europe, since the cultivar does not grow well in Northern European climates. However, squash cultivation began to spread across the globe. Like other Maya cultivars, squash was introduced to the world by Portuguese and Spanish traders.

CORN, COTTON AND CHOCOLATE: HOW THE MAYA CHANGED THE WORLD

Investigation of the historical record indicates that the cultivated species of *Cucurbita* were unknown in Western Europe prior to 1492. Evidence has recently been found of botanical knowledge of at least two species, *C. pepo* and *C. maxima*, that were recognized by herbalists in the early 16th century.

Depictions of *C. pepo* were found in *Grandes Heures of Anne of Brittany*, a French devotional book printed between 1503 and 1508. A depiction of *C. pepo* is included in *De Historia Stirpium Commentarii Insignes* in 1542 by Leonhart Fuchs, a German botanist.

The Maya trading network had spread the squash across the Americas. The squash was waiting on the shore when the first European settlers arrived. Northeastern Native American tribes grew pumpkins, yellow crooknecks, patty pans, Boston marrows, and turbans. Southern tribes raised winter crooknecks, cushaws, and sweet potato squashes. European settlers in the New World were introduced to squash by the Native Americans.

Different species of squash were introduced into the U.S. in the 19th century. Varieties of *C. maxima* traveled to the U.S. from Central America in the 1800s. They are listed in a seed catalog of 1828 and were probably the first *C. maxima* variety offered to American farmers. The Hubbard was introduced about 1855.

The period from 1880 to 1900 saw great horticultural development of modern squash varieties. The Fordhook zuchinni, Perfect Gem summer squash, and delicata winter squash became available to growers. Table queen acorn squash, a well-known variety today, was introduced in 1913. Zucchini came back from Italy in 1921, transported on its return trip to America by Italian immigrants. Cocozelle, an heirloom variety of zucchini, also from Italy, was introduced in 1934.

WORLD PRODUCTION OF SQUASH

Squash cultivation has spread to most the world and today squash is grown commercially in 110 countries. The world production of squash exceeds 20 million metric tons per year. The top ten producers of squash are led by China followed by India. Total production of both countries represents over 60% of the world total.

TOP 10 PRODUCERS OF SQUASH IN METRIC TONS

RANK	COUNTRY	PRODUCTION
1	China	6,140,840
2	India	4,424,200
3	Russia	988,180
4	USA	778,630
5	Iran	695,600
6	Egypt	658,234
7	Mexico	522,388
8	Ukraine	516,900
9	Italy	508,075
10	Turkey	430,402

CORN, COTTON AND CHOCOLATE: HOW THE MAYA CHANGED THE WORLD

THE SQUASH, A TECHNICOLOR FRUIT THAT CLIMBS ON A VINE

The Maya cultivated an amazing variety of squash plants. The squash is a fruit and a special type of berry, but it is eaten as a vegetable. Squash has more varieties of shapes and colors than any other fruit. Their great variety in colors, color patterns, and shapes, ranging from light green or white to deep yellow, orange, and dark green; from solid to striped, and from flattened to cylindrical to crookneck varieties; combined with their special aroma and taste, offers humans a unique visual and culinary experience.

Squash are members of the *Cucurbita* genus. *Cucurbita* species fall into two main groups. The first group are annual or short-lived perennial vines and are mesophytic, i.e. they require a continuous water supply. The second group is perennials growing in arid zones and so are xerophytic, tolerating dry conditions.

Cultivated *Cucurbita* species were derived from the first group. Growing 5 to 15 meters (16 to 49 feet) in height or length, the plant stem produces tendrils to help it climb adjacent plants and structures or extend along the ground.

The yellow or orange flowers on a *Cucurbita* plant are of two types: female and male. The female flowers produce the fruit and the male flowers produce pollen.

Cucurbita fruits are large and fleshy. Certain domesticated specimens can weigh well over 300 kilograms (660 pounds). The current world record for a *Cucurbita* was established with 911.2 kilograms (2,009 pounds) for an Atlantic Giant pumpkin.

WHAT DOES THE WORLD REALLY FEEL ABOUT THE SQUASH?

The squash has been assimilated into world cultures. The squash and its relationship with the human condition has been analyzed by scholars. They have assessed western literature and culture, then extended their analysis to non-Western cultural settings.

They discovered that the squash has complex semiotic associations with sex and sexuality, fertility, vitality, moisture, creative power, rapid growth, and sudden death.

Cucurbits also figure prominently in the symbolism and cosmologies of many non-Western societies. And you thought that squash was just an ordinary food.

WHAT IS IN A NAME?

The English word "*squash*" comes from the native American word "askutasquash", which means "a green thing eaten raw". This is a word from the Narragansett language, which was documented by Roger Williams, the founder of Rhode Island, in his 1643 publication: *A Key into the Language of America.*

Squash goes by different names in different countries, but not as many as other cultivars. The term squash is a name given by native Americans to a Maya cultivar that was distributed across the Americas prior to European contact. However, many countries have adopted this native American word. The Dutch, Italian, French, Danish, Irish, Norwegian, Swedish, Finnish and Somali all use the term squash. The British call them marrows, the Spanish use *calabaza* and

CORN, COTTON AND CHOCOLATE: HOW THE MAYA CHANGED THE WORLD

the Germans use *quetschen*. In India, the name for squash is *ghia* and the Japanese enjoy the squash and call it *kabocha*.

SQUASH AS A WORLD FAVORITE FOOD

Squash is a favored food in over a hundred countries extending from China to Europe and is a part of favorite local dishes. Foods that can be made using squash include biscuits, bread, cheesecake, desserts, donuts, granola, ice cream, lasagna dishes, stews, pancakes, pudding, pumpkin butter, salads, soups, and stuffing. And don't forget about your aunt's squash casserole.

There are 121 recipes from China listed on the internet. It is popular in Australia and New Zealand. France has favorite squash recipes as does Russia and African countries. In India, squashes are cooked with seafood. In France, squash are traditionally served as a gratin and as soups. In Italy, zucchini and larger squashes are served in a variety of regional dishes, squashes are made into a pie filling and as a sauce for pasta. In Japan, squashes are eaten boiled with sesame sauce, fried as a tempura dish, or made into balls with sweet potato.

ZUCCHINI, ARE YOU REALLY A MAYA CULTIVAR? FUNNY, YOU DON'T LOOK MAYA.

The popular zucchini squash went through a complete makeover when Italian horticulturalists changed the color, shape and taste of a Maya cultivar. Zucchini, like all squash, has its ancestry in the Americas. The zucchini traveled to Italy as a yellow squash and Italian agronomists worked their magic. Four hundred years later, when this specimen of *Cucurbita* returned to America, it was a specimen that had a long cylindrical shape and was striped green. It was completely unlike the original Maya cultivar that traveled to Italy. People were confused, they thought the zucchini was native to Italy. It sure did not look like other Maya cultivars and it had that Italian name.

Probably, the change in the appearance of the zucchini occurred in the very late 19th century, near Milan. The zucchini was formerly referred to as green Italian squash. The alternative name for zucchini in Europe is courgette, from the French word for the vegetable. The French snubbed zucchini for a long time until chefs learned to choose small fruits which are less bland and watery. The first records of zucchini in the United States date to the early 1920s. It was almost certainly brought over by Italian immigrants and probably was first cultivated in California.

That was less than 100 years ago, and the zucchini's bland taste, combined with its incredible abundance has led to a bewildering variety of food applications. Zucchini can be sautéed, baked, poached, stuffed, eaten raw, and of course baked into bread. Its flowers can be eaten stuffed and are a delicacy when deep-fried, as tempura.

HALLOWEEN PUMPKINS: HOW SQUASH CHANGED A RELIGIOUS HOLIDAY

The pumpkin, a really large squash, has carved out a name for itself in history. The name, pumpkin, is derived from the Latin or Greek word for a large fruit.

The Maya culture, which was replete with complex ritual intercourse between priests and the gods, would be happy if they envisioned the ritual and pomp that is heaped on their lowly pumpkin during the modern Halloween holiday.

CORN, COTTON AND CHOCOLATE: HOW THE MAYA CHANGED THE WORLD

The large orange sphere is hollowed out and carved into fantastical figures that represent the wayward spirits that prowl the Halloween night. When the interior is lit with a flickering candle the image of the specter carved into the pumpkin shell is eerily exaggerated. According to many scholars, Halloween or All Hallows' Eve is a Christianized feast originally influenced by western European harvest festivals, and festivals of the dead with pagan roots.

One reason that the carved pumpkin became popular is that it was traditionally believed that the barrier between the physical and spirit worlds becomes thinner on Halloween night and contact with the souls of the dead is more readily made. The lanterns were both symbolic of such wandering spirits and were connected to Halloween lore related to warding off demons.

HOW DID THE LEGEND OF THE HALLOWEEN PUMPKIN BEGIN?

There is an Irish legend about a trickster named Jack who decided one day to play a trick on the Devil. He trapped the Devil in a turnip and paraded him around town. Eventually, Jack let the Devil out and the Devil put a curse on Jack and turned him into a spirit in hell. On Halloween night, the Devil releases Jack to terrorize the countryside.

To protect themselves, the Irish would place a turnip carved with a face outside their house to scare Jack into believing it was the Devil. They called the carved turnip, "Jacks lantern". The carved turnip has traditionally been used in Ireland at Halloween, but immigrants to North America carved the native pumpkin with a face, which is much softer and much larger, making it much easier to carve than a turnip. The carved pumpkins became known as "Jack-o'-lanterns".

The carving of the pumpkin has become a major art form during the Halloween celebration. The art has taken on a life of its own. The art of carving demons and ghouls into the façade of the pumpkin has reached high levels of realistic art. But whatever its origins, it's undeniable that over the last century or so, the particularly American pumpkin variety of the Jack-o-Lantern has become inextricably associated with Halloween.

COOKING THE PUMPKIN

While a broad range of squash is popular in cuisine around the globe, the pumpkin has found a special place among the tastes of the world and are very versatile in their uses for cooking. Most parts of the pumpkin are edible, including the fleshy shell, the seeds, the leaves, and even the flowers.

In colonial New England settlers sliced off the tops of pumpkins, removed the seeds, filled the interior with honey, milk, and spices, and then baked the pumpkin in the hot coals of an open fire. The contents were then scooped out and served as custard. Pumpkins were therefore the crust and not the filling of the early precursors of pumpkin pie. Settlers also used pumpkins in beer, breads, puddings, cookies, and pumpkin sauce, made with pumpkins stewed with butter, vinegar, and spices.

The Pilgrims were also known to make pumpkin beer. They fermented a combination of persimmons, hops, maple sugar and pumpkin to make this early colonial brew. In early colonies, pumpkin shells were used as a template for haircuts to ensure a round and uniform finished cut. Because of this practice, New Englanders were sometimes nicknamed "*pumpkin heads*".

CORN, COTTON AND CHOCOLATE: HOW THE MAYA CHANGED THE WORLD

When ripe, the pumpkin can be boiled, baked, steamed, or roasted. In its native North America, it is a very important, traditional part of the autumn harvest, eaten mashed and making its way into soups and purees. Often, it is made into pie, various kinds of which are a traditional staple of the Canadian and American Thanksgiving holidays. In Canada, Mexico, the United States, Europe, and China, the seeds are roasted and eaten as a snack.

Pumpkins that are still small and green may be eaten in the same way as squash or zucchini. In Guangxi province, China, the leaves of the pumpkin plant are consumed as a cooked vegetable or in soups. In Australia and New Zealand, pumpkin is often roasted in conjunction with other vegetables. In Japan, small pumpkins are served in tempura. In Italy, it is paired with cheese as a savory stuffing for ravioli.

Squash blossoms are eaten in all Mediterranean cuisines, usually stuffed with soft cheese, battered and fried. In Spain and Italy, they are also made into fritters. In the southwestern United States and Mexico, pumpkin and squash flowers are a very popular food item. They are dredged in a batter then fried in oil. They are a popular summer time treat.

THE PUMPKIN IN LITERATURE

Because of its relation to the spirts of Halloween, the magic related to the pumpkin has played a major role in books, legends, and fairy tales that deal with spirits, goblins, wizards and magical traits. In some of the accounts the pumpkin is used either as a magical drink, a symbol, a part of the anatomy of sub-humans, a horse carriage and a deadly missile.

The role of the pumpkin in literature ranges from a kindly spirit to the evil device of a ghoul. These tales have been a part of the culture for over 300 years.

THE LEGEND OF SLEEPY HOLLOW

The *Legend of Sleepy Hollow* is a scary story written by Washington Irving and tells the dreadful tale of a headless horseman chasing down a frail schoolmaster.

The legend relates to the tale of Ichabod Crane, a lean, lanky, and extremely superstitious schoolmaster and a headless horseman. One midnight, Ichabod rides his horse home through the woods. As he passes a purportedly haunted spot, his active imagination is engaged. He then detects that he is being followed by a tall rider dressed in black. He goes into flight when he notices that his pursuers head is not on his shoulders, but on his saddle.

The head is a horrifically carved pumpkin and in a frenzied race to a covered bridge where the headless rider is supposed to "vanish in a flash of fire and brimstone". Ichabod rides for his life and crosses a bridge that is supposed to be the boundary of the ghoul. However, to his horror, the ghoul continues across the bridge, rears his horse, and hurls his flaming pumpkin head into Ichabod's terrified face. In the morning, all that is found is a broken pumpkin. Ichabod disappears forever.

CINDERELLA

Pumpkin stories extend from the horrific to the wonderful fairy tale of *Cinderella*. In this feel-good story, Cinderella's fairy godmother turns a plain pumpkin into a beautiful carriage. The only problem is that the rental agreement runs out at midnight when the carriage reverts to a big pumpkin. But all is not lost as the prince finds her lost shoe, locates Cinderella and they live happily ever after.

PEANUTS AND THE GREAT PUMPKIN

In the classic cartoon strip, *Peanuts*, created by the great Charles M. Schulz, the main character Charlie Brown, is friends with Linus Van Pelt. Linus has a strong belief in the Great Pumpkin appearing at Halloween. He waits in the pumpkin patch on Halloween night to no avail. The great pumpkin never appears. "There is always next year" says Linus.

PUMPKIN JUICE

In some stories, drinking pumpkin juice has magical effects on its drinkers. In the Harry Potter novels, pumpkin juice is a favorite drink of Hogwarts School of Witchcraft and Wizardry. Juice from a pumpkin also has magical effects in the short story "Pumpkin Juice" by R.L. Stine from *Tales to Give You Goosebumps.*

PUMPKIN HEADS

Characters with a pumpkin for a head are brought to life by two popular authors. In Nathaniel Hawthorn's, *Feathertop,* from 1852, a witch turns a scarecrow with a pumpkin for a head into a man. In the Oz series of books, L. Frank Baum's character, Jack Pumpkinhead, has a large carved jack-o'-lantern pumpkin for a head and a wooden body that is brought to life.

VAMPIRE PUMPKINS

Just when you thought you knew all about pumpkins and their connection to the occult, we come up with a legend from Romania, the land of Dracula. The gypsy or Roma people believe that pumpkins can morph into a vampire during the light of a full moon. Vampire pumpkins are a folk legend from the Balkans. One of the main indications that a pumpkin is about to turn into a vampire is said to be the appearance of a drop of blood on its skin.

These vampire pumpkins travel around the houses, stables, and rooms at night, all by themselves, but do no harm to people. Since it is thought that they cannot do great damage, people are not afraid of this kind of vampire.

THE SQUASH AS A MEDICINE

Various species of squash have applications in medicine. *Cucurbita* is used in cosmetics for dry and sensitive skin. The flesh of *Cucurbita argyrosperma* is used for treating burns and skin conditions, and its seeds are used as an anesthetic. It is used to promote lactation in nursing women.

CORN, COTTON AND CHOCOLATE: HOW THE MAYA CHANGED THE WORLD

High doses of *Cucurbita ficifolia* have been shown to be successful in reducing blood sugar levels. *Cucurbita* fruits are an important source for humans of carotenoids, vitamin A, and rhodopsin, all of which are important to good visual acuity. Cucurbitin is an amino acid and a carboxypyrrolidine found in *Cucurbita* seeds that can eliminate parasitic worms and in treating schistosomiasis

THE PUMPKIN AS ANIMAL FOOD

The many uses of the pumpkin include its use as an animal food. Data from the University of Nebraska shows that pumpkins are a good source of energy and are high in crude protein and digestibility, and have high moisture content which makes them a great feed supplement when mixed with grazing crops.

Chickens, pigs, and goats love pumpkin, and the added vitamins and nutrients will benefit them in the long run. Raw pumpkin can be fed to poultry, as a supplement to regular feed, during the winter to help maintain egg production, which usually drops off during the cold months.

Canned pumpkin is often recommended by veterinarians as a dietary supplement for dogs and cats that are experiencing certain digestive ailments such as constipation, diarrhea, or hairballs. The high fiber content also helps to aid proper digestion.

THE SQUASH AND ITS PART IN CHANGING HISTORY

The world has adopted Maya squash as its own. It is enjoyed as food in over 100 countries. The world production of squash exceeds 20 million metric tons per year. The squash has many varieties in various colors, shapes, and sizes. The pumpkin, a favorite food, has changed religious holidays and is storied in books and legend.

CORN, COTTON AND CHOCOLATE: HOW THE MAYA CHANGED THE WORLD

CHAPTER 19: THE SUNFLOWER

Botanical name: *Helianthus annuus*   **Maya name:** *lol*

Memories of a youth

After my experience as a batboy for an industrial league baseball team in the late 1940s, I'm still mystified with the metaphysical connection between sunflower seeds and baseball players.

Over the years, I have watched literally thousands of baseball games on television and from the grandstands. I am amazed at the number of players, big league, minor league and even little leagues, who practice the habit of eating sunflower seeds.

The lower level leagues survived until the 1950s when during the late 1940s, baseball expanded as a post-war pastime. Everybody wanted to into the act. There were the major leagues, and then there were level A leagues, then B, C and D leagues. And then televised baseball was a true game changer.

In the late forties, baseball teams in Georgia included the "Atlanta Crackers", Macon "Whoopee's" and the "Savannah Sand Gnats". Georgia had teams in level A leagues and D leagues. The A league teams played in the Southern Association and South Atlantic League. The D level leagues included The Georgia State League, Georgia-Alabama League, Georgia-Florida League and the South-Eastern League. In Georgia, 37 Georgia towns had baseball teams. That's a lot of teams from an agriculture state.

Then there were the industrial leagues that were teams sponsored by big business corporations, such as Westinghouse, Coca Cola and the Ford Motor Company. My father worked for the Ford Motor Company. These teams were popular until their demise in the 1950s.

Dad was a number cruncher and he loved baseball. Therefore, he combined his vocation with his love of the game. He was the official scorekeeper for the Ford Motor Company industrial league team and I became the team's official bat boy. The team played at night and on Saturdays.

Officially the team was staffed with Ford employees who allegedly worked at the Ford manufacturing plant. However, several players were "ringers". These were men who had previously played major league baseball. They were paid by Ford so, technically, they were employed by Ford, but they did not work at the plant.

The star of the team was named "Red", he was a former major leaguer and had a close association with the Ford family. Rumor had it that he became so close to the wife of the "big boss" in Detroit, that he was shipped down to Atlanta. In Atlanta, he was treated like a rock star.

During the games, I was always very busy when the Ford team was at bat. I was occupied chasing down foul balls, retrieving bats tossed by a batter when he got a hit, keeping the bats in proper order, and I also helped a batter choose the perfect bat that guaranteed him a hit. When our team was in the field, I took a seat in the dugout and watched a phenomenal show performed by the manager and some of the bench players. While concentrating on the field action, they were eating sunflower seeds. I had watched these grown men consume the seeds many times and was always mystified at how they could crack open a seed, extract the inner

CORN, COTTON AND CHOCOLATE: HOW THE MAYA CHANGED THE WORLD

edible portion and spit out the two halves of the outer shell without thinking. It was an automatic mechanism.

The process of eating a sunflower seed by the team manager while concentrating on the field action was a total mystery to a twelve-year-old bat boy. Often, my attention was riveted on the manager and his routine of cracking the seeds, consuming the seed and spitting out the hulls. I calculated the number of seeds that he processed. I counted his action in cracking, ejecting, and swallowing the seeds at a rate of three per minute during routine play. My research indicated that he would increase his output to five or six per minute when the action sped up.

I tried to eat the sunflower seeds and only succeeded after using two fingers to hold the seed and use my front teeth to split the seed. Then I would extract the edible interior seed with my tongue, chew the delicious tidbit, and awkwardly spit out the seeds. I was 12 years old and never seemed to master the automatic process of cracking, consuming and spitting out the hulls. To this day, I have not mastered the skills and dexterity of a baseball player when eating sunflower seeds.

I achieved a certain skill level, but it was slow. I could place a seed in my mouth, crack and accurately spit out the hulls. My best time for performing this task was almost one minute. Plus, I was totally concentrating on the seed and not paying attention to field action.

Over the years, while watching baseball games, I am still fascinated while watching the consumption of sunflower seeds by the players. I'm always interested in close-ups of the seed consuming managers. In today's game, there is still an automatic rhythm of cracking a seed, splitting the hulls and ejecting the hulls, without any thought while plotting the next move on the field.

There is an unbreakable bond between baseball and the sunflower. There is magic in the process of consuming sunflower seeds that enhances the ability of a manager to envision a solution for a situation on the playing field. I think that the magic in the sunflower seeds is part of the mystery of the plant. It is a plant that follows the track of the sun across the sky and was chosen by Maya agronomists to domesticate for its magical qualities.

THE MAYA AND THE SUNFLOWER

The original source of the sunflower as a cultivar has been debated. Certain experts considered the sunflower to have been of North American origin, but recent studies have proven that the domesticated sunflower has its origin as an ancient Maya cultivar. Archaeological, linguistic, ethnographic, and ethno-historic studies have demonstrated that the sunflower entered the cornucopia of Maya cultivars as early as 2600 BC. Evidence indicates that its cultivation was widespread in Mesoamerica extending as far south to the as El Salvador.

Archaeological evidence of the sunflower in ancient Maya sites has been rare for several reasons. First, its usage in Maya cooking was not conducive to the deposition of detritus in archaeological sites. Second, tropical climatic conditions have poor properties for preservation of organic materials and they just rot away. In recent years, new evidence for Maya cultivars has come to light with advanced paleo-ethno botanical recovery techniques. Evidence of sunflower seeds have been found in Mesoamerica in situations where the preservation was especially good and have been recovered for testing.

CORN, COTTON AND CHOCOLATE: HOW THE MAYA CHANGED THE WORLD

MAYA USE OF THE SUNFLOWER

The Maya had several ways of preparing the nourishing sunflower seed as food. The most common way was to eat them fresh or toasted on a *comal*. The seeds were also ground into meal, mixed with maize flour and water to make a gruel known as *atole*. *Atole* is made by toasting the combined masa on a *comal*, then adding water. The resulting blend varied in texture, ranging from porridge to a thin liquid consistency. The mixture was poured into a gourd and became a portable meal to be carried into the fields by farmers or on the trail by travelers.

In cooking, the sunflower seed was used by the Maya just like other seeds and nuts, similar to the peanut and pumpkin seeds. They were used as a condiment in cooking stews and other dishes. The seed was ground or pounded into flour for cakes, mush or bread. Some dishes were prepared by mixing ground sunflower meal with vegetables including beans, squash, and corn.

Non-food uses of the sunflower include a purple dye for textiles, body painting and other decorations. Parts of the plant were used medicinally for purposes ranging from snakebite to body ointments. The oil of the seed was used on the skin and hair.

THE SUNFLOWER TRAVELS THE WORLD AND COMES BACK HOME AGAIN

In the early 16th century, the Spanish explorer, Monardes, brought the sunflower to Spain and it spread throughout Europe. The Spanish did not consider the sunflower as a food source, but was considered an unusual and beautiful flower that was grown for 200 years as an ornamental plant. The sunflower became widespread throughout Western Europe and was prized as a giant flower.

The person who brought the plant to the attention of the world was a Russian Czar. In 1698, Peter the Great, on a trip to Western Europe, became so enamored with the sunflower, that he carried its seeds back to Russia. There, the Russian church forbade animal fat oil during lent so the sunflower oil became popularly adopted.

An English patent was granted for producing oil from sunflower seeds in 1716 and this was the first commercial application on record. But this great idea would have to wait and it was the 19th century before the sunflower became popular as a cultivated food plant.

One of history's ironies is that when the native Maya cultivar came back to its home continent, it returned home as a changling. The plant had been genetically altered by Russian agronomists. The plant breeding material that returned the sunflower to America came from the gardens of Mennonite Russia immigrants. During the 1880s, the Mennonites sold their Russian-developed giant sunflower seeds to U.S. seed companies. Seed companies began offering the 'Mammoth Russian' in their catalogs, a variety that was a popular seed until the 1970s. In the United States, the first commercial use of the sunflower crop was as high-moisture stored fodder for poultry and the first sunflower oil was produced in Missouri during 1926.

By the early 1980s, the United States was producing sunflowers on over five million acres. Then by a quirk of history, the sunflower that had gone from the Yucatán to Russia and back would return to Europe once again. Cholesterol had become a health threat and European demand for sunflower oil increased to a level that Russian exporters of sunflower oil could not meet European demand. Europeans imported sunflower seeds from the U.S. and crushed them in European mills. The sunflower was back in style.

CORN, COTTON AND CHOCOLATE: HOW THE MAYA CHANGED THE WORLD

In the 1990s, and sunflower oil got a boost from an unexpected source: The makers of potato chips. The demand started with what was called the "Mediterranean Diet". Sunflower producers answered the demand by adopting a mutant sunflower, one created by Soviet agronomists. This was a cultivar that produced a healthy oil. It had higher levels of monounsaturated oleic fatty acids, and lower levels of polyunsaturated fats, and no trans fats. Today, farmers in the United States almost exclusively grow this sunflower cultivar.

In the 21st century, the Maya cultivar has made its mark on the world. It has made the transition from a decorative garden flower to a world class food product. It is now the third most popular vegetable oil in the world

WORLD SUNFLOWER SEED PRODUCTION

The cultivation of sunflowers as oil plants first emerged in the 19th century. Today they are grown worldwide in regions with a warm to moderate climate. The major sunflower seed oil producers in the world are the same countries that were the leading producers in the 19th century. Russia and Ukraine are back on top of the production list. Leading with 8.39 and 7.99 million tons respectfully. The total of world production is 37 million tons.

TOP 10 PRODUCERS OF SUNFLOWER SEEDS IN METRIC TONS

RANK	COUNTRY	PRODUCTION
1	Ukraine	8.39
2	Russia	7.99
3	Argentina	3.34
4	China	2.37
5	France	1.57
6	Romania	1.40
7	Bulgaria	1.39
8	Turkey	1.37
9	Hungary	1.32
10	United States	1.26
	WORLD TOTAL	**37.07**

THE SUNFLOWER IS THE SUM OF ITS PARTS

Considered to be giant daisies, sunflowers belong to the *Helianthus annuus* genus that lists about 67 species. It possesses a large inflorescence (flowering head), and its name, sunflower, is derived from the flower's shape and its image is often used as an analogy to depict the sun.

The plant has a rough, hairy stem, broad, coarsely toothed, rough leaves and circular heads with multiple flowers. The heads consist of many individual flowers which mature into seeds. What is usually called the "flower" on a mature sunflower is actually a "flower head" of numerous florets or small flowers crowded together. The outer petal-bearing florets are sterile and can be yellow, red, orange, or other colors. The florets inside the circular head are called disc florets, these florets are the ones which mature into seeds.

Each individual sunflower floret, contains its own ovary, stigma, style, and anthers. Attached to the outer ring of florets are the long ray petals, which are a greenish color when immature and

CORN, COTTON AND CHOCOLATE: HOW THE MAYA CHANGED THE WORLD

deepen to a yellow or orange color when fully mature. A single sunflower head that measures 12 inches (30 cm) across the head could have as many as eight thousand florets. Sunflowers commonly grow to heights between 5–12 ft. The tallest sunflower confirmed by Guinness World Records is 24 feet (8.0 m).

Sunflowers do not have special soil or climatic needs. They grow in hot deserts such as the Mojave, the swamps in Florida, and the woodlands in the Pacific Northwest. All they need is a full day of sunshine and loose fertile soil offering good drainage.

When forming a picture in their minds of a sunflower in bloom, most people think of a bright yellow flower. However, with the multitude of varieties cultivated in recent years, sunflowers bloom in a constellation of golden hues, not just bright yellow. Sunflowers are grown in many shades of yellow, brilliant yellow orange, white, deep bronzed scarlet, pinkish red, and even light brown.

Maya farmers used ancient farming practices to grow their typical native crops called "the three sisters" (corn, beans, and squash). However, there was a fourth sister in the mix sunflowers. Sunflowers are excellent companion plants when planted in vegetable gardens, because they draw beneficial insects to the garden that keep pesky bugs out. Rather than planting the sunflowers close together in multiple rows, the Maya chose to plant them around the perimeter of their garden about nine paces apart.

THE SUNFLOWER CONQUERS RUSSIA, CHANGES ITS RELIGIOUS PRACTICES AND CREATES A CHANGE IN HOW THE WORLD COOKS

Peter the Great had a great curiosity about science and technology and traveled to Western Europe in 1698. He wanted to learn the latest improvements in science and technology. He traveled to Holland, where he became so enamored with the giant yellow flower, that when he returned to Russia, he carried sunflower seeds with him. Russian farmers were unfamiliar with the cultivar and it did not catch on until the Russian Church made a momentous decision. During Lent, the Russian Orthodox Church forbad its adherents from consuming animal fat oils. However, sunflower oil, a vegetable oil, was not on the prohibited list and the Russian people wholeheartedly adopted the oil of the sunflower. The Maya cultivar changed Russia's religious practices.

By beginning of the 19th century, Russia manufactured sunflower oil on a large commercial scale. Russia was awash with the giant flowers, growing them on over two million acres. Their agronomists evolved two unique hybrids of the species. So, by 1830 the time was ripe for the sunflower to make a triumphant return home to the Americas. America embraced the sunflower as a homeboy and the rest is history.

THE USE OF SUNFLOWER AS FOOD

Uses of the sunflower as food have not significantly changed from the Maya world. Sunflower seeds are commonly eaten as a snack rather than as part of a meal.

Seeds sold by the bag are either eaten "plain" or with a variety of flavorings including barbecue, pickle, hot sauce, bacon, ranch, and nacho cheese. Dehulling is commonly performed by

CORN, COTTON AND CHOCOLATE: HOW THE MAYA CHANGED THE WORLD

cracking the hull with one's teeth and spitting them out while keeping the kernel in the mouth and eating it.

Sunflower seeds can enhance the flavor and texture of any food from salads to sauces, stuffing, cakes, cookies, bread and candy and can be used as garnishes or ingredients. Dehulled kernels and can be sprouted and eaten in salads. The seed can also be processed into sunflower butter, an alternative to peanut butter.

Sunflower seeds are ground to make flour and combined with wheat flour to make pancakes and baked items. In Germany, it is mixed with rye flour to make Sonnenblumenkernbrot (sunflower whole seed bread), which is popular in German-speaking Europe.

Sunflower oil has good emulsifying quality, so it is ideal for making mayonnaise and vinaigrette. Sunflower oil can be used directly in cooking as it is ideal for sautéing, and shallow frying, but It is not well suited for deep frying because the oil breaks down at temperatures more than 340 F (170C).

MEDICINAL USES FOR SUNFLOWERS

As well-known by the Maya, the sunflower has medical applications, and European practitioners have found medicinal uses for the sunflower. They include their use as a remedy for pulmonary infections and is widely used for colds and coughs. In the Caucasus, the seeds have served as a substitute for quinine in the treatment of malaria, and used as a diuretic and expectorant. Sunflower pith has been used by the Portuguese in making *moxa*, which was used in the cauterization of wounds and infections.

THE MANY USES OF THE SUNFLOWER

Today, sunflowers are used for purposes that were unimaginable a generation ago. Because of its semidrying properties, in Eastern Europe, where sunflower oil is plentiful it has been used in paints, varnishes and plastics. Sunflower oil is used in the manufacture of soaps and detergents. It is used as a pesticide carrier, and in the production of agrichemicals, surfactants, adhesives, plastics, fabric softeners, lubricants and coatings.

The seed is also sold as food for birds, and seeds have been processed as a livestock feed. Leaves of the sunflower are used as cattle feed, while the stems contain a fiber which may be used in paper production. Sunflower oil, is cheaper than olive oil and is used in the production of margarine and biodiesel. The pith of the sunflower head is ten times lighter than cork and is an important ingredient in the production of life jackets and life belts.

THE SUNFLOWER MYSTERY: HELIOTROPISM AND MATHEMATICAL SPIRALS

A popular misconception is that sunflower heads track the sun as it travels across the sky. That is true of immature flower buds. However, the mature flowering heads assume a fixed position with its face pointing to the east toward the rising sun. The choreographed alignment of sunflower heads in a field give some people the false impression that the flowers are constantly tracking the sun. The uniform alignment results from heliotropism during the immature development stage.

CORN, COTTON AND CHOCOLATE: HOW THE MAYA CHANGED THE WORLD

The buds are heliotropic until the end of the bud stage, and finally assume a permanent position facing east. Their heliotropic motion is a circadian rhythm, synchronized by the sun, which continues even if the sun disappears on cloudy days. The heliotropic motion of the bud is performed by the pulvinus, a flexible segment just below the bud, due to reversible changes in turgor pressure caused by osmosis.

The composition of the cluster of flower petals at the center of the flower follow a unique mathematically based spiral. The flower petals within the sunflower's cluster are arranged in a spiral pattern. Generally, each floret is oriented toward the next by approximately 137.5 degrees, the Golden Angle, producing a pattern of interconnecting spirals, where the number of left spirals and the number of right spirals are successive Fibonacci numbers. The Fibonacci sequence is 1, 1, 2, 3, 5, 8, 13, 21, 34, 55…, where each number is the sum of the previous two numbers. When this occurs, the angle between successive leaves or botanical element is close to the Golden Angle. Typically, there are 34 spirals in one direction and 55 in the other. On a very large sunflower there could be 89 in one direction and 144 in the other. This pattern produces the most efficient packing of seeds within the flower head.

So, the beautiful yellow flower possesses unique solar induced movement and a mathematical based spiral within its composition. It has a special place in the plant kingdom.

NAMES FOR THE SUNFLOWER

The name for the sunflower, has also taken a journey with twists and turns. Most Maya cultivars have a name that is a variant of the original Maya name. However, the term sunflower was originated in Europe and "sunflower" is the assigned name in various languages The Maya called the sunflower *lol*. Native Americans called the plant by various names such as *raw-zi* by the Omaha tribe and *wak-cha-zi* by the Dakota tribe.

In 1565, it was given the name *heliotrope*. The literal translation was "sunflower". This is the name that stuck before Carl Linnaeus tidied things up in 1735, by publishing the *Systema Naturae*. Carl Linnaeus was a Swedish botanist, physician, and zoologist, who formalised the modern system of naming organisms called binomial nomenclature. He is known as the "father of modern taxonomy".

Linnaeus shortened the Latin names, and named the sunflower: *Helianthus annuus*. The scientific name of the sunflower genus is a combination of two words "*Helios*" meaning sun and "*Anthos,*" meaning flower. Prior to his work, every living thing had a long descriptive Latin name.

So, every culture has translated the name into their own language. French, call it *tournesol*, the Swedish, Danes and Norwegians call it *solsikke*, Spanish and Italians call it *girasol* and the Germans call it *sonneblume*. But the Zulu language got it right, they call it sunflower.

BASEBALL PLAYERS AND SUNFLOWER SEEDS

The love of the game of baseball means excellent hitting, great fielding, swift running and eating sunflower seeds. The bond between baseball and eating sunflower seeds is a long-term relationship. How did it all began? And why did it have to be sunflower seeds?

CORN, COTTON AND CHOCOLATE: HOW THE MAYA CHANGED THE WORLD

Sunflower seeds are enjoyed by players, coaches, and managers. From Little Leagues to the majors, it's rare to see a single pitch thrown without at least one emptied shell being orally expelled by someone.

But, when did players start eating sunflower seeds? Are they a taste choice? Were they selected because of the dexterity required to extract the seed from the hull? Does the concentration on the process of seed removal assist in focusing on the game?

The use of sunflower seeds has become an alternative to chewing tobacco for major baseball players. That would be an explanation for the big-league player, but how about the little guys. Are they just trying to be like the big-league players, because avoiding tobacco is not an excuse for the little league consumer? Where did the association between baseball and the sunflower come from?

Back in the 1940s and 1950s, Hall of Fame players Enos Slaughter and Stan Musial were known to consume sunflower seeds, but that does not mean they were the first habitués. The use of sunflower seeds predated the habit of the two hall of famers. But it wasn't until 1968, that the fad really caught on, when baseball legend Reggie Jackson began eating the Maya cultivar. Prior to their conversion to eating sunflower seeds, baseball players chewed and smoked tobacco. The change to sunflower seed became popular with kids after seeing their heroes do it. The sunflower became the "chew of choice" for the little leagues.

In 1998, after former Indians player Brett Butler, a smokeless-tobacco user, contracted throat cancer, Major League Baseball barred teams from providing their players with tobacco products, although players were still free to use their own. All tobacco use was banned in the minor leagues that same year. The teams now provide more healthful chewing alternatives to tobacco. In a single season, a team will go through 12 cases of sunflower seeds and 10 cases of Bazooka bubble gum.

Who knows whether it was because of the increased awareness of the dangers of tobacco use, or simply the satisfaction of removing the nutritious seed from its salty hull? Players started following Reggie's lead, much to the chagrin of Major League grounds crews, who found the discarded shells difficult to clean up. In the 21st century, sunflower seeds remain a prevalent part of the game. Just ask the grounds crew who must sweep the floor of a dugout.

THE POPULARITY OF THE SUNFLOWER AS A SYMBOL OF BEAUTY

The sunflower has long been admired as a symbol of beauty. Considered the most cheerful flower in the world, the sunflower is a symbol of light, hope, and innocence. The beauty and dignity of the yellow bloom has been selected as a symbol that represents the pride of relationships with the sun and the home. The sunflower is the state flower of Kansas, one of the city flowers of Kitakyushu, Japan, and the national flower of Ukraine and Russia. However, not everyone held the sunflower as a thing of beauty. Many U.S. farmers considered the sunflower a weed. In 1972 the state of Iowa officially declared the sunflower a noxious weed.

The sunflower is often used as a symbol of green and it is the is symbol of the Vegan Society. During the late 19th century, the flower was used as the symbol of the Aesthetic Movement, it's image was carved into chairs, painted on ceramics and used as an architectural detail.

CORN, COTTON AND CHOCOLATE: HOW THE MAYA CHANGED THE WORLD

THE SUNFLOWER AND ART. IS ART IMITATING LIFE?

The sunflower is not only grown for its seeds and oil. For over 260 years the sunflower was considered only as thing of beauty and was used as a garden flower, the flower itself is favored for its cheery sun-like appearance, brilliant colors and frequently appears as a familiar motif in advertisements, logos, T-shirts, clothing designs, artist's drawings and paintings.

The sunflower has an aesthetic appeal to artists and lovers of nature's beauty. There is a fascination with the mysterious syncopated movement when an entire field of sunflowers turns and tracks the sun. The bright yellow and orange colors and the symmetrical shape composed of a multi-textural composition appeals to the eye of the beholder.

Painting the sunflower has been the subject of famous artists and has also made artists famous. The accounts of artists and the sunflower are the stuff of legends. The sunflower has played a major role in the lives of artists and buyers of art.

Vincent Van Gogh was a Dutch painter that painted numerous canvases with sunflower themes. The colors he used are vibrant and express emotions typically associated with the life of sunflowers: bright yellows of the full bloom to arid browns of wilting and death. Van Gogh led a tragic life and came to a tragic end. Bad luck also found its way into the market for his art. He never sold a painting while he was alive, but after his death his paintings grew in popularity.

Vincent Van Gogh may have been responsible for energizing interest in sunflowers after a 1987 exhibit of his later paintings at the Metropolitan Museum of Art in New York. His works included 15 paintings of sunflowers. His painting titled "Sunflowers", created in 1888, included 14 sunflowers of both the single and double petal variety. In 1990, a Van Gogh painting of sunflowers sold for $82,500,000. At the time, a record-setting dollar amount for a work of art.

Mexican artist, Diego Rivera, spent years studying in Paris and was influenced by Van Gogh's work. The sunflower series influenced Rivera to introduce the Mexican native sunflower into his important works. Diego Rivera's artwork is heavily woven into the fabric of the Mexican people that it has maintained a lasting impression. Rivera's piece "Sunflowers" depicts two children playing with dolls beneath a patch of sunflowers.

THE SUNFLOWER AND ITS PART IN CHANGING WORLD HISTORY

Born in the Yucatán, the sunflower made a round trip to Europe and back to its home continent before it was re-adopted by Americans. It has become the third most popular vegetable oil in the world. The heliotropic seed has made its mark on the world as a food, an oil and for its beauty. It changed the religion in Russia, promoted a magic habit with baseball players and became a symbol for beauty. The world grows 37,000,000 metric tons each year.

CORN, COTTON AND CHOCOLATE: HOW THE MAYA CHANGED THE WORLD

CHAPTER 20: SWEET POTATOES:

Botanical name: *Ipomoea batatas* **Maya name:** *Iis*

Memories of a youth

Thanksgiving in our house was always a grand affair. However, in 1944, Thanksgiving Day was a different holiday, the world was at war. Our boys were away overseas, some never to return. But, victory was swinging in America's favor. In June of 1944, our troops had invaded Normandy, Paris was liberated in August, and in November we were fighting the Germans near their homeland.

On the Homefront, during World War II, everyone experienced Thanksgiving in new and different ways. Gasoline rationing prevented people from getting enough fuel to travel to distant family gatherings. It was difficult to cook the holiday feast without key ingredients. What formerly had been a holiday of comforting predictability became a day full of obstacles. However, at our house the menu for that Thanksgiving Day was predictable and bountiful, because we had a victory garden and raised our own chickens.

In 1944, Thanksgiving was officially declared to be held on the fourth Thursday of November. President Franklin Roosevelt decided the economy would benefit from a longer Christmas shopping season. Congress then decreed that henceforth Thanksgiving would fall on the fourth Thursday in November.

Celebrating Thanksgiving changed that year. Wartime restrictions on meat, butter, and sugar rendered traditional Thanksgiving recipes impossible. Meat rationing began as military needs grew. Good cuts of meat had disappeared from butcher shops. Even hamburger was absent. When meat was available, shoppers flooded stores and stores ran out of the supply of meat before they ran out of customers.

Other foods and ingredients were rationed: cooking oil and fats, cheese, dried beans, ketchup, coffee, canned fruits and vegetables. Heavy cream went missing, meaning there was no whipped cream for pumpkin pie. If the major items were missing from the holiday meal, my mother probably lacked the minor ones: cinnamon, nutmeg, cloves, allspice, ginger, paprika, and others, had vanished. The man at the supermarket said, "If your turkey isn't spicy, blame it on Hitler."

Speaking of turkeys, the war effort had resulted in a shortage of turkeys. Every boy serving on the front lines was to be served a hot turkey dinner on Thanksgiving. So, there went our Thanksgiving turkeys. However, we were very glad that the boys on the front lines were getting a hot Thanksgiving meal. In our home, we were fortunate that we raised chickens. We decided that we would substitute four chickens for the missing Thanksgiving turkey.

My mother prepared a feast that was incomparable to that prepared by our neighbors. The menu consisted of a combination of classic Northern and Southern Thanksgiving dishes. My mother and father were not Southerners; they had moved south from New York at the beginning of the war. My father was employed by the Bell Aircraft factory. He produced the famous B-29 Super Fortress.

CORN, COTTON AND CHOCOLATE: HOW THE MAYA CHANGED THE WORLD

So, my family life was founded on dual cultures: The Southern culture in which we were immersed and the northern culture of my parent's background. Differences in the cultures were reflected in the menu for our Thanksgiving dinner.

It was my responsibility to maintain the Victory garden and to care for our chickens. When mother was considering the menu for the meal she reviewed the types of produce grown in our Victory garden. She selected potatoes, rutabagas, and green beans. I inquired why she did not use the sweet potato. I loved the Southern sweet potato dishes prepared from the tuber. She agreed. She had never used sweet potatoes for Thanksgiving dinner, but she thought it would be a good idea.

In our little town, the main occupation of the population was working at the Bell Aircraft bomber plant. Due to the war effort, the plant worked three daily shifts around the clock and Thanksgiving was not a holiday. So, we rescheduled Thanksgiving dinner from Thursday to Sunday. Sunday was my Father's day off from the plant.

Our dinner guests gathered for our big feast. The guest list consisted of my mother and father, my three siblings, my grandfather, and family friends, Bill and Mary. Everyone was very impressed at the delicious food being served at the meal. In times of rationing this was a sumptuous feast. We had bypassed rationing and delivered a Thanksgiving meal fit for a king and it had all come from our own backyard.

In addition to the chickens, the table was spread with cornbread dressing, mashed potatoes, sweet potato casserole, mashed rutabagas, green beans, cranberry relish, and plenty of gravy. The Northern culture was responsible for the rutabagas. The Southern culture was the source of the cornbread dressing and the delicious sweet potato casserole.

You might say that our grand Thanksgiving meal was a result of being patriotic by planting our Victory Garden and raising chickens. However, the Yankee influence of rutabagas was outscored by the delicious Southern cooking including the sweet potato casserole and cornbread dressing. This was the first time that my mother attempted to cook with the sweet potato. It was such a success that she prepared this dish for the next 50 years.

That Thanksgiving we benefited from the hard work of Maya agronomists because they domesticated the sweet potato that we enjoyed that Thanksgiving and for many Thanksgiving dinners afterwards. The wonderful tuber is now enjoyed by the entire world.

THE MAYA AND THE SWEET POTATO

The ancient Maya domesticated the sweet potato early in their civilization during the archaic period. Widespread cultivation of the vegetable was practiced around 3000 BC. Ancestors of the sweet potato are no longer found growing in the wild. The wild Mexican potato, *Ipomoea trifida*, is an ancestor and the closest wild relative of cultivated sweet potato (*I. batatas*).

Sweet Potatoes were one of the important crops in the Maya diet, and they were among the Mayas three most prominent root crops including cassava and jicama. The sweet potato was a high yielding crop and was distributed throughout the Maya domain.

SWEET POTATO DISHES PREPARED BY THE MAYA

Sweet potatoes were an important part of the Maya diet and are still used in traditional Yucatec cuisine. It is unusual to find accounts of everyday Maya life recorded by Spanish chroniclers.

CORN, COTTON AND CHOCOLATE: HOW THE MAYA CHANGED THE WORLD

However, two notable scribes recorded the Maya use of the sweet potato in their cuisine. The consumption of the sweet potato during the time of early European contact were direct extensions of traditional Maya food ways.

The Spanish Bishop of the Yucatán, Diego de Landa, wrote that the Maya used sweet potatoes to "extend" their maize based *posole* and *atole* when maize was scarce, usually just before the maize harvest. The sweet potatoes were cooked, mashed, and added to these traditional gruels as a thickener and nutrient. The combination was sweet and appetizing.

The Spanish priest and chronicler Bartolome de las Casas, who also ministered to the Maya, described a recipe for sweet potatoes. The procedure involves washing them after the harvest, curing them in light shade for a week to ten days, and then roasting them in their skins. Prepared in this way, they were said to taste *"as sweet as if they had been dipped in a jar of jam."*

A SWEET MAYA MUSICAL INSTRUMENT

The musical instrument called the ocarina is nicknamed the "sweet potato", ironically the Maya also invented the famed musical instrument. The ocarina is an ancient vessel flute device used by the Maya starting in the Pre-classic period. Hernán Cortez introduced the instrument to European courts. It became popular in Europe as a toy musical instrument.

THE SWEET POTATO MEETS THE WORLD

The saga of the sweet potato began well before European contact. The sweet potato spread across the pacific long before Columbus made landfall and was known to be grown in Polynesia hundreds of years before the discovery of America. Sweet potatoes from the Cook Islands have been radiocarbon-dated from 1000 AD. Studies indicate that it probably traveled to central Polynesia around 700 AD, and was transported from the Americas by Polynesians with their strong maritime tradition.

The first Europeans to taste sweet potatoes were crew members on Christopher Columbus' first voyage. The crew was served the sweet vegetable by the indigenous Taino people. The Taino populated the Caribbean Islands adjacent to the Yucatán. The sweet potato was eagerly embraced by the Spaniards and brought it back to Spain as early as 1500.

The sweet potato initially traveled to Spain and then to Italy, from there it spread to Austria, Germany, Belgium and England prior to the arrival of the first "Irish" potatoes from Peru. It took 200 years for the English to accept Irish potatoes as being fit for human food, but the sweet potato immediately became a rare and expensive delicacy. Reportedly, Henry VIII is said to have enjoyed sweet potatoes. The English initially imported their sweet potatoes from Spain, and called them Spanish potatoes.

In the early 17th century, the conquistadors transported them from New Spain's Pacific coast to the Philippines. The sweet tubers traveled west on the Spanish galleons sailing from Acapulco to the Philippines, and from there they spread to India, China and Malaysia.

Before George Washington became a general and the first U.S. President, he was a sweet potato farmer. George Washington Carver developed over 100 different products from sweet potatoes, including an alternative to corn syrup, instant coffee, mayonnaise, and cosmetics.

CORN, COTTON AND CHOCOLATE: HOW THE MAYA CHANGED THE WORLD

The sweet potato is now popular across the world and the populations of tropical countries are the greatest consumers. The New World, the original home of the sweet potato, grows less than three percent (3%) of the world's supply. Sweet potatoes have been an important part of the diet in the United States for most of its history, especially in the South.

SWEET POTATO, THE SUPER FOOD OF THE FUTURE CHANGES THE GLOBAL DIET

Robert Malthus, writing in the late 18th century, stated that the growth of population increases at a rate greater than that of the food supply. That was before industrialization and the green revolution. Sweet potatoes may be on their way to disprove the Malthusian theory.

Population numbers are increasing and the food supply must play catch up. A global dietary modification is in the works, and sweet potatoes are emerging as the super food of the future.

Sweet potatoes produce more pounds of food per acre than any other cultivated plant, including corn and the Irish potato and are more nourishing because they contain more sugars and fats. The orange tuber also yields more calories per acre than almost any other major food crop, and can be grown in poor soil with little water. Sweet potatoes produce 10.3 million calories per acre. Compared to the sweet potato, corn produces 7.5 million calories per acre, rice produces 7.4 million calories per acre and wheat produces a mere 3 million calories per acre.

An increase in the tonnage produced per acre enhances the chance of future success for the promising tuber. Average tonnage in the world is currently 13.2 tons per hectare. Israel has reported yields of 80 tons per hectare, using improved farming techniques to produce large yields.

Historically, sweet potatoes have replaced many native crops in Africa and Asia. Their talent for growing on marginal soil and requiring little water enhances their attractiveness in combating world hunger. Given the calories-to-area ratio projections, the high yield and the nutritional value required to feed future generations, sweet potatoes are due for a renaissance.

SWEET POTATO CHANGES COLOR TO IMPROVE AFRICAN HEALTH

The sweet potato is a major food source of food in Africa. Nigeria, Uganda, Tanzania and Rwanda and they are world leaders in sweet potato production. However, health problems have developed from the extensive consummation of the tuber. The sweet potato in question is not the familiar sweet potato with orange flesh, but the variety with white flesh. This type of potato is affecting the health of the people of Africa.

A move is underway to alter the type of sweet potato that is grown and eaten in Africa. The move is intended to replace the white with the orange fleshed variety. The white fleshed tuber is deficient in vitamin A, while the orange fleshed version has 14,187 international units (IU) per 100 grams. Minimum daily requirements for humans are 5000 IU per day.

The sweet potato has the most vitamin A of any of the major food crops. Corn has 214 IU of vitamin A, wheat has 9 IU, and the potato has 2 IU. The deficiency of vitamin A in a diet compromises the immune system and can cause blindness, disease and premature death. Vitamin A deficiency affects over 30 million children in Africa. USAID has a program underway to encourage the farming of the yellow sweet potato to change the health of Africa.

CORN, COTTON AND CHOCOLATE: HOW THE MAYA CHANGED THE WORLD

WORLD PRODUCTION OF SWEET POTATOES

More than 135 million metric tons of sweet potatoes are grown worldwide. China is by far the largest producer, nearly half of which is fed to animals. The rest of Asia accounts for 6 percent, Africa 5 percent, Latin America 1.5 percent, and the United States 0.45 percent.

The following chart indicates the importance of the sweet potato in the diet of the world.

TOP 8 PRODUCERS OF SWEET POTATOES IN METRIC TONS

RANK	COUNTRY	PRODUCTION
1	China	81.7
2	Uganda	2.8
3	Nigeria	2.8
4	Indonesia	2.0
5	Tanzania	1.4
6	Vietnam	1.3
7	India	1.1
8	United States	1.0

THE SWEET POTATO, BOTANICAL DESCRIPTION

The sweet potato (*Ipomoea batatas*) is a dicotyledonous plant that belongs to the family Convolvulaceae. It is a large, starchy, sweet-tasting root vegetable. The young leaves and shoots are sometimes eaten as greens. Of the more than 1,000 species of Convolvulaceae, *Ipomoea batatas* is the only crop plant of major importance. The sweet potato is only distantly related to the potato and does not belong to the nightshade family.

The genus *Ipomoea* that contains the sweet potato also includes several garden flowers including the morning glory. The plant is an herbaceous perennial vine, bearing alternate heart-shaped or palmately lobed leaves and medium-sized sympetalous flowers. The edible tuberous root is long and tapered, with a smooth skin whose color ranges between yellow, orange, red, brown, purple, and beige. Its flesh ranges from beige through white, red, pink, violet, yellow, orange, and purple.

THE SWEET POTATO AS POPULAR CUISINE

Columbus brought sweet potatoes back to Spain, introducing them to the taste buds of Europe. The native name for the sweet potato was *patata*. Therefore, Europeans referred to the sweet *patata* as the potato, which often leads to confusion when searching for old sweet potato recipes. It wasn't until the 1740s that the term sweet potato began to be used by American colonists to distinguish it from the white or Irish potato.

First, let's get something straight, the yam is not a sweet potato. True yams are native to Africa. When slaves were transported to North America they adopted sweet potatoes as a substitute for the tuber they had eaten in their homeland and called it by the familiar name, yam. In the 21st century the sweet potato is still incorrectly called a yam.

The vegetable is prepared in numerous ways depending on the customs and the tastes of the population.

CORN, COTTON AND CHOCOLATE: HOW THE MAYA CHANGED THE WORLD

The Americas: The sweet potato is often served for Thanksgiving dinner in the United States. Sweet potato dishes represent traditional American cooking, and recipes include candied sweet potatoes as a side dish consisting mainly of sweet potatoes prepared with brown sugar, maple syrup, molasses, orange juice, marshmallows or other sweet ingredients.

Sweet potato casserole is a dish consisting of mashed sweet potatoes in a casserole dish, topped with a brown sugar and pecan topping. Sweet potato pie is a traditional favorite dish in Southern cuisine and is similar in many ways to pumpkin pie.

Sweet potato fries or chips are another common preparation offered in restaurants as alternatives to regular Irish potato fries. Baked sweet potatoes are an alternative to baked potatoes and are often topped with brown sugar and butter.

Europe: In Spain, the sweet potato is called *boniato*. On the evening of All Souls' Day, in Catalonia, it is traditional to serve roasted sweet potato and chestnuts, and sweet wine. The occasion is called La Castanyada. The sweet potato is also used in making cakes.

France: A sweet potato soufflé recipe is a favorite choice for a delicious, savory side dish. Seasoned with thyme, onions, and garlic, as well as a generous handful of Gruyere.

Britain: A rich and creamy sweet potato soup is popular. A combination of cheese and sweet potatoes makes this into a rich, smooth, comforting soup.

China: Sweet potatoes, typically of the yellow variety, are baked in a large iron drum, and sold as street food during winter.

Korea: Sweet potatoes are baked in foil or in open fire, typically during winter, baked sweet potatoes are called "Goguma". Sweet potato starch is used to produce *dangmyeon* (cellophane noodles). Sweet potatoes are also boiled, steamed, or roasted, and young stems are eaten as *namul*. Pizza restaurants such as Pizza Hut and Domino's in Korea are using sweet potatoes as a popular topping.

Japan: Roasted sweet potato is called *yaki-imo*, boiled sweet potato is the most common way to eat it at home. Also, its use in vegetable tempura is common. *Daigaku-imo* is a baked sweet potato dessert.

Asia: Sweet potato cooked with rice, is popular in Guangdong, Taiwan and Japan. It is also served in *nimono* or *nitsuke*, boiled and typically flavored with soy sauce, mirin and dashi.

Malaysia and Singapore, Sweet potato is often cut into small cubes and cooked with yam and coconut milk (santan) to make a sweet dessert called *bubur caca*.

Philippines, Sweet potatoes are an important food crop in rural areas. They are a staple among impoverished families in provinces, since they are easier to cultivate and cost less than rice the tubers are boiled or baked in coals and may be dipped in sugar or syrup. They can also be cooked in vinegar and soy sauce and served with fried fish.

India: In some regions of India, fasts of religious a nature are an occasion for a change in normal diet, with a total absence from cooking, and at that time the sweet potato is eaten. A popular method of preparation is roasted slow over kitchen coals at night and eaten with some dressing.

CORN, COTTON AND CHOCOLATE: HOW THE MAYA CHANGED THE WORLD

YOU MEAN THE SWEET POTATO IS NOT A YAM?

The Maya word for the sweet potato was *lis*. However, the honor for naming the sweet potato goes to the Taino culture. The first Europeans to taste sweet potatoes were members of Christopher Columbus's 1492 expedition. Later explorers found sweet potatoes under an assortment of local dialects, but the name that stuck was the indigenous Taino name of *batatas*. Therefore, Europeans referred to the sweet potato as the potato. It wasn't until the 1740's that the term sweet potato began to be used by American colonists to distinguish it from the white or Irish potato. The first record of the name "sweet potato" is found in the Oxford English Dictionary of 1775.

Carl Linnaeus, combined the native Taino name with Greek when naming the sweet potato: *Ipomoea batatas*. This is composed of the Greek words, *Ipomola* meaning a "binding weed" and adopted the Taino name unchanged.

In Argentina, Venezuela, Puerto Rico and the Dominican Republic the sweet potato is called *batata*. In Mexico, Peru, Chile, Central America, and the Philippines, the sweet potato is known as *camote,* derived from the original Aztec or Nahuatl word, *camotli.*

In Peru, the Quechua name for a type of sweet potato is *kumar*, strikingly similar to the Polynesian name *kumara* which has reinforced the scholarly suspicion that the similar names are an instance of Pre-Columbian trans-oceanic contact.

The sweet potato is known as *batato* in Spain, in France it is known as the *patate douce*, in German it is known as *batate* and Italian it is called *patate dolce.*

It appears that the Taino word was used in most languages.

WHAT? THEY EAT 1100 POUNDS OF SWEET POTATO EVERY YEAR?

The sweet potato is popular across the world, but has the greatest consumption in tropical countries. Sweet potatoes became popular after their introduction to Pacific Ocean islands, spreading from Polynesia to Japan and the Philippines. One reason for their popularity is that they were a reliable cultivar in cases of crop failure of other foods because of typhoon flooding.

Per capita production is greatest in countries where sweet potatoes are a staple of the human diet, the rate of consumption is led by Papua New Guinea with about 1100 pounds per person per year, followed by the Solomon Islands at 350 pounds then Burundi and Rwanda at 286 pounds and Uganda at 220 pounds.

The rate of consumption in Papua is over 20 pounds per week, that's 3 pounds per day and that is a lot of sweet potatoes. Consumption in the American South is 7.3 pounds per capita. Compared with sweet potato consumption in the US, Papua eats 150 times the consumption of sweet potatoes in the U.S.

THE SWEET POTATO AND THE REVOLUTIONARY WAR

The sweet potato is an almost nutritionally perfect tuber and was a staple that provided substantial nutrition for soldiers during the American Revolutionary War. The sweet potato was an essential food for all the colonies in the days before modern preservation. One colonial physician called them the " vegetable indispensable."

CORN, COTTON AND CHOCOLATE: HOW THE MAYA CHANGED THE WORLD

The sweet potato aided Revolutionary War Hero General Francis Marion and his troops achieve victory. Marion's guerrilla warfare tactics included hiding out in the swamps, where he sallied forth to ambush British soldiers. This elusive behaviour earned him the nickname "The Swamp Fox".

Francis Marion may not have known the specifics of sweet potato nutrition, but as a farmer he understood that they are healthy and tasty. The sweet potato travelled well with his ragtag brigade of Patriot soldiers. Many accounts tell of Marion and his men dining on roasted sweet potatoes, served on pine bark plates.

The famous painting "Sweet Potato Dinner" depicts Continental General Francis Marion hosting a British general at his camp hidden deep in the swamps. When the British general Tarleton arrived, he was surprised to find the entire force dining solely on a meal of sweet potatoes, because no other food was available. When the British officer returned to Charleston, he resigned from the army rather than fight an enemy that was willing to fight for a cause while living on so little food."

The painting was executed in 1840 by John Sartain. Later Currier and Ives did an engraving from the painting. During the Civil War, the image of the sweet potato dinner was engraved on the $10 bill of the Confederate States.

THE SWEET POTATO DURING THE CIVIL WAR

The American South has always been celebrated for its cuisine. The cuisine consists of a tasty blend of ingredients and cooking techniques connected to the region's rich soil. Before the Civil War nearly every large farm in the South had a sweet potato patch. However, during the Civil War, food shortages plagued the South, and empty cupboards required resourcefulness. Southern cooks turned to the sweet potato as a substitute for foods in short supply.

THE SWEET POTATO AS FOLK MEDICINE

Sweet potato roots and leaves are used in folk remedies to treat illnesses as diverse as asthma, night blindness, and diarrhea. Easily digestible, they are good for the alimentary system. It is believed they bind heavy metals, so they have been used to detoxify the system. It is also used for the treatment of anemia and is useful as a treatment for several premenstrual symptoms in women as well.

SWEET POTATOES AS A NUTRITIOUS SUPER FOOD

The *Center for Science in the Public Interest* named sweet potatoes as its No. 1 Super Food, saying they are, "*...one of the best vegetables you can eat.*" These deep orange-fleshed nutritional powerhouses contain high amounts of dietary fiber, naturally occurring sugars and complex carbohydrates, protein, vitamins A and C, iron and calcium. The sweet potato digests slowly, causing a gradual rise in blood sugar so you feel satisfied longer.

THE MANY USES FOR SWEET POTATOES

The sweet potato has practical applications other than use as a food. In South America, the juice of red sweet potatoes is combined with lime juice to make a dye for cloth. By varying the proportions of the juices, every shade from pink to black can be obtained.

CORN, COTTON AND CHOCOLATE: HOW THE MAYA CHANGED THE WORLD

George Washington Carver, the American botanist and inventor, developed over a hundred sweet potato products. Carver's inventions included sweet potatoes as the basis for instant coffee, mayonnaise, laundry soap and cosmetics. All parts of the sweet potato plant are used for animal fodder.

THE SWEET POTATO AS BIO FUEL

Sweet potatoes yield more ethanol per acre than corn, and they can produce more than six times as much fuel per acre as corn. Corn gets 300 gallons of ethanol per acre and sweet potato tubers can get 1,800 gallons out of the same amount of land.

THE SWEET POTATO IN SONG

The sweet potato has been featured in songs by notable artists. The legends of music had an affinity for the sweet potato. Glenn Miller recorded "Sweet Potato Piper". It was first performed by Bing Crosby, Dorothy Lamour and Bob Hope in the movie *On the Road to Singapore*.

A popular song titled: "Sweet Potato Pie" has been recorded by the legendary singers Ray Charles and James Taylor. An all-female singing group called Sweet Potato Pie records popular bluegrass music.

WORLD CHANGE SPARKED BY THE SWEET POTATO

The sweet potato entered the world early in the game. The world has adopted the tuber and it changed the eating habits of hundreds of millions around the world. it is the favorite food of Oceania and Africa. Each year, 130 million tons are produced; that's 280 billion pounds or 4 pounds for every person on the planet. The vegetable, with its high growth capacity and nutritional value, is emerging as the super-food.

CORN, COTTON AND CHOCOLATE: HOW THE MAYA CHANGED THE WORLD

CHAPTER 21: TOBACCO

Botanical name: *Nicotiana* **Maya name**: *k'uuts*

Memories of a youth

Larry White and I were walking home from the park. We were fast friends and neighbors. As we were strolling along, I glanced down and I could not believe my eyes. There, lying in the gutter was a full package of cigarettes. In one fell swoop, I quickly scooped up the prize. What a prize! A complete package of *Wings* cigarettes. Larry was amazed, he said, "let's go and smoke one of the cigarettes." I agreed and we went back to the park.

It was 1944, we were seven years old, and had never smoked a cigarette. Much less ever been in possession of an entire package of cigarettes. The war had made the acquisition of cigarettes very difficult and they were rationed. We settled down at a picnic table and lit up a cigarette. We puffed on those cigarettes, coughing and sneezing as we attempted to inhale. After our adventure, Larry and I walked to our homes.

Emboldened by my newfound package of cigarettes, I walked into my house with a cigarette dangling from my lips. My mother was in the kitchen when she saw my grand entrance.

"My god, Jimmy," she said. "What are you doing with that cigarette in your mouth?"

I answered, "I found this pack of Wings cigarettes and I thought I would start smoking.".

My mother had the fastest right hand in our little town. With a single quick movement, she snatched the cigarette from my mouth and the package from my hand. She said, "Well, let's see what your father has to say about your new cigarette habit."

At the dinner table that evening, my mother said to my father, "Well, Father, Jimmy walked into the kitchen this afternoon with a cigarette in his mouth. He thinks he is going to start smoking cigarettes."

My father leaned back in his chair and said, "Why smoke cigarettes? You want to act like a man, why not smoke like a man?" He pulled two large cigars from his pocket. "Here, he said why not light up a stogie?"

I was thrilled, being offered a real cigar by my father! That was unbelievable. I took the cigar from his hands and unwrapped the treasure. My father even offered to light my cigar, even as he lit his own. I puffed on my cigar as my father held a match to its front.

I leaned back in my chair, ready to enjoy the sweet savory smoke of the large stogie. I drew in my breath and then exhaled large clouds of white smoke. Everyone at the table including my mother, my father, my older sister, my younger sister and my brother were all watching with silly smiles on their faces. I planned to entertain them with my perfect performance of smoking a cigar.

After several minutes of smoking I decided to attempt to blow smoke rings in the air. Just as I was concentrating on forming my lips into a circle in preparation for blowing smoke rings, a strange feeling came over me. I began to feel dizzy. Then things started spinning around the room. I looked at my mother and father, they had started laughing. Things spun faster as I

CORN, COTTON AND CHOCOLATE: HOW THE MAYA CHANGED THE WORLD

attempted the smoke ring routine. Suddenly, everything seemed out of control. I felt sick to my stomach and knew what was coming next.

I had to make it to the bathroom, I had to make it to the toilet and I did not have much time to waste. Swinging my legs off the chair I turned toward the bathroom. As I stood, the floor started swaying back and forth, as the room continued to spin. I had to make it to the bathroom. As I started walking toward the bathroom my legs became like rubber and everything moved in slow motion.

I don't remember making the trip to the bathroom, but I remember my head being stuck in the toilet. I have never been so sick in my life. Everything that I had for supper, lunch and breakfast passed into the toilet. I recall lying on the cool bathroom floor and swearing that I will never smoke a cigar again.

Of course, my family was gathered around my pitiful little corpse stretched out on the bathroom floor. I will never forget the sound of their hilarious laughter. It's been seven decades since I smoked that cigar offered by my father, and I haven't smoked a cigarette or a cigar in all that time.

The Maya agronomists, who domesticated and nurtured the horrible tobacco plant, would also be laughing at my seven-year-old plight. They produced tobacco, strong tobacco, and enjoyed the drugs that were part of the tobacco plant. They would agree that a seven-year-old had no business smoking a cigar.

MAYA AND TOBACCO

The Maya really enjoyed smoking a good cigar; in fact, they were so addicted to tobacco that the herb became an integral part of their social and spiritual life. The curse of tobacco as it exists today began with the achievements of Maya agronomists and the addictive habits of the Maya population.

The habitual of tobacco use could not have existed without the creative cultivation techniques practiced by Maya agronomists. Before 2000 BC, the Maya developed tobacco into a valuable cultivar that found an important niche in their culture. Ethnographical and archaeological evidence indicates that the world-wide custom of using tobacco was first practiced by the Maya. This custom served the Maya as a popular recreational pastime, but also had significant religious and mythological implications.

The Maya appreciated tobacco for its powerful effects on the sensory system, including mood altering and hallucinogenic conditions. Tobacco smoking anchored Maya rituals of religious and social significance and the Maya considered tobacco as an essential part of their physical, social, and spiritual well-being. Sensory experiences induced by smoking tobacco solidified relationships between humans as well as the relationship between humans and the sacred spirit world.

THE MAYA AND THEIR TASTE FOR TOBACCO

Tobacco was more than just a cultivar to the Maya. The process of growing and processing tobacco became an important industry in their society. One in which the herb was developed into a product suitable for domestic consumption and for trade. The taste for tobacco evolved into a dependence caused by the effects of nicotine, the pleasure of smelling the rich odor of pungent tobacco and feeling the nasal passage pricked sharply and brushed by smoke.

CORN, COTTON AND CHOCOLATE: HOW THE MAYA CHANGED THE WORLD

The ancient Maya smoked a species of tobacco that was more potent than commercially available in today's smoking world. They developed two species of wild tobacco plants into cultivars: *Nicotiana rustica* and *Nicotiana tobacum*. The Maya habitually used *Nicotiana rustica*, which has a much higher nicotine content than *Nicotiana tobacum*. Nicotine is the principal agent of tobacco that affects the central nervous system.

Nicotiana tobacum contains 2 to 3% nicotine while *Nicotiana rustica*, the favorite brand of the Maya, has been found to contain up to 10% nicotine. The difference in the quantities is significant in its effect on the user of *Nicotiana rustica*; it is the difference between a mildly pleasant sensory experience and the experience of an intense hallucinogenic and intoxicating state. The Maya became intoxicated and experienced hallucinogenic episodes while smoking *Nicotiana rustica* tobacco. This species continues to be smoked in some parts of Mesoamerica.

THE MAYA AND THEIR TOBACCO CULTURE

Very little information is available related to the historic tobacco culture practiced by the Maya. However, experts are certain that the cultivation and processing of tobacco, was developed by Maya agronomists through millennia of growing tobacco.

The culture of growing tobacco and smoking cigars has been practiced by the Maya since time immemorial. In the 21st century tobacco is still one of the most important plants cultivated by the Maya. Today's methods of growing the herb in the isolated rainforest villages of the Lacondon Maya mountains is similar to the methods used by the ancient Maya. The Lacondon are isolated from the outside world and continue to live in the same way as their ancient ancestors. Their population comprises a few hundred Maya who preserve the ancient ways, and they are heavy smokers.

The methods of raising tobacco used today are analogous to those used by the ancient Maya. The Lacondon Maya sow tobacco seeds in pots or small isolated plots. Late in the year, young tobacco sprouts are transplanted in the fields. Tobacco plants are then allowed to mature and in late spring are cut by the farmer.

The Lacondon cure the tobacco by a method that has changed little over the centuries. The tobacco leaves are suspended on a rack of wood rods and permitted to dry in the sun for about two weeks. The tobacco leaves are then pressed between two large flat stones. The rock pressing process is repeated for about a month, completing the curing process, the tobacco is now ready to be made into cigars.

The ancient Maya preferred smoking a cigar made with long, thick tobacco leaves, like the cigar fabricated and smoked by the Lacondon Maya. This type of a cigar has three parts: filler, binder, and wrapper. The filler is the inner core that forms the body and shape of the cigar. The binder is the leaf in which to the filler is wrapped. The wrapper or outer covering consists of a ribbon shaped leaf wrapped spirally around the binder. The cigar is now ready to be enjoyed as a smoke.

PECULIAR METHODS USED BY THE MAYA TO CONSUME TOBACCO

The ancient Maya enjoyed tobacco in other ways besides smoking. Chewing, licking and drinking tobacco were sometimes used in addition to smoking. Tobacco chewing consisted of chewing tobacco leaves or by consuming powdered green tobacco mixed with lime and chilies.

CORN, COTTON AND CHOCOLATE: HOW THE MAYA CHANGED THE WORLD

Another method of consuming the herb was drinking tobacco as a juice. The tobacco brew was produced by steeping or boiling tobacco leaves to form a soup-like drink. This brew was then consumed by mouth or taken through the nostrils. Using this method of ingesting tobacco, the active ingredients are absorbed more quickly when they are directly exposed to the absorptive receptors of the mouth and nose.

The drinking of tobacco juice sometimes irritated the stomach, leading to an unusual method of ingesting tobacco by rectal injection. Enema syringes and enema rituals are displayed throughout Maya art. An example of this type of tobacco usage is depicted on the painting on a large polychrome Maya vase, dated from 600 to 800 AD. In the scenes illustrated on the vase, a man is depicted carrying a large enema syringe and then shown having a woman applying the syringe to him in the appropriate location. Applying the liquid mix through the anus delivers the narcotic rapidly to the human absorption receptor system, without irritating the stomach.

MAYA WRITTEN RECORDS OF MAYA USE OF TOBACCO

The evidence that tobacco was deeply embedded in the Maya culture is reinforced by numerous scenes depicting the act of smoking in Maya art. In addition to graphic art found on painted vases, tobacco smoking is depicted in murals, in sculpture and referenced in ancient Maya books, called codices. In the Madrid codex, an illustrated Maya manuscript from the post-classic period, three pages show separate deities smoking large cigars and include compound hieroglyphs that indicates the term "smoking".

In a sculptured panel at the ancient city of Palenque, the carving depicts an elderly man in profile, identified as god L, and he is shown smoking a large funnel shaped cigar and is blowing curls of smoke from the cigar. One of the earliest examples of smoking in ancient Maya art is a ceramic container made in early classic Maya style. The vessel shows figures of god K and god L smoking cigars. This symbiology of smoking by the gods provides a link between religion and cultural affairs during the early classic period. Multiple examples of Maya painted vases display images of man and gods smoking cigars and using tobacco in other ways. These paintings add to the body of evidence that the Maya were avid aficionados of tobacco use.

SCIENTIFIC EVIDENCE OF MAYA TOBACCO USE

Scientists have discovered the first physical evidence of Maya tobacco. The evidence was contained in an ancient painted Mayan vessel. To make this discovery, the researchers had a unique opportunity when they discovered a 1,300-year-old vessel decorated with hieroglyphics indicating the contents of the vessel. Investigation indicated that the interior of the vessel had unmodified residue that had been protected from contamination. The residue was collected, analyzed and was found to be tobacco. To archaeologists, this was a big find.

The small clay vessel bears Mayan hieroglyphics reading, "the home of his/her tobacco". The vessel was made around 700 A.D. in the Mirador Basin in Guatemala. The discovery provides unequivocal evidence for agreement between a specific hieroglyphic representation of the vessels content and the vessel's actual contents. The same analysis has revealed that the tobacco consumed by the Maya was *Nicotiana rustica*. This is the first hard evidence supporting the fact that Mayans smoked tobacco.

TOBACCO AS MAYA MEDICINE

CORN, COTTON AND CHOCOLATE: HOW THE MAYA CHANGED THE WORLD

The Maya used tobacco as a medicine in multiple ways. Tobacco treatments were applied in the form of smoke vapor and as a liquid by medicine men and healers in the curative rites performed during their healing rituals.

The weed was applied topically and internally as a cure for a range of maladies extending from headaches to tape worms. Tobacco was used to treat miscarriages, snakebite infections and wounds, and was ingested to fight parasites.

MAYA TRADE SPREADS TOBACCO TO THE AMERICAS

The Maya custom of tobacco smoking was spread to every other native culture in North and South America. In addition to growing tobacco for their own use the Maya grew tobacco as a trade good. Tobacco was disseminated throughout Mesoamerica, the Caribbean, Central America and was introduced to the North and South American cultures via the Maya trading routes.

The North American Indians cultivated various types of tobacco for hundreds of years but their mild species were replaced by *Nicotiana rustica* as part of the trading activities of the Maya. *Nicotiana rustica* was the tobacco grown in the Mississippi Valley as early as the first millennium BC. It is important to note that the use of a pipe for smoking was used by North American Indians while the cigar continued to be the smoke of choice for the Maya.

MAYA TOBACCO MEETS THE WORLD AND THE NASTY WEED SPREADS GLOBALLY

When the conquering Spaniards first encountered the Maya, they also found ardent tobacco smokers. The Maya habitually used the exotic herb and engaged in the nasty habit that was totally unknown to the Western world. The sight of people smoking brought astonishment to the Europeans as this was their first exposure to the habit, but it soon to spread across the globe and changed the habits of the world.

The first Europeans to witness the act of smoking were probably two Spaniards from the crew of Christopher Columbus' ships. On his first voyage, the men were put ashore on a Caribbean island to survey the countryside. According to the logbook of Christopher Columbus the scouts gave a description of an encounter with native smokers: *"...They were carrying glowing coals in their hands as well as good smelling herbs, they were dried plants rolled in a large dry leaf... They set one end on fire and inhaled and drank the smoke on the other. It is said that in this way they became sleeping and drunk but they got rid of their tiredness. The people call the small muskets... tobaccos...."*

Wherever they traveled, the conquistadors encountered the custom of tobacco usage by the Maya. Accounts by Spanish chroniclers provided many incidents of encountering Maya smoking and chewing tobacco. Tobacco became an important asset in the relations between the conquistadors and the native population. The Spanish grew accustomed to the use of tobacco and became habitual smokers too.

In 1530 Friar Bernardino de Sahagun, writing in New Spain, clarifies the between sweet *Nicotiana tabacum* and coarse *Nicotiana rustica*. *Nicotiana tabacum* is the species currently used worldwide as the source of commercial tobacco.

CORN, COTTON AND CHOCOLATE: HOW THE MAYA CHANGED THE WORLD

Records indicate that in 1518 tobacco was imported as an ornamental plant to Spain and five years later traveled to Lisbon. In 1531, European cultivation of sweet broadleaf *Nicotiana tabacum*, transplanted from the Yucatán, was grown in Santo Domingo and Cuba. This product provided a tobacco source for the Spanish market and trading purposes.

In some ways, the more things change the more they stay the same. There was a determined anti-smoking lobby in Europe as early as the 16th century. One of its outspoken members, an Italian traveler, during a visit to the New World in 1541, raised his angry voice: *"what a wicked poison from the devil this must be! I have entered the house of an Indian who had taken this herb, which is called… Tabaco and immediately perceiving the sharp, fetid smell… I obliged to go away in haste and seek some other place."*

In 1560, 29-year-old, Jean Nicot de Villemain, France's ambassador to Portugal, wrote of tobacco's medicinal properties, describing it as a panacea. When Nicot returned to France, he brought *Nicotiana rustica* plants to the Royal court and introduced snuff tobacco to the French. The plant was first called *Nicotina* after the ambassador himself, Jean Nicot. The term *nicotine* later came to refer specifically to the chemical in the plant.

Despite the anti-smoking lobby and the displeasure of the leaders of the Spanish clergy, the nasty habit of tobacco smoking spread rapidly among the conquistadors. The recent inhabitants of the New World soon became addicted. The tobacco habit was exported to Europe by Spanish, Portuguese, and Dutch Sailors. Sailors also adopted the habit of chewing tobacco. Chewing tobacco was a more convenient use of tobacco than smoking because chewing allowed the sailors hands to be freed for working and avoided the threat of fire on the flammable ships.

Early in the 16th century, Spain had a lock on the tobacco market. About 1575, the Dutch, to break Spain's monopoly over tobacco sales, began smuggling tobacco from the West Indies into Europe, mainly to England. The Dutch themselves took up the habit with enthusiasm and became avid smokers.

It is difficult to say when the tobacco plant and the habitual use of tobacco first reached the European general population. It is likely that tobacco's first introduction to Europe occurred in Spain, France, Portugal and Holland before the year 1560, and it probably first spread to fellow sailors while socializing at port cities. These would have included sailors employed by Sir Francis Drake. In 1565, tobacco reached the shores of England, transported there by the raiders of Sir Francis Drake. They had plundered the Spanish Main, and their plunder included "a great store of tobacco". The herb was carried home and introduced to avid users in England.

In 1586 tobacco arrived in English society when some Virginia colonists returned to England and began smoking pipes using Indian tobacco. The sight of men smoking caused a sensation among observers. William Camden, a contemporary witness, reports that *"These men who were thus brought back were the first that I know of that brought into England that Indian plant which they call Tabacca and Nicotia."*

The habit of smoking was not accepted among the British without resistance. King James I expressed royal displeasure and indignation about the use of tobacco. In 1604, he wrote a pamphlet of entitled *Counterblaste to Tobacco*. He wrote, *"the British should not imitate the Indians in so vile and stinking customs… Why do we debase ourselves as to imitate the beastly Indians…"* Good King James was not very successful in his anti-tobacco campaign. However, the English use of tobacco continued full of enthusiasm.

CORN, COTTON AND CHOCOLATE: HOW THE MAYA CHANGED THE WORLD

The nasty habit caught the British by storm and soon smoking and the use of tobacco became the rage of the British Isles. The popularity of smoking was emphasized in a report published in 1612. The report described the vast number of shops that were selling tobacco in the City of London. The report states that upward to 7000 houses are making a living in the tobacco trade. With the great popularity of tobacco usage in London and on the Continent, it soon became evident that the custom of tobacco smoking was here to stay in both the New World and the Old World.

In 1614 King Philip III of Spain established Seville as the tobacco center of the world. Attempting to prevent a tobacco glut, Philip required that all tobacco grown in the Spanish New World to be shipped to a central location in Seville. Ships sailed up the Guadalquivir river to the port in Seville with their holds full of tobacco.

European use of the cigarette began in Seville, Spain. Paper wrapped cigarettes were improvised by the beggars of Seville in the 17th century. The beggars would pick up discarded cigar butts, shred the tobacco, and roll up the bits in scraps of paper. Thereby, the beggars invented the most popular method of smoking tobacco in the world today. These "poor man smokes" became known as *papeletes,* from the papers used to make them or cigarillos. The term *cigarette* is the French term that is used for a small cigar, rolled up in a paper wrapper that is made of finely cut tobacco. The world's first tobacco processing plant was constructed in Seville. Eventually the plant became the Royal Tobacco Factory of Seville, which was the world's largest tobacco processing factory until the 1950s, when it became the University of Seville.

Tobacco was first grown as a cash crop in North America. In 1612, the settlers of the first English colony in Jamestown, Virginia grew tobacco and it was their main source of money. In 1614, the first sale of native Virginia tobacco was to England. The Virginia colony entered the world tobacco market, under English protection. Starting in 1619, in the English Colonies of Virginia and Maryland, tobacco was being used as currency. The herb continued to be used as a medium of exchange for 200 years in Virginia, and for 150 years in Maryland.

In 1730, the first American tobacco factories were constructed in Virginia which were small snuff mills. Founded in New York City during 1760, Pierre Lorillard established a tobacco plant or a "manufactory" in New York City for processing pipe tobacco, cigars, and snuff.

In 1776, the American Revolution was ignited by the taxes imposed on tea by the British. However, another grievance of the colonists was the severe British tax on tobacco leading to the Revolutionary War, whichwas also locally known as "The Tobacco War." Growers on the "tobacco coast" along the Chesapeake Bay found themselves perpetually in debt to British merchants. This was a good reason to revolt.

While tobacco was a major cause of the revolution it also served as a financial solution for funding the fledging American government. Tobacco helped finance the Revolution by serving as collateral for the loan that Benjamin Franklin acquired from France. The security for the loan was 5 million pounds of Virginia tobacco. George Washington once appealed to his countrymen for aid to the Colonial army, "If you can't send money, send tobacco". During the war, it was tobacco exports that the fledgling government used to build up credits abroad. When the war was over, the American government turned to tobacco taxes to help repay the Revolutionary War debt.

CORN, COTTON AND CHOCOLATE: HOW THE MAYA CHANGED THE WORLD

In 1785, the westward pioneering movement was in full motion. The country was moving west and Conestoga wagons loaded with settlers left Pennsylvania for new homes in the western parts of the nation. Drivers of the wagons rolled tobacco into thin ropes for smoking on the long trip. The Conestoga wagon was referred to as the "stogie" and the long thin cigars smoked by the drivers lead to the nickname "stogies" for cigars.

The cigar became popular in England and in 1826, the country imported only 26 pounds of cigars that year. The cigar becomes so popular that within four years England would be importing 250,000 pounds of them annually. During the Crimean War, 1853-1856, British soldiers learned the cheapness and convenience of Turkish cigarettes, called p*apirossi*. They adopted the cigarette habit and transported the practice of cigarette smoking back to England. London tobacconist Philip Morris began making his own cigarettes. Old Bond Street soon becomes the center of the retail tobacco trade. Fears were first raised about the health effects of smoking in England and in 1858 an article in The Lancet, the British Medical Journal, reports the dangers of the weed.

In 1848, U.S. soldiers coming back from the Mexican war acquired a taste for the darker, richer tobacco favored south of the boarder in cigarros and cigarillos, leading to an explosive increase in the use of the cigar.

TOBACCO AND THE AMERICAN CIVIL WAR

During the Civil War, 1861-1865, tobacco is provided as part of the basic rations supplied by both the armies of the North and South and many Northerners were introduced to tobacco this way. Under the pressure of war, tobacco manufacturing quickly shifted from the south to New York City which became the North's tobacco-manufacturing center.

Confederate and Union soldiers found a plentiful supply of tobacco along their route of march. Since much of the fighting took place in the tobacco rich regions of the South, soldiers often helped themselves. In the quiet moments between battle, Confederate and Union soldiers would exchange goods. The traditional swap was Northern coffee for Southern tobacco.

During Sherman's march, Union soldiers, now attracted to the mild, sweet "bright" tobacco of the South, raided warehouses for some chew on the way home. Some of this sweet "bright" made it all the way back to the North. Bright tobacco became the rage in the North and tobacco addiction spread further across the country.

The first federal tax on tobacco was instituted to help pay for the Civil War. The tax yielded about three million dollars. In 1863, Congress passed a law calling for manufacturers to create cigar boxes for transporting cigars. The boxes make it convenient for Internal Revenue Service agents to paste Civil War excise tax stamps on the boxes.

HIGHLIGHTS IN THE POPULARITY OF TOBACCO

In 1871 the first smoking ban was introduced when smoking was banned on the floor of the U.S. House of Representatives.

The first American cigarette factory opened in 1864 and produced almost 20 million cigarettes; however, the cigarettes were hand rolled. The smoking habit accelerated with the invention of the automatic cigarette-rolling machine. James Albert Bonsack was granted the first automatic rolling cigarette machine patent in 1880. Readymade cigarettes were a luxury item, but because of their convenience, they became increasingly popular.

CORN, COTTON AND CHOCOLATE: HOW THE MAYA CHANGED THE WORLD

In the manual fabrication process a skilled manual cigarette roller could produce only about four cigarettes per minute. This rate of production was insufficient to satisfy the market demands. However, Bonsack's machine could produce 200 cigarettes per minute, rolling 120,000 cigarettes in a ten-hour shift, revolutionizing the cigarette industry.

Oscar Hammerstein received patent on a cigar-rolling machine in 1883. This is the same year the U.S. ends the Civil War excise tax on cigars, helping to usher in the 40-year Golden Age of cigar smoking.

In 1884 James Buchanan Duke takes his tobacco business national and forms a cartel that eventually becomes the American Tobacco Company. Duke emerges as the president of the new company and buys two Bonsack machines to increase production. In 1884, Duke produces 744 million cigarettes, more than the total 1883 national production by all producers. Duke's airtight contracts with Bonsack allow him to undersell all competitors.

The American Tobacco Company, based in Durham, North Carolina, wisely made the connection between baseball, America's favorite pastime, and tobacco. In 1899, Bull Durham becomes the most famous trademark in the world, giving rise to the baseball term, "bull pen", stemming from a Bull Durham advertisement painted behind the Yankees warm up area. The term "shooting the bull" was derived from the act of chewing tobacco and expectorating the juice. The Bull Durham name was advertised all over the world, and was even painted on the Great Pyramid of Egypt.

The anti-smoking tide begins to turn against tobacco in 1890 when a total of 26 U.S. states and territories outlaw the sale of cigarettes to minors. The 20th century was a game changer for tobacco usage. The century was very good to tobacco and worldwide sales of tobacco accelerated. In the United States, 4.4 billion cigarettes were sold that year. There were approximately 300,000 cigar brands in the U.S. and 6 billion cigars were sold. Four in five American men smoked at least one cigar a day.

TOBACCO HELPS WIN WORLD WARS

America enters World I In April of 1917, and the U.S. joins the fight in the trenches of France. The use of cigarettes exploded during World War I, where cigarettes were called the "soldier's smoke". Prior to World War I, smoking cigarettes as opposed to cigars, had been perceived as effeminate by men, and unrefined by women. Smoking in the trenches changed that when soldiers overseas were given free cigarettes every day. Virtually an entire generation of young men returned from the World I addicted to cigarettes.

Those opposed to sending cigarettes to the doughboys were accused of being traitors. Tobacco supporters included General John J. Pershing who said, *"You ask me what we need to win this war. I answer tobacco as much as bullets. Tobacco is as indispensable as the daily ration; we must have thousands of tons without delay"*. The War Department bought the entire output of Bull Durham tobacco. Bull Durham advertised, *"When our boys light up, the Huns will light out."*

As the twentieth century progressed the smoking habit increased. In 1910 the per capita adult cigarette consumption in the U.S. was 151 cigarettes per year and per capita cigar consumption was 77 per year. By 1920, the U.S. had a per capita smoking rate of 477 cigarettes and a per capita cigar consumption of 80 per year. In 1930, the U.S. had an annual per capita smoking rate of 977 cigarettes, twice the 1920 rate. By 1940 the smoking rate had skyrocketed and

CORN, COTTON AND CHOCOLATE: HOW THE MAYA CHANGED THE WORLD

cigarette consumption had risen to 2,558 cigarettes per capita, or nearly 600 percent the cigarettes consumed in 1930.

American joined World War II in 1941, and as part of the war effort, President Roosevelt makes tobacco a protected crop and tobacco is distributed to the troops as part of their rations. General Douglas McArthur makes the corncob pipe his trademark by posing with it on dramatic occasions such as his wading ashore during the invasion and the re-conquest of the Philippines.

Cigarettes were included in soldiers' C-Rations. Tobacco companies sent millions of free cigarettes to GI's, consisting of mostly the popular brands and the home front had to make do with off-brands. Tobacco consumption is so fierce that a tobacco shortage develops. By the end of World War II, cigarette sales are at an all-time high.

Before the war, tobacco companies were selling their cigarettes mainly to men, but everything changed during the war. At home, production increased and cigarettes were being marketed to women. More than any other war, World War II brought independence for women. Many of them went to work in factories as "Rosie the Riveter" and started smoking for the first time while their husbands were away in the military.

In the 21st century tobacco continues to change the world. Tobacco related deaths accounted for 100 million deceased in the 20th century. If similar trends continue, that number could jump to one billion dead in the 21st century.

The tobacco habit has spread around the world. Smoking is incredibly popular in China where over a third of the world's smokers now reside which is 300 million smokers. Over 50,000 cigarettes per second are consumed throughout the country, which adds up to 3.73 billion cigarettes every 24 hours, and upwards of 1.7 trillion cigarettes a year. China suffers one million deaths per year from tobacco use, a number which is expected to double by 2025. It is estimated that as many as 100 million Chinese men presently under the age of 30 will die from tobacco use. With the U.S. decline in smoking, American cigarette companies are selling most of their product abroad. Cigarette manufacturers are now making more money selling to foreign countries than selling to Americans.

However, cigarette smoking still accounts for 1 out of every 5 deaths each year in the United States. That's approximately 443,000 bodies which means it is the leading cause of preventable death in the country. Public Health studies revealed that the levels of nicotine in major cigarette brands rose by 11 percent in the early 21st century. The concentration of nicotine was intensified, and cigarettes themselves were modified to give more nicotine per puff.

ANTI SMOKING LAWS COVER THE GLOBE, WELL ALMOST

The smoking habit continues around the world and is expanding in developing countries. The deaths and health issues caused from secondhand smoke is a menace hanging over the people who are close to the smoker. The anti-smoking lobby has become empowered.

Smoking currently has been totally or partially prohibited in 113 countries around the world. The anti-smoking laws range from total prohibition in the country of Bhutan to local regulation by cities or states in the United States. The anti-smoking forces are gathering strength, especially with the threat of damage to health from second hand smoke.

CORN, COTTON AND CHOCOLATE: HOW THE MAYA CHANGED THE WORLD

However, in the United States, the federal government has led the anti-smoking movement by creating smoking prohibitions in federally controlled buildings and on transportation systems. The federal government has left the smoking regulations up to the individual states, therefore, smoking bans in the United States are entirely a product of state and local laws. Thus, the existence and aggressiveness of smoking bans varies widely throughout the United States ranging from total smoking bans to no legal smoking regulation at all.

In 1970, a federal law was passed requiring a stronger health warning on cigarette packages: *"Warning: The Surgeon General Has Determined That Cigarette Smoking Is Dangerous to Your Health"*. In 1997 President Clinton outlawed smoking in all Federal buildings in the executive branch. During the 1990s, U.S. Department of Transportation banned smoking on all U.S. international flights. In 1975, Department of Defense stopped the distribution of free cigarettes in the C-rations and K-rations of troops.

As of November 2012, 28 of the total 50 States had banned smoking in all general workplaces and public places, including bars and restaurants. Of the 60 most populated cities in the nation, all but 17 ban smoking in all bars and restaurants. In 2012, data indicated that 81.3% of the U.S. population is covered by bans on smoking in workplaces, and/or restaurants, and/or bars, by a state, commonwealth, or local law.

For the last 25 years, countries around the world have slowly climbed onboard the non-smoking train. While the permitted limits of smoking vary greatly in countries across the globe, most countries have some nationally mandated laws.

WORLD PRODUCTION OF TOBACCO

The growing of tobacco has spread to more developing countries each year. Production of tobacco leaf increased by 76% between 1971 and 2013. The increase in production was almost entirely due to improved productivity by developing nations. During that period, production in developed countries decreased. China's increase in tobacco production was the single biggest factor in the increase in world production. China's share of the world market increased from 17% in 1971 to 43% in 2014. Every year 7.4 million tons of tobacco is produced throughout the world.

TOP TOBACCO PRODUCING COUNTRIES IN THE WORLD

RANK	COUNTRY	PRODUCTION
1	China	3,200,000
2	India	875,000
3	Brazil	810,550
4	United States	345,837
5	Indonesia	226,700
6	Malawi	151,150
7	Argentina	148,000
8	Tanzania	120,000
9	Zimbabwe	115,000

CORN, COTTON AND CHOCOLATE: HOW THE MAYA CHANGED THE WORLD

THE NATURE OF THE WEED

Nicotiana is the genus of plants whose dried leaves are processed into tobacco. The plant belongs to the *solanceae* or nightshade family which encompasses familiar vegetables like the Irish potato and the eggplant. The nightshade family consists of 73 species and all but two are native to American continents.

The tobacco leaf is used in cigars, cigarettes, snuff, pipe tobacco, and chewing tobacco. The chief commercial species, *Nicotiana tabacum*, is native to Mesoamerica, but has been cultivated so long that it is no longer known in the wild.

Nicotiana rustica, native to the Yucatán, is the species that was used by the Maya. This species is now grown chiefly in Turkey, India, and Russia. It contains up to nine times more nicotine than common species of *Nicotiana* such as *N. tabacum*. *Nicotiana rustica* leaves have a nicotine content as high as 9%, whereas *Nicotiana tabacum* leaves contain about 1 to 3%.

The addictive alkaloid nicotine is considered the most characteristic constituent of tobacco. Nicotine is the third most widely consumed psychoactive substance in the world, which is due to the spread of tobacco.

Nicotiana tabacum is a robust annual branched herb growing up to 8.2 feet (2.5 m) high with large green leaves and long trumpet shaped white-pinkish flowers. All parts are sticky and covered with short viscid-glandular hairs which exude a yellow secretion containing nicotine. Leaves vary in size; the lower leaves are the largest and are up to 24 in (60 cm) long. The leaves decrease in size toward the upper stalk, the upper one is the smallest and is elliptic shaped.

TOBACCO BECOMES THE GREATEST KILLER IN WORLD HISTORY

Tobacco has gone much further than enticing people into a nasty, unhealthy habit. The Maya habit of smoking has spread around the globe and has claimed more lives than have been lost in all the 1349 wars in recorded history. Smoking is practiced by some 1.22 billion people; and nearly 80% of the world's smokers live in low middle-income countries.

The World Health Organization estimates the yearly global death toll as a result of tobacco usage is currently 6 million persons (including exposure to secondhand smoke) and drains $500 billion annually from the global economy in lost productivity, misused resources, and premature deaths. Unchecked, the yearly death toll is expected to rise to 7 million by 2020 and will increase to more than eight million per year by 2030. More than 80% of those deaths will be in low- and middle-income countries.

According to the World Health Organization (WHO), tobacco caused 100 million deaths in the 20th century. It is predicted that by the end of the 21st century, tobacco will have killed one billion people.

Whichever estimates you use, tobacco is responsible for more deaths than the greatest wars of the 20th century plus the other 1347 wars in recorded history.

SURE FIRE METHODS TO STOP SMOKING PERMANENTLY

CORN, COTTON AND CHOCOLATE: HOW THE MAYA CHANGED THE WORLD

Even in the 15th and 16th centuries, smoking was considered to be a filthy, noxious and nasty habit that caused negative health effects. Powerful rulers were dead set against the use of tobacco. They were determined to stop smokers by royal decree and if that did not work they would permanently terminate their nasty habit by deadly execution.

The list of countries placing the death penalty for tobacco usage extended across the world. The nasty habit and menace to health was dealt with by maiming, exile or death. If these techniques did not stop smoking, then nothing would. They actually did not, even though they were severe.

In Mongolia, in 1617, the Emperor orders the death penalty for those using tobacco. In 1628, Shah Safi of Persia punishes merchants for selling tobacco by pouring hot lead down their throats.

In 1633, Sultan Murad IV of Turkey orders tobacco users executed as infidels. As many as 18 offenders a day were executed. A year later in Russia, Czar Alexis puts a stop to the habit by creating penalties for smoking: the first offense is punished by whipping, a slit nose, and transportation to exile in Siberia. The penalty for the second offense is execution.

In 1638, China the use or distribution of tobacco is made a crime punishable by decapitation. In 1643, Russia Czar Michael hardens the line against smokers; he declares smoking to be a deadly sin. Violators are flogged or have their lips split or their noses taken away. Later in 1674, Russia places the death penalty on smokers. Czar Peter the Great of Russia, cleared the air in 1725, he advocates smoking and repeals the Romanoff smoking bans.

WHAT'S IN A NAME?

The Maya, the world's first smokers, used the term *K'uuts* for tobacco. The conquistadors called the herb, *tabacca*, adopted from the Taino word, *tabago*, for a pipe used to smoke tobacco. The term tobacco was adopted around 1588, a loan from the Spanish word *tabaco*, influenced by the Taino word. The name for tobacco, was born in the islands off the coast of the Yucatán, and it stuck to the noxious weed.

In 1753, Swedish Botanist Carolus Linnaeus gave the weed its botanical name. He named the plant genus *Nicotiana* after Jean Nicot, the 16th century French ambassador to Lisbon, Portugal. Linnaeus described two species, *Nicotiana rustica* and *Nicotiana tabacum*.

Tobacco, cigarettes and cigars have many names, several of which are slang, probably because of their popularity.

TOBACCO NAMES

The names for tobacco are not as numerous as the word for the cigarette or cigar. English terms include weed and leaf. However, foreign words sound quite similar to tobacco. In French, it is *tabac*, in Dutch it is *tabak*, in German it is *tabak*, in Norwegian it is *tobakk* and in Japanese it is *tabako*.

CIGARETTE

The names referring to the cigarette are numerous, many of them slang, and slang words referring to the cigarette often have nothing to do with tobacco.

CORN, COTTON AND CHOCOLATE: HOW THE MAYA CHANGED THE WORLD

The names include fag, weed, cancer stick, death stick, gasper, coffin nail, cig, smoke, reefer, butts, dugans, straights, and bogeys.

Foreign names for cigarettes are as follows. In French, it is *ciggarette*, German it is *zigarette*, Spanish it is *cigarillo*, Dutch it is *sigaret*, Italian it is *sigaretta* and in Norwegian it is *sigarett*.

CIGARS

Somehow the cigar and its names are elevated above the street names given to cigarettes. They actually have their roots based in historic episodes or quality of tobacco origins.

The names for cigars include, corona, stogie, cheroot, claro, Havana, panatela, perfecto, tobie, seegar, cabbage leaf, el ropo, stoker, and stinker.

Foreign names for the cigar stick close to the original Taino word sound. In French it is *cigare*, German it is *zigarre*, Dutch it is *sigaar*, Italian it is *sigaro*, Russian it is *sigara*, Spanish it is *cigarros* and Swedish it is *cigarr*.

HEY MACK, CAN YOU SPARE A SMOKE?

If the danger to your health was not enough to daunt you from smoking, then the prices of buying cigarettes should turn you away. The price of cigarettes and cigars has grown exponentially during the 21st century.

However, it does not appear that the high costs of using the weed is a deterrent to smoking. The purchase prices of cigarettes and cigars have risen to record levels. Smoking was a reasonably priced way to impair one's health until the turn of the 21st century, when the prices went off the Richter Scale.

The cost of cigarettes has risen from a 1970 cost of $0.60 per pack to a 1990 cost of $3.00 then to $4.00 per pack in 2000. They are now positioned at the high price of $14.00 per pack in some markets. These are U.S. prices, where the costs vary from $4.25 in Missouri to $14.00 in New York City.

Internationally, if you want to save money on smoking you can move to Ukraine where they cost a mere $1.43 per pack. Avoid Norway where they charge $13.20 per pack. Cigarettes are cheap in South America, Asia and Africa, where they range from $1.00 to $2.00 per pack.

The price of the beloved cigar has increased even more than the cigarette. The game changed when the U.S. embargoed Cuba in 1960. While that ban still is in place, Cuban cigars have become a valuable product. In the 1960s cigars sold for a mere $ 0.25 to $1.00 for domestic brands and $ 2.00 for imported cigars. The cost has gone up. Domestic cigars are $5.00, imported cigars are $80.00 to $100.00 and Cubans are $250.00 each.

At a recent Christies Auction, vintage Cuban cigars went for $460.00 per cigar. Now, that is a buyer that really loves a good cigar.

CIGAR BOXES AS ART OBJECTS

This was the beginning of "cigar box art". Cigar box art has today grown into a collector's dream. They pursue a goal of acquiring the beautiful labels, each a miniature work of art created through lithography printing process that would be impossible to duplicate today. Antique cigar labels are some of the most beautiful collectibles that you can find.

CORN, COTTON AND CHOCOLATE: HOW THE MAYA CHANGED THE WORLD

Cigar boxes also became the primary part of popular homemade musical instruments. They became the body of guitars and fiddles. The earliest cigar box instruments were extremely crude and primitive, but they are works of art.

STRANGE AND DEADLY OCCURRENCES DUE TO THE SMOKING HABIT

The anti-smoking lobby had more than the health of smokers to generate their efforts towards stopping smoking. People misused the cigarette in various other ways to introduce misfortune to themselves and death to others.

1771: A French government official is condemned to be hanged for permitting foreign tobacco to enter the country

1830: The Prussian Government enacts a law that smoking cigars in public, be smoked while confined in a sort of wire-mesh contraption designed to prevent sparks setting fire to ladies' "crinolines" and hoop skirts.

1902: In New York, Topsy, the ill-tempered Coney Island elephant, kills J. F. Blount, a keeper, who tried to feed a lighted cigarette to her. She picked him up with her trunk and dashed him to the ground, killing him instantly.

1904: In New York City, a judge sends a woman is sent to jail for 30 days for smoking in front of her children.

1911: In New York City, the Triangle Shirt Waist Factory caught fire resulting in a deadly tragedy. It is believed that a carelessly discarded cigarette started the fire on the 9th floor. The fire killed 146 garment workers, mostly young immigrant women. It was the worst workplace disaster in NYC history until 9/11.

1912: The luxury liner Titanic, called "unsinkable", struck an iceberg and sank killing more than 1500 passengers. The ship did not possess enough lifeboats to save all the passengers. As the ship sank, men in tuxedos are observed in the lounge, smoking cigarettes, as they awaited their fate.

1904: In New York City, a woman is arrested for cigarette smoking in an automobile. "You can't do that on Fifth Avenue," the arresting officer says.

1906: In Kentucky, a group called the "Night Riders" formed. They were a group of angry farmers who donned hoods and rode horses at night to terrorize other farmers who sold tobacco to the price-gouging American Tobacco Company. They burned barns and fields and lynched people.

SALUTING THE JOYS OF TOBACCO: ALL HAIL THE CIGAR

Despite the billions of habitués, plus all the advertising hoopla and the perceived pleasure that tobacco brings to the user, not that much is written about the joys and pleasures of tobacco. However, the one mode of smoking that has been glorified is the cigar. That rolled up cylinder of the heavenly smoke producing herb has been glorified by statesmen, writers, wags, and philosophers.

It is indeed odd that the smelly smoke-producing cigar has so many high achieving devotees who have sung praises to the cigar. The quips, quotes, and comments are entertaining and thought provoking. Enjoy some of the world-class thoughts on the art of enjoying the cigar.

CORN, COTTON AND CHOCOLATE: HOW THE MAYA CHANGED THE WORLD

Rudyard Kipling
"And a woman is only a woman, but a good cigar is a smoke."

Will Rogers
"Our country has plenty of five-cent cigars, but the trouble is they charge fifteen cents for them."

Groucho Marx
"Given the choice between a woman and a cigar, I will always choose the cigar."
"A woman is an occasional pleasure but a cigar is always a smoke."

H.L. Mencken
"There are no ugly cigars, only ugly smokers."

Sigmund Freud
"Sometimes a cigar is just a cigar."

Mark Twain
"If I cannot smoke in heaven, then I shall not go."
"It's easy to quit smoking. I've done it hundreds of times."

A message sent to Winston Churchill from the manager of Dunhill Tobacco Shop, whose shop had just been bombed.
"Your cigars are safe, Sir."

W.C. Fields
"I never smoked a cigar in my life until I was nine"

James Woods
"Aficionado my ass...I just love to smoke cigars"

Raul Julia
"Why pay $100 on a therapy session when you can spend $25 on a cigar? Whatever it is will come back; so what, smoke another one."

THE TRAVAILS OF SMOKING CIGARETTES MEMORIALIZED IN SONG

Directly opposite to the glory and praise heaped upon the cigar, the cigarette has been the subject of scorn by singers and songwriters. The cigarette as the prime subject of a song is a rare thing but they are mentioned as part of sad ballads usually linked with drinking coffee or whiskey. The songs are sung by lonely men and women searching to regain something that has been lost like their youth, a lover or the bottom of a bottle. The songs that mention cigarettes are deep in longing and nostalgia.

Famous songs that cite cigarettes were sung by famous artists like Johnny cash in "Folsom Prison Blues", the blue songs by Tom Waits and Simon and Garfunkel's ballad of "America".

Songs that feature the dangers of cigarette smoking are few but they have become classics in their strict but plaintive lessons of the perils of cigarettes. One enduring one was made popular by The Sons of the Pioneers in 1947, and by Jim Croce more recently.

CORN, COTTON AND CHOCOLATE: HOW THE MAYA CHANGED THE WORLD

Once I was happy and had a good wife
I had enough money to last me for life
I met with a gal and we went on a spree
She taught me smoking and drinking whiskey

Cigarettes, whiskey, and wild, wild women
They'll drive you crazy, they'll drive you insane
Cigarettes are a blight on the whole human race
A man is a monkey with one in his face

In 1947 a song was introduced that spelled out the horrors of smoking and the song has been a standard for the anti-smoking lobby. The song, "Smoke! Smoke! Smoke! (That Cigarette)," Was written by Merle Travis for singer Tex Williams and became a national hit. The lyrics tell the tale of an addicted smoker.

Now I'm a feller with a heart of gold
And the ways of a gentleman I've been told
The kind of guy that wouldn't even harm a flea
But if me and a certain character met
the guy that invented the cigarette
I'd murder that son-of-a-gun in the first degree
Smoke, smoke, smoke that cigarette
Puff, puff, puff and if you smoke yourself to death
Tell St. Peter at the Golden Gate
That you hate to make him wait
But you just gotta have another cigarette.

The song is used in lawsuits as a defense in person's health that is harmed by cigarettes. The defense claims that the song proves that plaintiffs knew that cigarettes were dangerous. It has become the anthem of the tobacco defense attorneys.

TOBACCO AND ITS PART IN CHANGING HISTORY

Tobacco is the Maya cultivar that did not bring something good into the world. Tobacco is the world's favorite narcotic. Tobacco has killed more people that all the wars and plagues in history. The effects of this nasty habit are still on going in the 21st century. Tobacco-related deaths accounted for the demise of 100 million people in the 20th century. If similar trends continue, that number could jump to one billion dead in the 21st. Smoking is practiced by some 1.22 billion people; and nearly 80% of the world's smokers live in low middle-income countries. That's enough about how it has changed the world.

CORN, COTTON AND CHOCOLATE: HOW THE MAYA CHANGED THE WORLD

CHAPTER 22: TOMATOES

Latin name: *Solanum lycopersicum*. **Maya name**: *p'aak*

Memories of a youth

Entering our backyard on early summer mornings was a sensory delight, one that was pleasing to my senses of sight and smell. The cool morning air was perfumed by a fresh bouquet of honeysuckle, clover, grass and the spicy scent of vegetables growing in our Victory Garden. The light from the morning sun energized droplets of dew suspended from the ends of leaves and blades of grass. The dew sparkled like diamonds, at times the magnification of the early sunlight by the droplets of dew was blinding. This combination of a visual delight and a sensory bouquet created a fantasyland for my seven-year-old eyes. This was my domain.

I was the guardian and caretaker of our victory garden and our chicken coop. World War II had resulted in rationing and food shortages and people converted their backyards into mini farmsteads. Most families boasted a small victory garden; however, my Irish grandfather planted a large victory garden, and we were the only family in the neighborhood that maintained a hen house. The garden and the hen house kept us supplied with a bounty of vegetables, eggs, and chicken for the table. The yield of the garden and the chickens provided plenty of stuff for my mom to preserve in Mason jars.

I had a valuable job. My family had made a seven-year-old workhorse out of me. I loved the responsibilities. Caring for the chickens was a standard set of chores. Feeding and watering the critters was a bit of a bore, but gathering their eggs was always fun. Finding a dozen or so eggs in the hen's nests each day was a surprise, and presenting them to my mom was always a pleasure.

However, my greatest task and the source of my greatest adventures were tending the victory garden. We did not have a large variety of vegetables, but they were all staples. We grew potatoes (my grandfathers' favorite food), rutabagas, beans, squash, cucumbers, corn, and beautiful red tomatoes.

The big red tomatoes were the pride of our garden and these fruits required the most care and protection. In addition to the standard gardening chores including pulling weeds and watering the plants, another vital task was required. This was a task that needed courage, planning, and swiftness of hand.

The tomato was the succulent fruit that attracted the ugliest, sneakiest, and destructive creature in gardening lore: the predatory tomato hornworm or *Manduca quingue maculeta*. These horned caterpillars are the largest in the South and grow to over four inches in length. Four inches long is a huge bug. Especially when confronted by the small hand of a seven-year-old hornworm hunter.

If not impeded in their relentless munching on the plants, these green monsters can consume an entire tomato plant. Their march across the tomato plants is highly visible and the munched area gives away the location of the destructive omnivorous monster.

My principal task, as master of the garden, was to detect and destroy this greedy and insatiable horned monster. My mission was to intercept the green monster before they consumed my grandfather's beautiful red tomatoes.

CORN, COTTON AND CHOCOLATE: HOW THE MAYA CHANGED THE WORLD

The garden was laid out with two rows of staked tomatoes, with ten plants in each row. The advantage to this arrangement was that it established a compact area for hornworm surveillance that could be easily covered each morning. I would move down between the two rows of tomato plants equipped with a mason jar half filled with soapy water. Immersing the green monster in soapy water resulted in a quick death.

I would move down the rows, turning over the leaves of tomato plants in a systematic manner. Moving down the line, I would inspect the bottom of each tomato leaf. Some days I would come up empty without a single sighting. The encounters were always stressful and if I did not encounter any hornworms, it was always a big relief.

Not all mornings were uneventful, sometimes I encountered the feared green enemy. I would turn over a leaf, and there it was! The surprised green hornworm would rise on its rear legs to confront me. As an experienced hunter of tomato worms, I had speed on my side. The capture of the reared up green caterpillar involved a quick grab of his back to snatch him up before he could grasp my fingers with several of his five pairs of legs.

The clean snatch of the creature would result in the hated caterpillar flying into the mouth of my jar of soapy water. As the culprit sank to the bottom of the jar it met with sudden death. There was no mercy and I took no prisoners. Some days I would encounter several of the beasts. At the end of a morning dispatching several hornworms, I was elated but exhausted because my actions had saved the tomatoes. During my term as a guardian of the Victory Garden, I did not permit the destruction of a single tomato plant by the green monsters.

To this day, some seven decades later, the tomato is still my favorite fruit. I consume at least one per day. I feel, in my heart, that this is a love affair that began while serving as the guardian of big red tomatoes in our Victory Garden. This love of tomatoes links me directly to the Maya agronomists who cultivated this storied fruit.

THE MAYA AND THE TOMATO

Wild tomatoes are a small green inedible berry whose habitat is western South America, where they are distributed from Ecuador to northern Chile. Wild tomatoes grow in a variety of habitats, from near sea level to over 3,300 m in elevation. There is genetic verification that reveals that wild tomatoes are the ancestor of the domesticated tomato, but there is no evidence that the wild varieties were ever eaten in their lands of origin.

Somehow the little green berry found its way to the Yucatán. It was possibly transported by birds that carried the seeds to the north. Once in the hands of the Maya, the little green berry was cultivated by Maya agronomists. They used their talents to transform the tomato from the inedible berry into a world culinary favorite, the big red delicious tomato.

The tomato became a Maya cultivar and the domestication of tomatoes was accomplished in approximately 100 BC. The first tomatoes probably looked more like yellow cherry tomatoes, before they became the luscious red globules we know and love today.

The Maya adopted the tomato as part of its basic food group along with maize, squash, chilies, and beans. The tomato was used in sauces combined with chilies, in cooked dishes such as stews and were made into fillings for tortillas.

The tomato is considered as a healthy food, because it has large amounts of Lycopene, a vital anti-oxidant that helps fight against cancerous cell formation as well as other kinds of health

CORN, COTTON AND CHOCOLATE: HOW THE MAYA CHANGED THE WORLD

complications and diseases. The tomato has so much of this anti-oxidant that it derives its red color from the nutrient.

The Maya also used the tomato for medical purposes. A cocktail was prepared of tomato juice and was drunk slowly for sore throats throughout the day. The tomato was used as a treatment for burns, it was cut into wedges and was rubbed over the burned area. The acid from the tomato takes the pain away.

THE TOMATO IS INTRODUCED TO THE WORLD

When the Spanish conquistadors arrived in the early 16th century, the Maya had spread the tomato across Mesoamerica and the Caribbean, but It had not spread into North or South America

As early as 1493, Christopher Columbus was the first to transport the tomato to Europe. After colonization, the Spanish distributed the tomato throughout their colonies in the Americas. They also took it to the Philippines, from there it spread to Southeast Asia and then the entire Asian continent. When the Spanish brought the tomato to Europe, it was easily grown in Mediterranean climates and was eaten in Europe shortly after being introduced.

In 1496, Columbus transported the tomato to Naples. The Italians first adopted the tomato as a decorative plant, and then began to eat the fruit. Not surprisingly, the first time that the tomato was used in European cooking was in Italy.

The earliest discussion of the tomato appeared in an herbal book written in 1544 by Pietro Andrea Mattioli, an Italian botanist. The account suggested that a new type of eggplant had been brought to Italy, that when mature, was blood red or golden in color. However, it wasn't until ten years later that tomatoes were named in print by Mattioli as *pomi d'oro*, or "golden apple". The earliest cookbook with tomato recipes was published in Naples in 1692, although the author apparently obtained the recipes from Spain.

By the mid-18th century, tomatoes were widely eaten in Europe, and before the end of that century, the Encyclopedia Britannica stated the tomato was "in daily use" in British kitchens in soups, broths, and as a garnish.

The tomato took nearly 300 years to make a round trip from the Yucatán and return to North America. The fruit was popular in Europe before it returned to America. However, since tomatoes are related to the nightshade family, many people thought they were poisonous. Thomas Jefferson, a remarkably progressive Virginia farmer as well as a remarkable statesman, grew tomatoes in 1781.

Tomatoes were used as food in New Orleans as early as 1812, doubtless through French influence, but it was another 20 to 25 years before they were grown for food in the northeastern part of the country.

North Americans believed tomatoes were poisonous until 1820, when Colonel Robert Gibbon Johnson disproved that myth during a public demonstration on the courthouse steps in Salem, New Jersey. On September 26th, 1830, Johnson stood on the steps of the Salem courthouse, with a basket of the potentially toxic fruit. Despite warnings that its poison would turn his blood into acid, he told several hundred spectators that he planned to eat the entire basket, and

CORN, COTTON AND CHOCOLATE: HOW THE MAYA CHANGED THE WORLD

survive. Johnson did eat the entire basket and indeed survived. Women in the crowd fainted at the ghastly sight of the red tomatoes slipping so easily, so evilly down Colonel Johnson's throat, the sight became so ominous that the local fire department band played a dirge.

After Johnson's demonstration, the tomato became popular. By the close of the twentieth century, the tomato was widely cultivated as a food plant, and had become a key feature of dishes consumed in America.

Civil War was a game-changer for the tomato. The need for nonperishable food was a priority and canneries boomed, filling contracts to feed the Union army. Tomatoes, which grew quickly and held up well during the canning process, rose to the occasion. After the war, demand for canned products grew and with more tomatoes being canned than any other vegetable. This meant that more farmers needed to grow them.

The use of the tomato blossomed in the 19th and 20th century. The tomato is now grown and eaten around the world. It is used in diverse ways, including raw in salads, and processed into ketchup, canned tomatoes, tomato sauce, barbeque sauce, tomato juice or tomato soup. In the 21st century, the tomato is enjoyed around the world.

THE TOMATO NOW REIGNS AS THE WORLD'S FAVORITE FRUIT?

The tomato, a bright red Maya cultivar has become our favorite fruit. Call it the "ta-mah-toe" or call it the "toe-may-toe" anyway you call it, it's all American and born in Yucatán. The tomato has been proclaimed number one in the race to be the world's favorite fruit. The luscious red cultivar has moved ahead of the ever-popular Chiquita banana, an Asia cultivar, to become the number one in the world. Annual world production of tomatoes is 161,800,000 tons and the world production of bananas is a close second at 152,000,000 tons. The once champion banana has slipped into second place.

After a few hundred years in European cuisines, the tomato has firmly implanted itself as a major player the cuisines of many nationalities. Italian cooking has become synonymous with tomato sauce. Pizza would be lost without it. Where would Mexican restaurants be without salsa? Tomato soup, tomato slices on a burger and ketchup are all highly integrated uses for the versatile fruit in American culture. Additionally, millions of Americans grow tomatoes in their backyards each year. From one continent to another, the tomato has crossed over cultural barriers to become the world's favorite fruit.

THE U.S. SUPREME COURT HANDS DOWN A DECISION TO TURN THE TOMATO INTO A VEGETABLE

The tomato is a large berry and is botanically classified as a fruit. However, in 1893 the Supreme Court of the United States reversed the field on Mother Nature and classified the tomato legally as a vegetable. In the supreme court case of *Nix vs Hedden*, the plaintiff wished the United States Supreme Court to declare that the tomato be classified as a fruit rather than as a vegetable, as defined by U.S. government customs for the purposes of taxation.

The court rejected the botanical truth that the tomato is indeed a fruit. Instead the Supreme Court justices ruled that the tomato was a vegetable. The Court referenced Webster's dictionary as a basis of proof. The dictionary described the tomato as a vegetable. No, a botanist was not offered as a witness. The court rejected the botanical truth that the tomato is a fruit.

CORN, COTTON AND CHOCOLATE: HOW THE MAYA CHANGED THE WORLD

The decision handed down by the Supreme Court legally changed the tomato from a fruit into a vegetable. That decision was 120 years ago. The tariff on imported vegetables is still the law in the 21st century. Maya agronomists produced a fruit that has a worldwide popularity; they would be surprised that the Supreme Court would reverse Mother Nature, their partner in agronomy, and change history.

TOMATO AS THE STATE FRUIT OR VEGETABLE? WELL, MAKE UP YOUR MIND.

The Jersey Tomato was adopted as the state vegetable by the state of New Jersey in 2005. The Jersey tomato's ride through the Legislature began after a group of fourth-graders wrote letters urging lawmakers to adopt a state fruit. Their beloved blueberry won out, and the tomato lost out. However, New Jersey took advantage of the 1887 Supreme Court decision that the tomato is a vegetable not a fruit. The New Jersey legislature then accepted an offer they could not refuse and voted the tomato in as the state vegetable. However, the "Jersey Tomato" does not actually exist as a variety, it has become extinct.

Tennessee and Ohio selected the tomato as the state fruit. Arkansas took no chances and adopted the tomato as the state fruit and the vegetable.

WORLD PRODUCTION OF THE TOMATO

Tomatoes are now the most widely grown "vegetable" in the world and are cultivated as far north as Iceland and as far south as the Falkland Islands. Tomato seedlings have even been grown in space. Tomato seeds, which spent six years circling the earth in a satellite, have been compared with others which had stayed at home. No significant differences were found in the growth of plants from the two lots of seed. The world has adopted the tomato as a popular food. The Maya cultivar is grown in numerous countries with China leading the way followed by the United States and India. The leading consumers are Mediterranean countries with 132 -220 pounds (60-100 kg) eaten per capita per year. Americans eat about 80 pounds a year (36 kg).

TOP 10 TOMATO PRODUCING COUNTRIES IN METRIC TONS

RANK	COUNTRY	PRODUCTION
1	China	50,000,000
2	India	17,500,000
3	United States	13,206,950
4	Turkey	11,350,000
5	Egypt	8,625,219
6	Iran	6,000,000
7	Italy	5,131,977
8	Spain	4,007,000
9	Brazil	3,873,985
10	Mexico	3,433,567

CORN, COTTON AND CHOCOLATE: HOW THE MAYA CHANGED THE WORLD

THE BOTANY OF THE TOMATO

The tomato is an American plant with an American name. The tomato is the edible fruit of the cultivated varieties of *Solanum lycopersicum*, which belongs to the nightshade family, *Solanaceae*. The tomato is now grown worldwide; thousands of types of tomato cultivars have been developed with varying fruit types. Cultivated tomatoes vary in size, from cherry tomatoes, 0.4–0.8-inch diameter (1–2 cm) up to beefsteak tomatoes, which are up to 4 inches (10 cm). Most tomato cultivars produce red fruit, but there are several cultivars with yellow, orange, pink, purple, green, black, or white fruit. They vary in shape from almost spherical through oval and elongated to pear-shaped. The fruit is a soft, succulent berry, containing two to many cells of small seeds surrounded by jellylike pulp. Most of the tomato's vitamin C is found in this pulp.

Tomato plants are generally many branched, spreading 24–72 inches (60–180 cm) and recumbent when fruiting, but a few forms are compact and upright. Leaves are hairy, strongly odorous, and grow up to 45 cm long. The flowers are yellow, 2 cm across, pendant, and clustered. Tomatoes are one of the most common garden fruits in the United States and have a reputation for out producing the needs of the grower.

The heaviest tomato ever, weighing 7 lb. 12 oz. (3.51 kg), was of the cultivar "Delicious", grown by Gordon Graham of Edmond, Oklahoma in 1986. The largest tomato plant grown was of the cultivar "Sungold" and reached 19.8 m (65 ft.) in length, grown in Mawdesley, Lancashire, UK, in 2000.

I SAY TOMATO AND YOU SAY "MATER"

It all started with the Maya, they named the tomato, *paa'k*. When the Spanish first encountered the tomato, it was in Tenochtitlan, the Aztec capital city. They saw the fruit being sold in the market. The Aztec called it *xitomatl*. In the Aztec language, Nahuatl, the word *xitomatl* gave rise to the Spanish word "tomate" and that is where the English word *tomato* comes from.

Old German folklore claimed that witches used plants of the nightshade family to evoke werewolves, a practice known as lycanthropy. The common German name for tomatoes translates to "wolf peach". Carl Linnaeus took note of this legend when he gave the tomato its Latin name, *Solanum lycopersicum,* which literally means, "edible wolf peach". But there was confusion in the scientific naming of the tomato. In 1768, Philip Miller moved it to its own genus, naming it *Lycopersicon esculentum.* This name came into wide use, but was in breach of the plant naming rules. Philip Miller had the name wrong and it has been returned to *Solanum Lycopersicum*.

The name for tomato in other languages is slightly different, but basically sticks to the original Spanish/Nahuatl name. In French, it is *tomate*, in Dutch it is *tomaatti*, in Russian, Swedish and Danish it is *tomat,* in Japanese it is *tomato* and in Spanish it is *tomate.* However, the Italians call it p*omodoro*, or golden apple.

The tomato has become our favorite fruit. Call it the *ta-mah-toe* or call it the *toe-may-toe* or as a Southerner would call it a "mater", any way you say it's all American and born in Yucatán.

THE TOMATO CHANGED ITALIAN CUISINE, AND THE WAY THAT WE EAT

CORN, COTTON AND CHOCOLATE: HOW THE MAYA CHANGED THE WORLD

The most famous Genoan, Christopher Columbus, made the most significant contribution to embellishing Italian food. After his famous first voyage, he brought back many of the rich bounties of the New World including the tomato. Before his adventure, tomatoes were not part of Italian cuisine. Today it is hard to imagine Italian food without tomatoes!

Much of the cuisine we enjoy in America today originated in Naples and Sicily. They created some of the world's most popular foods. The history of Italian cooking was shaped by the pairing of tomatoes with pasta.

The tomato was born to meet pasta, and tomato sauce altered the history of pasta forever. The first recipe for tomatoes with pasta was not written until 1839. When Ippolito Cavalcanti, Duke of Buonvicino, offered a recipe for "vermicelli co le pomadoro", tomatoes had arrived.

Before the advent of tomato sauce, pasta was eaten without sauce and it was eaten with the fingers. Many believe that the liquid sauce demanded the use of a fork. At first, pasta was consumed using a long wooden spike, but this eventually evolved into three spikes, a design better suited to gathering the noodles. Thus, the introduction of the fork. A simple noodle and tomato sauce shaped the history of manners as well as the history of food.

Pizza, a world-famous food, originated in the city of Naples. Pizza has a humble beginning as a peasant food. It kept the poor people of Naples fed through the winter when not much else was available.

The story goes that it was created by a restaurant owner in Naples to celebrate the visit of Queen Margarita, the first Italian monarch since Napoleon conquered Italy. The owner made the pizza from three ingredients that represented the colors of the new Italian flag, consisting of red, white, and green colors. The red is the tomato sauce, the white was the mozzarella cheese, and the green was a fresh basil topping. Yes, you guessed it, Margarita Pizza was born, and it is still the standard name for fresh tomato with basil pizza.

In the late 1800's, a significant change occurred in American food ways. First and most significantly, was the mass immigration from Europe and the blending of cultures. Italian immigrants introduced pizza and spaghetti with red sauce, these dishes soon became symbols of the lively Neapolitan culture.

There is controversy as to which pizzeria was the first in the United States. It is widely believed to be Lombardi's in Little Italy, Manhattan established by Gennaro Lombardi in 1905. Amazingly, at that time, the cost for a whole pizza was only five cents. However, it was still too expensive for many people and they charged less money for a part of the pie. This is how the "pizza by the slice" was born in the U.S.

THE ITALIAN TOMATO EARNS A PEDIGREE

The tomato holds a reverential position in Italian cuisine, culture, and lore. Italy even has laws that protect the pedigree of qualified tomatoes. The law establishes a protected denomination of origin for tomatoes just as the French do with wine grapes.

In Italy, the most famous variety of tomato is the San Marzano. Ask any Italian, and he'll tell you that this plum tomato is nothing less than God's juicy Italian gift to the world. They love the San Marzano tomato for its sweetness, its low acidity, its meaty flesh and, mercifully, its low seed count. The San Marzano tomato has received a pedigree from the European Union.

CORN, COTTON AND CHOCOLATE: HOW THE MAYA CHANGED THE WORLD

Only canned San Marzanos grown in the Valle del Sarno are in compliance with Italian law can be labeled "Pomodoro San Marzano dell 'Agro Sarnese-Nocerino DOP". The most important label to look for here is "DOP" which stands for Denominazione d'Origine Protetta (Protected Designation of Origin). This is a certification bestowed by the European Union and administered by the Italians that guarantees the can of San Marzano you are buying is the real deal. This is the highest pedigree bestowed by the EU.

Italy is protective of its tomato products as well as their tomatoes. Recently, Italian police raided a supermarket and seized tons of canned tomato paste. The labels on the cans stated that the tomato paste was "processed in Italy". The tomatoes were actually processed in Italy, as stated on the can, but they were not grown there. The tomatoes were grown in China and shipped to Italy as concentrated paste. The paste was then diluted with water and canned in Italy.

The Italian government felt that the label was misleading because they did not state the country of origin. Italy has now introduced a law that requires the country of origin be printed on the label of cans.

Chinese pirates picked the wrong country in their attempt to sell bogus Italian tomato sauce. Italy was not a patsy. Italy has a worldwide reputation in the culture and cooking of quality tomatoes for 500 years. They know their tomatoes and their ability to negotiate.

The cultivar has initiated a heated tomato war between the two countries. One country is known for its quality food and the other for its cheap knockoffs. Maybe Marco polo can decide the winner. The Maya cultivar is only a pawn in this war of foods.

ALL HAIL KETCHUP, THE SLOW-MOVING TOMATO SAUCE

By any measure, tomato ketchup, a sweet and tangy sauce made from tomatoes, is the most popular condiment in America. The history of ketchup is fascinating and complicated. Food historians generally agree that the predecessor of our ubiquitous all-American tomato-based condiment was a Chinese sauce.

In the 17th century the Chinese mixed up a concoction of pickled fish and spices, they called it *kôe-chiap* or *kê-chiap*. By the early 18th century, the sauce made it to Malaysia and Singapore where it was discovered by English explorers. The Indonesian-Malay word for the sauce was *kĕchap*. That word evolved into the English word "ketchup". The term used for the sauce varies and it is sometimes spelled "catsup" in American english. British colonists brought ketchup to North America where Americans experimented with the sauce, using a variety of additional ingredients, including beans and apples. It became popular throughout the United States in the early nineteenth century.

After the Civil War, commercial production of ketchup rapidly increased. As the century progressed, tomato based ketchup began its ascent in popularity. Ketchup was popular long before fresh tomatoes were eaten. While many continued to question whether it was safe to eat raw tomatoes, people were less hesitant to eat tomatoes as part of a highly-processed product that had been cooked and infused with vinegar and spices.

In 1896 the New York Tribune reported that tomato ketchup was America's national condiment. Until 1900, ketchup was mainly used as an ingredient for savory pies and sauces, and to

CORN, COTTON AND CHOCOLATE: HOW THE MAYA CHANGED THE WORLD

enhance the flavor of meat, poultry, and fish. It then became famous as a condiment following the appearance of french fries, hamburgers, sandwiches, hot dogs and grilled meat.

The relatively high viscosity and plastic nature of ketchup can make pouring it from a glass bottle somewhat difficult and unpredictable. Thus, the lines from the song by Carley Simon, *Anticipation* is played in the background of a series of Heinz ketchup ads in the 1970s. Ketchup is a world favorite as well as an American favorite. Globally, the market for the red stuff is worth $3.3 billion.

PLAYING KETCHUP, CHINA GRABS THE LION'S SHARE OF TOMATO PRODUCTION

China now grows more tomatoes than any country in the world. The country grows a staggering 48,572,921 metric tons of the red fruit. The great majority is used for processing into ketchup, pasta sauce and salsa. However, while they are the world's highest producer of the fruit, it is amazing is that the Chinese people do not eat the tomato raw.

The story of how China's tomato industry grew surely must rank as one of the weirdest of the country's economic boom. To begin with, the Chinese themselves shun tomatoes. In China, about the only way you can get a person to eat a tomato is by slicing it and liberally sprinkling sugar over each slice. When the Spanish brought New World cultivars to china, chili peppers and sweet potatoes quickly became firmly entrenched in the Chinese diet, but the tomato did not find a place in the cuisine and became an outcast here. We say tomato, the Chinese say "foreign eggplant".

Most of the tomatoes are grown in the province of Xinjiang, in northwest China bordering Russia, and formerly referred to as "Chinese Turkestan." It is also at the crossroads on the ancient trade route between the East and the West, the Silk Road. In the 1950s, the government of China established a program to create work for thousands of soldiers and ex-convicts who had been sent to make the region more culturally Chinese and to keep an eye on the Soviets and ethnic minorities. The Chinese government gave small plots of land to tens of thousands of tomato farmers.

At harvest, the contrast between the antiquated Chinese transportation infrastructure and the sleek modern American tomato processing facilities presents a stark contrast. The ripe tomatoes are collected in gunnysacks, dumped into trailers, and driven by truck, motorcycle, and even donkey cart to ultramodern, Italian-designed tomato processing factories.

There, using the standard method for creating industrial tomato paste, most of the tomatoes are heated to about 200 degrees, which causes them to blow up. The resulting paste is partially evaporated and flows into sterile drums. The drums go by rail across the country to the east coast and are shipped around the world.

The precipitous rise of the country's tomato industry, which scarcely existed a decade ago, is wreaking some havoc. The Senegalese claim that cheap Chinese tomato paste is driving their farmers out of business. Turks, Australians, and Russians have similar complaints. The Italians are especially unhappy. The Silk Road, which Marco Polo used to bring pasta to Italy, has turned into a pipeline for cheap tomato paste.

HEIRLOOM TOMATOES, WHAT ARE THEY?

CORN, COTTON AND CHOCOLATE: HOW THE MAYA CHANGED THE WORLD

Much is written about heirloom tomatoes. The heirloom tomato is an non-hybrid cultivar of tomato. It also refers to the age of the cultivar, although there is some debate over this definition. Some say heirloom tomato seeds must be at least 100 years old, others say 50 years.

A "true" heirloom tomato is a cultivar that has been handed down from one family member to another for many generations, or a cultivar that was introduced many years ago, and has been saved, maintained and handed down. Most agree that an heirloom tomato is not grown in modern large-scale agriculture. The trend of growing heirloom tomatoes in home gardens has gained popularity over the last couple of decades. They come in a variety of colors, shapes and sizes and are extremely flavorful.

COMPANION PLANTS FOR THE TOMATO

Companion plants are specimens that are grown along with tomatoes that provide protection from pests and enrich the growth of the tomato. Plants that assist in the growth of others range in their type of assistance including attracting beneficial insects, naturally regulating pests, repelling harmful insects, providing nutrients, and in some cases, simply provide a shaded microclimate or climbing support. Tomatoes have several companion plants that are beneficial to their growth, including asparagus, basil, chives, oregano, parsley, marigold, sunflower and zinnia.

Marigolds are an example of an excellent companion plant for tomatoes and can be used to deter Mexican bean beetles, squash bugs, thrips, tomato hornworms, and whiteflies. The root of the marigold produces a chemical that kills roundworms as they enter the soil.

DEFINITIONS OF THE SLANG WORDS FOR TOMATO

The term tomato has entered the English language as a slang term. The word ranges from the description of a pretty woman to a boxing term.

Tomato: The term used to describe a beautiful woman.

Tomatoes: The term used to describe a large pair of woman's breasts.

Tomato: In the boxing industry, an inexperienced fighter or a fighter who is past his prime.

THE BENEFITS OF LYCOPENE

The latest buzz surrounding tomatoes is the benefit of lycopene, the major carotenoid contained in tomatoes that is responsible for the deep red color. Similar to beta-carotene, lycopene has been touted as a potent anti-oxidant, a molecule which snuffs out cancer-causing free radicals. Tomatoes are an excellent source of lycopene, and numerous studies have confirmed that people who consume increased amounts of tomato products experience marked reductions in cancer risk. Results from cancer research have induced tomato breeders at the University of Florida to produce high lycopene cultivars.

THE BIGGEST FOOD FIGHT IN THE WORLD STARRING THE RIPE TOMATO

From Spain to Greece to Italy, and across the globe, food fights have become something of an annual ritual. It's all in the name of tradition, of course. The ripe tomato is the star player in the biggest event of them all.

CORN, COTTON AND CHOCOLATE: HOW THE MAYA CHANGED THE WORLD

The largest and best-known food fight is the "Tomatina", it is the poplar tomato war fought in the tiny Spanish town of Buñol, located not far from Valencia. Every year, on the last Wednesday in August, thousands of locals and tourists pile into the narrow town square, the Plaza del Pueblo. They arrive well before noon to wait the first trucks laden with overripe tomatoes.

Right at midday, a rocket marks the start of battle. The first load of the juicy red ammunition is poured into the square as trucks dump tomatoes in abundance into the Plaza del Pueblo. The chaos begins and the sky turns dark with vegetal projectiles. The tomatoes are imported from Extremadura, where they are less expensive and of inferior taste. They are grown specifically for the holiday.

In 2013 the Town Hall of Buñol decided on limiting the fight to 20,000 revelers, with 5,000 tickets allotted to locals of the town of Buñol and 15,000 tickets allotted to foreigners.

The participants' use of goggles and gloves are recommended. The tomatoes must be crushed before being thrown to reduce the risk of injury. It is estimated that 150,000 tomatoes are used as food fight ammunition, that is nearly 48 tons of squishy red fruit.

After exactly one hour the fight is terminated with the firing of the second rocket. Rivers of tomato juice flow freely in the streets and the whole town square is colored red. The city has turned the cleanup operation of the red juice into a science. Just after the last tomato splats to the pavement, an army of volunteers turns on the hoses, strip the protective plastic from the buildings, and scrub down the pavement.

Fire trucks then hose down the streets. Participants use hoses to remove the tomato paste from their bodies, some go to the pool of "los peñones" to wash. After the cleaning, the village cobblestone streets are pristine due to the acidity of the tomato juice and its ability to clean street surfaces.

THE TOMATO AND ITS PART IN CHANGING HISTORY

The tomato is now the world's favorite fruit indicated by the 161,800,000 metric tons the world grows each year. The red delicious fruit was considered poisonous in America until the 19th century when it finally adopted this native cultivar. In Italy, which adopted the tomato in the 16th century, the tomato was awarded a pedigree and it is the basis of Italian cooking. The tomato was declared a vegetable by the U.S. Supreme court and is the state vegetable of New Jersey.

CORN, COTTON AND CHOCOLATE: HOW THE MAYA CHANGED THE WORLD

CHAPTER 23: THE TURKEY

Botanical name: *Meleagris gallopavo*   **Maya name:** *uu lum*

Memories of a youth

My sister Janice and I would often hike up Kennesaw Mountain, an hour-long walk from our home and was always full of adventures. Kennesaw Mountain was the site of a furious battle fought during the Civil War. During our visits, we explored entrenchments lining the side of the mountain which were positioned in horizontal rows ascending the mountainside. These were the battlements where confederate soldiers fought and died in their successful defense of this strategic mountain fortress. The trenches did their job as the confederates held off the attacking Yankee troops. The northern army was forced to bypass Kennesaw Mountain and continue their march to Atlanta.

The war had ended some 85 years before our visits, but the hillsides and the trenches were still littered with rusted armament. We would navigate the mountainside searching for Civil War relics. However, on one visit to the mountain we encountered some treasure that was not related to the long-ago battle between Americans.

Returning home, we were walking down a dirt road bordered by farmlands. As we strolled along, we saw a quick movement ahead on the dirt road. The movement was followed by several more quickly moving shapes. They were small figures and made peeping sounds. We approached the bushes where the small creatures had taken cover. We pulled back the bush and to our surprise saw four baby turkeys huddled together and shaking in fear. They were staring up at us. This was a big surprise for us too for we had ever seen baby turkeys. In addition, they were white feathered specimens.

We wondered where the little guys lived. We looked around and did not see a barn or farmhouse. Furthermore, we did not see a mother turkey. Apparently the four siblings had wandered off and were lost. Concerned for their survival, we scooped them up and placed them inside our jackets and brought them home with us.

"What are you going to do with those turkeys?" My mother inquired.

I responded, "Well we'll build them a Turkey run and raise them for next Thanksgiving's dinner."

And we did build them a nice turkey run. It had a 10-foot-by-10-foot wire enclosure and a nice turkey house constructed of wood. The little guys were happy in their house. I really took good care of them. I fed them before school and again after school. I know that this may have been overdoing it, but they ate all the chicken feed that I spread out. They really grew fast. After a few weeks, they begin to look like little turkeys. We were very pleased; our project was working. We would be having a nice turkey dinner for Thanksgiving. Our first mistake was giving names to the little fellows. We called them Roy Rogers, Gene Autry, Hop-along-Cassidy, and Gabby Hayes.

Every morning when I approached the turkey run, I whistled and call the names, "Roy, Gene, Hop-along and Gabby". They would come out of the house making immature gobbling noises. They are glad to see me and their food. These friendly communications occurred each morning and I bonded with my little turkey friends.

CORN, COTTON AND CHOCOLATE: HOW THE MAYA CHANGED THE WORLD

Sadly, everything comes to an end. Early one morning I approached their run. Whistling and calling them names. I did not get my usual response. Not a single sound came from their house. As I approached the fenced area I saw a horrid sight, one that I have never forgotten. My little friends were dead. They had all been killed. They were executed in horrible manner. They had been dismembered by an animal with a blood lust. Their little heads that had been severed and their legs had been separated from the bodies. It was a real tragedy. The parts of their bodies were scattered across the fenced area.

The culprit must have been a mink or a weasel, animals that kill for pleasure. I collected the remnants of my little friends and gave them a proper burial. That ended my adventure with turkeys and their charming ways. I still have a place my heart for the little chaps. Maya farmers who domesticated the turkey would not be surprised, their turkeys faced even more challenging predators that lived in the rainforest.

THE MAYA AND THE TURKEY

When the Maya wanted to cook a turkey for dinner they had their choice of the type of turkey to select. They could select the wild ocellated turkey, *Meleagris ocellata,* or the domesticated turkey, *Meleagris gallopavo.* It required a Maya hunter to bring down a *Meleagris ocellata* turkey dinner, but the domesticated turkey, the *Meleagris gallopavo,* could be collected as the dinner entree by going into the garden of a Maya house and calling the bird to come to its fate.

The difference in the selection process for the type of turkey to cook involved the science of animal domestication. The *Meleagris gallopavo* was an amiable creature that was domesticated by the Maya. The ocellated turkey was never domesticated for this bird possessed that certain wild streak possessed by certain creatures that cannot be tamed.

The domestic turkey became a mainstay in the culture of the Maya. It was a backyard animal and was easily accessible while the ocellated turkey is still a hunted wild bird. The Maya turkey is the ancestor of all domestic turkeys consumed in the world today. This is the species that the Europeans brought back with them to Europe. All domestic turkeys originated in the Maya domain.

ARCHAEOLOGICAL EVIDENCE OF TURKEY DOMESTICATION BY THE MAYA

The actual date of domestication of the turkey has been debated by archaeologists. Recent detective work by archaeologists has shed light on an early date of domestication. Researchers at the University of Florida found that the turkey, one of the most widely consumed birds worldwide, was domesticated by the ancient Maya as early as 2,500 years ago. The discovery of turkey bones at the ancient Maya archaeological site of El Mirador in Guatemala opened the door for a new look at the dating of turkey domestication.

This discovery of the turkey bones is significant because the Maya did not have many domesticated animals. The Maya domesticated the turkey, the dog, the Muscovy duck, and the stingless bee. Maya agronomists had cultivated a wide variety of nutritious domesticated plants, however, most of their animal protein came from hunting and gathering of wild resources such as game, fish, and shellfish. The turkey was a major source of protein.

The El Mirador turkey skeletons indicated the presence of male, female, and sub-adult turkeys which indicates traits of domestication. The evidence indicated the presence of reduced flight

CORN, COTTON AND CHOCOLATE: HOW THE MAYA CHANGED THE WORLD

morphology of the birds, the small bumpy nodules on the birds' ulnas, the forearm bones where flight muscles attach, are undeveloped in the turkey skeletons, suggesting that the birds didn't fly much and must have been domesticated. This trait indicated that the El Mirador turkeys were raised in captivity for a long enough to result in physical changes in the bird's bone structure. This evidence supports an argument for the origins of turkey husbandry or at least captive rearing by the Maya for an extended period in the Pre-classic period.

The archaeological sourced bird bones were processed at the DNA Laboratory located in the Department of Archaeology at Simon Fraser University in Canada. Two replicable DNA fragments were obtained for sample, the sequences clearly match most closely with *M. gallopavo* rather than *M. ocellata*, confirming the early domestication of the turkey by the Maya.

THE TURKEY AS A PART OF THE MAYA CULTURE

The turkey was a critical part of the Maya culture. The turkey was also important in the world of Maya ritual and, like corn, remains important today in ceremonies for curing, planting, and praying for rain. The bird served as a sacrificial object in offerings to the gods. They were a major food source and their feathers, bones and other byproducts were used for practical purposes. Turkey feathers were made into quills and used to write in the books that chronicled the religious rituals and sciences of the Maya. The byproducts were also used to make medicines, musical instruments, personal adornments, and tools.

THE TURKEY AS AN ESSENTIAL DIET AND AS A RITUAL FOOD

One of the classic dishes that was served as part of rituals invoking the gods of the four directions, called the *bacabs*, was a special turkey stew. The *bacabs* are creator gods and have many functions, but are primarily the "Lords of the Winds", each seated at a corner of the world and holding up the sky. The stews are traditionally made from turkey and were the color of the related *bacab*. In the traditional Maya ritual, east is yellow, west is red, north is white, and south is black. The center, our world of plants, is green.

Turkey dishes were a popular meat during antiquity and the bird is still important in Maya cooking today. The turkey was used to make rich spicy stews, turkey soups, turkey tamales, turkey tacos and in other various dishes.

THE TURKEY AS A SACRED BIRD ILLUSTRATED IN THE CODICES

The turkey has the honor of being a subject of illustrations in the Maya codices. While it was an important species in the Maya economy it is also frequently shown in the codices. The frequency of the image in the codices is due to the turkey being a bird of sacrifice. In the Dresden Codex, a whole turkey is pictured as an offering. The Dresden Codex also shows the sacrifice of a turkey by decapitation. The illustration pictures a priest holding a headless bird in his hand while standing before an altar. The writing of Friar De Landa confirms that the turkey was a sacrificial offering.

CORN, COTTON AND CHOCOLATE: HOW THE MAYA CHANGED THE WORLD

THE TURKEY IN PAINTED MAYA ART AND MODELS.

The Maya painted turkeys, distinguished by the wattle falling down the front of the face and by bumps on the head, on cylindrical vases dated from 250 to 800 A.D. Maya art of the period also depicted the rain god, Choc, with a turkey protruding from his nose. The ancient San Bartolo murals, dated from 100BC, include painted murals that illustrate turkeys taking part in the rituals. Maya artists created alabaster vases in form of the turkey as the birds were the quintessential animals for feasting and for sacrificial offerings. The Maya even made turkey-shaped tamales!

THE TURKEY MEETS THE WORLD

The European credited with the discovery of domesticated turkeys was none other than Christopher Columbus. He was on his fourth voyage in 1502, when he landed on a group of islands off the coast of Honduras. The natives presented him with turkeys which he called *gallina de la tierra*, or "land chicken". He tasted turkey and found the flesh good enough to take a few specimens back to Spain.

The turkey was a big success in Spain. The Royal court wanted to increase the availability of the bird, so in 1511, the Bishop of Valencia required that each ship returning from the West Indies bring back 10 birds, five males and five females. Turkeys quickly became an important food for the upper-class due to its superior taste over game birds and its less stringy texture. Up to that time, nobility dined on peacock and pheasant both of which have stringy flesh.

From Spain, the turkey spread to the remainder of Europe. Turkeys were sent to Italy by 1520 and by 1531 they were offered as presents among the nobility. Italians readily adopted the turkey and the first known recipes for the bird appeared in Italian cookbooks.

The 16th-century English navigator, William Strickland, is credited with introducing the turkey into England. In 1526, he acquired six birds from Native Americans and sold them in Bristol. The bird proved to be a great hit in England. Previously, the feathered diet of English aristocrats included tough and chewy morsels including cormorants, swans, cranes, herons, storks, and the great bustard. Henry VIII was the first English king to enjoy turkey, although Edward VII made eating turkey fashionable at Christmas.

Prior to the late 19th century, the exotic turkey was something of a luxury in Britain, with the smaller goose or beef more common at a Christmas dinner among the working classes. In Charles Dickens' *A Christmas Carol* (1843), Bob Cratchit had a goose before Scrooge sent Tiny Tim to buy the "prize Turkey". "What, the one as big as me?" Tiny Tim asked Scrooge.

In an ironic twist, the domestic turkey was sent with colonists from England to Jamestown, Virginia. When the Pilgrims sailed to North America in 1620, they took a few domesticated turkeys with them on the Mayflower. In New England, the "European" turkey was introduced to the local turkeys where it interbred with wild turkeys to become the ancestor of the modern holiday gobbler.

In the centuries since the first Thanksgiving, America has grown fond of the turkey. The huge, flightless, ugly-looking, domesticated turkey is more popular in North America than anywhere else in the world.

CORN, COTTON AND CHOCOLATE: HOW THE MAYA CHANGED THE WORLD

The intensive farming of turkeys from the late 1940s has dramatically reduced the price of the turkey, making it more affordable for the average American. In 1930 it took a week's wage to buy a turkey. Now it takes less than an hour.

The color of the original breed is the bronze hue of their feathers, but since 1960 the color of turkeys has changed. Bronze feathers have been changed to white feathers. In the 1920's turkeys were being selected for a larger breast and in the 1950s, breeders began to raise turkeys with fewer dark pinfeathers. By the 1960s, the Large or Broad Breasted White Turkey was developed. Now all commercial turkeys have white feathers and large breasts.

In the 21st century, all the world loves the turkey. 5,400,000 tons are produced each year. The Bronze bird of the Maya has changed. It now has white feathers and cannot fly.

WORLD PRODUCTION OF THE TURKEY

The turkey is raised by farmers around the world. The United States is the world's largest turkey producer and largest exporter of turkey products. Domestic consumption in the U.S. is higher than any other country. The total consumption per capita has risen from 8.1 pounds in 1980, it peaked at 18 pounds in 2007, and the average was 16 pounds per capita in 2015. Canada follows the U.S. with 9.1 pounds per capita and Europe with 8.3 pounds per capita. The U.S. consumer loves the delicious bird.

The United States leads the world in turkey production with 2.592 million metric tons (MT), while the European Union produced 2.030 million metric tons (MT), Brazil produced 0.520 million MT and Canada produced 0.165 million MT. The following chart illustrates the rankings.

TOP TURKEY PRODUCING COUNTRIES IN METRIC TONS

RANK	COUNTRY	PRODUCTION
1	United States	2,592,000
2	EU-27	2,030,000
3	Brazil	520,000
4	Canada	165,000
5	Russian Federation	105,000
6	Mexico	13,000
7	South Africa	8,000
8	China	6,000

The total tonnage produced is 5,400 million metric tons, which is a lot of turkey. The Maya cultivar has changed the way the world eats. They are eating a healthy kind of flesh.

THE TURKEY AND THEIR BIOLOGY

A turkey is a large bird in the *genus Meleagris*. One species, *Meleagris gallopavo* is native to the forests of North America. The domestic turkey, a large poultry bird, is a descendant of this species. The other living species is *Meleagris ocellata* or the ocellated turkey, is native to the forests of the Yucatán Peninsula.

CORN, COTTON AND CHOCOLATE: HOW THE MAYA CHANGED THE WORLD

Turkeys are classed in the taxonomic order of *Galliformes*; they are relatives of the grouse family. Males of both species have a distinctive fleshy wattle hanging from the underside of the beak, and the protuberance that hangs from the top of the beak is called a snood. They are among the largest birds in their ranges.

The turkey is raised throughout temperate parts of the world and is a popular form of poultry; partially because industrialized farming has made it very cheap considering the large amount of meat it produces. The female domesticated turkey is referred to as a hen and the chick as a poult or turkeyling. In the United States, the male is referred to as a tom, while in Europe, the male is a stag. The average lifespan for a domesticated turkey is ten years if left alone until this age.

THE BEHAVIOR AND THE LOOK OF THE MODERN TURKEY

Maya agronomists would not recognize their turkey dressed in their 21st century costumes. The Maya turkeys could fly up to 55 miles per hour and could run 20 miles per hour. The commercial turkey is a completely different bird than its ancestors. Times have changed and the new 21st century turkey is specifically bred for white feathers and a huge breast. It cannot fly at all, it cannot run and it even cannot have sex. The breasts of the new version of the turkey are too large for it to fly or even run.

In the 1940s, selective breeding produced birds with broader, meatier breasts, causing the turkey's bodies to become disproportionate. It became difficult for them to stand, and even more impossible for them to mate. The male cannot mate due to the large size of his breasts; they are too large for the male to mount the female.

In the mid-20st century, canvas saddles were strapped on the backs of female breeding turkeys for preventing damage from the feet of the males attempting to mate. It became apparent that the male's breasts had become too big to mate properly. The saddles were abandoned in the 1950s and replaced with artificial insemination.

How do turkeys feel about being forcibly subdued and manually masturbated? They don't seem to mind at all, it appears that they find it pleasing. Some tom turkeys actually get so excited by the mere arrival of the milkers or masterbaters that they cannot be milked in time.

Although the natural color of the turkey feathers is bronze, commercial species have been bred to have white feathers because consumers did not like the dark pinfeathers. Most birds reach a weight of 22 pounds (10 kg) after 15 weeks, due to the constant availability of formulated feed and ample water.

Turkeys are highly social and become very distressed when isolated. Adult turkeys can recognize "strangers". Placing any alien turkey into an established group of birds will almost certainly result in that individual being attacked, sometimes fatally.

Maturing males spend a considerable proportion of their time sexually displaying. This is a display similar to that of the wild turkey and involves fanning the tail feathers. The birds "sneeze" at regular intervals, followed by a rapid vibration of their tail feathers. Throughout the display, the birds strut about slowly, with the neck arched backward, their breasts thrust forward emitting their characteristic "gobbling" call.

CORN, COTTON AND CHOCOLATE: HOW THE MAYA CHANGED THE WORLD

Only tom turkeys make the classic gobbling call, while hen turkeys make a clicking noise. Turkey hens are usually sold as whole birds, while toms are processed into products such as cutlets, tenderloins, turkey sausage, turkey franks, and turkey deli meats. Virtually all turkeys now consumed in America are strains of broad breasted whites that have been specially bred.

Many people consider the flesh of the turkey, especially the breast meat, to be bland and tasteless. The modern commercial turkey has been bred for various characteristics: docility, early maturity, maximum gross weight, and color of the carcass. However, flavor of the flesh is not one of the valued traits.

It would be easy to blame the industry to the lack of flavor, but it is part of what consumers demonstrate that they want. Americans consistently choose lower prices and greater quantity in their food. In the 21st century, the modern commercial turkey reflects that trend.

WHAT'S IN A NAME

The Maya called their big bird by the name *Uu Lum*. American Indians had names for the turkey that basically translated as a "big bird". When Europeans discovered the turkey, they called it by different names. Columbus called it: *gallina de la tierra*, or "land chicken. The British referred to the bird as *turkeycock.* The French called the turkey *coq d'Inde*, meaning rooster of India. This has been shortened to *dinde*, the modern French word for turkey. Once the bird began to strut its stuff across the European continent, every language settled on a different name. The result was a muddle. Adding to the confusion was that people mistook the word for "turkey" as referring to the equally odd-looking guinea fowl that were being imported from West Africa about the same time.

None of the adopted names in any language relates or sounds like the original Maya, Aztec, or Spanish word for the turkey. The Mexican spanish got close. They use the name *guajolote*, from the Nahuatl word *huexolotl*.

European names are diverse. In German, it is *truthahn*, in Italian it is *polo d'india* or *tacchino,* in Spanish it is *pavo*, in Swedish it is *kalkon*, in Danish it is *tyrkeit* and in Japanese it is *toruko.* South Americans refer to the turkey as *peru*.

In 1728, the Swedish naturalist Carl Linnaeus tried to classify the turkey. Even Carl did not get it right. When he cobbled together the Latin name *Meleagris gallopavo,* he missed the mark; *meleagris* is a guinea fowl, *gallus* is a chicken, and *pova* is a peacock. All in all, the turkey had Linnaeus confused, but the name stuck, as the official botanical Latin nomenclature.

THE TURKEY AS A FOOD GROUP

People of all ages of all ages love to eat turkey because of its profile as a healthful, "comfort" food. The naturally mild taste of turkey readily combines with different seasonings, making it an ideal choice in spicy ethnic dishes, as a substitute for higher-fat meats in favorite recipes and in turkey deli meats. Ground turkey has a high appeal among all ages, genders and economic levels.

Turkey can be used in so many cooking methods, including stovetop, oven, microwave and grill. There is a wide range of cuts and products available such as ground turkey, turkey ham, turkey

CORN, COTTON AND CHOCOLATE: HOW THE MAYA CHANGED THE WORLD

franks, turkey pastrami, turkey sausage, turkey bacon and deli turkey make this protein easy to incorporate into any meal. The trend of low-fat, low cholesterol diets has greatly increased the use of turkey in modern meals. Turkey is increasingly packaged in smaller portion sizes that are perfect for singles or small families. A national study on turkey consumption found that nearly half of U.S. consumers eat turkey at least once every two weeks.

Creative chefs have combined the turkey with other fowl made into elaborate dishes known as turducken. That is a duck stuffed inside a turkey and then a chicken stuffed into the duck. Vegetarian analogues made from tofu are known as tofurkey.

For nearly 500 years, the turkey has been adopted as a major food by numerous countries and their cuisines reflect the many dishes that have been developed by creative cooks.

THE GREAT MAYA TURKEY DAY: THANKSGIVING

Turkey is a popular dish for celebrating the holidays. The bird is the main course at Christmas and Easter, but the consumption of the turkey on Thanksgiving Day eclipses all other holiday feasts. For Americans, Thanksgiving is traditionally a day for families and friends to get together and enjoy a lavish meal. Thanksgiving Day is a time to give thanks for what they have received and a popular time to visit family and friends. While today's Thanksgiving celebrations would hardly be recognizable to attendees of the original 1621 harvest meal, it continues to be a day when Americans come together around the table, albeit with some updates to pilgrim's menu.

English colonists and Wampanoag native Americans got together for a harvest festival in 1621. Harvest festivals are a common tradition in many cultures. In late fall, when the crops are in and the livestock need to be slaughtered, it's time for one last feast before the lean times of winter. In the second half of the 1600s, celebrating such thanksgivings after the harvest became more common and started to become annual events.

On September 28, 1789, the first Federal Congress of the United States passed a resolution asking that the President of the United States recommend a day of Thanksgiving. A few days later, President George Washington issued a proclamation naming Thursday, November 26, 1789, as a *"Day of Publick Thanksgiving"*. This was the first-time Thanksgiving was celebrated under the new Constitution of the United States.

Subsequent presidents issued Thanksgiving Proclamations, but the dates and even the months of the celebrations varied. An official date was not established until President Abraham Lincoln's 1863 Proclamation stating that Thanksgiving would be commemorated on the last Thursday of November.

However, in 1939, during the great depression, the last Thursday in November fell on the last day of the month. Concerned that the shortened Christmas shopping season might dampen the economic recovery, President Franklin D. Roosevelt issued a Presidential Proclamation moving Thanksgiving from the last Thursday to the second Thursday of November. Three years later, in December 1941, a joint session of Congress changed the date to the fourth Thursday in November and President Roosevelt signed the resolution on December 26, 1941. That's how the day is celebrated in the 21st century.

CORN, COTTON AND CHOCOLATE: HOW THE MAYA CHANGED THE WORLD

PARDONING THE DOOMED TURKEY

The president of the United States has been traditionally presented with a live turkey at Thanksgiving. Since the last part of the 20th century the president has pardoned the Presidential turkey. This is a great honor for the Maya bird.

The turkey pardoning ceremony takes place in the White House rose garden. The turkey is placed on the table. He may be patted, but not poked by the 30 or more guests. The turkey then is pardoned from a certain death in a mock magnanimous gesture performed by the President of the United States.

The custom began with President John F. Kennedy when he spared the life of the turkey he received in 1963. He stated, *"we will let this one grow"* and he sent the bird to live out its life on a farm. At least one headline in the Los Angeles Times referred to it as a pardon, but Kennedy did not formally refer to it as such.

The first President on record issuing a "pardon" to his turkey was Ronald Reagan, who pardoned a turkey named Charlie and sent him to a petting zoo in 1987.

In 2013, President Obama pardoned Popcorn, a 38-pound (17 kg) turkey from Badger, Minnesota. Popcorn won an online contest over its identically sized stable mate, Caramel, who was also spared.

The presidential pardon lives on as do the turkeys selected as the presidential bird. The Maya turkey may not have been the cause of Thanksgiving, but they are the star of the feast.

THE MAYA TURKEY FEEDS ASTRONAUTS ON THE MOON

The Maya turkey satisfies the hunger of people all over the world and has even been served as an entrée in outer space. When Neil Armstrong and Edwin Aldrin sat down to eat their first meal on the moon, their foil food packets contained roasted turkey and all the trimmings. One of the dinner options for Commander Christopher Ferguson aboard Atlantis, the last NASA shuttle to fly into space, was smoked turkey and turkey tetrazzini.

THE TURKEY TROT. MAY I HAVE THIS DANCE?

The Maya use dances in their rituals, but they would not have recognized the dance named after their turkey. The turkey lent its name to a popular dance craze in the early 1900s. The basic step of the dance was to imitate turkey-like movements. The dance consisted of four hopping steps sideways with the feet well apart, first on one leg, then the other with a characteristic rise on the ball of the foot, followed by a drop upon the heel. The dance was embellished with scissor-like flicks of the feet and fast trotting actions with abrupt stops.

From 1900 to 1910, the Turkey Trot was done to fast ragtime music popular in the decade, such as Scott Joplin's Maple Leaf Rag. Irene and Vernon Castle raised its popularity by dancing the Turkey Trot in the Broadway show, "The Sunshine Girl".

It achieved popularity chiefly because of being denounced by the Vatican. It was thought that the positions assumed by the dancers were offensively suggestive. Furthermore, conservative members of society felt the dance was demoralizing and tried to get it banned at public functions, which only served to increase its popularity.

CORN, COTTON AND CHOCOLATE: HOW THE MAYA CHANGED THE WORLD

IS THE TURKEY REALLY STUPID?

The turkey's alleged stupidity has given rise to derogatory terms about the bird in the English language. An example of the suspicious IQ of the turkey comes from reputable poultry researchers. They talk of domesticated turkeys standing in the rain looking upward to heaven and not having the sense to go inside out of the rain. Raindrops block their nostrils, and the result is that the turkeys die by drowning. Surely this is the ultimate act of stupidity. This gives rise to the expression that a person is "too dumb to get in out of the rain."

WORDS CREATED BY THE TURKEY

The use of the word turkey as a synonym for failure and worthlessness it is not easy to trace, but it has a long history. The word turkey is an all-purpose term of derision that is traced to the American theater. Walter Winchell, gossip columnist for the New York Daily Mirror, and Groucho Marx the comedian, used the term for theatrical failures. In the theatre, anything that did not live up to expectations was termed a "turkey".

The term turkey has multiple meanings all connoting a tendency for failure. Today, to be called a turkey is obviously a pejorative, but in an earlier time it was a slang word meaning a coward. Turkey has become a political term for mockery of all levels of U.S. elected officials.

TALKING TURKEY

Based on an old joke, the expression "talking turkey" has come to mean to speak frankly. It is also suggested that it arose because the first contacts between Native Americans and settlers often centered on the procuring of wild turkeys, to the extent that Indians were said to have asked whenever they met a colonist, "you come to talk turkey?".

TURKEY GOBBLE

The term "gobble" probably comes from imitations of the loud gurgling sound made by male turkeys. What it actually refers to is talking rapidly, indistinctly, incoherently, or nonsensically.

GOBBLEDYGOOK

The term "gobbledygook" is an insult to bureaucratic jargon at government meetings. Texas Senator, Maury Maverick, who won the seat vacated by Vice President Lyndon B. Johnson, issued an order banning *gobbledygook* language. Asked where he got the term, Senator Maverick responded: "*I was thinking of the old bearded Turkey gobbler back in Texas who was always gobbledy-gobbling and striking a pose with ludicrous pomposity. At the end of every gobble there was sort of a gook.*"

THE TURKEY SHOOT

The "Turkey Shoot" has come to signify a simple task or a helpless target. The term came from hunters shooting wild turkeys that were roasting in the trees. They're easily killed in roost because while the one being killed falls dead; the others sit still as if waiting their turn to be shot.

The most famous "turkey shoot" was in the Pacific during World War II. The Battle of the Philippine Sea (June 19–20, 1944) was a decisive naval battle of WW II eliminated the Imperial Japanese Navy's ability to conduct large-scale carrier actions. The battle was nicknamed: "The

CORN, COTTON AND CHOCOLATE: HOW THE MAYA CHANGED THE WORLD

Great Marianas Turkey Shoot" by American aviators. The battle involved the severe losses inflicted upon Japanese aircraft by American pilots and anti-aircraft gunners. Compared to a loss of only 30 American aircraft, 350 Japanese planes were downed. During a debriefing after the air battles a pilot from USS Lexington remarked *"Why, hell, it was just like an old-time turkey shoot down home!"*

HERDING TURKEYS: LONG DISTANCE DRIVES FEATURING THE TURKEY

Originally, the turkey had the ability to be a strong walker. This trait was used for transporting the big bird. The amiability, sturdy constitution, and long strong legs of the birds enabled them to be herded over long distances. They are hardy and able to negotiate difficult terrain that included swimming.

Before the 20th century, turkey drives were common in United States and in England. In that day, roads were not in good condition and wagons could only hold a few birds. There were no refrigerated trucks, so turkeys could not be slaughtered on the farm. Therefore, thousands of turkeys were forced to walk to their own hanging. In Europe and America turkeys were driven on foot to market as a herded mass.

As early as 1691 European drovers were reported driving turkeys from France to Spain in flocks like sheep. In 18th century Europe turkeys typically walked 100 miles or more from the farm to the market. In England, turkeys were walked to the city markets. To prevent them from flying away one wing was cut. Turkeys wore shoes for the journey, their feet were dipped in thick pitch or booties were made of sacking to protect them during their march.

In the United States, turkey drivers used similar techniques for transporting turkeys. The turkeys were herded into large groups. Ideally a drive of 20,000 turkeys employed 4 to 6 drovers. The drovers carried long whips with strips of red flannel tied to the ends which were used to flick the birds into line.

A walk by some 1000 turkeys that were driven from Missouri to Denver, took place in 1863. Two boys were employed to drive the turkeys the 600 miles to their destination. These armies of turkeys at best averaged one mile per hour, but their speed increased toward nightfall when the birds began to roost in trees where they could not be besieged by foxes, coyotes, and humans. If the birds were not successfully regrouped promptly each morning upon leaving their roosts they scattered in the woods and could not be recovered.

THE TURKEY DROP

A turkey festival once held in Yellville, Arkansas was known as the "Turkey Drop". During this festival, turkeys were thrown from a moving aircraft flying 1000 feet above the ground. They would plunge down through the air at 50 miles per hour, crash to the ground, then be chased down, cornered and captured by local youths. This was obviously a horrible event for the turkeys.

Turkeys would flutter down to the ground with some crashing into telephone poles. They would try to run on broken legs before being set upon by a gang of kids who captured and fought over the bird. Each year 10 to 12 turkeys would be dropped from an airplane. Townspeople would gather below and try to catch take one to take home to eat. Public outcry from across the country resulted in cancellation of the Turkey Drop.

CORN, COTTON AND CHOCOLATE: HOW THE MAYA CHANGED THE WORLD

TURKEY SHOOTS

During the 19th century, the "Turkey Shoot" was an important part of the American Christmas tradition. Shooters paid money to participate in the turkey shoot. The event involved marksmanship with a target that was not a paper cutout, but a real live turkey. A plank was placed at some distance from the shooters with a hole cut in it with the head of the turkey thrust through the opening with his body hidden behind it. Only the turkey's head is visible and is the target. The sportsmen fired at this mark. If blood was drawn, the marksman was entitled to the turkey.

This custom goes back to colonial times when colonial shooters fired a single musket ball at the bird. This type of the contest at 60 yards of distance between the shooter and the bird was a challenge. However, modern precision firearms make hitting the target quite easy thus only the head was the target.

The practice of shooting at captive turkeys went out of fashion due to the efforts in 1866 of the American Society for the Prevention of Cruelty to Animals. The practice was considered inhumane.

THE MAYA TURKEY INVENTS THE FROZEN TV DINNER

Turkey farmers owe a huge debt of gratitude to a combination of dumb luck and a Maya turkey. The fortuitous intersection of fate involved Carl Swanson, Pan Am airways and an abundance of frozen turkeys. The positive result of this fateful confluence was the invention of the frozen TV dinner, an innovation that changed the way America serves and eats their meals.

During the Depression, Swanson decided there was money to be made in turkeys, and then during World War II, turkeys became even more profitable because of the scarcity of other kinds of meat. Swanson decided to corner the turkey market and begin a massive buying campaign. However, farmers discovered that it was easy to raise turkeys and after the war ended, the bubble burst because of the glut of turkeys on the market. Swanson was left with a huge quantity of turkeys and no market in sight. He had big troubles

He decided to keep them frozen until he could figure out what to do. His cold storage facilities were filled and it became necessary to rent cold storage rail cars for the overflow of frozen turkeys. In a stroke of luck, one of Swanson's distributors was a firm that prepared food packages for overseas flights on Pan American Airways. These portable meals were packed in aluminum trays and heated on board the aircraft in convection ovens. However, this product was not marketed to the public. The public was not even aware of the methodology of cooking and serving prepared frozen dinners. This idea was the spark that ignited a change in the way that America dinned.

A Swanson executive proposed that Swanson make a similar frozen meal for consumers. He knew that the consumer was interested in a faster and more convenient method of food preparation. Swanson named his creation a "TV dinner" because the container looked like a television and he associated the meal with television viewing. Television was the new and exciting technology that was entering mainstream American life. In the spring of 1951, a few thousand meals were test marketed in cities from Omaha to Chicago. It was a risky venture because frozen foods were not yet a significant part of American dining.

CORN, COTTON AND CHOCOLATE: HOW THE MAYA CHANGED THE WORLD

The idea of prepared meals that could be eaten in front of the television set intrigued consumers. The concept was so successful that within three years Swanson was selling 13,000,000 turkey dinners annually, and it was a whole dinner including the sides, dressing, gravy, and, of course, the turkey. The Swanson Company has celebrated over 50 years producing the TV dinner and turkey remains the most popular frozen entree. So, a great idea combined with luck and the Maya turkey changed the way that America dinned.

THE TURKEY AND ITS PART IN CHANGING HISTORY

The turkey has become the mother of all birds. It is the star of all big American holiday feasts. The turkey is consumed by hundreds of millions of people in countries around the world, dining on the 5,000,000 metric tons produced each year. The turkey has changed colors and its size to accommodate the wants of the consumer. The bird has produced legendary phrases and terms and it invented the frozen TV dinner.

CORN, COTTON AND CHOCOLATE: HOW THE MAYA CHANGED THE WORLD

CHAPTER 24: VANILLA

Botanical name: *Vanilla planifolia*   **Maya name:** *sool*

Memories of a youth

On Sundays, our neighbor, Mr. Rakestraw, always had a family gathering. The whole Rakestraw clan would show up for Sunday dinner. Mrs. Rakestraw was a wonderful cook. The menu was pure Southern cooking. She made delicious cornbread, corn on the cob, sweet potato pie, fried okra, fried chicken and peach cobbler. To top off that wonderful peach cobbler dessert, Mr. Rakestraw made the most delicious vanilla ice cream I have ever eaten.

His recipe was different from other ice creams. He first made a vanilla egg custard with eggs and cream, added the remainder of the ingredients and placed the whole concoction in a hand operated ice cream making machine. The only missing component was someone to provide the energy for turning the hand crank of the machine. The process took about an hour, turning the crank and properly freezing the ingredients to produce the delicious vanilla ice cream that only Mr. Rakestraw could make. The hand crank power was usually provided by yours truly.

Somehow, I would always wander by their house just as Mr. Rakestraw would have his batch of raw ingredients prepared and ready to be poured into the ice cream churn. I had a job as the churn-cranker assured by my perfect timing.

I would show up and say, "Mr. Rakestraw, do you need any help pouring the batch into your churn?"

Mr. Rakestraw would always feign a look of surprise and say: "Well, hello Jimmy. Yes, I can use a little help and you know, my arm is sore from working. I could use some help in turning the crank."

The ice cream machine consisted of a wooden tub enclosing a container that held the ice cream mixture. An exterior crank turned the paddles located in interior of the container. I would step forward and help him pour his mixture into the machine. Then I would help pack the outer area of the container with ice and sea salt, assume my regular seat and start cranking the handle.

Around noon Mr. Rakestraw's relatives would start arriving for dinner. Mr. Rakestraw would greet them and then sit down near me and we would talk. He considered me to be unique because I went to Catholic school in Atlanta and rode the Greyhound bus both ways to the city each day. Our conversations usually concerned my knowledge of the ways of the big city, Atlanta. Mr. Rakestraw was an intelligent man with a deep Southern drawl. He was very well spoken using correct but drawling grammar. However, to a Yankee he would appear to be a redneck. He was in his fifties and I was 12 years old. However, he always spoke to me as an equal and did not talk down to me.

During our conversations, he told me that he had never been to Atlanta, some 18 miles to the south. He had little interest in that city; however, he was a big fan of the Atlanta crackers baseball team. He listened to their games on radio, but never once considered going to Atlanta and attending a game.

CORN, COTTON AND CHOCOLATE: HOW THE MAYA CHANGED THE WORLD

Mr. Rakestraw had a curious way of describing our little town. When he referred to the downtown square he would always refer to the town center as "Marietta, Georgia". I always wanted to ask him why he always included the name of the state when he referred to our little town. Georgia is the largest state east of the Mississippi river, so the state lines are hundreds of miles away.

While we chatted, his family would continue to arrive, and soon Mrs. Rakestraw would announce that dinner was served. I would always be invited to join the Rakestraw family for Sunday dinner. I would genteelly refuse, using my duty of as chief ice cream churner as the reason. However, I considered myself to be critical part of the team making the best vanilla ice cream in the world.

Toward the end of the meal, Mr. Rakestraw would come over and sit next to me. He would always inquire about the state of the ice cream. "Well, Jimmy, how is our ice cream coming?"

I would respond. "Very good Mr. Rakestraw, the crank is getting harder to turn. I think it's ready."

He would answer; "Well let me take a little peek."

He would remove the lid and pull out the interior paddles. As he withdrew the ice cream machine paddles the thick creamy heavy ice cream would adhere to the paddles. Withdrawing the beautiful ice cream would release the scent of fresh vanilla and would make me salivate. As usual, Mr. Rakestraw would announce that this batch of vanilla ice cream was probably the best he ever made. He would then carry the churn with its delicious contents into the kitchen. There it would be placed in bowls along with the peach cobbler for dessert.

When Mr. Rakestraw went into the kitchen, I would lean back in my chair and rest my arm. I did not want to rub my arm because someone would think that I was tired from turning the handle of the ice cream churn. Like clockwork, Mr. Rakestraw would reappear through the kitchen door. He would be carrying two large bowls of perfect vanilla ice cream. Wordlessly he would hand me a bowl and then take a seat in his chair. He did not speak until he had tasted a spoonful of our ice cream. He would look over at me. He would always say the same thing, "Damn, that is good ice cream." He would then look up at the sky and say, "Sweet Jesus, please forgive my language."

I would then taste a spoonful. The vanilla flavor transported by the frozen egg cream exploded on my taste buds. It was so cold that I almost got a brain freeze. This may not have been heaven, but it probably was the best ice cream ever made on earth.

Sitting here today, in my memory, I can still taste that delicious homemade vanilla ice cream. A Sunday afternoon, homemade vanilla ice cream and a conversation with Mr. Rakestraw makes a perfect memory. Little did Maya agronomists know, growing their vanilla orchids in forest gardens, what pleasure they would bring to our little town of Marietta, Georgia.

THE MAYA AND VANILLA

For many years, the homeland of the vanilla orchid has been debated by botanists. However, genetic evidence recently uncovered by botanical gumshoes has targeted the source of the vanilla orchard as a Maya cultivar. Maya agronomists cultivated the climbing vanilla orchid in their forest gardens which were agricultural management systems employed for genetically altering native plants in the surrounds of the rainforest.

CORN, COTTON AND CHOCOLATE: HOW THE MAYA CHANGED THE WORLD

Forest gardens were maintained to propagate the cultivars of the forest and were developed by Maya agronomists as a variegated garden that genetically altered tree species including avocado, cacao, chicle, mango, papaya and mahogany, plus the vanilla orchid, *Vanilla planifolia.*

The Maya collected different species of wild vanilla from the rainforest and propagated them. This process meant that species previously geographically separated were able to be hybridized in the same protected environment. The result was an evolutionary cultivar that refined the flavor of the vanilla bean.

The Maya cultivation of the orchard was especially difficult because of the sensitive nature of its pollination. The success of Maya agronomists was aided by the symbiotic relationship between the vanilla orchid and its natural pollinator, the local species of Melipona bee. The bee had a unique method of pollinating the orchid flower. Pollination was required to propagate the fruit that produces vanilla.

The Maya harvested the long brown bean produced by the orchid. The fragrant rich vanilla beans are the pods or fruits from the tropical climbing orchid that yields vanilla.

The ancient Maya believed that the vanilla drink had aphrodisiac qualities. Modern research, however, has not established its role in the treatment of sexual dysfunctions. The Maya used vanilla as a perfume when mixed with copal resin, burned as a savory incense and was used to treat insect bites and heal wounds.

Most importantly, the Maya enjoyed the flavor of the vanilla, especially when mixed with a chocolate drink. Its evolutionary journey began as a Maya cultivar inside the tropical forests of the Yucatán and the flavoring spread across the world.

THE WANDERING TRAVELS OF THE VANILLA ORCHID. HELLO WORLD, HERE I COME

The travels of the vanilla bean have been traced and it has left behind a fragrant trail. Vanilla first left the Yucatán during the early 1500s on ships bound for Spain. The Spanish originally believed that it only had value as a perfume. It wasn't until Cortes arrived in 1519, that the Spaniards learned that vanilla was added to flavor chocolate drink.

When Hernan Cortez met with the Aztec Emperor Montezuma in Tenochtitlan, he observed that the Emperor enjoyed a royal beverage of vanilla-scented chocolate. The Spanish tried this vanilla flavored drink themselves and were so impressed by the new taste sensation that they took samples back to Spain.

It was vanilla rather than the chocolate that made a big hit as a flavor, and by 1700 the use of vanilla had spread over all of Europe. Mexico became the leading producer of vanilla for three centuries. Within half a century, Spanish factories were preparing vanilla-flavored chocolate. For two centuries, Europeans continued to use vanilla only in combination with the cocoa bean. Until the early 17th Century, when Hugh Morgan, a creative apothecary in the employ of Queen Elizabeth invented chocolate-free, all-vanilla-flavored sweetmeats. The Queen adored them.

By the next century, the French took a liking to the flavor and began using it as an ingredient in pastries, cakes, beverages and to flavor ice cream. This treat was discovered by Thomas Jefferson in the 1780s, when he lived in Paris as American Minister to France. He was so thrilled with the ice cream, that he copied down a recipe. Jefferson was said to have a carried his favorite 18-step recipe for an ice cream delicacy back to America. Vanilla became popular in the U.S.

CORN, COTTON AND CHOCOLATE: HOW THE MAYA CHANGED THE WORLD

In 1806, the first vanilla orchid to flower in Europe was grown in the London collection of Charles Greville. Cuttings from that plant went to Netherlands and Paris. The French transplanted the vines in their overseas colonies. Until the 19th century, Mexico was the world's chief producer of vanilla. In 1819; however, a French Admiral was responsible for introducing vanilla to Tahiti, then shipped vanilla fruits to the islands of Réunion and Mauritius. After Edmond Albius discovered how to pollinate the flowers quickly by hand, the pods began to thrive. Soon, the tropical orchids were sent from Réunion Island to the Comoros Islands and Madagascar. By 1898, Madagascar, Réunion, and the Comoros Islands produced about 80% of world production.

Vanilla came late to recipe books when in 1824, the first American recipe for vanilla ice cream is found in Mary Randolph's, *The Virginia Housewife.* By the latter half of the century, the demand for vanilla skyrocketed. Not only was it the flavor of choice for ice cream, but it was an essential ingredient in soft drinks. Among these adherents of vanilla was Atlanta chemist John S. Pemberton's and his soft drink, "Coca-Cola". Today, the Coca Cola Company is the world's largest consumer of vanilla.

In the 21st century, vanilla is the most popular flavor in the world. The taste for vanilla is a worldwide favorite. The United States is the world's largest consumer of vanilla flavoring, followed by Europe. Each year, about 8500 tons of vanilla is produced worldwide. Vanilla, is one of the most expensive of the world's spices.

THE SEARCH FOR THE HOMELAND OF VANILLA

The origin of the Tahitian vanilla orchid had long eluded botanists. Known by the scientific name *Vanilla tahitensis*, Tahitian vanilla is found to exist only under cultivation. Natural, wild populations of the orchid had never been encountered until recent scientific studies traced the original homeland of the vanilla orchid.

Madagascar and Indonesia grow most of the world's crop, but the question remained, where did the orchid originate? Botanists from the University of California traced Tahitian vanilla back to its true origins. DNA analysis corroborated what the historical sources said, that vanilla was a trade item brought to Tahiti by French sailors in the mid-19th century. They used vanilla cuttings from the Philippines. The genetic data confirmed that the closest relatives to Tahitian vanilla were two species that grow naturally only in the tropical forests of the Maya domain: *Vanilla planifolia and Vanilla odorata.* The legends proved to be true, the home of vanilla lies deep in the forest gardens of the Maya rainforest.

MAKE MINE VANILLA, THE MOST POPULAR FLAVOR IN THE WORLD

For 500 years, vanilla has seduced kings, comforted millions and is now the most popular flavor in the world. Another Maya cultivar, chocolate comes in second. Vanilla was popular with the Maya and it still leads the pack of the world's favorite flavors.

Vanilla is appealing because it conjures up feelings of comfort and familiarity when included as a flavoring in foods ranging from ice cream and yogurts, to muffins and cakes, to pastries, confections, and other desserts. Most people don't realize that it can also act as a flavor enhancer. It increases our ability to taste other flavors by intensifying those flavors.

THE BIOLOGY OF VANILLA

CORN, COTTON AND CHOCOLATE: HOW THE MAYA CHANGED THE WORLD

The main species harvested for the vanilla bean is *Vanilla planifolia*. Although it is native to Mexico, it is now widely grown throughout the tropics.

The vanilla orchid grows as a vine, climbing up a tree, pole, or other support. It can be grown in a forest, in a plantation, or in a "shader", in increasing orders of productivity. Its growth environment is referred to as its terroir, and it includes not only the adjacent plants, but also the climate, geography, and local geology. Left alone, it will grow as high as possible on the support, with few flowers. Vanilla vines grow to be 30-50 feet tall, when supported by a host tree or posts, and is grown in a hot, moist, tropical climate. Vanilla is the only edible fruit of the orchid family, the largest family of flowering plants in the world. There are over 150 varieties of vanilla plants.

Distinctively flavored compounds are found in the fruit or seed pods, which result from the pollination of the flower. These seed pods are roughly a third of an inch wide by six inches long. Their color when ripe is brownish red to black. The fruit, a seed capsule, if left on the plant, ripens and opens as it dries. The phenolic compounds crystallize, giving the fruits a diamond-dusted appearance, it then releases the distinctive vanilla smell. Inside of these pods is an oily liquid full of tiny black seeds.

Each flower produces one fruit and *V. planifolia* flowers are hermaphroditic: They carry both male (anther) and female (stigma) organs; however, to avoid self-pollination, a membrane separates those organs. The flowers can be naturally pollinated only by bees of the Melipona genus found in Mexico.

WORLD PRODUCTION OF VANILLA

The world production of vanilla has a much smaller tonnage number that any other Maya cultivar. Only 10,000 tons of the flavoring is produced each year. However, a little bit goes a long way. Last year, the world's largest vanilla-producing country was Madagascar, with an output of more than 3,500 tons of vanilla, barely edging out Indonesia, and far above the 390 metric tons from Mexico the original home of the flavor.

TOP 10 VANILLA PRODUCING COUNTRIES IN METRIC TONS

RANK	COUNTRY	PRODUCTION
1	Madagascar	3500
2	Indonesia	3400
3	China, mainland	1350
4	Papua New Guinea	400
5	Mexico	390
6	Turkey	290
7	Tonga	202
8	Uganda	170
9	French Polynesia	60
10	Comoros	42

WHAT DO YOU CALL VANILLA?

The Maya started it all, they referred to the vanilla bean as *Sool*. The Aztec inherited the love of vanilla from the Maya, named the fruit *tlilxochitl* or "black flower". The Spaniards adopted the

CORN, COTTON AND CHOCOLATE: HOW THE MAYA CHANGED THE WORLD

flavor and compared the vanilla bean pods to a little sheath or *vaina*, which is derived from the Latin word, vagina. They called it "vainilla", or "little pod". The name stuck and the word vanilla entered the English language in 1754, when the botanist Philip Miller wrote about the genus in his *Gardener's Dictionary*.

The names assigned the flavor around the world adopted the name originated by the Spanish. The French call it *vanille*, in Danish it is *vanille*, in German it is *vanilla*, in Finnish it is *vanilja*, in Russian it is *vanil*, in Spanish it is *vainilla*, and Zulu it is vanilla. Even the Zulu got it right.

OK, WHAT IS THE DIFFERENCE BETWEEN VANILLA AND FRENCH VANILLA?

What's in a name? Vanilla bean varieties are often named for the location where they're grown, like Madagascar, Tahiti and Mexico. However, the location where it was cultivated was not the way French vanilla got its name. The name came from the culinary magic produced by French chefs, and refers not to a variety of vanilla, but to the classic French method of making ice cream using an egg-custard base. French vanilla, of course, is both a taste and a scent that transcends the flavor of ice cream.

Today, when we refer to French vanilla, it is when the vanilla flavor is caramelized and cooked custard-like, with a slightly floral scent. Vanilla is the pure form of the extract from the orchid fruit. The difference between the two is that French vanilla has cream and eggs.

JUST HOW MANY TYPES OF VANILLA ARE THERE?

Ancient Maya agronomists developed what was the perfect flavoring. In the 21st century, they would be surprised to learn that multiple varieties of the vanilla orchid are being grown in exotic locations across the world, each with its own distinctive flavor. All of them are originally from the forest gardens of the Yucatán.

Just like grapes grown for wine, vanilla beans develop different flavors depending on where they're grown. As the French say about wine, the *terroir* modifies the flavor. The flavor of the beans varies with the location of their growth and is influenced by the local climate, geography, and geology.

Tahitian vanilla: Tahitian beans have a fruity, floral flavor with cherry and anise-like notes, which means they work well with fruit and are excellent in ice creams, custards and drinks.

Mexican vanilla: Is bold and dark with tones of smoke. Mexican beans have a sweet, creamy flavor, but with a bit of a spicy character, like clove or nutmeg. The flavor pairs well with spices like cinnamon and cloves, as well as chocolate and spicy chilies, salsas or barbecue sauces.

Madagascar vanilla: Dark, full bodied and rummy with a hint of tobacco. Perfect for recipes that might be flambéed or if you need a vanilla to stand up to powerful flavors that might overshadow it.

Bourbon vanilla: This vanilla comes from Madagascar's Bourbon islands, their sweet, creamy flavor is thought of as classic. This is a great all-purpose vanilla for using in any sweet or savory dish.

CORN, COTTON AND CHOCOLATE: HOW THE MAYA CHANGED THE WORLD

India vanilla: The beans are huge and very oily, with a very muted, woodsy quality. This vanilla will stand up well to spices in a dish where the presence of cloves, rosemary, cinnamon, or thyme may threaten to eclipse other vanilla varieties.

Indonesian vanilla: These beans are thick, oily, pliable, and it's the oddest. The scent of this vanilla is somewhat fermented and the overall scent profile is one you would associate with prunes. When cooked, the vanilla flavor becomes more pronounced, perfect for stewing fruit, or in pies and compotes.

SYNTHETIC VANILLA

One of the sad truths about vanilla is that while the world enjoys the flavor, production of natural vanilla cannot satisfy the world's demand. Maya agronomists would be shocked to know that science has imitated Mother Nature and developed a synthetic vanilla.

Artificial vanilla flavoring was developed to satisfy the shortage of natural vanilla. Synthetic vanilla is composed of artificial "vanillin". Vanillin is the component in natural vanilla that produces the wonderful flavor.

In the 21st century, the production of artificial vanillin greatly exceeds the amount of natural vanilla produced. Vanillin and vanilla extracts have an estimated annual total volume of 16,000 metric tons. The advantage of vanillin is not only in the quantity, but in the low price of the artificial flavoring. Natural vanilla costs about $682 per pound while artificial vanillin costs about $4.50 per pound.

Artificial vanilla flavoring is alleged to have a richer flavor profile than natural vanilla. The largest use of vanillin is in the flavor industry, and as a very important key note for many different flavors. The ice cream and chocolate candy industries together comprise 75% of the market for vanillin.

Vanillin is also used in the fragrance industry, in perfumes, and to mask unpleasant odors or tastes in medicines, livestock fodder, and cleaning products.

VANILLA AS FOOD FLAVORING

Vanilla extract is derived from the vanilla pod and is produced by steeping it in alcohol and water. Only vanilla extract has the true flavor and aroma of vanilla pods.

When preparing to use vanilla in a recipe, several choices are available for the cook to choose from. The five main commercial preparations of natural vanilla are:

Whole vanilla pods: The whole ripe fruit of the vanilla orchid.

Vanilla Powder: Ground pods, pure or blended with sugar, starch, or other ingredients.

Vanilla extract: Vanilla in an alcoholic solution. Both natural and imitation forms of vanilla contain at least 35% alcohol.

Vanilla sugar: a packaged mix of sugar and vanilla extract.

CORN, COTTON AND CHOCOLATE: HOW THE MAYA CHANGED THE WORLD

Pure vanilla powder: Pure natural vanilla powder or paste.

BARTENDER, MAKE MINE A VANILLA EXTRACT ON THE ROCKS

Vanilla extract is processed in ethyl alcohol and is bottled in a suspension of alcohol. This provides vanilla extract with the same alcohol proof as vodka. So, vanilla extracts have the same proof as Absolute vodka or Captain Morgan rum and yet it can be purchased in a supermarket next to the giant birthday cake candles. Without an age limit. Who in the world permitted this?

One must travel back in time to the years just before Prohibition was enacted. Seeing the writing on the wall, flavor extract trade groups and manufacturers, realized that the only way to save their industry was to create legal loopholes allowing them to continue operating. Vanilla extract relies on alcohol to extract the essential flavors from the vanilla bean and suspend them in a stable solution, it's also required by law to have an alcohol content of at least 35 percent. Vanilla extract is also the only flavoring deemed important enough for the federal government to officially define standards for it.

In 1919, the Eighteenth Amendment was made the law of the land, and the U.S. was an alcohol-free country. Seeing their last chance to avert disaster, vanilla manufacturers flooded congressmen with telegrams saying that their industry and also the food industry would be ruined if they were held to the same laws as liquor. By the time the Volstead Act went into effect the following year, it included a clause that made an exemption for flavor extracts if they were deemed non-potable and a reasonable person wouldn't want to drink them straight.

In 1933, when Prohibition was repealed, the argument was presented for defining vanilla extract as something completely different from liquor. Today, even at 35% alcohol, which is 70 proof, vanilla extract is a food product under the jurisdiction of the Food and Drug Administration and not the stricter governmental regulations for liquor.

In the end, it was all about the money. Alcohol used in liquor is taxed at $13.50 per gallon. Flavoring manufacturers also pay that amount, but because their product is not used as an alcoholic beverage, they're entitled to a "drawback" or refund of $12.50 per gallon. So, while Absolute vodka pays the U.S. government $13.50 per gallon it makes with an alcohol content of 40 percent, a vanilla flavoring company pays $1.00 for every gallon of vanilla extract that it produces a produce with the same percentage of alcohol.

However, to qualify as a flavoring, a vanilla extract still must be judged non-potable. The unenviable job of testing vanilla extracts to make sure that no sane, mature, or mentally and emotionally healthy person would want to drink them straight? The Food and Drug Administration tests them to assure they're not going to end up the next big thing at high-school parties across America.

THE UNFORGETTABLE TASTE OF THE "NILLA" WAFER AND "NANNA" PUDDING

Memories of childhood and the pleasures of your mother preparing "nilla" pudding or "nanna" pudding will be never forgotten. The vernacular speech of the children from the American South has altered the name of vanilla to "nilla" and banana to "nanna". These names live on in legend.

CORN, COTTON AND CHOCOLATE: HOW THE MAYA CHANGED THE WORLD

The wonderful concoction of vanilla wafers and bananas joined into a pudding brings back fond memories. Nanna pudding is that delightful combination composed of layers of bananas, vanilla pudding and vanilla wafers. Vanilla wafers are small golden vanilla flavored cookies made by Nabisco. "Nilla" is the brand name owned by Nabisco that is associated with the cookies.

Nanna pudding is a Southern dish, but when did it become that way? To find out you just look for that point in time when writers started calling the dish "an old Southern favorite". Banana pudding was a dish served across the nation during the late 19th century. The initial pudding recipe did not include vanilla wafers, it used sponge cake, lady fingers or crumbs. It was not until the 1920's that it became more popular in the south than other parts of the nation.

Nabisco may not have come up with this popular use for its product, but they soon picked it up and ran with it. By the 1940s the company was publishing a recipe for banana pudding printed on the side of its Vanilla Wafers boxes. They were still called vanilla wafers, not "Nilla Wafers". Nabisco didn't adopt that brand name until the 1960s.

During the 1950s and 1960s vanilla wafers, steadily eclipsed other banana pudding fillings like sponge cake. After World War II, the Southern identity of banana pudding took hold, and by the 1950s, newspaper writers were routinely associating the dessert with the South. Perhaps the real mystery is not why banana pudding became a Southern thing, but why other parts of the country let such a delishous and convenient dessert slip out of their repertoire. This childhood memory will live on forever.

VANILLA PERFUME

The Maya believed that vanilla had the power of an aphrodisiac. This was also believed by 18th century Europeans. During the 1700s, physicians recommended vanilla to male patients to ensure potency. That may be the reason that vanilla is the magic ingredient in high end perfumes. There may be a masculine corollary. Men say that the sweet, welcoming odor has a euphoric effect that sets a sensual mood.

Vanilla is used to produce numerous fragrances, but they are not all vanilla perfumes. Shalimar is the grand dame of vanilla perfumes is is likely the sexiest and most enticing vanilla perfume you will find on the market.

VANILLA AND ITS PART IN CHANGING HISTORY

Maya vanilla is the world's favorite flavor. The flavoring is popular all over the world and we enjoy the 10,000 metric tons of vanilla produced each year. Coca cola is the largest consumer of vanilla in the world. The flavoring introduced the legendary nanna pudding and is used in expensive perfumes.

CORN, COTTON AND CHOCOLATE: HOW THE MAYA CHANGED THE WORLD

CHAPTER 25: MAYA CULTIVARS CHANGE THE WORLD

When the great navigator steered his three caravels into the turquoise waters of the Caribbean, his fortuitous mistake forever linked the decadent Old World with the unspoiled treasures of the New World. European contact not only changed the Americas, but forever changed Europe, Asia and Africa.

The collision of the two civilizations had formidable consequences for the entire globe. When the New World was conquered by European powers, the character of the New World's people was transformed forever, and not for the better. However, the Old World was changed for the better, enriched by New World gold, new lands, cultural changes and especially the cultivars that improved the life style of its people and financed the rise of European nations.

In return, the Old World brought some animals and cultivars with the New World, but also decimated indigenous civilizations by delivering crowd diseases that led to the "Great Dying." European diseases annihilated most of the Native American populations. Europeans benefited from this mass disaster by populating the vast lands of the Americas.

The cultivars developed by the Maya were not a fluke of history. They were intentionally developed by an ancient scientific society. Thousands of years before Columbus landed, the Maya had a sophisticated culture and one of the most advanced scientific, technological and agricultural civilizations in the world.

Their grand cities were wonderments of art and architecture and were replete with magnificent high-rise structures. The cities were home to urban populations of over 100,000 people. During the same time period, Europe was deep in the throes of the dark ages and London was a dirty river trading town with a population of 9000, while Classic Maya cities were the largest and most sophisticated cities in the Western World.

Six centuries before Spanish explorers landed in the New World, the Maya civilization outstripped the carrying capacity of their land. This abuse of their habitat, combined with a natural environmental disaster, resulted in the collapse of the Maya civilization. The Classic Maya had developed advances in science, technology and agriculture that far outpaced similar achievements in Europe. Maya scientific advances have now been surpassed by centuries of European scientific and technical achievements. However, Maya intellectual magic achieved in agronomy has not been surpassed.

If the greatest intellectual feat of the Maya was the invention of the number zero, proclaimed as one of the singular accomplishments of the human era, then their development of unique cultivars was a comparable intellectual accomplishment that has astounded contemporary agronomists. Archaeologists and biologists have argued for decades about how Maya agronomists developed their magic cultivars in the Yucatán, an area totally isolated from the rest of the world.

Mother Nature generously endowed the Yucatán with unique indigenous plants that were domesticated by the Maya. Their cultivars were the result of the conscious biological manipulation of the native specimens by dedicated agronomists. The development of maize was mankind's first and greatest feat of genetic engineering. After European contact, the inventive products of Maya agronomy were disseminated around the globe and have changed the course of history.

CORN, COTTON AND CHOCOLATE: HOW THE MAYA CHANGED THE WORLD

It has been long been proclaimed that the booty of gold and silver collected during the conquest was the greatest treasure that flowed from the Americas. That was true in the short run, but time and world agriculture, changed by Maya cultivars, has altered the calculus of that comparison. The financial worth of Maya cultivars has increased over the centuries at a greater rate than any other resource from the Americas.

The sum of the financial value generated by Maya cultivars in a single year is now greater than all the gold and silver taken from the New World. Maya cultivars constitute the most important food and fiber crops in the 21st century. Their increased value has forever changed the balance of financial worth between the Maya cultivar and the precious metals taken from colonial America.

If the basic needs of people in the 21st century can be expressed in terms of food, and clothing, Maya cultivars are providing 60% of the food for the world's population and cotton fibers, also a Maya cultivar, provide 90% of the textile fibers around the globe.

The fruit and vegetables consumed by most people across the world had their origin as Maya cultivars. It was a real game changer when Maya cultivars altered the dietary customs of the entire world. Maya cultivars not only changed the source of food for most the earth's population, their cotton fibers changed the way the people of the world clothe themselves. Maya cotton has the unique capability of producing cooling clothes in a hot climate and warming garments in a cold climate.

Cultivars originating from the Yucatán far exceed the contribution of cultivars originating from Europe, Africa, and Asia. Only the Middle East comes close to matching the number of cultivars that have been derived from Maya agronomists. The entire earth changed its diet when most of the world's population came to rely on cultivars originating in a small isolated area of our planet.

Maya cultivars have changed the tastes of the world and they are prepared using completely different methods in diverse geological areas throughout the world. Maya cultivars are flexible and can be prepared to suit local tastes. Each country has developed cooking that satisfies cultural tastes and the effects of the local environment.

MAYA CULTIVARS, AS A TEAM OR ALONE, CHANGE THE WORLD FOREVER

The effects of Maya cultivars on the world's societies has altered history. The Maya cultivars have proven to be a source of power and great wealth, but have also induced great poverty, misery, and exploitation. They have started wars, overthrown monarchies, altered political boundaries, inspired the Industrial Revolution, started college systems, promoted deadly habits, sparked sporting empires and changed cultural speech, music and lifestyles. Is all this change beyond the scope of mere agricultural products? Follow the trail of these historic Maya inventions as they play their part in changing the history of the world.

World changes prompted by Maya cultivars can be categorized by the facets that have altered global food security, wealth, politics, education, technology and culture. Significant change has been produced by Maya cultivars with the influence of an individual cultivar or when combined with other cultivars as a team to promote historical modifications. The Columbian Exchange introduced Maya cultivars that introduced historical changes.

THE COLUMBIAN EXCHANGE: THE MECHANISM FOR CHANGE

CORN, COTTON AND CHOCOLATE: HOW THE MAYA CHANGED THE WORLD

When Christopher Columbus discovered America, his efforts initiated significant changes in the environment and culture of the world. The ecological and demographic consequences of this great merger continue into the 21st century. The introductions of new flora, fauna, and ideas started a synergistic chain reaction in politics, technology, health, and cultures that started in 1492 and continues in force today. This great swap of resources and cultures is called the "Columbian Exchange", and the Columbian Exchange is all about Maya Cultivars.

In the Columbian Exchange, Europe gained access to numerous new sources of food and fiber. Most of these new crops were Maya cultivars. This great exchange between the New World and the Old World, altered the history of our planet forever. Including the great dying of Native Americans, the re-peopling of the western hemisphere by European immigrants, the worldwide improvement in food security and significant historical changes produced by Maya cultivars.

The term, Columbian Exchange was coined in 1972 by historian Alfred W. Crosby, in his book, *The Columbian Exchange: Biological and Cultural Consequences of 1492*. This book changed the outlook of historians. When the book and its concept first appeared, it was distained by historians. It has now become one of the foundational works in the field of environmental history and after over forty years it remains one of the major resources in the study of world history. The concept of the Columbian Exchange is the inspiration for historical examinations into the results of what occurred when two different cultures, separated by time and space, finally collided.

European contact and the interchange between the two hemispheres introduced a wide variety of agriculture products to Europe producing increases in population. European explorers returned to Europe with Maya cultivars and other American crops, which became important elements contributing to the health and wealth of Europe. Europeans trading American cultivars with peoples in tropical Asia and Africa introduced Maya cultivars to lands where high crop yields and the nutritional value of Maya crops resulted in the development of native populations. Maya cultivars thrived in poor soils that were unable to produce large yields of native crops.

The initial motives of the European adventurers were economic, nationalistic, and religious. Biological change was not in their playbook. The least of their concerns involved biology. Their primary mission involved enrichment of the crown, expansion of empires, and conversion of the heathen. They had no intension of spreading Old World pathogens to the New World. Instead, they established a virtual biological pipeline between Europe and America. The time depth view of their imperial operations reveals that spreading disease was their morbid endowment to populations dying in their wake.

The Columbian Exchange repopulated America, Europe and Africa. Before the exchange, everyone in the Americas was a Native American. Everyone in Eurasia and Africa and their distant ancestors were born on those continents. Not a single person in the world shared a common ancestor with Native Americans for a period of at least 10,000 years. The Columbian Exchange resulted in the spread of human populations that altered the demography of the world either through voluntary or forced migration through slavery.

During the period from 1500 to 1800, the largest contingent of migrants to the Americas consisted of Africans, involuntarily transported. A smaller, but still sizable migration involved Europeans who traveled to the Americas to colonize the lands depopulated by Native Americans who had died from infectious Europeans diseases. The pace of migration accelerated during the nineteenth century when Europeans traveled in massive numbers to the western hemisphere. Those migrations have profoundly influenced modern world history.

CORN, COTTON AND CHOCOLATE: HOW THE MAYA CHANGED THE WORLD

THE COLUMBIAN EXCHANGE: WHO CONTRIBUTED THE MOST CULTIVARS TO THE WORLDS, THE MAYA OR THE REMAINDER OF THE WORLD?

The worldwide production of important agricultural crops displays the broad acceptance and popularity of Maya cultivars. The list of the world's most important crops indicates how Maya cultivars have changed how the world is fed. Their acceptance began during the Columbian Exchange with indigenous America animals and plants that had never seen by Europeans and European plants and animals coming to the New World that America had never seen.

The official inventory of plants listed in Crosby's book, includes a lengthy combined list of specimens that were sent to the Americas from the continents of Africa, Europe, and Asia, designated as the Old World. Comparing the list of Afro-Eurasian contributions with a list of cultivars originating in the Americas indicates a difference in quality and quantity. A review of the list indicates that the research team compiling the official combined Afro-European list was Eurocentric. The listing of the cultivars originating from Afro-Eurasian sources has a total of 46 agricultural crops. The official list of Old World specimens does not identify contributions from specific geographical areas of the Afro-Eurasian world, so basically, the tally of cultivars involved in the Columbian Exchange was actually a comparison of worldwide cultivars versus cultivars developed by Maya agronomists.

To clarify the comparison, I have prepared a modified, geographically-based list of cultivars contributing to the Columbia Exchange. The modified lists are grouped by geographic origins and categorize the major cultivars that originated Europe, Africa, the Middle East and Asia.

AFRO-EURASIAN CULTIVARS

EUROPE	ASIA	MID-EAST	AFRICA
Artichoke	Apple	Barley	Coffee
Asparagus	Apricot	Cantaloupe	Collard Greens
Beet	Banana	Carrot	Okra
Broccoli	Black Pepper	Grape	Watermelon
Cabbage	Citrus	Lentils	Yams
Cauliflower	Coconut	Lettuce	
Pear	Cucumber	Oats	
Turnip	Garlic	Olive	
	Hemp	Onion	
	Mango	Peas	
	Oats	Rye	
	Onion		
	Peach		
	Rice		
	Soybean		
	Sugarcane		

CORN, COTTON AND CHOCOLATE: HOW THE MAYA CHANGED THE WORLD

The modified Afro-Eurasian list of cultivars includes 16 indigenous plants from Asia, 11 from the Middle East, 5 from Africa, and only 8 from Europe. A review of the European agricultural contributions indicate that Europe did not contribute a single high-yield cultivar on the official list of popular modern cultivars. The Africa-Eurasian consortium of food producing crops indicates that the Middle East and Asia produced important high yield cultivars including wheat, rye, barley and rice.

The following table indicates the modified list of cultivars originating in the Americas where Maya cultivars are listed separately from other native North and South American cultivars.

MAYA AND NORTH AND SOUTH AMERICAN CULTIVARS

MAYA	NORTH AMERICAN	SOUTH AMERICAN
Agave	Black raspberry	Canistel
Amaranth	Blueberry	Cashews
Arrowroot	Cranberry	Potatoes
Avocado	Jerusalem artichoke	Strawberries
Cassava (manioc)	Pecans	Yerba mate
Common beans	Prickly pear	
Chia	Wild rice	
Chicle		
Cherimoya		
Chili peppers		
Chocolate/Cocoa		
Cotton		
Guava		
Henequen		
Jicama		
Maize (corn)		
Papaya		
Passion fruit		
Peanut		
Pineapple		
Sapodilla		
Squash		
Sugar-apple		
Sunflower		
Sweet potato		
Tobacco		
Tomato		
Turkey		
Vanilla		

Contributions of American cultivars listed in the Exchange include a total of 29 Maya cultivars from Mesoamerica, 8 from North America and 5 from South America. An analysis of the cultivars

CORN, COTTON AND CHOCOLATE: HOW THE MAYA CHANGED THE WORLD

indicates that crops originating in the Americas offer a superior selection of nutritious cultivars when compared with the Old-World specimens. Maya agronomists, with 29 cultivars, lead in the competition for the total number of world-class cultivars. These crops include maize, cassava, sweet potato, tomatoes and the peanut. These are leading production crops in the world. One of South America's 5 cultivars on the list is the all-important white or Irish potato.

MAYA CULTIVARS CHANGE THE GLOBAL GAME PLAN AND NOW FEED MOST THE WORLD

Maya cultivars as a group combined to change the global game plan of nourishing the world. It is not surprising that cultivars from superior Maya agronomy have played a role in changing the world's food supply. The world population is currently over 7,000,000,000. That's seven billion, and Maya Cultivars currently feed 60% of the world's population. Cassava, alone, feeds 500,000,000 people daily and maize (corn) is the highest produced grain in the world.

The expectation that population growth will always exceed the food supply has a long history extending back to Malthusian logic. Malthusianism is the idea that population growth is exponential while the growth of the food supply is arithmetical. Surprisingly, during the period from the 1950s to the 1990s, a period which experienced the most dramatic increase in human population, per capita world food production actually increased.

The United Nations Food and Agriculture Organization has published a study forecasting world food production through 2050. The FAO forecasts that agriculture production increases can accommodate food demand and the rising world population. Malnutrition will be minimized, but will still be a problem in developing countries. The forecasted food supply is contingent upon high yielding Maya cultivars carrying the load as leading food producers, as well as several other factors, including improved agricultural methods that increase crop yields while minimizing environmental impact, improved irrigation, availability of productive land, and pest management.

MAYA CULTIVARS CHANGE THE POPULATION OF THE WORLD

The Maya cultivars playing in the Columbian Exchange increased world human population because of the global spread of nutritious food crops. A well-nourished world with enhanced food security was a key factor contributing to the over-population of the world. Maya cultivars have been directly responsible for the accelerated change in population growth. That change is directly reflected in the growth that world population has experienced since the onset of the Columbian Exchange. The Columbia Exchange changed the nature and composition of world agriculture and the growth of world population.

A better-nourished world has been the principal contributing factor in the expansion of world population. Accelerated growth began in the eighteenth century and has continued into the 21st century. Unlike changes that have been brought about by a single cultivar. World population growth has been a result of the composite team work of multiple Maya cultivars.

The Columbian Exchange and the introduction of Maya cultivars to the world induced a surge in world population. In the year 1500, as the Eurasian population was recovering from the bubonic plague, the world population stood at about 425 million. By 1600 it had increased more than 25 percent to 545 million. Human population increased less rapidly during the next century, reaching 610 million in 1700.

CORN, COTTON AND CHOCOLATE: HOW THE MAYA CHANGED THE WORLD

Thereafter, due to enhanced nutrition, population increased at a faster rate than ever before. By 1750 the population stood at 720 million; the world population reached one billion in 1810 and 1930 saw the world at 2 billion. In 1960 the 3 billion mark was passed, in 1980 it passed 4 billion, in 1990 the 5 billion mark was passed, in 2000 population passed 6 billion and 2010 saw the 7 billion mark surpassed.

Projections for the future indicate a slowing of the increase of growth. In the past, ten-year periods have produced an increase of a billion people; however, the rate is slowing to the longer period of 15 years to increase the population by a billion people. A world with a population of 8 billion is expected in 2025 and 10 billion in 2050.

The reduced change in the projected rates of future population growth contradict the precepts of Malthusian logic. Reverend Robert Malthus wrote in 1798 that food production tends to increase arithmetically, while population increases at a faster geometric rate. Malthus argued that people may choose to reduce population growth; however, Malthus stated, food production can only be increased by slow, difficult methods such as reclaiming unused land or intensive farming. Reverend Malthus did not have the benefit of fully appreciating the positive effect that the new Maya cultivars had on increased crop yields. Nor did he know about the future impact of the agricultural revolution and new technology that included pesticides, refrigeration, mechanized farm equipment, and large trans-oceanic shipments of food.

An analysis of the annual tonnage yielded by the world's leading agriculture producers indicates why Maya cultivars have changed the way that the world is nourished. They compose most of the cultivars producing the largest agricultural tonnage in the world.

TOP MAYA CULTIVARS THAT CHANGED THE WAY THE WORLD IS NOURISHED IN METRIC TONS

MAYA CULTIVAR	ANNUAL PRODUCTION
Maize	1,006,000,000
Cassava	256,404,000
Tomato	161,800,000
Sweet potato	106,500,000
Peanut	40,016,000
Sunflower	37,000,000
Chili peppers	31,131,000
Beans	41,970,000
Squash	15,633,000
Pineapple	24,000,000
Papaya	12,355,000
Chocolate	10,000,000
Vanilla	10,000,000
Turkey	5,400,000
Avocado	4,000,000
TOTAL	**1,760,209,000**

The highest-ranking grain producer in the world is maize, producing more tonnage than either rice or wheat. Twelve of the world's top twenty agricultural yielding crops are Maya cultivars. The table above indicates the annual tonnage of the top Maya cultivars in world production. That's

CORN, COTTON AND CHOCOLATE: HOW THE MAYA CHANGED THE WORLD

almost 1.8 BILLION metric tons or 3,520,000,000,000 pounds of food. That's enough quantity to provide every man, woman and child on the planet with 489 pounds of food per year.

HEY! WE'RE NUMBER ONE! MAYA CULTIVARS BECOME THE MOST POPULAR IN THE WORLD

Six Maya cultivars have become the world's most popular food choice in their category. Popular Maya cultivars include maize, the tomato, the chili pepper and cotton fiber. Tobacco, a curse on mankind, is the world's most popular narcotic. Vanilla is the world's favorite flavor and chocolate is the second most popular flavor.

Maize is the world's most popular grain. World production is 1,006,000,000 metric tons. Maize is more productive than rice, wheat and rye.

Tomato is the world's most popular fruit. The delicious red Maya cultivar has attained world popularity and 161,800,000 metric tons are produced each year.

Chili Peppers have become the world's favorite spice. They have outpaced black pepper in yearly production with 31,131,000 metric tons of chili peppers produced.

Cotton has become the world's most popular and important fiber. It is by far the most produced fiber and it clothes 90 percent of the world. Yearly production of the Maya fiber exceeds 26,829,000 metric tons per year.

Tobacco is the world's favorite narcotic. Nicotine has made slaves of habitués across the world with 6,100,000 metric tons of the noxious weed grown each year.

Vanilla has become the world's favorite flavor. While only 10,000 metric tons of this cultivar are produced each year, which is not very much, but a little goes a long way.

Chocolate as a flavor, is in second place, with a yearly production of 10,000 metric tons.

That's a total of six Maya cultivars that lead the world in popularity in their category and they all originate from a small isolated corner of the planet. Now, that's something to brag about.

MAYA CULTIVARS REVERSE A HISTORICAL LEGEND: THE FABLED TROVE OF CONQUISTADOR TREASURE CHANGES FROM GOLD TO GREEN

The precious metals garnered by the conquistadors from the Americas has long been considered more valuable than a collection of plants from the Yucatán. The legendary concept of the great value of the swag collected by the conquistadors is based on fanciful, extravagant and exaggerated stories of the precious metal exploited from the New World. What is the actual value of the bonanza of gold and silver that made Spain the richest country in Europe?

What is the truth and what is legend relative to the bountiful treasure looted from the New World? What was the worth of this treasure in financial terms and what became of the fabulous

CORN, COTTON AND CHOCOLATE: HOW THE MAYA CHANGED THE WORLD

trove? Is the precious metal still the greatest treasure gleaned from the New World? It now appears that Maya cultivars have changed the metrics.

The dissemination of Maya cultivars and the passage of time has changed the total financial value of the riches that came out of the New World. The new leader in great wealth is not the color of gold or silver, but it is green as in the color of Maya cultivars. Maya cultivars now cover the world with bountiful harvests in the form of food and fiber. The financial value of one year of world harvest of Maya cultivars is greater than the value of all the gold and silver that was looted from the New World.

The amount of precious metal exploited by the conquistadors appeared to be a legendary bonanza, but the exact amount of precious metal excavated from the New World is unknown. Because of the poor record keeping it is difficult to estimate the amount of precious metals taken from the New World. However, using records from the USGS and the Gold Council the total amount of gold and silver excavated before 1831 equals 5,640,000,000 ounces of silver and 43,000,000 ounces of gold. This includes the precious metal from the conquest, ancient gold and silver from Rome and Egypt and the amounts excavated throughout the world after the 16th century. and is a conservative value. Using modern day prices of gold and silver, with silver at $24.08 per ounce and gold prices $1200 per ounce, the total equals $187,000,000,000 U.S. dollars.

Calculating the financial value of one year's production of major Maya cultivars, using prices from the Food and Agricultural Organization (FAO), equals a total of $580,800,000,000 U.S. dollars. The current worth of Maya cultivars per year is over three times the total value of all the precious metal taken from the New World.

Comparing these figures indicates that the new champion of wealth generated from New World goes to the Maya cultivars. When you consider that the value of precious metals is at an all-time high per ounce, and that the total amount of existing of gold and silver is historically fixed, the dollar amount of the harvest of Maya cultivars will increase each year and it will forever be the champion.

MAYA CULTIVARS CHANGE THE MASS OF THE HUMAN BODY

The impact of Maya cultivars in providing nutritious food has changed the size and shape of humans throughout the world through improved nutrition. The human physiognomy has changed in a modern form of evolution. Research spanning 300 years of height and nutrition data have summarized their findings into what has been termed as a new form of evolution, known as "technophysio-evolution".

Advancements in body mass occurred quickly and have had a significant impact on the human body. In the last century, the shape and size of the body itself has changed. These changes have increased body size by over 50%, and have greatly improved the robustness and capacity of vital organ systems. Little did the Maya agronomists suspect that their cultivars would change the mass of the human body.

MAYA CULTIVARS, AS STAND-ALONE CATALYSTS, CHANGE THE WORLD

The changes in the world related to the combined effects of Maya cultivars have been defined. Following are some of the changes induced by individual cultivars. The change is sometimes subtle, but often, they are quite dramatic.

CORN, COTTON AND CHOCOLATE: HOW THE MAYA CHANGED THE WORLD

MAYA TOBACCO, THE WORLDS FAVORITE NARCOTIC, CHANGES THE WORLD'S DEATH RATE AND BECOMES THE GREATEST KILLER IN HUMAN HISTORY

The changes in the world and the fate of its people are not all due to the influence of multiple Maya cultivars. A single Maya cultivar is responsible for changing the health and morbidity rates of the world population. That cultivar is the nasty weed known as tobacco.

In time depth, tobacco has been a bad actor ever since it made slaves out of the Maya. The Maya enjoyed smoking a good cigar; in fact, they were so addicted to tobacco that the herb became an integral part of their social and spiritual life. The curse of tobacco, cast out into the world, began with the addictive habits of the Maya population.

The ancient Maya smoked a species of tobacco that was more potent than that which is commercially available today. The Maya used *Nicotiana rustica* which has nine times more nicotine content than *Nicotiana tobacum*. The increased nicotine caused the Maya to become intoxicated and experience hallucinogenic episodes.

After European contact, the nasty habit of tobacco smoking spread rapidly among the conquistadors and they soon became addicted. The tobacco habit spread to Europe, and the use of tobacco became the rage of the British Isles. Addiction grew among the British so that in 1612, a British report stated that in London upward of 7000 houses were making a living in the tobacco trade. Tobacco usage grew in many forms including cigarette, cigar and pipe smoking as well as chewing tobacco. Once the purview of men, tobacco began attracting women into its addiction

During World War I the use of cigarettes exploded. Soldiers overseas were given free cigarettes in their C-rations every day. Virtually an entire generation of young men returning from World War I were addicted to cigarettes.

During World War II, cigarettes were again included in C-Rations. GI's returning home were addicted to tobacco. On the home front, tobacco production increased and cigarettes were being marketed to women. Many of them started smoking for the first time while their husbands were away in the military. By the end of the war, cigarette sales are at an all-time high. Addiction grew to new heights.

As the twentieth century progressed the filthy smoking habit increased. In 1910 the per capita adult cigarette consumption was 151 cigarettes per year and per capita cigar consumption was 77 per year. By 1920, per capita smoking rate grew to 477 cigarettes and per capita cigar consumption was 80 per year. In 1930: the U.S. had a per capita smoking rate of 977 cigarettes, twice the 1920 rate. By 1940 the smoking rate had skyrocketed, cigarette consumption raised to 2,558 cigarettes per capita, nearly 600 percent the consumption of 1920. The nation became addicted to tobacco.

The World Health Organization (WHO) estimates the yearly death toll because from tobacco usage is currently 6 million persons and drains $500 billion annually from the global economy in lost productivity, misused resources, and premature deaths. Unchecked, the yearly death toll from tobacco is expected to rise to 7 million by 2020 and will increase to more than eight million per year by 2030. More than 80% of those deaths will be in low-income and middle-income countries. Smoking is practiced by some 1.22 billion people.

CORN, COTTON AND CHOCOLATE: HOW THE MAYA CHANGED THE WORLD

Tobacco has gone much further than enticing people into a nasty, unhealthy habit. The Maya habit of smoking has spread around the globe and has currently claimed more lives than have been lost in all the 1349 wars in recorded history. According to WHO, tobacco caused 100 million deaths in the 20th century. It is predicted that by the end of the 21st century, tobacco will have killed one billion people

MAYA COTTON, THE WORLDS FAVORITE FIBER, CHANGES THE WORLD IN MULTIPLE WAYS

More than any other Maya cultivar cotton has changed the course of the world in multiple ways. Some of the historical changes were for the good and some were bad and some were very ugly. The good changes include the way cotton clothes the world, inspired the Industrial Revolution and created land grant colleges turning the USA into a technological powerhouse. The bad change includes igniting the American civil war and the ugly is its role in increasing slavery.

THE COTTON GIN RAISES COTTON PRODUCTION AND INCREASES SLAVERY

During the late 18th century, cotton was the major raw material used in the world textile industry. United States cotton growers could not satisfy the demand of the modern mills. They were inhibited by the process of hand powered preparation of raw cotton into a fiber suitable for the industrialized weaving machines. Eli Whitney invented a simple machine to process cotton fiber and enabled abundant quantities of American cotton to change the path of world history. His invention, the cotton gin, reduced the production time for preparing bales of cotton.

The cotton gin reduced the cost of cotton processing leading to the demand for increased cultivation and more workers to plant, harvest and process the fiber. In 1791, cotton production in the USA totaled 2,000,000 pounds. Whitney's invention grew the American cotton industry enormously. By 1801 the annual production of cotton reached over 50 million pounds, and by the early 1830s the USA produced most the world's cotton.

The tragic side of the boom was that the demand for cotton and the attendant labor increased the slave population in the American South from 654,121 persons in 1790 to 3,954,511 persons in 1860. The use of the cotton gin resulted in a 600% increase of American slavery between 1790 and 1860 and lead the country headlong into the American civil war.

MAYA COTTON LEADS THE USA INTO CIVIL WAR AND THE ABOLITION OF SLAVERY

The ego of the antebellum South was fueled by the riches gleaned from cotton and the practice of slavery. Arrogance and their cavalier culture were the principal reasons that led the south into their misguided secession from the Union.

Civil War hostilities began on April 12, 1861, when Confederate forces fired upon Fort Sumter in the harbor of Charleston, South Carolina. President Lincoln issued the Emancipation Proclamation on January 1, 1863, declaring that all slaves in the confederate states would be forever free, which made ending slavery a major goal of the war. Concerned that a presidential proclamation would be insufficient, the President pushed for a constitutional amendment. The Thirteenth Amendment to the United States Constitution outlawing slavery was passed by the Senate on April 8, 1864.

CORN, COTTON AND CHOCOLATE: HOW THE MAYA CHANGED THE WORLD

The defeat of Southern forces in the noble defense of their homeland lead to General Robert E. Lee's surrender of the confederacy to General Grant on April 9, 1865. The total number of dead at war's end was 620,000, a total of more than all the combined fatalities of all American wars. The conflict had lasting positive effects on American history and the characterization of its identity as a nation. The American Civil War consolidated the Union, passed the 13th amendment to the U.S. Constitution confirming the ablation of slavery and freed the slaves. Maya cotton was just a pawn in the civil war, a valuable commodity that drove the greed and power of the Southern aristocracy.

MAYA COTTON SHAPES MODERN HISTORY ACCELERATING THE INDUSTRIAL REVOLUTION

The Industrial Revolution was born in Britain during the 18th century and changed the world. The introduction of technology to the textile industry was a major turning point in history. Cotton supplied the raw material and inspired the Industrial Revolution.

By the 1840s, Britain's colonies could not supply the vast quantities of cotton fibers needed to meet the demands of the industrialized factories. American cotton offered an unlimited supply for the demand plus it was a superior type of fiber. The unlimited supply of Maya cotton from America accelerated advances in the Industrial Revolution and spurred new inventions for textile manufacturing. The team of cotton and textile production were the key forces in evolving innovations in industry during the first Industrial Revolution and the subsequent phases of the revolution.

The first Industrial Revolution was fueled by cotton enhancing innovations in textile machinery, iron manufacturing, and steam power. The initial wave of technology gave way to the second Industrial Revolution in the transition years from 1860 to 1914.

During the 1890s, the United States, became the leading industrial nation in the world. The innovations of the second Industrial revolution blossomed into the third Industrial Revolution. Scientific innovation accelerated exponentially enhancing the concept of globalization as the world grew smaller and became a digital society. Maya Cotton evolved global society into a world based on renewable energy, digital tools, and fueled the series of innovations that lead to the internet. Maya cotton was in the right place at the right time.

MAYA COTTON SPARKS THE LAND GRANT COLLEGE SYSTEM AND MAKES THE USA BECOME A TECHNOLOGICAL SUPERPOWER INDUCES

When Maya cotton fueled the Industrial Revolution, it accelerated the need for technology based educations. Cotton introduced an advanced educational system that changed the United States into a world super power.

The Industrial Revolution began century Great Britain, but within a few decades it spread to the United States. The Industrial Revolution evolved quickly in America and increased the demand for skilled labor and technical capabilities. These requirements ushered in a new imperative for technological capabilities in higher education. Existing American universities did not include science, engineering or agricultural sciences as part of their curriculum. Something new was required.

The need for expertise in science and engineering became apparent to American leaders in business and government. Leaders in the United States senate determined that the nation must

CORN, COTTON AND CHOCOLATE: HOW THE MAYA CHANGED THE WORLD

a develop university system that will provide technically trained professionals to support the burgeoning industrialized society. This concept signaled the creation of the land-grant college system.

The history of the ground breaking land-grant college system is intertwined with the success of America as a technological giant and is considered a historic breakthrough in higher education. Arnold Toynbee, the noted British historian, once observed that the land-grant idea is the one original contribution of American higher education.

The land grant system began in 1862 with a piece of legislation known as the Morrill Act. This act of congress established land grant colleges with the intention that they would teach mechanical and agriculture engineering. This act created colleges that have grown into international giants in science and engineering.

They are ranked among the leading universities in the world. One of the land grant colleges is currently ranked as the number one university in the world. Sixty-nine land-grant colleges were founded and their influence on American higher education has been formidable. They carry out pioneering research in physics, aerospace sciences, digital sciences, medicine, bioengineering, agricultural science, and other fields. Nearly two-thirds of all doctoral degrees are awarded by land-grant universities, and they have graduated nearly 300 Nobel Laureates.

The Industrial Revolution was the fuse that created the land grant college system which turned America into a scientific giant. The fuel that ignited and sustained the Industrial Revolution was Maya cotton.

MAIZE, THE MOST POPULAR GRAIN IN THE WORLD, CHANGES CULTURE AS A POPULAR WHISKEY AND INVENTS NASCAR

Maize has assumed a prominent place throughout the world. It is the most produced grain in the world, it is a popular food, it is made into a legendary whiskey, and it changed American culture and started a sports empire. Maize has enabled billions of people to consume a sufficient quantity of food. It is more than a source of energy, it has become a key ingredient in the cuisine of countries across the face of the earth.

MAIZE WHISKEY, ERR, CORN WHISKEY CHANGES AMERICAN TASTES AND CULTURE

Maya agronomists could have never conceived that their amazing cultivar would be the basis of one of the legendary alcoholic beverages in world history. Corn whiskey is an American alcoholic liquor made from corn mash. The mash is then distilled in copper pot stills. The process is based on traditional methods that produced the legendary moonshine whiskey, the predecessor of quality bourbon whiskey.

BOURBON, THE ALL-AMERICAN MAYA WHISKEY

The art and skill of distilling and ageing corn whiskey into a sophisticated liquor was a bit of magic. This changeling became known as Bourbon whiskey. Before it became a gentleman's drink, this alcoholic corn beverage evolved from a rough and tumble whiskey made in the backwoods of America.

Bourbon whiskey is a barrel-aged distilled spirit made primarily from corn. It has been legally produced since the 18th century. The use of American corn for the mash and American oak for

CORN, COTTON AND CHOCOLATE: HOW THE MAYA CHANGED THE WORLD

forming the barrels was a logical and fortuitous combination. The creative use of native materials was part of the cognitive genius of Scotch-Irish settlers in America.

The smooth alcoholic beverage produced from the Maya cultivar has a pedigree that is protected by law. Bourbon whiskey made from Maya maize is now sold in more than 100 countries. Maya maize has changed American law and the taste of fine cocktails around the world.

MAYA CULTIVAR INVENTS NASCAR

The greatest legends surrounding the production and delivery of moonshine whiskey were the escapades of the brash drivers who raced their high-octane cars down twisting mountain roads. These motorized daredevils evaded government blockades, while delivering moonshine into the cities.

The battle between the moonshine trippers and the revenuers basically came down to an automobile race. Historically, the greatest stock car drivers, racecar builders, and mechanics were a part of the business of running moonshine. They have been romanticized by folk tales and the media.

The runners loved to compete and they would race against each other on the local highways. Then, somebody got the bright idea to excavate a crude oval track out of a cow pasture. The rest is history. The cars continued to improve, and by the late 1940s, stock car races featuring these cars were being run for pride and profit. These races became popular entertainment for audiences in the Southern United States,

William France, Sr., founded NASCAR in 1948. The organization has grown larger than he ever dreamed. NASCAR is second only to the National Football League among professional sports franchises in terms of television ratings.

NASCAR, like so many elements of American heritage, has its roots in a culture that embodied the American values of independence, self-sufficiency and mastery of craft, not to mention a love of corn whiskey and the raw mechanical power of the internal combustion engine. NASCAR is a sport of the masses. Maya maize can be proud of being part of this American heritage.

THE MAYA PEANUT BRIGADE ELECTS AN AMERICAN PRESIDENT

The peanut changed world history when a death in the family caused an American Naval officer to be called home to his family peanut farm. Destiny took a hand and the peanut farmer became the President of the most powerful country in the world.

James Earl Carter was born in plains, Georgia and grew up on his family peanut farm. Rather than being a peanut farmer Jimmy envisioned a career as an officer in the U.S. Navy. At eighteen years of age the young Jimmy Carter left his home in plains to attend Georgia Tech. In 1943, the U.S. Naval Academy admitted him as a cadet. After graduation from Annapolis, he was selected to be a part of the new nuclear submarine program for the Navy. Lieutenant Carter's star was quickly rising in the Navy nuclear program.

CORN, COTTON AND CHOCOLATE: HOW THE MAYA CHANGED THE WORLD

When his father passed away in 1953, fate stepped in and the Maya cultivar called the future American president back to his roots. Carter was a very conscientious man, family came first, and he resigned his Navy commission and returned to Georgia. He made the peanut business into a successful enterprise, and then began his career in politics. Carter entered the political arena in 1962 as a local school board member, then as a Georgia state Senator. In 1970 he was elected as the Governor of Georgia.

In 1976, he ran as a Democratic candidate for the president of the United States. He was swept into presidential office by groups of volunteers from Georgia and across the nation. These volunteers became known as the "Peanut Brigade". Against all odds, their momentum carried Jimmy into office as the 39th President of the United States.

Jimmy Carter served one Presidential term. During his presidency, he made significant advances in world peace and changed history. His legacy includes the Camp David Accord treaty and the SALT II nuclear arms treaty.

After his Presidency, his peace-keeping and humanitarian efforts made Jimmy carter renowned as the most successful former president in history. Jimmy Carter was awarded the Nobel Peace Prize in 2002 for his efforts to find peaceful solutions in international conflict. America and world peace owe this change to the Maya peanut.

MAYA PINEAPPLES INVENT THE GREENHOUSE, CHANGE HOSPITALITY, ALTER WORLD ARCHITECTURE AND OVERTHROW THE HAWAII MONARCHY

The pineapple has attained worldwide popularity as a delicious fruit. However, the pineapple is unique among catalysis of historical change. Changes introduced by most other Maya cultivars usually occur in relation to the benefits of consuming the cultivar. Changes evolving from the pineapple emerged from activities related to cultivation of the plant. The first pineapples consumed in Europe were a hit and Europeans entered into a competition to grow this tropical fruit.

THE PINEAPPLE INVENTS THE GREEN HOUSE

When Christopher Columbus returned to Europe with a pineapple, it created a taste sensation and the tropical fruit became an aristocratic delicacy. The problem with the acquisition of pineapples was that obtaining a fresh fruit was almost impossible. The lengthy sea voyage from the distant tropics made obtaining a viable fruit for European consumption an impossibility. The race was on to develop technology for building a greenhouse for cultivating the Maya fruit. Gardeners began to seek an appropriate environmental envelope or greenhouse for growing the pineapple. However, nearly two centuries would pass before European horticultural technology could grow a pineapple.

Greenhouse design was perfected by an Englishman, William Paxton. His designs enabled the environmentally controlled greenhouse to admit maximum light and maintain a watertight envelope. His designs not only evolved into successful greenhouse systems, but they have also revolutionized modern agriculture.

Artificial environments in greenhouses have changed how crops are grown in northern climates. Presently over one million acres of greenhouses are producing a variety of crops, most of them Maya cultivars. Tonnage of greenhouse grown crops exceeds 300,000,000 tons per year.

THE PINEAPPLE CHANGES WORLD ARCHITECTURE

CORN, COTTON AND CHOCOLATE: HOW THE MAYA CHANGED THE WORLD

In building the greenhouse, William Paxton introduced modular glass systems, industrialized iron structures, and the appropriate interior environment to construct an efficient building envelope for growing pineapples. Paxton was a renaissance man whose cognitive mind enabled him to transfer the principals of organic structures into innovative building systems, environmental technology and aesthetic designs. His genius not only revolutionized greenhouse design but changed the architectural, structural, and construction practices of the world

Paxton was not an architect or engineer, but his cognitive instincts guided his development of the innovative architectural and structural systems used in the construction of the Crystal Palace building which housed the 1851 International Exhibition in London.

The Crystal Palace became the epitome, not only of greenhouse design, but of monumental glass architecture buildings. The Crystal Palace became the quintessential archetype for glass-clad structures in the 19th century and extrapolated design concepts into 21st century architecture. The towering glass clad skyscrapers that are the hallmark of modern cities are due to the changes made by the pineapple.

THE PINEAPPLE OVERTHROWS THE MONARCHY OF HAWAII

The Kingdom of Hawaii was established during the years from 1795 to 1810. The Kingdom continued until the end of the 19th century. The first appearance of the pineapple in the Kingdom of Hawaii was in 1813, when a Spanish advisor to the King of Hawaii, brought the famous fruit back to Hawaii.

Queen Liliuokalani was the last reigning monarch of the Kingdom of the Hawaiian Islands. In 1893, local businessmen and politicians, composed primarily of American and European residents with interests in pineapple and sugar production on the islands, carried out a coupe d'état in order to benefit from more favorable trade conditions for fruit and sugar exports to markets in the United States. They overthrew the queen and took over the Kingdom of Hawaii.

Hawaii was annexed by a joint resolution of Congress and in 1900 Hawaii became an official territory of the United States. Queen Liliuokalani was forced to give up her throne. The high U.S. tariff on fruit was lifted. Pineapple production flourished.

The overthrow of the Kingdom of Hawaii and the subsequent annexation of Hawaii has been cited as a major instance of American imperialism. The change in governments was a product of greed, and was perpetrated by pineapple growers who wanted to increase their profits. The Maya cultivar was a part of the conspiracy to steal the islands.

THE PINEAPPLE BECOMES THE UNIVERSAL SYMBOL OF HOSPITALITY

When Christopher Columbus first encountered the pineapple on the Caribbean island of Guadeloupe, the natives of Guadeloupe had a custom of placing pineapples outside the entrances to their dwellings as symbols of welcome, friendship and hospitality. Europeans soon adopted the symbiology and it was later adopted by the American colonies.

The rarity and expense of the pineapple became a symbol of wealth, hospitality, and luxury and an iconic image of success. The pineapple was adopted as a design element for artists, architects, designers and craftsman throughout the colonies and in Europe. The delicious pineapple has changed the way the world displays their hospitality. It has become a symbol of welcome for the world.

CORN, COTTON AND CHOCOLATE: HOW THE MAYA CHANGED THE WORLD

CHOCOLATE INVENTS THE MICROWAVE, BECOMES BIG BUSINESS AND DOMINATES THE CHRISTIAN HOLIDAYS

Chocolate was a sacred food for the Maya and its consumption was reserved for the elite and religious rituals. In the 21st century, chocolate has not changed its role as an elitist. It is the second most popular flavor in the world and modern culture would not be complete without a gift of chocolate for a religious holiday. It is ironic that Christian holidays are being celebrated by a pagan cultivar. Chocolate has changed the technology of cooking since it invented the microwave oven. The Maya cultivar has become a big business with over $98,000,000,000 in annual worldwide sales.

CHOCOLATE INVENTS THE MICROWAVE OVEN

A melted chocolate bar was the basis for the invention of the microwave oven. The first microwave oven was an accidental discovery prompted a Maya cultivar.

A Raytheon scientist was experimenting with a new magnetron which is a vacuum tube device that releases microwave energy. While working with the device, he noticed that the chocolate bar in his pocket had melted. He attributed the melted chocolate to the microwaves being generated by the machine and, like any good scientist, he conducted more tests.

He realized that microwaves issued from magnetrons might be able to heat up food at incredibly fast rates. The results led engineers to redesign the microwaves in a safe enclosure and violá, the microwave oven was born.

CHOCOLATE, A MAYA CULTIVAR AND A PAGAN PRODUCT, TAKES POSSESSION OF CHRISTIAN HOLIDAYS

Chocolate was the sacred food at pagan Maya ceremonies and has become, ironically, the most celebrated food gift for Christian holidays. Considering that chocolate was domesticated by the Maya, who according to Christian dogma are heathens, it appears that the Christian holidays have been taken captive by the sweet and succulent heathen cultivar.

Chocolate for Easter
Easter, the greatest feast day in the Christian calendar, is a religious high holiday and a day of gifting children with a tradition of baskets filled with chocolate candy.

Chocolate for Valentine's Day
Saint Valentine was a Christian martyr who died in 269 AD. The tradition of gifting a box of chocolates on Valentine's day has become well established.

Mother's Day chocolate
Mother's Day is not a religious holiday, but it is the celebration of appreciation for everyone's Mother. If you are a mother, you're entitled to receive a gift of chocolate on Mother's Day.

CORN, COTTON AND CHOCOLATE: HOW THE MAYA CHANGED THE WORLD

Chocolate for Halloween
In addition to the chocolate treats given to children, chocolate makers have produced products for adults that make this Americas best selling candy holiday.

Chocolate for Christmas Day
Christmas is a grand holiday for religious and commercial enthusiasts and a time for giving boxes of luxury bonbons and collections of fine chocolate bars.

Chocolate, once the elite food of the gods, has found its place in modern celebrations. However, they now celebrate a different God.

THE CHILI PEPPER, THE WORLDS MOST POPULAR SPICE, CHANGES WORLD TASTES, INVENTS CHILI CON CARNE AND WINS A NOBEL PRIZE

The chili pepper is the most popular spice in the world. They were hot stuff in the world of the Maya and continue to have the right stuff as it makes changes to the modern world. The colorful Maya cultivar changed the taste of the world as it spread across the globe. It is the procreator of legendary chili con carne, earned a Nobel prize and, would you believe, empowered chili hand grenades. Over 31,000,000 metric tons of the capsicum laden cultivar are produced each year.

MAYA CHILI PEPPERS CHANGE THE TASTES OF THE WORLD

Just how did the chili pepper make so many changes in cuisines throughout the world? During the Columbian Exchange, chili peppers were disseminated across the world and were quickly adopted into the cuisine of disparate cultures, making a great difference in the tastes of food around the world. The chili, a quintessential spice, has been changing tastes for 500 years.

The chili has always been a part of Mexican cuisine. However, can one imagine how Indian or Thai food would taste without the zest of chilies? The food of numerous countries completely changed with the introduction of the chili pepper into their cuisine as chilies bring life to food.

THE SAGA OF CHILI CON CARNE, A LEGEND CREATED BY THE CHILI

The legendary dish called "chili con carne" is much more than just a recipe prepared with hot chili peppers. It has become a symbiology that represents a way of life, a philosophy and has a pedigree defended to the death by chili aficionados. The dish has inspired debates, duels, cook offs and multiple arguments, both verbal and written, that extol the merits of the Famous Bowl of Red.

The dish is a spicy stew containing chili peppers, meat, and tomatoes. Competitive chili cooks are forbidden to include beans, marinate any meats, or discharge firearms in the preparation of chili for official competition. Chili con carne is not a Mexican dish, it has a Tex-Mex origin. Mexicans do not hold any claim to the spicy recipe and they highly distain the dish. The only thing certain about the origins of chili con carne is that it did not originate in Mexico.

CORN, COTTON AND CHOCOLATE: HOW THE MAYA CHANGED THE WORLD

CHILI IS THE BIGGEST GAME IN TOWN: THE CHILI CON CARNE COOK OFF

The chili cook-off, an event started by chili con carne aficionados, may be the most competitive event in history. A chili cook-off is a lifestyle, a battle of wits, with guarded recipes and a competition between fierce cooks who are the ultimate chili heads. It is also a well-loved social event.

The enthusiastic cooks possess special recipes containing secret ingredients. They prepare their own recipe in a special way for their unique pot of chili con carne. The most famous chili completion, of course, is held in Texas.

THE CHILI PEPPER AS A WEAPON

The chili is famous as a spice but it also can serve as a potent weapon, and it has since the time when Maya warriors used the cultivar in "hand grenades." The potent ingredient in the weapon is the burning caused by the chili pepper

The Scoville scale is the measurement of the pungency or spicy heat of chili peppers. The higher the Scoville Heat Units (SHU) number in a chili pepper, the hotter the pepper is to human receptors. The capsaicin levels in superhot chilies have been have been used as a deterrent and a defense.

The ancient Maya used the chili pepper as a chemical weapon during warfare. They applied the toxic qualities of the capsaicin in chili to create an early version of the hand grenade. The weapon was fabricated from a hollowed-out pumpkin. The pumpkin was then filled with hot ashes and ground hot chilies. The missile was tossed at the enemy. When the grenade hit the ground, it smashed and burst open, creating clouds of toxic smoke that caused choking, irritation of the eyes and throat and disrupted the enemy.

Extract of capsaicin in an aerosol can, usually known as capsicum or pepper spray, has become widely used by police forces as a non-lethal means of incapacitating a person, and in a more widely dispersed form for riot control, or by individuals for personal defense.

CHILI PEPPER TEAMS WITH A HUNGARIAN SCIENTIST TO WIN A NOBEL PRIZE

The discovery of vitamin C was a great scientific and medical breakthrough and a great boon for mankind. The solution involved the chili pepper and a Hungarian Scientist. Scientists found that vitamin C was the solution for preventing and curing scurvy. However, the isolation of vitamin C from the sugars in citrus fruit presented a difficulty in obtaining pure vitamin C.

CORN, COTTON AND CHOCOLATE: HOW THE MAYA CHANGED THE WORLD

Then the chili pepper came to the rescue. In 1933, a Hungarian scientist, Doctor Albert Szent-Gyorgyi, set about to find natural sources to isolate vitamin C. Szent-Gyorgyi solved the problem by making imaginative use of the local Hungarian specialty, paprika, made from a bell pepper. He tested the cultivar in the laboratory and found that the bell pepper was a treasure chest full of vitamin C.

In 1937, just four years after the discovery of vitamin C, Szent-Gyorgyi received the Nobel Prize for his seminal work. So, the discovery of vitamin C was a joint venture between two cultures: the Hungarian and the Maya.

THE TOMATO, THE MOST POPULAR FRUIT IN THE WORLD, IS SHUNNED AT FIRST, GETS AN ITALIAN PEDIGREE, AND IS DECLARED A VEGETABLE BY DECREE OF THE U.S. SUPREME COURT.

The tomato has changed the way the world chooses its favorite fruit. Yes, it is a fruit and not a vegetable. The world has adopted the tomato as its favorite fruit. America, now a bastion of tomato lovers, took nearly three centuries to accept the tomato. The tomato was the subject of a flawed decision by the U.S. Supreme court, declaring the fruit to be a vegetable. Italy has been a longtime lover of the tomato and it has given the fruit a pedigree and foiled a plot by the Chinese to sell faux Italian tomato sauce. The Maya cultivar is grown in numerous countries with a total world production equal to 145,751,507 metric tons.

TOMATO: THE MAYA CULTIVAR, CHANGES THE RACE FOR TOP FRUIT IN THE WORLD

The big surprise in the race for top spot in the world of fruit is that the tomato is now the number one favorite. The luscious red cultivar has moved ahead of the ever-popular Chiquita banana, to become number one in the world. World production of tomatoes is 161,000,000 tons and the world production of bananas is a close second at 154,000,000 tons. You can call it the "ta-mah-toe" or call it the "toe-may-toe" anyway you call it, it's all American and born in Yucatán.

WHAT? YOU SAY TOMATOES ARE POISONOUS?

Americans believed tomatoes were poisonous until 1820, when that myth was disproved during a public demonstration on the courthouse steps in Salem, New Jersey. On September 26th, 1820, Colonel Robert Gibbon Johnson stood on the steps of the courthouse in Salem, with a basket of the potentially toxic fruit. Despite warnings that its poison would turn his blood to acid, he told several hundred cheering spectators that he planned to eat the entire basket and survive. Johnson ate the entire basket and indeed survived. After Johnson's demonstration, the tomato became popular. By the close of the twentieth century, the tomato was widely cultivated as a food plant, and has become a key feature of dishes consumed in America and around the world.

U.S. SUPREME COURT RULES THE TOMATO IS A VEGETABLE

The tomato is botanically classified as a fruit. However, in 1893, the Supreme Court of the United States legally classified the tomato as a vegetable. In the supreme court case of *Nix vs. Hedden*, the plaintiff wished the United States Supreme Court to declare that the tomato be

CORN, COTTON AND CHOCOLATE: HOW THE MAYA CHANGED THE WORLD

properly classified as a fruit rather than as a vegetable for the purposes of avoiding the vegetable tax on the tomato. The court decided that the tomato was a vegetable.

That court decision was over 120 years ago, when the Supreme Court legally changed the tomato from a fruit into a vegetable. The tariff on imported vegetables, including the tomato, is still the law in the 21st century. Maya agronomists would be surprised that the Supreme Court would reverse the ways of mother earth, their partner in agronomy, and change history.

THE TOMATO BECOMES A STATE VEGETABLE. WAIT LET ME GET THIS STRAIGHT. I THOUGHT IT WAS A FRUIT.

It all started in 2005, when a group of fourth-graders wrote letters to the New Jersey legislature urging lawmakers to adopt a state fruit. However, the blueberry won out, not the beloved Jersey tomato. Lawmakers, looking to glorify the Jersey tomato, found that there was not an official state vegetable in the Garden State so the state legislature took advantage of the flawed 1893 U.S. Supreme Court decision stating that the tomato is a vegetable not a fruit. Tennessee and Ohio have also selected the tomato as the state fruit. Arkansas took no chances and adopted the tomato as the state fruit and the vegetable.

THE ITALIAN TOMATO EARNS A PEDIGREE

In Italy, the most famous variety of tomato is the San Marzano. Canned San Marzanos, when grown in the Valle del Sarno in Italy in compliance with Italian law can be labeled *"Pomodoro San Marzano dell 'Agro Sarnese-Nocerino DOP"*. The most important label to look for here is "DOP" which stands for *Denominazione d'Origine Protetta* (Protected Designation of Origin). This is a certification bestowed by the European Union and administered by the Italians that guarantees the can of San Marzano you are buying is the real deal. The DOP is the highest pedigree bestowed by the European Union.

MARCO POLO, BRING THE PASTA, THE CHINESE ARE BRINGING THE SAUCE

Chinese food pirates picked the wrong country to be a patsy with their attempt to slip bogus Italian tomato sauce onto the market. Italy is protective of its tomatoes, as well as their tomato products. The Italian police raided a supermarket and seized tons of canned tomato paste. The labels on the cans stated that the tomato paste was "processed in Italy". While, the canned tomatoes were processed in Italy, as was stated on the can's label, the tomatoes were grown in China.

All hell broke loose in Italy. However, European Union courts ruled that the canned tomatoes were legal and not misleading. The Italian government felt that the label was misleading because they did not state the country of origin. Italy has now introduced a law that requires that the country of origin be printed on the label of cans. The Maya cultivar has initiated a heated tomato war between the two countries. One country is known for its quality food and the other for its cheap knockoffs. Maybe Marco polo can decide the winner. The Maya cultivar is only a pawn in this war of foods

CORN, COTTON AND CHOCOLATE: HOW THE MAYA CHANGED THE WORLD

MAYA VANILLA, THE MOST POPULAR FLAVOR IN THE WORLD CHANGES THE WORLDS SWEET TOOTH

For 500 years, Maya vanilla has seduced kings and comforted millions. Vanilla is now the most popular flavor in the world. Another Maya cultivar, chocolate comes in second. Vanilla was popular with the Maya and it still leads the pack of the world's favorite flavors. Vanilla is appealing because it conjures up feelings of comfort and familiarity when included as a flavoring in foods. Memories of childhood and the pleasures of your mother preparing "nanna" pudding will be never forgotten. These names and the pleasures of childhood live on in legend.

HENEQUEN BECOMES THE MOST POPULAR ROPE IN THE WORLD, MAKES THE YUCATAN RICH AND HIRES THE TEXAS NAVY FOR PROTECTION

The Maya discovered a myriad of purposes for all parts of the agave plant. However, the rope made from the agave was the most enduring and important use of henequen fibers. Maya engineers constructed the longest bridge in the ancient world using henequen ropes as cables on a suspension bridge at the river city of Yaxchilan on the border between Guatemala and Mexico.

Spaniards introduced the henequen fiber to Europe before 1560. The fiber became a popular mainstay on sailing ships with navies around the world. Henequen ropes were strong and resistant to deterioration from microorganisms found in saltwater.

The agave plant was considered by the Spanish to be too valuable to share with other countries and they protected the cultivar. However, the plant was taken from the Yucatán to the state of Florida in 1836 and were it spread to tropical areas around the world. Once the fiber from the Maya cultivar spread across the world its uses greatly expanded. Its applications grew from making rope and general cordage to a multitude of other uses.

Mérida, Mexico, was said to have more millionaires than any other city in the world due to the wealth from the fiber was known as "Green Gold." During the time when the Yucatán area of Mexico was independent from Mexico, the Republic of the Yucatán hired the navy of the Republic of Texas to protect its coast.

THE MAYA TURKEY, THE MOTHER OF ALL BIRDS, BECOMES THE KING OF THE HOLIDAYS, AND INVENTS THE TV DINNER

All the world loves the turkey. The bird is grown around the world and loved for its mild flesh. The Maya turkey is the ancestor of all domestic turkeys consumed in the world. The United States is the world's largest turkey producer and largest exporter of turkey products. Domestic consumption in the U.S. is higher than any other country and the total world production of turkey per annum is 5400 million metric tons. Which is a lot of turkey.

The United States, the European Union, Brazil, Russia, Mexico, Canada and Australia all consume millions of tons of turkey per year. It is a popular dish for celebrating the holidays and

CORN, COTTON AND CHOCOLATE: HOW THE MAYA CHANGED THE WORLD

is the main course at Christmas and Easter, but the consumption of the turkey on Thanksgiving Day eclipses all other holiday feasts.

The turkey lent its name to a popular dance craze in the early 1900s. The basic step of the dance was turkey-like movements which was done to fast ragtime music.

The turkey and its hunt prompted the term "turkey shoot", an expression for an easy kill. The most famous turkey shoot was during WWII. The Battle of the Philippine Sea was a decisive naval battle of World War II. The battle for control of the air was nicknamed, *The Great Marianas Turkey Shoot* by American aviators for the severely disproportional loss ratio inflicted upon Japanese aircraft by American pilots in which 350 Japanese planes were downed compared to a loss of 30 American aircraft.

The turkey changed the way that the world eats its meals by inventing the TV dinner and has made many changes to the world, its customs, its amusements, the way language is used and the way we celebrate holidays.

CASSAVA FEEDS 500,000,000 PEOPLE PER DAY, AND IS THE WORLDS LEADER IN FOOD ENERGY PER ACRE

Maize was the main food source for the Maya. But, there was something missing from the overall equation in their food supply. Cassava was the forgotten cultivar missing from the Maya food supply and over the centuries, cassava has proven that it had the right stuff.

In the 21st century, after maize and rice, cassava is the third largest source of food carbohydrates in the tropics, and is the basic food source for 500,000,000 people. World production of cassava root is approaching 300,000,000 tons. That is almost 9 pounds for every human on earth.

No continent depends as much on cassava in feeding its population as does Africa.

CHICLE INTRODUCES A BAD HABIT AND CHANGES THE CUSTOMS OF THE WORLD

Maya chicle in the form of chewing gum introduced the nasty habit that changed the world's customs. The habit of chewing gum has enveloped billions of people worldwide. Globally, a total of 3.74 trillion sticks of gum are chewed each year, producing a worldwide chewing gum industry worth $19 billion. The chewing of gum has been called "the cause of the downfall of the western world" a comment that was made by people who are disgusted by gum smacking individuals and by "gum chewing do-nothings".

Chicle was introduced to the world in the 19th century. However, the nasty habit caught on. Children were encouraged to buy chewing gum, and sales increased when illustrated sports cards were included in the packs.

Chicle has changed laws of the world. There is a strictly enforced ban on chewing gum and importing chewing gum into Singapore. Only chewing gum of therapeutic value prescribed a doctor is allowed in the country.

CORN, COTTON AND CHOCOLATE: HOW THE MAYA CHANGED THE WORLD

PAPAYA, THE DELICIOUS FRUIT, IS A HEALTHY FOOD, A MEAT TENDERIZER AND SAVED A THE HERO OF A CLASSIC MOVIE

The papaya was first cultivated by the Maya thousands of years before the classic period. The ripe papaya is popular around the tropical world when eaten as a raw fruit and its juice is a favorite refreshing drink.

Papaya is used as a meat tenderizer and for various medical purposes including digestive remedy, cancer issues and kidney ailments.

THE PAPAYA SAVES INDIANA JONES

The Maya cultivar played a key role in the making of a classic adventure film. During the filming of the movie classic: *Indiana Jones and the Raiders of the Lost Ark.* The actor, Harrison Ford, who played the Indiana Jones character, injured his back while performing stunts. The injury caused the movie to shut down. The only solution appeared to be back surgery for Harrison Ford. The surgery and recovery period would delay the movie for months.

The director, Stephen Spielberg, then learned of the curative powers of an enzyme derived from the papaya fruit. For spinal injuries, chymopapain, a purified enzyme derived from the papaya plant, is injected into the disk space to reduce the size of the herniated disks. He consulted with a doctor who applied the enzyme to the spine of Harrison Ford. The enzyme worked like a charm. In a few days, Harrison was back, working in front of the cameras. Papaya saved the show.

SQUASH BECOMES A FAVORITE FOOD AROUND THE WORLD, THE ZUCCHINI CHANGES ITS STRIPES AND THE PUMPKIN CHANGES THE WAY THAT THE WORLD ENVISIONS HORROR

Squash was the firstborn of Maya cultivars. The basic Maya foods were composed of the triad of maize, beans and squash and they became the foundation of Maya agriculture. Maya agronomists were the first to cultivate the five species of squash that are popular throughout the world today.

Squash is a favorite food in over a hundred countries from China to Europe. There are 121 recipes from China alone listed on the internet.

CORN, COTTON AND CHOCOLATE: HOW THE MAYA CHANGED THE WORLD

The zucchini is a Maya cultivar, but it would not be recognized by a Maya today. This variety of squash had a complete makeover when Italian horticulturalists changed the color, shape and taste. The zucchini traveled to Italy as a yellow squash and then the Italians worked their magic. When this squash specimen returned to America four hundred years later it was a long cylinder shaped green striped specimen.

The pumpkin may be the most popular of the squashes. The carving of the pumpkin into fantastic shapes has become a major art form during the celebration of Halloween. The image of the pumpkin has assumed the personification of evil throughout the world. The pumpkin has assumed a place in world legend including the great pumpkin as a cartoon to horrific tales in literature and its role as a vampire.

MAYA BEANS ARE ADOPTED BY THE WORLD AND EARN A PEDIGREE

Maya agronomists developed several bean species that have been adopted by the world and their beans are included in the cuisine of a hundred counties. Italians came to love the Maya bean and it has become such a quality cultivar in the Venetian region that it was given a POD pedigree by the European Union. The bean has earned its Protected Designation of Origin.

A whopping total of 42 million metric tons of dry and green beans are produced worldwide each year. That's 84,000,000,000 pounds of beans each year or 12 pounds for each inhabitant on the planet. There is a lot of Maya beans consumed each year.

SUNFLOWERS BECOME A FAVORITE FOOD, CHANGE RELIGIOUS HABITS, BRING BEAUTY TO ART AND SOOTH THE GAME OF BASEBALL

Spanish explorers brought the sunflower to Spain in 1569 and it spread throughout Europe. The Spanish did not consider it to be a food source, but was considered a beautiful and unusual flower and was grown for 200 years as an ornamental plant.

However, the sunflower has made its mark on the world. A Russian czar introduced the Sunflower to Russia where the sunflower seed became popular as an oil and changed the religious habits of the Russians. It is the third largest most popular vegetable oil in the world.

One of history's ironies, is that in the late 19th century the native Maya cultivar returned to its home continent. When it returned, it had changed. It was genetically altered and its properties had been heightened by the intervention of Russian agronomists.

To some observers, the sunflower appears to be alive. The buds of the Sunflower are heliotropic, and the flower follows the track of the sun. Painting the sunflower has been the subject of famous artists and has made artists famous.

The love of the game of baseball means excellent hitting, great fielding, clever running and eating sunflower seeds. The bond between baseball and eating sunflower seed has a long-term relationship.

SUMMARY: WORLD CHANGES AS THE RESULT OF GROWING A MAYA CULTIVAR.

This chapter has summarized the world changes generated by Maya cultivars. Some changes are the result of the actions due to teams of cultivars and others are the result of the action of single cultivars. The changes are significant and the world will never be the same. The ancient

CORN, COTTON AND CHOCOLATE: HOW THE MAYA CHANGED THE WORLD

Maya agronomists would be surprised and pleased. They did not ever realize that "the other parts" of the world even existed.

CORN, COTTON AND CHOCOLATE: HOW THE MAYA CHANGED THE WORLD

EPILOGUE: REMEMBER THE FUTURE TO ANTICIPATE THE PAST

The philosophy of the Classic Maya was based on the thesis: "R*emember the future to anticipate the past".* That philosophy is valid in the 21st century. When considering the earth's future, it is important to remember the Maya philosophy and recall that the Maya civilization collapsed when they over-stripped their land and became vulnerable to environmental change.

The world has an opportunity to learn from the mistakes that doomed the Maya. By remembering the future, we can learn from our past mistakes. We must protect the land and the environment and like the Maya, our hand must be gentle on the soil.

Maya cultivars have the capabilities to enhance the world's food security and defy Malthusian logic. Success means that the world's food supply must be increased and the population growth decreased to attain the balance within the world order.

Bountiful Maya cultivars can increase world food security without over-stripping the world's land mass. The worlds future depends on the ability of its inhabitants to maintain a balance between population and food supply and Maya cultivars offer the potential to become super-foods for satisfying the demands of the growing population.

Corn can be hybridized to enhance its yield, while sweet potatoes and cassava have the capabilities to yield more calories per acre than other conventional crops. These agronomic talents combined with advances in agriculture technology can solve future issues of world food security.

The third Industrial Revolution is continuing into the fourth. We are presently in the digital age where technological advances are out-pacing Moore's law. That law states that technological innovations would double every two years. The third Industrial Revolution has proved that Moore's observations were understated, technology is advancing at a faster rate than anticipated.

Cotton, a Maya cultivar, initiated the first Industrial Revolution and started the land grant college system, an educational system that is one of the major factors in accelerating the ongoing Industrial Revolution. This educational system has enhanced the growth of universities and made the USA into a technological superpower. In a ranking of the best global research universities, the U.S. had a total of 181 ranked Universities, China had 87, Britain had 81, Germany had 50 and Italy had 38. The Maya cotton inspired land grant colleges have 37 schools on the list of best global research universities.

America's research universities and scientific institutions are best in their class, allowing the nation to focus its ingenuity where it's most needed. U.S. Universities are graduating creative technologists and provide a pipeline of talent into technology centers. Of the 9 largest technological companies in the world, 8 are based in the U.S. Given the growing importance of the technology sector, that's a big deal. America is spending the money to keep its leadership intact: 30% of all research and development dollars in the world are spent in the U.S.

Maya cultivars are doing their part to balance the worlds food supply and population, influencing the continuing industrial revolution and enhancing America as the world's technological leader.

Six Maya cultivars enter the future as world favorites including: the favorite fiber, spice, grain, fruit flavor and narcotic. As the future looms, Maya cultivars are still changelings in world affairs. Maya agronomists should be pleased with their accomplishments.

BIBLIOGRAPHY

Adams, Richard E. W. *Prehistoric Mesoamerica*. Boston: Little, Brown and Company, 1977.

Alcorn, Janis B. Huastec *Mayan Ethnobotany*. University of Texas Press. Austin: 1984.

Aveni, Anthony F. *Skywatchers of Ancient Mexico*. Austin: University of Texas Press, 1980.

Ayala Falcon, M. "*Lady K'awil, Goddess O, and Maya Warfare*," In Ancient Maya Women, ed. Traci Ardren.: Altamira Press, Walnut Creek. 2002

Barnhart, Edwin. "*Indicators of Urbanism at Palenque*." In Palenque: Recent Investigations at the Classic Maya Center, edited by Damien B. Marken. Berkley: Altamira Press, 2007.

Barnhart, Edwin. *The Palenque Mapping Project: 2000 Field Season Final Report.* Crystal Waters, FL: The Foundation for the Advancement of Mesoamerican Studies, Inc. (FAMSI), 2000.

Baudez, Claude. *The Ancient Civilization of Central America*. Translated by James Hogarth. London: Barrie & Jenkins, 1970.

Bell, E. E. *Engendering a Dynasty: A Royal Woman in the Margarita Tomb, Copan*, In *Ancient Maya Women*, ed. Traci Ardren.: Altamira Press, Walnut Creek 2002

Baudez, Claude, Sydney Picasso. *Lost Cities of the Maya*. Translated by Caroline Palmer. New York: Harry N. Abrams, Inc., 1992.

Berlow, Lawrence H. *The Reference Guide to Famous Engineering Landmarks of the World: Bridges, Tunnels, Dams, Roads and Other Structures.* Phoenix: The Oryx Press, 1998.

Bernal, Ignacio. *A History of Mexican Archaeology:* The vanished civilizations of Middle America. London: Thames and Hudson, 1980.

—. *The Olmec World.* Translated by Doris Heyden and Fernando Horcasitas. Los Angeles: University of California Press, 1969.

Blake, Michael. *Maize for the Gods*. University of California Press. Berkley. 2015.

Bourbon, Fabio. *The Lost Cities of the Mayas: The life, art, and discoveries of Frederick Catherwood.* New York: Abbeville Press, 2000.

Castello Yturbide, Teresa. *Presencia de la Comida Prehispanica*. Mexico City: Fomento Cultural Banamex, 1987.

Camacho, Escobar MA, Jiménez-Hidalgo E, Arroyo-Ledezma J, Sánchez-Bernal EI, Pérez-Lara E, *Natural history, domestication and distribution of the turkey (Meleagris gallopavo) in Mexico.* Revista Universidad y Ciencia. 2011

Ceram, C. W. Gods, *Graves and Scholars: The Story of Archaeology*. New York: Alfred A. Knopf, 1975.

Emboden, W.A. (1979) "*Nymphaea ampla and Other Mayan Narcotic Plants.*" Mexicon

CORN, COTTON AND CHOCOLATE: HOW THE MAYA CHANGED THE WORLD

Chan, Roman P. *Cultura y Ciudades Mayas de Campeche*. Mexico City: Editora del Sureste, 1985.

Coe, Michael. *Breaking the Maya Code*. New York: Thames and Hudson, 1999.

— *The Maya*. 4th Edition. London and New York: Thames and Hudson, 1966.

Coe, Sophie D. & Michael D. *The true history of Chocolate*. Thames and Hudson. New York 1996.

Coe, Sophie D. *Americas first Cuisines*. University of Texas Press. Austin, 1994.

Coe, Michael, and Mark Van Stone. *Reading the Maya Glyphs*. New York: Thames & Hudson, 2001.

Corona-M E. *The Pleistocene bird record of México*. Acta Zoologica Cracoviensia 45special issue. 2002

Craven, Roy C. *Ceremonial Centers of the Maya*. Tallahassee: The University Press of Florida, 1974.

de la Vega El Inca, Garcilaso. *Royal Commentaries of the Incas and General History of Peru*. Translated by Harold V. Livermore. Austin: University of Texas Press, 1987.

Demerest, Arthur. *Ancient Maya.* Cambridge: Cambridge University Press, 2004.

Diamond, Jared. *Collapse*. New York: Penguin Books, 2005.

—. *Guns, Germs and Steel*. New York: W. W. Norton & Company, 2005.

Diaz, José Luis *Ethnopharmacology of Sacred Psychoactive Plants Used by the Indians of Mexico*. Annual Review of Pharmacological Toxicology. 1977

Dienhart, John M. *The Maya Hieroglyph for Cotton Mexicon*. 1986

Dreiss, Meredith L. and Greenhill, Sharon Edger. *Chocolate, Pathway to the Gods*. The University of Arizona Press, Tucson. 2008.

Evans, R. Tripp. Romancing the Maya: *Mexican Antiquity in the American Imagination 1820-1915*. Austin: University of Texas Press, 2004.

Feldman, Lawrence H. *A Tumpline Economy: Production and Distribution Systems in Sixteenth-Century Eastern Guatemala*. Culver City, CA: Labyrinthos, 1985.

Fitzsimons, Neal. *The Greatest Bridge Spans in the World. Engineering History*, Baltimore: Self Published, 1995.

Emboden, W.A. "*Nymphaea ampla and Other Mayan Narcotic Plants*." Mexico, 1979.

Folan, William J., et al. *Coba: A Classic Maya Metropolis*. New York: Academic Press, Inc., 1983.

Foster, Lynn V. *Handbook to Life in the Ancient Maya World*. New York: Oxford University Press, 2002.

CORN, COTTON AND CHOCOLATE: HOW THE MAYA CHANGED THE WORLD

Freidel, David, Linda Schele, Joy Parker. *Maya Cosmos: Three Thousand Years on the Shaman's Path.* New York: Perennial, 2001.

Fussell, Betty. *The Story of Corn.* New York. Alfred A Knopf. 1992

Gentilcore, David. *Pomodoro*! Columbia University Press. New York. 2000

Gerlach Nancy & Jeffery. *Foods of the Maya.* University of New Mexico Press. Albuquerque. 1994.

Gill, Richardson B. *The Great Maya Droughts: Water, Life and Death.* Albuquerque: University of New Mexico, 2000.

Glassman, Steve. *On the Trail of the Maya Explorer.* Tuscaloosa: The University of Alabama Press, 2003.

Graham, Ian. *Alfred Maudslay and the Maya.* Norman: University of Oklahoma, 2002.

Guderjan, Thomas H. *The Nature of an Ancient Maya City: Resources, Interaction and Power at Blue Creek, Belize.* Tuscaloosa: The University of Alabama Press, 2007.

Hammond, Norman. *Ancient Maya Civilization*.: Rutgers University Press, New Brunswick, 1988.

Harlow, George. *"Hard Rock."* Natural History Magazine, August 1991.

Harris, Kate *Trees of Belize. Belize*: Bay Cedar Publishing. 2009.

Hellmuth, Nicholas. *Monster und Menschen in der Maya-Kunst.* Graz: Akademische Druck- u. Verlagsanstalt, 1987.

Hellmuth, Nicholas. *Beans of the Maya.* FLARR. 2014.

Hellmuth, Nicholas. *Maize of the Maya.* FLARR, 2014.

Henderson, John S. *The World of the Ancient Maya.* Ithaca: Cornell University Press, 1981.

Herman, Arthur. *How the Scots Invented the Modern World.* Three Rivers Press. New York, 2001.

Hobhouse, Henry. *Seeds of Change.* Sidgwick & Jackson. 1985. New York.

Howell SNG, Webb S, *A guide to the birds of Mexico and northern Central America.* New York: Oxford University Press. 1995

Hunter, Bruce C. A. *Guide to Ancient Maya Ruins.* Norman: University of Oklahoma Press, 1986.

Hymans, Edward, and George Ordish. *The Last of the Incas.* New York, 1963.

James, Peter, Nick Thorpe. *Ancient Mysteries.* New York: Ballantine Books, 1999.

Kirby, Richard, Sidney Withington, Arthur Darling, Fred Rick Kilgour. *Engineering in History. New York:* Dover Publications, 1990.

King, Chris. *Entheogens, the Conscious Brain and Existential Reality: Part 1.* Journal of Consciousness Exploration & Research. 2012

CORN, COTTON AND CHOCOLATE: HOW THE MAYA CHANGED THE WORLD

Krupp, E. C. *Echoes of the Ancient Skies*. New York: Harper & Row, 1983.

Laws, Bill. *Fifty plants that changed the course of History*. Firefly Press. Buffalo. 2010.

Leon-Portilla, Miguel. *Bernardino de Sahagun: First Anthropologist.* Translated by Mauricio J. Mixco. Norman: University of Oklahoma Press, 2002.

—. *Pre-Columbian Literatures of Mexico*. Norman: University of Oklahoma Press, 1975.

Leopold AS, *Wildlife of Mexico: the game birds and mammals.:* University of California Press. Berkeley.1959

Mallan, Chicki. *Guide to the Yucatán Peninsula including Belize*. Chico, CA: Moon Publications, 1989.

Mann, Charles C., *1491, New Revelations of the Americas before Columbus*. Vintage Books, New York, 2011.

-*1493, Uncovering the New World Columbus created*. Alfred A. Knoff, New York 2011

Marsh, Carol. *William Wrigley, jr*. Chicago. Gallopade International

Mason, Gregory. *Columbus Came Late*. New York: The Century Co., 1931.

Maudslay, Alfred P. *Biologia Centrali-Americana*. Facsimile edition prepared by Dr. Francis Robicsek. 5 vols. New York: Milpatron Publishing Corp., 1974.

McKillop, Heather. *In Search of Maya Sea Traders*. College Station: Texas A&M University Press, 2005.

Meyer, Carolyn, Charles Gallenkamp. *The Mystery of the Ancient Maya*. New York: Atheneum, 1985.

Miller, Arthur G. *Maya Rulers of Time: A Study of Architectural Sculpture at Tikal, Guatemala*. Philadelphia: University of Pennsylvania, 1986.

Miller, Loretta Scott. *A Yucatán Kitchen*. Pelican Publishing. Gretna. 2003.

Miller, Mary Ellen. *Maya Art and Architecture*. New York: Thames & Hudson, 1999.

Moll, Roberto Garcia. *Palenque 1926-1945.* Mexico City: Instituto National de Antropologia, 1985.

Morley, Sylvanus, George W. Brainerd, and Robert J. Shearer. *The Ancient Maya*. 4th Edition. Stanford: Stanford University Press, 1983.

LaFeber, Walter. Inevitable revolutions: *The United States in Central America.:* W.W. Norton. New York.1993.

Morley, Sylvanus. *The Ancient Maya. 2nd Edition*. Stanford: Stanford University Press, 1946.

Mathews, Jennifer P. *Chicle: The Chewing Gum of the Americas, From the Ancient Maya to William Wrigley.:* University of Arizona Press. Tucson 2009.

CORN, COTTON AND CHOCOLATE: HOW THE MAYA CHANGED THE WORLD

McDonald, J. Andrew and Brian Stross. *Water Lily and Cosmic Serpent: Equivalent Conduits of the Maya Spirit Realm.* Journal of Ethnobiology. 2012

McKenna, Terence *Food of the Gods.* London: Rider. 1992

Morley, Sylvanus, George W. Brainerd. The Ancient Maya. 3rd Edition. Stanford: Stanford University Press, 1956.

Murphy, Francis S. *Dragon Mask Temples in Central Yucatán.* Hong Kong: Scribe Ltd., 1988.

Nicholson, Irene. *Mexican and Central American Mythology.* Rushden, England: The Hamlyn Publishing Group Ltd., 1983.

O'Kon, James. *The Lost Secrets of Maya Technology.* New Page Press. New York. 2012.

O'Kon, James. *The Hidden Codex.* KDP Publishing, New York, 2016.

O'Kon, James. "Bridge to the Past." Civil Engineering Magazine, January 1995.

—. "*Computer Modeling of the Seventh Century Maya Suspension Bridge at Yaxchilan.*" Computing in Civil Engineering. Reston, VA: ASCE Press, 2005.

—. "*Computer Simulation of 7th Century Maya Suspension Bridge.*" Computer Applications and Quantitative Methods in Archaeology. Berlin: Deutsches Archaologischens Institut, 2007.

—. "*Forensic Engineering Research Uncovers Lost Maya Engineering Landmarks.*" Structural Engineering Institute of the American Society of Civil Engineers. Reston, VA: ASCE Press, 2007.

—. "*Journal and Sketches of the Puuc Region of the Yucatán.*" Atlanta: Self-published, 1990.

—. "*Journal and Sketches of Travels on the Usumacinta River.*" Atlanta: Self-published, 1989.

—. "*The Maya: America's First Water Resource Engineers."* Environmental and Water Resources: Milestones in Engineering History. Reston, VA: ASCE Press, 2007.

O'Kon, James, et al. *Guidelines for Failure Investigation.* Washington DC: American Society of Civil Engineers Press, 1989.

Osmanagich, Sam. *The World of the Maya.* Piscataway: Euphrates, 2005.

Pagden, A. R. *The Maya: Diego de Landa's Account of the Affairs of the Yucatán.* Chicago: J. Phillip O'Hara, Inc., 1975.

Parsons, Jeffrey R. *Prehistoric Settlement Patterns in the Texcoco Region, Mexico.* Ann Arbor: University of Michigan, 1971.

Perera, Victor, Robert D. Bruce. *The Last Lords of Palenque.* Berkley: University of California Press, 1982.

Pilcher, Jeffery M. Planet Taco, *A global History of Mexican Food.* Oxford University Press. New York. 2012.

Poirier, Rene. *Engineering Wonders of the World.* Paris: Barnes and Noble, Inc., 1957.

CORN, COTTON AND CHOCOLATE: HOW THE MAYA CHANGED THE WORLD

Pollock, H.E.D. *The Puuc*. Cambridge: The Carnegie Institution of Washington, 1980.

Pool, Christopher. *Olmec Archaeology and Early Mesoamerica*. Cambridge: Cambridge University Press, 2007.

Prescott, William H. *History of the Conquest of Mexico*. 3 vols. Boston: Phillips, Sampson and Company, 1859.

—. *History of the Conquest of Peru*. 2 vols. Boston: Phillips, Sampson and Company, 1859.

Proskouriakoff, Tatiana. *An Album of Maya Architecture*. Washington: Carnegie Institution of Washington, 1946.

Ramirez de Alba, Horacio. "*El cemento y el concreto de los Mayas*." CIENCIA Ergo Sum, 1999.

—*Estudio del Concreto Maya*. Toluca, Mexico: Universidad Autonoma del Estado de Mexico, 2000.

Renfrew, Colin, Paul Bahn. *Archaeology: Theories, Methods and Practice*. New York: Thames and Hudson, Inc., 1991.

Rice, Prudence. *Maya Political Science, Time, Astronomy and the Cosmos*. Austin: University of Texas Press, 2004.

Robicsek, Francis. *The Maya Book of the Dead: The Ceramic Codex*. Charlottesville: University of Virginia Art Museum, 1981.

—. *The Smoking Gods: Tobacco in Maya Art, History and Religion*. Norman: University of Oklahoma Press, 1978.

Robin, C. "*Gender, farming, and long-term change: Maya Historical and Archaeological perspectives*," In Current Anthropology, Wenner-Gren, 2006

Schele, Linda, David Freidel. *A Forest of Kings: The Untold Story of the Ancient Maya*. New York: William Morrow and Co., 1990.

Schele, Linda, Mary Ellen Miller. *The Blood of Kings. New York*: George Braziller, 1986.

Schorger AW. *The wild turkey: its history and domestication*. University of Oklahoma Press. Norman. 1966

Sharer, Robert J. *The Ancient Maya. 5th Edition*. Stanford: Stanford University Press, 1994.

Sherratt, Andrew. *The Cambridge Encyclopedia of Archaeology*. New York: Crown Publishers, 1980

Smith, Andrew. *The Tomato in America. University of South Carolina Press*. Columbia 1994.

Smith, Andrew F. *Peanuts, The Illustrious History of the Goober Pea*. University of *Illinois Press. Urbans 2002.*

-*The Turkey, An American Story*. University of Illinois Press. Urbans 2006.

Soustelle, Jacques. *The Olmec's: The Oldest Civilization in Mexico*. Norman: University of Oklahoma Press, 1985.

Sorenson, John L., Carl L. Johannessen. *World Trade and Biological Exchanges Before 1492.* Sorenson and Johannessen. Eugene 2013.

Spinden, Herbert J. *A Study of Maya Art: Its Subject Matter & Historical Development.* New York: Dover Publications, Inc., 1975.

Stephens, John Lloyd. *Incidents of Travel in Central America, Chiapas and Yucatán.* 2 vols. New York: Harper and Brothers, 1841.

—. *Incidents of Travel in Egypt, Arabia, Petraea, and the Holy Land.* New York: Harper and Brothers, 1837.

—. *Incidents of Travel in Yucatán. 2 vols.* New York: Harper and Brothers, 1843.

Stirling, Matthew W. *Indians of the Americans.* Washington DC: National Geographic Society, 1955.

Stuart, George E., Gene S. Stuart. *The Mysterious Maya.* Washington, DC: National Geographic Society, 1977.

Tate, Carolyn. *Yaxchilan: The Design of a Mayan Ceremonial City.* Austin: University of Texas Press, 1993.

Tedlock, Barbara. *Time and the Highland Maya.* Albuquerque: University of New Mexico Press, 1982.

Thompson, J. Eric. *Maya Hieroglyphic Writing: An Introduction. 3rd Edition.* Norman: University of Oklahoma Press, 1971.

Thornton, Erin, Emery, Kitty. et al. *Earliest Mexican turkeys (Meleagris gallopavo) in the Maya region.* PLOS, one. 2012

Ulloa, Mauricio, Stewart, James McD. *Cotton Genetic resources in Western States of Mexico Genetic Resources and Crop Evolutions.* 2006...

Vargas, Ayala, Helmer Dagoberto, Helmer. Le Ik, *Chili peppers from Guatemala.* Universidad de San Carlos de Guatemala. 2014

Warman, Arturo. *Corn Capitalism.* University of North Carolina Press. Chapel Hill 2003.

White, C. *"Gendered Food Behavior among the Maya,"* In Journal of Social Archaeology, Sage Journals, 2005

Yafa, Stephan. *Cotton, The Biography of a revolutionary Fiber.* Penguin Books. New York. 2005

CORN, COTTON AND CHOCOLATE: HOW THE MAYA CHANGED THE WORLD

Made in the USA
Columbia, SC
14 September 2020